JOHNS, MARKS, TRICKS, AND CHICKENHAWKS

JOHNS, MARKS, TRICKS, AND CHICKENHAWKS

Professionals and Their Clients Writing About Each Other

Edited by **R.J. MARTIN, JR.** and **DAVID HENRY STERRY**

SOFT SKULL PRESS · BERKELEY | AN IMPRINT OF COUNTERPOINT

Sterry, David H.
Johns, Marks, Tricks and Chickenhawks : professionals & their clients writing
about each other / David H. Sterry and R. J. Martin, Jr.
pages cm
ISBN 978-1-59376-507-1 (pbk.)
1. Male prostitutes—United States. 2. Prostitutes—United States.
3. Prostitution—United States. I. Martin, R. J. II. Title.
HQ119.4.U6S74 2013
306.74'30973—dc23
2012040828

Cover design by Shane Lukas
Interior design by Elyse Strongin, Neuwirth & Associates, Inc.

SOFT SKULL PRESS
An imprint of COUNTERPOINT
1919 Fifth Street
Berkeley, CA 94710
www.softskull.com
www.counterpointpress.com

Printed in the United States of America
Distributed by Publishers Group West

10 9 8 7 6 5 4 3 2 1

CONTENTS

3 Mansions, Hotels, and Luxury Condominiums

4 Cyberspace

5 The Brothel

6 Peep Shows, Strip Clubs, and Adult Theaters

ACKNOWLEDGMENTS

First and foremost, we would like to thank all of our contributors. We feel honored that they shared their stories with us. We would also like to thank our team at Soft Skull and Counterpoint Press. Working with our editor, Liz Parker, has been a joy. Many thanks are also due to our lovely and talented agent, Jim Levine, and the awesomely amazing Kerry Sparks, of the Levine-Greenberg Literary Agency. As always, massive props to the Snow Leopard, the one and only Arielle Eckstut. We would also like to thank Richard Eion Nash, without whom none of this would've happened. Finally, platitudes of gratitude to Leslie Levitas, Colman Conroy, and Eric Singer for editorial assistance.

JOHNS, MARKS, TRICKS, AND CHICKENHAWKS

INTRODUCTION

Obsidian hair and copper skin, she walks toward me as I cruise in my beat-to-shit car through the seedy groin of the Tenderloin. She's wearing jeans and a T-shirt. All the other hos sashaying down the stroll are like kabuki cartoon caricatures of hookers: glittery miniminimini-skirts, mammoth jackedup décolletage spilling tit flesh out of halter tops, machete heels, and painted razor nails. That's why I notice her. She looks like somebody I might hang out with. She doesn't look like a lady of the night. But I know she's working. I have ho dar. Every time I see someone working, my spider senses start tingling. I'm 23. I've been retired from the sex business for six years. There was no gold watch, severance package, or golden parachute.

It hits me suddenly. I could just pay this girl to have sex with me. It strikes me how odd it is that I've never considered buying sex, when I sold so much of it. Looking back, I wonder how could this have been. First, this was before you could look at a world full of women selling sex just by going to one of a million sex-selling websites. Second, everywhere else I lived, you had to know where the hookers were and go find them. Not in San Francisco. Here, they're walking right down Geary like they own the place. Also, for the past six years I'd been sleeping-on-people's-couches, living-in-damp-basements, crashing-in-the-student-center dirt poor. That's how I lived rather than go back to selling sex again. It saved my life at a time when I didn't have any money or people, but it left me bent, spindled, and mutilated.

1

So for the first time since I left the sex business, I have cash in my pocket and I am face-to-face with a woman I am actually attracted to who would give me sex for money. Plus, when I was a provider, all the clients I had sex with for money were at least old enough to be friends with my parents. So it just didn't seem like the kind of sex I wanted for myself. Fun sex. As opposed to sex for profit.

As I cruise in my beat-to-shit car I realize I don't want a professional. I was a professional. I know what it means to be a professional and have sex. It means that no matter how much you look like you're into it, there's almost always a part of you that isn't quite totally there. A part of you who is watching yourself performing acts of sex. And most times you're lying to the customer. Pretending that their stories are fascinating, pretending that they're charming, beautiful, and intelligent, pretending to be really turned on and happy, when you're not. Like when you work in an office. No matter how much fun you're having, you're still at work. You're almost always painfully conscious of that. There were very few times when I was selling sex for money that I completely lost myself in a moment of true sexuality. No matter how good it felt physically, I always had that very conscious awareness that it was my job to turn myself into whatever would keep the customer satisfied. Customer satisfaction. Customer gratification. Customer elation. Customer orgasm.

But now I'm 23. I have money in my pocket. It hits me like a velvet glove that I could pay this excellent-looking young woman, who, under different circumstances, I could be dating, to have sexual intercourse with me. I never for one second wonder whether it's right or wrong. I just know that I want to be a great, great customer. I had a couple of clients who taught me so much about life and love and sex and they were so sweet and fun and nice to me. As opposed to the customers who demeaned, polluted, and punished me. Who made me get naked and dressed me up in a French maid's apron and made me clean their houses while they had wild sex with each other and snickered at me for $200 an hour. Which was $1,000 in 2012 money. That was a gigantic amount of money to me at that time. Just before I became a prostitute/rent boy/industrial sex technician, I fried chicken for a living. Now that was a terrible job. Wickedly hot, stinking and greasy, boiling oil spattering and burning your arms and hands. Plus you have to wear a ridiculous little paper hat, and you always, always, always, no matter how much you scrub, scour, and shower, have a thick patina of rancid stench surrounding you like a wet fart fog. But since I retired from the chicken-frying business, I have gone into fried chicken restaurants and felt absolutely no moral qualms about it. It was just a normal business transaction. Problem is, when I walk into a fried chicken restaurant, I get nauseous. I ate so much fried chicken when I worked at that fried chicken restaurant, I almost sprouted wings. It makes my stomach turn now, that deep-fried funk. I can't eat industrial fried chicken anymore. It makes me physically, emotionally, spiritually sick. I do not, thankfully, feel the same way about sex. Before I entered the sex business I craved sex. While I was in the sex business I craved sex. After I got out of the sex business I craved even more sex. During college, when I was an industrial sex technician retiree, I had many girlfriends. Perhaps "girlfriends" is not the right word. I always had a girlfriend. But I was also having sex with lots of other women. I always had five or six women friends who I really liked, and if it was late at night and I was in their dorm and I knocked on their door, there was a decent chance they'd have sex with me. That just was kind of the way it was at that time in history.

Even at that moment, trolling down the ho stroll in my beat-to-shit car, I have a girlfriend. She's smart, funny, and attractive, an underachiever who doesn't value herself enough and lets me boss her around and puts up with my shit. I have sex with her as often as she'll let me, which is quite often. She thinks that we are in a monogamous relationship. From everything I've observed, she, in fact, *is* in a monogamous relationship. But I am not. She asks me sometimes if I'm having sex with anybody else. And I lie to her. It's very easy. It doesn't hurt anybody. But it does make it hard to be very close to her. I feel bad. About the lying. But not bad enough to forgo having sex with other women. Especially not Obsidian Copper.

3

Introduction

I slow my beat-to-shit car. She's walking slow and casual, like she has nowhere to go in her jeans and T-shirt. I'm having shockingly vivid visions of what she'll look like naked underneath me as my fully inflated member enters her. It makes me sex drunk.

I stop. She looks like she could be on her way home from her job at Barnes & Noble, or on her way to see an independent rock band play at some cool club. I roll down the window. She leans down so her head is in the frame of the car window. It's like she's on my TV.

"Hey, how you doing?" Obsidian Copper has the darkest shiniest eyes. And hair. A tiny little a smile flirts on her lips. A tiny little twinkle flashes in her fired-glass black eyes. Like she thinks the whole thing is rather amusing. I like that. That's how I tried to be when I was an industrial sex technician.

"I'm better now that I'm looking at you." Writing it down now it seems like a cheesy line, but I really did mean it. I actually did feel better looking at her. I had just watched pornography and I was vacant, hollow, brittle, bitter, agitated, jangly, unsettled, unhappy, and dissatisfied in the worst sense of all those words. Now I feel better. Just looking at her.

"I bet you say that to all the girls," Obsidian Copper chuckles in the most endearing way. "Are you with the cops?"

This talk of law enforcement kick-starts my central nervous system, a jolt of adrenaline squirts out of my glands, my fight-flight alarm rings, buzzes, and beeps. This is fun. Like I'm the star of a really cool movie.

"Do I look like a cop?" I raise my eyebrows in a droll ho-stroll smirk.

"That's exactly what a cop would say," she shoots back with a sly copper deadpan.

"No," I state, "I'm not now, nor ever have I been, with the police."

Obsidian Copper opens the door and gets in my beat-to-shit car. Smells of grit, used booze, bus exhaust, and the Tenderloin waft in with her. But underneath is a fresh clean smell of somebody who's cleaned herself recently with a nice soap and hasn't covered the

4

whole thing up with toxic, eye-stinging perfume. When I smell her I want to have sex with her even more.

"Where to?" I ask.

"Just start driving," she says, like we're in some '30s noir movie, in which she's the dangerous dame and I'm the lovelorn palooka.

I'm liking her more every second. I start driving.

"So," I say, "I actually used to work in the business." It feels like a good icebreaker. I want her to know that I'm in the people-who've-sold-sex club. I feel so simpatico with Copper Obsidian. It's so easy to talk to her. I don't have to think about making some kind of future with her. Or whether she likes me. I just want to be a good customer. I want to look down at all that copper and obsidian as she services me.

"Really?" Obsidian Copper doesn't seem surprised at all. I suspect it would take a lot to surprise her.

"Yeah, when I was younger. In Hollywood. But I worked with an agency." I want to say more. But I don't quite know what to say. It's also kind of shocking because I've never actually told anyone this before. I am quickly realizing that this is part of the appeal of hiring an industrial sex technician. It's someone you can tell anything to. It's someone you can do anything with. Or to. Of course I understood all that intellectually, and I saw it over and over again with my clients. Coma Girl. The 82-year-old who wanted cunnilingus just once before she dies. The judge in diapers. But I never thought about it before from a consumer's perspective. It's very liberating. A couple of years after I got out of the sex business I became a marriage counselor. People wanted to tell me all their problems. They wanted me to listen. They wanted to be understood. When I was an industrial sex technician, about half of the women who hired me didn't really even want sex. They wanted me to listen. They wanted to be understood. Often while I was naked. And they had all their clothes on. Many of them wanted me to touch myself. While I was naked. And they had all their clothes on. It made me smile when I realized that often the only difference between being a top-of-the-food-chain industrial sex technician and being a marriage counselor was that I had all my clothes on, I wasn't abusing myself, and I was being paid much less money.

"So, what kind of donation are you looking to make?" I love how that word has become part of the hooker/ho/industrial sex technician jargon. Donation. Like I'm helping endow the Prostitute Scholarship Fund. They do this, of course, because if I were a cop, they couldn't say they were trying to get paid for services. It was just a donation to the Ho's Retirement Home.

I admire how skillfully she shifted into business mode. I don't have to negotiate. My customers just always had my money there. But Obsidian Copper has changed the dynamic. The meter's running. Time's money. Money makes the world go round. And she is here to get P-A-I-D. I am shaken by a profound realization that this is going to be different than the sex I have with my girlfriends. Many of them gave me lots of love with the sex. Sometimes they would want to have sex for a long time. But as a client, I am going to have to pay for every second of sex. And there will be no love. It definitely changes the interaction for me. It doesn't seem quite so sexy anymore.

"I have $100. I'm not sure what the going rate is. That's what I was making."

I'm driving. Away from the Tenderloin up the hill into the overpriced air of Nob Hill. I glance over at Obsidian Copper. Her face is wide, her cheekbones flat, her skin smooth and beautiful. If you tarted her up, she could probably be a model.

I have a pumping rush of sexcitement. This is so much better than feeling vacant, hollow, brittle, bitter, agitated, jangly, unsettled, unhappy, dissatisfied in the worst sense of all those words. I hadn't yet figured out why I was watching all that porn and feeling that way. I just felt compelled by a force I could not quite control. Driving around negotiating how much I'm going to pay to have sex with Copper Obsidian is so much more fun, my mind flooded with images of me taking her from behind, like an animal, letting the monster loose.

"$150. That's what the going rate is now. In case you're wondering. Are you sure you don't have $150?" Her voice is exactly the same as when she was talking before. It's quite a skill. To go from casually chatting to business negotiation without feeling like there's a hustle going on. And, of course, that is the art of the hustle. I think that word is misunderstood. Or maybe it just has many meanings. Yes, a pool hustler hustles people by fooling them. But in the end he has to have great skill. Same with being an industrial sex technician hustler. You have to actually have game. Deliver the goods. Otherwise you're a thief, and eventually someone's going to crack your head open. Which may happen anyway, because the whole thing is an under-ground industry, prohibition being what it is, the means of produc-tion being in the hands of gangsters as the War on Whores rages.

"I'm sorry," I say, because I am. "I really only have $100."

Obsidian Copper looks at me with those deep hard raven eyes, sizing me up, weighing risk and reward, her face a still lake on a warm day when nothing is moving. She is impenetrable. She is a closed book. Finally she says, "You don't have a place, right?"

"No, I don't have a place."

"Take a right up here." Her voice is as flat as her face.

"Where we going?" I realize I'm quite excited that I don't know where I'm going with Obsidian Copper. But at the same time I'm acutely aware that this could be some elaborate setup to kill me and slice me into little bloody pieces and dump me into the bay. Which makes my heart jackhammer, pulse spike, and nerve synapses jangle. This is such a high. Like rock climbing. Or whitewater rafting. Or bungee jumping.

"Down by the water."

"So, we're gonna do it . . . in the car?"

"In the car," she says like she says everything else, in a dry straight line.

"So," I ask, "$100 is good?"

"Sure." I have no idea if she's bitter or happy, disgruntled or gruntled.

"Next time I'll have more."

"Sure." This time she's got a small but obvious sneer smeared on her lips. Like she's heard that line a billion times before. That's when I wonder if maybe something happened to her. Like something happened to me. I got raped. Just before I got into the sex business. And now I'm wondering if something happened to her. Maybe not. Maybe she's putting herself through grad school.

"What your heritage?" I ask. I want to know. And I do feel a surging urge to help her. This is the first real appearance of the character who will greatly affect the next fifteen years of me having sex with prostitutes/hos/industrial sex technicians.

Sir Save-A-Ho.

He comes in all shapes and sizes, and almost anyone who's been in the business any length of time comes across one. A white knight in shining armor who thinks he can rescue the damaged, beautiful ho with the heart of gold and rehabilitate her, in the process earning her eternal gratitude and a lifetime of free sex.

"I'm half Mexican and half Indian."

"From India, or, you know Native American."

"Cherokee." When she says this she really looks Cherokee. I can see her people in teepees, hunting buffalo, living harmoniously with Mother Nature. Not treating her like it's our toxic playground wasteland. From gathering berries and growing corn and making pots to strolling through the Tenderloin selling your sex for money. My grandfather was a coal miner. In Newcastle, England. During the winter he would go down underground while it was still dark, suck down cancerous coal dust for twelve hours, and come back out when it was dark again. I wonder what our grandfathers would think of us, selling all that sex, and now buying it. I didn't ever think it was wrong to sell sex for money. But I did often feel depleted and wigged out and like my hard drive swallowed a virus when I was exposed to the sexual horrors I encountered as my clients played out insane, monstrous things. Looking at her now, all that obsidian and all that copper, I wonder if maybe there are some violence-inflicting, dead-by-30 skeletons lurking in her ancestral closet. I want to ask. But I don't want to be a stupid white man. It's really not stuff you chat about around the water cooler. Which is really what we're doing here. But I find myself wanting to be her friend. To dive beneath that copper lake and see what's in the hole in the bottom of her obsidian sea. I want to help. I want to save the ho.

"Wow," I say, "what's that like?"

"I don't know," she says dead flat, "I've never been anything else."

"Right," I chuckle. It's funny the way she says it. Of course she's right. It was kind of a stupid thing to ask. I kick myself mentally. "Where did you grow up?"

"Where did you grow up?" she bats back with a droll roll of her obsidian eyes.

"All over," I give her back some world-weariness of my own.

"Me too." She returns a tiny little copper nod.

"I'm surprised we never ran into each other there."

"Take a right up here, go down to the end of the block, turn the car around." And now we are back in business mode. Just like that. Snap of a finger. Flip of a switch. The meter's running, we're back on the clock, time to get this show on the road.

I park. It's very dark. It's a perfect spot. You can see someone coming from a long way off.

As soon as the car's in park, I give her $100. I always wanted to get paid right away when I was on the job. Then I could relax. Depositing the money into my pocket immediately made everything all good. The mantra of my employment counselor/pimp was:

Get the money up front.

So I make sure Copper Obsidian has her money up front. She seems to appreciate that. I realize I don't know her name. I want to know her name. But I figure she'll just give me a fake name. A *nom de ho*. And I don't want to be the cliché who asks her what her real name is. So I just avoid the whole name issue. Even though I really want to know her name.

She takes one leg of her pants off faster-than-the-human-eye-can-see fast. She's reclining the seat as far back as it will go. She's looking up at the ceiling. Not at me.

It's so abrupt. And so not sexy. Even though just looking at her is quite sexy, with just her leg and her vagina naked there in my fully reclined passenger seat. In fact, it's wildly exciting and diverting. It completely distracts me from the fact that my personal house is on fire.

But I'm not ready to fuck her. I'm not sure exactly what to say. So I just unzip my pants and take my not-hard cock out. It's very different from having sex with civilians. They usually want to kiss and touch, and some like to talk saucy and naughty.

Obsidian Copper lies there like a cadaver. So I try to get enough blood into my sad, flaccid penis so I can insert the thing into her prostitute vagina. The bloom seems off the rose in our relationship.

Obsidian Copper turns and looks at my unthrobbing manhood languishing in my hand like a comatose white worm. "Oh," she says, "do you want some head?"

Again I'm impressed with her business skills. That's exactly what I want. She's being everything a good industrial sex technician should be. This is what I always used to strive for when I was working. To give the customer exactly what was wanted. And get it done as quickly as possible. If it was bad I'd go off and gorge on day-old birthday cake and ice cream and lots of weed. If it was good I'd go play Ping-Pong or basketball or have sex with my coed girlfriend if she'd let me.

"Yes, please," I say with appreciation and enthusiasm, "I'd love some head."

She leans into my crotch and gets herself comfortable while at the same time opening a condom and putting the closed end into her mouth. She unrolls the condom with her lips around my suddenly awakening tool, and she works her hands and mouth like a combination suction machine/tourniquet, drawing the blood up and making sure it stays there.

I want to put my hands on her obsidian hair. I almost always do that when I'm with a civilian. But when I was on the job I had an incident where a man put my hair in his mouth and started sucking on it. So I can't stand having people touch my head like that. The flashback/muscle memory disturbs me in the worst way imaginable. So I think I should ask. Trying to be the best client I can be.

"Would it be okay if I touch your hair while you're doing that?" I sound like a nice person when I ask that. That makes me happy.

She stops for second and says, "Sure."

I have a feeling she says that word a lot.

I don't know how long exactly she weaves her fellatio magic. But it does feel so good that I forget it's a business transaction for a minute. Or two minutes. Or ten minutes. When time stops having any meaning, it's almost always a good sign. I discover another one of the real upsides of hiring a talented industrial sex technician. It just feels so darn good. And again, it completely makes me forget about all that raging, roiling, boiling, festering sickness that's growling like a filthy hungry monster chained in my basement.

I feel like I've already gotten my $100 worth.

Then she's leaning back into my reclined passenger seat, at the same time guiding my rigid sheathed penis right up to the tip of her womanhood. She licks her fingers and touches herself. Twice. She puts her legs up. I look down. She has such a great copper face. She's concentrating very intently on getting me inside her so that thrusting can begin and blastoff can be achieved. She does not look sexy in any way. She does not look like an actress in any of the pornographic movies I compulsively, obsessively watch. She does not make kissy lips. Or roll her eyes ecstatically. Or stick out her tongue orgasmically. She looks like a carpenter trying to nail a hammer into a wall. I wonder if that's what I looked like when I was trying to service my clients. I always tried to smile. I probably smiled too much. Like some hideous Joker rent boy.

I want her to look at me. I want to kiss her. But I never kissed anybody. Nobody I knew kissed anybody when they were on the job. It's too intimate. So I don't try to kiss her. But I want to kiss her.

Suddenly she has me inside her. Swoosh.

11

She looks at me and gives me a smile. It's very small. And very far away. Like she's a hologram smiling from another galaxy. Like she doesn't want to be there. That makes it sad. I know that feeling. But at the same time, she has her hand now on my ass and it's thrusting me forward at the same time as she's thrusting herself forward, and then pulling back, with lots of incredible swivel/gripping/suction action. Highly skilled. Efficient and effective.

I look down at her. She's looking straight up. Her face is a void. There's nothing there. Eyes doing that thousand-yard stare. It's kind of creepy and horrifying, but I can't take my eyes off her face. It's like the greatest train wreck you've ever seen: You don't want to look at it, but you can't turn away. While her body is devouring me, working me over like a finely tuned sex machine.

My soul and my body are in conflict. Her placid detachment is disturbing, and I want to help her feel better. Whereas the piston-thumping shaft-drive pyrotechnic thrusting is driving my body wild. I can hear my orgasm calling me. It's coming, and unless I stop it, it will be here soon. I want to stop it. I want to keep doing this all night, every night, for the rest of my life. But when I look at her face, I can tell she doesn't want to be having sex with me. I'm pretty sure I've only been having intercourse with her for maybe six or seven minutes. But I feel she's done her job, done her duty, and I should just let my orgasm come, so she can be on her way. Seems only fair. She's been so nice.

So I shut my eyes. I let her push me in, squeeze me superhuman tight, and suck me back the other way, all of my pleasure centers firing up, turning on, shooting and spraying.

My orgasm is upon me, it envelops, overwhelms, and overcomes me, it's shiveringly, otherworldly, transcendentally ecstatic.

Then it's over. And we're done.

She grips her fingers very tight around the top of the condom wrapped around my still-pumping semen organ. She has me out of her area so fast it makes the head of my penis spin. She's back in her pants before I'm even back in my seat.

"Can you take me back where you picked me up?" she says like she's a plumber who just finished snaking my drain.

It's very jarring to go from ecstasy to detachment in the bat an eyelash. It's like coming up from the depths too fast without enough oxygen. I'm having the sex bends.

I don't feel like she's a plumber who just finished snaking my drain. I feel like we just had sex. I want desperately to talk to her. I want to see where she lives. I want to buy her dinner. I want to go see some independent band at some cool club with her. I want to know her name. I want to know her.

"Sure," I say. "Are you okay?"

She turns her head a tiny little bit and looks at me and nods a tiny little nod, with a tiny little grin, like she's happy I asked. Then she says, "Sure."

I feel drained. Literally and figuratively. I want to go to sleep. And that vacant, hollow, brittle, bitter, agitated, jangly, unsettled, unhappy dissatisfaction is already creeping back.

"Hey," I say, "I really had a good time. And you're very skillful. I wish I had some more money to give you. I just wanted to say thank you for being . . . such a nice person."

"Sure," she says. But this conversation is clearly over. She looks a million miles away out the window.

I feel almost desperate for some kind of contact with her. To get inside of her heart and brain now that I've been inside of her vagina.

"Hey," I say as I park my beat-to-shit car back in the seedy groin of the Tenderloin, "can I get your number? I'd like to see you again."

"I don't have a number."

Soon as the car stops moving she's out the door and slams it shut.

I watch her walk away from me, until all that obsidian and copper disappears.

That's how I go from the supply to the demand side of the sex business. For the next fifteen years I have sex with more prostitutes/ hos/industrial sex technicians than I can count. Or maybe I can count them, but I choose not to. I spend tens of thousands of dollars having sex with the best of hos and the worst of hos.

Bad things keep happening. I get conned out of my beautiful house in the hills of Echo Park. I fall deep, deeper, deepest down the black hole of debt. I either dump or am dumped by all the girlfriends, the wife, and the fiancées.

Then one night in Harlem, I try to have sex for money with a transsexual/crackhead/thief masquerading as a female prostitute/ho/industrial sex technician. She takes me to a crack house. I am excited to go. Later I realized I wanted someone to kill me. I've never believed in suicide. You're forcing someone else to clean up the mess you made of your life and death. It seems selfish. Rude. But if someone else kills you, they're responsible for the cleanup.

So I find myself deep in the bowels of a Harlem crack house surrounded by a bunch of angry disenfranchised crackheads. The tranny thief, who I notice has an enormous Adam's apple (*How did I miss that? I find myself thinking*), punches me in the nose and demands my big gold fanny pack. I refuse. A rabid, drug-fueled mutant flies through the air like a prehistoric crackosaurus and cracks me over the head with a lead pipe.

Luckily, I come from a long line of hardheaded peasants, and you can basically use our skulls to pound in nails. So my head bends, but it does not break. Blood gushes down my face like a warm, wet red waterfall.

The circle of drug addicts stares at me with the deep confusion only crack addicts can muster. They gape at me like a school of crack fish. And I have an intense feeling of connection with them. Like we are all in the brotherhood (or transgenderhood) of bent, folded, spindled, and mutilated humans.

As all that blood gushes down my face and soaks my shirt, they look so funny, I start to laugh. I don't mean to. It's not like I think, *Oh, I should laugh now.* The laugh just comes out big and natural.

Then they start laughing.

Suddenly me and all my crackheaded brothers (and transgendered sister) are all laughing together. At that point in my life I have lots of money. So I pull out a $100 bill and hand it to them. They seem hypnotized by it. Like they haven't seen a $100 bill in so long that it throws them into a deep trance. I use this opportunity to take leave of my new crack buddies, slithering out of the crack house like a snake after he's delivered the apple in the Garden of Eden.

Ascending into the sweetness of the Harlem dawn, it feels so good to be alive. I have a blinding, flashing, eye-opening light bulb moment: I don't want to die. I realize that having a girlfriend, then a wife, then a bunch of fiancées, while having sex with all these prostitutes/hos/industrial sex technicians, is a very bad way to spend my time. It just keeps feeding the beast, which gets bigger and bigger and hungrier and hungrier. It stops me from giving and getting love from girlfriends, my wife, and then my bunch of fiancées. And I'm tired of having sex with people I don't know. Who don't like me. I want to have a life full of sex with people I love. Who love me. I want to be with somebody I can trust enough to have a kid with. And raise up that kid and have a family.

The next day I start my search for a professional therapist who can help me. It takes a long time, but I finally find a hypnotherapist in California. Which is pretty much the best place to find a hypnotherapist. Using Jungian/hypnosis-based creative visualization, she shows me how to recognize the impulse for sexual self-destruction and nip it in the bud ASAP. She helps me untangle my knots. She urges me tell my story. I write it down as best I can. Then I use many of the skills I developed as a sex worker/ho to find an agent. The agent helps get me a book deal. When all those words pour out, it sets me free. Embracing my raped inner ho makes it very clear that I didn't want to pay for sex anymore.

When I get my book deal, I make a pact with the universe. I will try to help other people from the sex business tell their stories. That's how we end up, my ex-agent/current wife/mother of my

15

child and me, running a writer's workshop for people either in or getting out of the sex business at a nonprofit in a basement in San Francisco. That begets *Hos, Hookers, Call Girls, and Rent Boys*. When that book comes out, my partner in crime R.J. and I are the object of enormous love and hate. From pillars and dregs of society, academics and illiterates, sex workers and johns, business leaders and food stampers, teenagers and octogenarians. From people who desperately want prostitution abolished. From people who desperately want prostitution decriminalized. Angry threats, violent e-mails, toxic rants. I live in a small faux-liberal town called Montclair, New Jersey. A very popular local website runs a little story about me and the book. They are flooded with vile, venomous, hate-speech-filled comments. If you scratch beneath the tolerance, with the anonymity of the World Wide Web all that ugliness comes pouring out. At first I take it personally. I let the barbs of hate make me bleed. To my great shame, I lash out once or twice. Then it hits me. This has nothing to do with me. This is about a post-puritanical culture that's incredibly uncomfortable when confronted with real, actual human whoring (as opposed to *Pretty Woman*–ish fantasies) and the exchange of sex for money. Then I keep reminding myself of the words of one of my heroes, Oscar Wilde: There is only one thing in the world worse than being talked about, and that is not being talked about.

When *Hos, Hookers* comes out, I do Sex Worker Literati shows all over the country, and once a month in New York City. Sex workers, either current or former, tell or read their stories. I discover a whole new galaxy of incredibly talented writers and performers who just happen to have been prostitutes/hos/industrial sex technicians. Lots of them ask me if we are going to put together another book. It becomes obvious that there are so many more voices out there. So I start collecting stories. I use all my networks to reach out to sex workers. Hos are by their nature brilliant and diligent networkers. They come flying out of the cyber-woodwork. Soccer moms and madams, junkies and MFA graduates, bluebloods and high yellas, purebreds and mutts, doctors and high school dropouts. I also go back to some of the amazing young women I met when I was brought to Washington, D.C., by the United States Department of Justice to do a writing workshop with survivors who were sexualized too young and too often, most of whom with absolutely no chance of having their voices heard in our society. Most of whom have been arrested and beaten and tortured. Most of whom are written about by social workers and academics and theorists and policy wonks and Hollywood writers doing either feel-good ho fairy tales, or gruesomely brutal stories that make the basic assumption: Hookers have to be saved, and they are disposable, illiterate, uneducated fodder for serial killers. Perhaps not so coincidentally, this mirrors what happens in real life. When the Green River Killer was caught, he said he killed prostitutes/hos/industrial sex technicians because he knew no one would miss them.

As I think about my life as a consumer and provider of sex for money, I realize how all those relationships changed me. With all these new writers at our disposal, we decide it would be crazy not to do a new book that focuses on those relationships. And, of course, I made a deal with the universe to help sex workers tell their stories. Don't want to mess with the universe.

Then I realize I'd like to have stories from customers about what it's like to pay for sex. Back-to-back, face-to-face, eye-to-eye with providers. So I go after johns, marks, tricks, and chickenhawks to get their stories. I ask everybody I know. And I know lots of perverts, freaks, and ne'er-do-wells. I put out the call all over the information superhighway. I lurk in online dens of iniquity. I solicit the famous and unknown. I am shocked at how few men (and women) are willing to say publicly that they have paid for sex. As if there are no customers in this billion-dollar industry. And so many times I get the same insulted response from guys: "Hey man, I don't have to *pay* for it." Like this is the litmus test for manhood. That's one reason there are so

17

many anonymous consumer stories. Apparently, at this moment in history, it's easier for people to say they sell sex than that they buy it.

Thanks for listening. If you have a story to tell, let me know. I'd love to hear it.

David Henry Sterry

1
The Street

HEY JOE

Jessica Bertucci

What started off as a late night hook-up right off of the track is now an eleven-year-old friendship and still going . . . When you meet someone turning tricks, you never know what to expect. Is he going to be nice? Are you ever going to see this person again? But on this night, I felt comfortable with this trick, and I felt like I could bring him to my apartment. Call me crazy, but even back in those days I always went off of my first mind, which is my best friend at times and my worst enemy as well. Joe is Chinese. He is about 56 years old and on the heavier side, but is what every real woman should have by their side no matter what. He is loyal and honest and will do whatever it takes to try and make things work. Me, on the other hand . . . not so much. Hahaha. So when I arrived at my place with Joe, he must've also felt comfortable. We did what I like to call "the unusual," and while sitting there afterward, my cat at the time, Mydro, launched full-force at Joe's balls. He screamed like a bitch and got dressed. I knew I would never see him again. Two to three years go by and—BOOM!—who do I run into? Joe! And I have been a pain in his ass ever since.

Since knowing Joe, a lot of things in my life have happened . . . Basically, my life has been up and down and all around. From getting kidnapped by pimps and going to jail to Joe helping me attend school. Epic fail but anyways . . . I have lied to Joe . . . stopped talking to Joe . . . reunited with Joe . . . borrowed from Joe . . . left the state, came

The Street

back, and guess what? Joe is still around! Now I am not saying Joe is dumb for still being around, but I can say that a lot of good things in my life would not have happened if it weren't for him. I wouldn't have some of the little sense I do have if it weren't for him as well.

I wouldn't trade Joe for any trick, brother, sister, mother, or father, or for that matter anything. He has been family to me when no one even noticed I existed. He has accepted me for the unstable, lying, good-for-nothing whore/basic person that I come from and the woman I am turning out to be!

JESSICA BERTUCCI was born and raised in Chicago. At age 11, she was placed in the child welfare system and moved to Harvey, Illinois, and eventually, Provo, Utah, where she attended high school before relocating back to Chicago. She identifies the streets as the place where she received most of her education. She loves to play video games and will "talk to people till they are blue in the face." After a difficult young adulthood, she takes pride in being free, off hard narcotics, and able to support herself. Her work appeared in *Hos, Hookers, Call Girls, and Rent Boys* (Soft Skull, 2009).

DIAMOND BRACELETS

Mattilda Bernstein Sycamore

You know those tricks who've had fifty years of practice sucking cock—and I do mean fifty years—and still it's sandpaper city? What's up with that? This straight boy on the street says I remind him of Alice in Wonderland, how sweet! Though I think my father molested me during that movie. Alice just kept falling and falling.

Three in the morning and of course I'm wired—remember the early '90s? Tweakin' and tweezin', tweakin' and tweezin'. Every time a trick hangs up on me, I gain a renewed faith in humanity—someone really cares! Looking worse in the mirror, do you believe in insurance? Aaron says there's an online community called pneumothorax .com—his collapsed lung finally has a home: Donna Karan Donna Karan Donna Karan.

Fighter jets and fire engines—oh, it's my mother's birthday! She leaves a message. Did she really say "I love you"? More sirens. I'm so dehydrated and Congress authorizes President Bush to wage war against Iraq while fighter jets just keep flying over and over. Everyone in the street stops to stare. But where are all those jets going?

The U.S. government is already talking about postwar occupation of Iraq, and the tendons in my feet and hands are burning. The sky is still so loud—is that a bomb? So much pain in my head, everybody's allergic to war. But wait—there's good news: The stock market is up 7.8 percent in two days and you've been invited to celebrate Disney's 100th anniversary with a four-day, three-night vacation stay in Orlando, Florida, near world-famous Walt Disney World. Plus, you'll enjoy three days/two nights on the white-sand beaches of Daytona—all for $99 per person. The confirmation for your invitation is Magical 752.

News brief: Someone on the phone sex line used the word "tender"! Apparently the roaches enjoy the base of my electric toothbrush, a safe, warm home for the fringe. I hate it when I get so exhausted that I can't function, and then I get depressed—wait, that happens every day. My trick loves this weather—we have this weather every night. If I stayed in bed for two months, who would feed me?

This trick says, "Wasn't it fun to watch the Blue Angels?" A taxi driver tells me air shows are America's number-one pastime. The toast at 7 AM is so dry, and I can feel my depression creeping up on me—HELP! There's a good-luck penny in the hallway—okay, everything's going to be fine. Sick, sick, sick, sick—kick!

My next trick has such pale skin, reminds me of when I was afraid of the sun too—was I that pale? My favorite moment is when I tell him his hair is soft. He says, "Thanks, I work on it." Felix's mixing takes me out of depression, through nostalgia and into the border area. Like I could cry, or fly. Which do I prefer—using a dildo and fucking up my hand, or using my dick and inflaming my jock itch? The bride is arriving soon, and I must please her. Over the phone, he says: "I just got in from Paris and I feel like shit, are you up for fucking?"

As soon as the trick walks in, I know I'm not going to be able to fuck him. He's working the receding hairline with a gooey gray ponytail and blue contacts to contrast his leather tanning-salon skin, Fila jumpsuit, big silver rings on all his fingers, and round tortoise-shell eyeglasses. This girl is married, with kids—and now she needs tea, then a shower. But God save the queen, he comes while I'm jerking him off. Then the best part is when he tells me about his town: He says the racial composition is twenty-five different shades of white, and the architecture is like Taco Bell–designed heaven.

In the depressed area of the trick's town, the houses go for $500,000, but to really fit in you need to own not only a pool, but an indoor pool, a north-south tennis court, and a two-story garage for the $500,000 RV. It's not just a gated community: They've got armed guards on patrol. Everywhere there are blue-haired ladies in designer jeans wearing enough diamond bracelets to get a hernia.

Did I mention the trick's umbilical hernia, a bubble of mushy skin oozing out of his belly button like a force field? Rich people are so glamorous. The next trick hands me a glass of tap water—the bitch doesn't know if he can get money out of the bank, but his apartment must be worth $3 million and the doorman has to unlock the elevator. This is just the San Francisco apartment.

Dreams of new houseplants, changing what it says on the computer screen, and stress, stress, stress! Did I mention Ralowe's show? We performed together at this hipster nightmare. He finished the night with layers of noise, drums that were just another instrument on top of the machines, and then Ralowe shaking his body and shouting rap vocals over the commotion. It was delicious. Everyone left.

Today the sun is filtering through the clouds, and I'm rooting for the clouds. Shit—here comes the sun—and is it really 4 PM? All the little memories loading me down   like I'm eating *tom kha* soup with Rue, and Jeremy introduced me to that soup. Buying plants together, going to visit the sea lions, and I can't bring myself to get rid of the stuffed animals, even though they just make me think of petting Jeremy, sweet Jeremy. I want to call him and tell him I miss him, but I don't want to call him.

I know it's dangerous to get all teary-eyed about the time when my white boyfriend introduced me to a Thai specialty, but that's how nostalgia works—nostalgia is dangerous. Kayti remembers when she used to say she was Persian, so people wouldn't know that she was Latina—people thought it was more glamorous to be from Persia; we both had a lot of Persian friends. Kayti says they were really from Iran, right?

Dreams that they've changed my front door, can I get out? I'm thinking about how many pairs of eyes we look into each day—there's this guy on the bus with beautiful gray eyes, I can't stop looking. I catch another eye in the back, just one, a blond guy. The bus arrives. At home, I jerk off so I don't have to think about hooking up.

I'm telling Justin and Owen about Jeremy, and then all of the sudden ten people show up at their house, I guess it's 2 AM. Owen says you switch so easily into social mode. I don't know what mode I'm in, suddenly I've got so much energy, and Xylor says I saw you earlier and I was telling somebody about your outfit—it was the most preposterous combination of colors I've ever seen, I even remembered the red socks, though it didn't make sense. The person I was talking to said, "Yeah, Mattilda likes red socks."

Ralowe starts free-styling and I'm dancing on top of the ottoman, it's all about the hands and body twisting and tensioning, breathe in, out. Almost falling off and recovering. I have so much energy, it's crazy—and too late, really. Xylor says, "I wonder why." I say, "No, that's not why." She looks at my eyes. "Well, maybe you're just a night person."

I'm so glad everyone goes outside to smoke, Billeil even checks to make sure. Ralowe and I leave, and I'm looking at the doors in front of the apartment. The apartment's so long and thin—was it made for immigrant workers, or did they subdivide it? Then I'm looking into the funeral home, and, wait, the door frame next door is gorgeous and Ralowe says he's exhausted. I'm getting exhausted too.

Just as I'm hailing a taxi, the bus comes. Ralowe tries to get on the back and the bus driver calls him out—get off the bus, he says. Ralowe gets off, I'm waving him to the front, and the bus driver speeds away. This woman says, "Just because they're black, they think they can get on for free." The bus driver, who's black, says, "Shut your mouth already." The woman looks at me, she says, "Your daddy raped you and that's why you're a faggot." I say, "My daddy raped me, but that's not why I'm a faggot." She says, "Your daddy raped you and that's why you're a faggot." I say, "Your problem is that you tasted shit, and then you just kept eating it." She gets off the bus.

I call Ralowe on his cell phone: "Honey, you should have asked me for a dollar." Ralowe says, "I'm gonna walk home." "All the way to

North Beach?" He says, "I'm gonna work on this song." I say, "Well, I'll call you when I get home, 'cause I've got a story for you." He says, "Don't call me because I don't have any minutes, I'll see you tomorrow." I say, "I might not get up in time." He says, "Then I'll see you Tuesday."

We're all crazy, holding it together with such fine threads. I'm waiting for the 90 at Van Ness and Mission, and I'm getting all emotional—it's not okay for a bus driver to make you walk home because you don't have enough money for the fare—and does the 90 ever come? Finally it pulls up, I can't believe it, and just as I get on the bus there's a ten-foot high ad for Tommy Hilfiger, the whole ad is this guy's abs and the Stars and Stripes. It's sickening and suddenly I'm horny in that desperate way.

MATTILDA BERNSTEIN SYCAMORE (mattildabernsteinsycamore.com) is most recently the author of a memoir, *The End of San Francisco* (City Lights, 2013). She is also the author of two novels, most recently *So Many Ways to Sleep Badly* (City Lights, 2008), and the editor of five nonfiction anthologies, including *Why Are Faggots so Afraid of Faggots?: Flaming Challenges to Masculinity, Objectification, and the Desire to Conform* (AK Press, 2012); *Nobody Passes: Rejecting the Rules of Gender and Conformity* (Seal Press, 2007); and *That's Revolting! Queer Strategies for Resisting Assimilation* (expanded edition, Soft Skull, 2008). In 2012, Mattilda moved to Seattle, and hopefully by the time you read this she will still love it. Always feel free to say hi.

Shawanda

My name is Shawanda. That's my real name, Shawanda. How I got started is my friend was doing it, her brother was hooking her up. So, you know, right place right time. Ha ha ha. He gave us some rock. He said he was going to fuck us up if we didn't smoke. So I figured it was better to just smoke instead of getting my ass ripped up. But then I got away from him. I was 13. But he showed me how to get paid. Everybody gots to get paid. The problem is, I gots to get all liquored up and get my smoke before I could work, and then when I'm done working, I gots to get liquored up and smoked up again. So that's a serious problem. But I can't stand to work for nobody. I don't want nobody messin' with my money. So everybody thinks they can run their games on me. This is my rule. You good to me, I good to you. I worked with this girl Cookie. She from Thailand. Cute little girl. Big earner. She pretended like she didn't speak no English. We worked doubles for a while and at the start of every date, she bat them big-ass eyes and say in her little baby girl voice, "You good to me, I good to you." She showed me how to milk the cow. Why rip some asshole off for a C when you can milk the cow for a C every week? But as soon as somebody mess with me, all bets is off. I can't stand me no bumzillions. That's what I call 'em. That's a bum, only a zillion times worst. With a bumzillions, you know, I take whatever I can get, fuck 'em, what they gonna do, go to the man and say, "A ho stole my shit!"? I don't think so. This here is my world. You come down to Shawanda's world, I give you whatever the fuck I want to give you. Fuck it. I want to get me a rich husband. A white man. A old white man. And I'd live in a big ole house, get my babies back, and just wait around for that motherfucker to die.

SHAWANDA is a sex worker based in Oakland, California. This is her first published work.

THE PROFESSIONAL CHICKEN

Perry Brass

I met Raymond on Market Street in San Francisco one evening in the mid-1960s. I was 18 years old and basically living on the streets, like a lot of queer kids were doing in those days and still do. I had come to San Francisco to escape my growing up in Savannah, Georgia, where at that time I was sure that the best I could hope for would be not to be murdered: a common end for gay men in the Deep South then— murder, suicide, or a slower version of either as you accommo- dated yourself to a lifetime of fear, self-loathing, and self-rejection. I wanted none of that. So at 17 I hitchhiked from Savannah to the city by the Golden Gate that offered me an amazing, embracing freedom. I met Raymond one lovely San Francisco evening in the fall. He was with a group of young *queens*—that is, guys who openly identified themselves to each other as gay. Raymond was not a queen: He was a chicken-hustler who kind of knocked you out with how cool and good-looking he was. He was slightly built and, almost indecently, nicely formed with young James Dean looks. His tight denim shirt, the standard hustler uniform, was left slightly unbuttoned so you could see some of his perfectly chiseled chest, with just a glimpse of either small pink nipple showing.

He had a way of smoking a cigarette or of walking into a room that could make your mouth water. He was being kept by a homely tall guy in his early 30s who already seemed like an old john—he had a mid-level office job and was as prissy as an old maid aunt. His name was Peter, and he had picked up Raymond in Union Square, a good hustler area: The better hustlers hung out there, rather than some of the scuzzier areas of Market Street. Still, Market Street was a great place to meet guys in the early evening. There were lots of people about and you quickly met friends, or *potential* friends, at almost any corner. I was immediately enchanted with Raymond, and the three of us went to a coffee shop, with Peter panting and making himself look like a fool all over Raymond, who would just wave him off, or simply smile at him when Peter said Raymond had the cutest ass he'd ever seen on a boy.

"You still don't get to use it," Raymond said softly. He didn't have to protest much, but he let it be known that like a lot of hustlers, he didn't get fucked but did the fucking. He also had a girlfriend and mentioned her often, even if no one ever got to meet her. That was Raymond's public palaver. In private, what hustlers did was another story. But one of the main rules of hustlers was that you didn't blow their story—their covers. If you did, it could be dangerous, although Raymond seemed so sweet and extremely young—in regular daylight, he easily looked 14—that you couldn't imagine him hurting you. (Although I found out later that he could defend himself, and did.)

Raymond didn't last long in Peter's extremely tacky care; he threw the kid out in a few days, because Peter was too pushy about fucking him, and as Raymond insisted, "I just don't go that route."

I started seeing him a lot back on Market Street in the early evening or Union Square in the late afternoon, and he told me about himself. He was past 20 (exactly where past was his business), but he was so fair-skinned and compactly built in a softly lean way that he had been doing the chicken bit forever—maybe six or seven years—and would continue doing it. His one problem was his smoking: It was aging him, and he didn't take care of his teeth—they were chipped and yellow already—but that added a street toughness to him which some men found appealing. He had nice manners, like he would usually address men as "sir," and he never raised his voice or came off strident and offensively macho.

The real kicker, I learned, was his origins: Raymond insisted he was Mexican, born and raised there, and he spoke beautiful, fluent Spanish. "Both my folks were Basques," he told me. "Basques are often blond. My family moved to Mexico before I was born. I go back sometimes. They think I'm studying here in the U.S. I hate school. It just wasn't for me, I kept getting into fights and I had to show guys all the time I wasn't chicken-shit or pussy. I started doing this"—he meant hustling—"in Texas, where some of my relatives live. Basque families are real close to each other—we're like a minority in Spain and everyplace else. I can speak Basque, too. It's a separate language."

When he told me this, I felt that he had shared something with me that didn't usually come out. His real name, he told me, was Ramón, and when he spoke Spanish (and became *Ramón*) his whole affect changed. He was no longer just a kid hustler, but relaxed into a deeper, really more beautiful self. He glowed. I heard him speaking Spanish to Latino kids who were either on the streets hustling or working menial jobs in restaurants. They were usually handsome Mexicans, with striking, hatchet-sharp Aztec features and silky, coal-black hair. *Ramón*, with his soft blond looks and shy diffident manner, stood out from them. I asked him once what they were talking about.

"Mostly how hard their life is. They wish they were back home, but it's too hard there for them. No jobs. They have to fight too much to stay alive. They don't want to just do work in the fields. It's still better for them here."

However, not all the Latino kids were nice to him, and we were once together on South Market Street when a small too-full-of-them-selves macho group of them started picking on him, and calling him a *maricón* to his face. I'm not sure how all this started, maybe with some kind of rumor, but it flared up and *Ramón* suddenly became just plain Raymond—and not about to take anything. He pulled a switch-blade out from his pocket and flicked it open, but casually, just to show it. I thought I was going to pass out from fear; then everything calmed down. The boys left and he put the knife away.

"I don't let people fuck with me," he said softly, making me quite aware of what he was capable of doing.

I'd decided early on not to make any moves on Raymond, and that incident definitely solidified my feelings. He had always insisted to me he was *straight*, and I was too much engaged in my own romantic quests to seek out straight kids. But worse was the feeling that if I had done it, it would have changed everything. Raymond telegraphed quickly that he trusted no one, and he never would have trusted me even to the slight extent that he did if I had tried anything. But we did hang out together when we saw each other, and I was sure he was as open with me as he could be with anyone else. He did tell me that when he made enough money, he called home from a pay phone and talked with his folks or his sister. He had a younger kid sister he liked. He told me she was so blond that people were sure she was a gringo, and she had a hard time insisting that she wasn't. He also told me at one point that his parents were gypsies, but *that* story I found hard to believe.

At the end of my first winter in San Francisco, I decided that I was tired of living hand-to-mouth there, and other kids I'd met told me that there were more jobs on the East Coast. I had a slight amount of training as an artist, so I thought I should move to New York where the "art jobs" were. I saw a notice on a North Beach coffee shop bulletin board for a ride to New York, and I called the guy—he was looking to share expenses and I had just about that much money saved up—and took it. After a few stops in other cities, I ended up in New York in the fall of 1966. I started hanging out in the Village near Washington Square, which at that point was very gay, especially on the west side of the Square. I saw several young guys there I knew from San Francisco who had the same idea: They were tired of the tight economy out west, and New York, as the Vietnam War heated up, had become awash in money and jobs. I quickly got one as a gofer in an art studio, making a tiny salary, but I could live cheaply enough to enjoy New York City. Finally, I met two other guys, Eric and John, there from the West Coast. They were in their late 20s, but really into 14- and

15-year-old boys. We would hang out in the Square, and mostly I was happy to have any kind of gay company, which was also a distinction of that period: like no matter what you specialized in, be it truck drivers, kids, sailors, black men, white guys with mustaches— anyway, you could hang out with other *gays* and talk together.

I was doing this one day when Raymond popped up. Eric and John both smiled generously at him. It became apparent that they'd had him in San Francisco and both of them had paid for him. He was cordial to them and joined us. A few minutes later, Eric and John left us to go to a movie, and I got to stay alone for a few minutes with Raymond. I asked him what he was doing in New York. He told me that things were going badly at home in Mexico for his parents and he decided that he really needed to make some money, and he could make a lot more money in New York "doing what I do" than in San Francisco where "kids were all over the place."

I guessed he meant "real" kids who actually were the age Raymond tried to be and previously could pass for, although in the bright daylight of the Square I could see that the past year had aged him and he no longer looked 14. He was now slipping closer to looking his real age. He was still very appealing though, and as we were talking, a john in his late 40s started looking at us.

Raymond's eyes gazed softly at the sidewalk, then he stared up at me. I could tell this was a signal that I should leave him for the transaction at hand, and I did. But I didn't go very far; I wanted to watch and did so from an angle across the street. The man, who was wearing a bulky beige raincoat and a hat, approached him and sat down. Raymond's eyes settled on him like they would on a pigeon, and he drew a cigarette out of his denim shirt pocket. The man offered him a light. Raymond accepted it, and about three minutes later, with hardly any words involved, the two of them walked off together.

I wasn't sure if I'd ever see Raymond again, but I did, either in the Square or standing on a corner on Greenwich Avenue near Tenth Street, which was also a good corner for hustlers back then. We would talk briefly between his tricks. He had begun working for a "service," which he gave me few details about. I think he wasn't proud of it—there was something about working for one that demeaned him, and I'd been told by other hustlers that if you worked for a service, it was usually expected of you that you did "other things" rather than just be "trade." In other words, some men would expect to fuck you if they offered you enough money, and if you didn't do it the service would quickly drop you.

Although I was making piddling money at the art studio, I felt bad for him. He was staying in a hotel near Times Square and looked tired and raw around the edges. His eyes were circled with dark rings and he was edgy; that charming kid part that he could do so well was getting burned away. The last time I saw him, he told me that he really wanted to return to Mexico. He'd been speaking with his sister, who told him that their mother was sick and their father wanted him home.

"I don't know what I'll tell him," he told me. "I'll have to make up all kinds of stories. I can't tell them what I do, and they'll want me to stay there and I don't want to do that either."

"What do you really want to do?" I asked. "I mean what do you want to do with your *life?*"

He shrugged. "I dunno. I want to get married sometime and have a family. But I don't know what I want to do exactly. I kind of drift along. A lot of kids do that. What's so bad about it?"

I noticed he had a book with him. It was, believe it or not, *The Catcher in the Rye.* I thought that was almost funny, and smiled. He seemed like Holden Caulfield's shyer, more ragged kid brother, from the other side of the tracks. I said goodbye to him, and he actually hugged me, which Raymond had never done before. I didn't see him again, and had almost stopped thinking about him, until I saw Eric again in midtown Manhattan. We just ran into each other by accident, and he asked me up to his place for lunch the next day. He was living with John in an apartment hotel close to the theater district. It was an old building with rundown apartments in which, I had a feeling, generations of struggling Broadway chorus girls and boys lived. Eric made lunch for me: a grilled cheese sandwich and Campbell's soup. I dug into my sandwich and suddenly remembered Raymond.

Eric looked downcast when I brought his name up. I asked him why.

"He's dead," Eric said. I was shocked. "He was killed somewhere outside of San Antonio, Texas, where his folks lived. I think a gang finally got to him. They have some bad gangs in that area."

I felt really terrible, close to crying.

"I thought his parents lived in Mexico, and were Basques."

"That was all bullshit," John said. "He made it up. He was just a gringo kid from some two-bit border town in Texas. He hated being a punky kid other kids picked on, so he made up that story. He was picked on a lot at home, too. His father was a son of a bitch who used to beat him. He was about as Mexican as I am." John smiled.

"But why'd he make up this story about being a Basque?" I asked.

Eric shook his head. "All hustlers do it. It gives them a story to tell because most of the time their real story is not very pretty— even though *they* can be. We liked Raymond a lot. He was cute and great in bed. All that bullshit about him being really straight—if he was, he was certainly doing a good job of acting 'gay' for *us*. We both had him several times, and fucked him when we wanted to. We paid him, sure, but that was part of the act. He was good with old men though—he had a string of them all over. They just dug his little-lost-boy act, and he was good at doing it. But, as we all know, you can't do that forever."

I finished my grilled cheese sandwich and thanked them both, then decided I never wanted to see these two guys again. There was something about them I could no longer stomach. I kept thinking, *Why didn't they help Raymond more if they knew all about him?* And I wished I could have; but maybe the truth was, he wouldn't let anybody do it. No matter what his *real* story was or what he did in bed with other men, he wanted to preserve his dignity, his sense of himself, and that meant keeping all of us away from him. His story was so sad that it haunted me for years, and I can still see his face, his sandy-blond hair, his shy, almost smiling eyes, and the way he walked with his tight denim shirt just slightly unbuttoned, with his hands deep in his pockets.

PERRY BRASS is a, poet, novelist, playwright, and activist. His father died at 42; his mother died at 60 of complications from adult-onset diabetes and plain stupidity. His father, a Southern Jewish gentleman, spoke fluent Yiddish and had no college education. He also hunted and fished and loved guns and adventure. Both his parents were exceptionally good-looking people with streaks of great stubbornness and evil tempers and a passion for not working for other people. Brass, for better and worse, has inherited all of this. He grew up in Savannah, Georgia, during segregation, when his own doctor had separate waiting rooms for white people and colored people. He quickly learned to question anything that anyone ever said while growing up. He escaped by hitchhiking to California when he was 17, and he lived a life on the streets. He lived in Germany in the late 1970s with his then-partner, a sergeant in the U.S. Air Force, learning a great deal about what it meant to be gay in the service. During the early 1980s, with his current partner, he lived in New Orleans for three years, and he has lived in New York on and off through most of his adult life. He has had a lot of shit-shoveling jobs in writing: copy, PR, editing everything from tech stuff to porn. He worked on the floor of an aircraft factory in Hartford, Connecticut, during the height of the Vietnam War. A year later, in New York, he worked in commercial art studios and ad agencies during the "Mad Men" period of knife-to-the-throat NY advertising and was constantly harassed for being queer. He describes it as the worst form of male prostitution he'd ever been involved in, either as a participant or an observer. He has published sixteen books, winning numerous awards for his poetry, plays, and fiction. He has had over sixty poems set to music by such composers as Chris DeBlasio, Fred Hersch, Ricky Ian Gordon, Paula Kimper, and Gerald Busby. He is featured in *All the Way Through Evening*, a documentary by Australian filmmaker Rohan Spong about young composers who've died of AIDS, named for his collaboration with Chris DeBlasio. In 1972, he co-founded the Gay Men's Health Project Clinic, the first clinic for gay men on the East Coast, still operating as New York's Callen-Lorde Community Health Center. His nonfiction books include *The Manly Art of Seduction* and *King of Angels*, a

Southern-gay-Jewish coming-of-age novel set in Savannah in 1963. He is a coordinator of the New York Rainbow Book Fair, the oldest LGBT book fair in the United States, and he's the treasurer of the Greater New York Independent Publishers Association. He believes that all people are created equal, and that our beliefs about God are based on the alpha dog system: God is the ultimate Alpha Dog. He believes that love is the most wonderful thing in the world; it is the only thing that changes human life.

Johns, Marks, Tricks, and Chickenhawks

WHO'S THE WHORE?
MY FIRST TIME HIRING A MONEY BOY
IN THAILAND

David Gilmore

My friend Darren and I walked past a couple of quiet gay bars, and a few guys came out to greet us enthusiastically. They were the so-called "money boys." Point of clarification for the paranoid: They are not boys. They are over 18.

Most of the sex trade one finds on the street is not appealing to me—they look too street-tough and saucy and at the same time are aggressively flirty. I'm attracted to refined little guys—shy, intellectual elves—and I was fairly certain I was not going to find anyone like that on this street side. So I just gave the friendly brush-off to the guys who solicited us. They wouldn't take no for an answer and surrounded us, walked with us and even stood in our way. The desperation level was making me sad. But we smiled and laughed and shook our heads, "No thank you . . . NO!" I had to actually pick one guy up and move him out of my way and give him a friendly spank for being in my way. I think he enjoyed it, actually.

I mentioned to Darren that if I saw someone who intrigued me, I might go for it, but had little idea how to make a smooth transaction happen. It's a complex move—you have to face your own issues of money, power, shame, illegality, then negotiate for what you want to do (if you even know) and do it all with someone who is likely not going to be speaking your language in a foreign currency that requires you to divide everything by thirty-five on the spot. You are

39

expected to do this with aplomb, smiling all the while. This is, after all, Thailand, the land of smiles.

We walked up another side road, and out came another gaggle of boys to solicit us. I stopped in my tracks as one would when being pursued by a pack of wild animals. *Hold your ground*, I told myself, *don't run . . . just back away slowly*.

At last, one guy appeared from behind the crowd who caught my attention. He was not one of the grabby ones. Looking over the top of his buddies, I smiled at him and he smiled back at me, revealing a mouthful of braces. Oh no, braces—too young! It is particularly challenging to judge ages in Thailand—their creamy, smooth skin seems to age so well in the tropical humidity that someone in their forties can look like they're twenty while we Westerners end up looking like hairy, sun-damaged lizards. I beckoned him with a backward nod of my head and asked him his age. He said 22. Taking him for his word, I put him back in the running for my maiden voyage.

In Thailand, the money boys are the "property" of the bar they hang out in. They sit at the bar waiting for customers to approach. The bartender or the bar owner makes the sale. The bar keeps track of them and I suspect offers some protection and validation that they are healthy and of age. It's all informal but nonetheless solid. At the very least, the bar provides witnesses should anything unsavory happen to the boy.

The other boys could see that I was focused on the one. I felt strangely like I was at a seafood restaurant picking out a lobster from a tank. The others backed away out of respect for the boy who might have a sale—a professional courtesy that didn't subject me to a territorial bitch fight. I was left standing alone with the boy in the street—Darren stood about 500 feet away, watching. The boy came closer and I asked his name. *Day-Arh* was the best I could make of what he said. It kind of sounded like "Dear." I told him I thought he was very cute and that later I would come back after my friend went to bed. He smiled and nodded and we said goodbye.

After dinner and a drag show at Tangmo, I walked Darren back to the hotel. He got into bed with a 101-degree fever. I, however, had a fever of another kind. I wanted to go out and hire my first money boy. I said goodnight to Darren, packed some lube and a condom into my shorts, and set out into the street.

I stopped in the ramshackle lobby of our gay hotel to talk to the owner, Phytoon, to ask him about money boys. He seemed like he either had been a money boy once or would have likely been part of that syndicate that keeps track of them. There was a certain friendly-netherworld quality to him. I smiled and approached him and told him I wanted to buy a money boy. He gave me back a half smile and a knowing look—clearly I wasn't the only one who had ever approached him about this.

His English was excellent, and so I barraged him with questions: "Phytoon, I want to do this but I'm not sure how. What do you pay them, how long do you get, and what are you allowed to do?" Feeling the power of being the one with all the information, he had me sit at the bar and laid it out for me in long form.

"Well, this is how you do it," he said, tapping his cigarette in the ash tray. "First you choose the boy you like, and then you go to him and negotiate with him about what he is willing to do. You can ask him anything about the details. Then you ask him how much. He'll tell you. You can negotiate with him, but around here it's usually about 1,000 baht. Then you have to pay the bar." He gave me a few more pointers and then, like a coach, he patted me on the shoulder and sent me into the alley leading to Day-Arh.

The conversation with Phytoon got me all excited. How easy is this? How simple? How forthright? What a great opportunity to be able to negotiate exactly what you want along with the price, and then actually do it. No shame, no skulking around, no hours in front of the computer.

Adrenaline was now coursing through my veins, and my pulse quickened as I turned up the deserted street where I last saw Day-Arh. The boys all saw me coming. But this time they stayed seated, and I heard one yell into the bar, "DAY-ARH—he's HERE!!" He came bouncing out of the murky disco bar with a cigarette in his hand. My

41

excitement was dashed seeing that he was a smoker. I hate the taste of smoke on someone. He came right up to me and saw the smile fall off my face. I frowned, *You smoke*. He quickly hid the cigarette behind his back and flashed a big smile at me as if to say, *Who ME? I don't smoke*. We both laughed. He immediately dropped it, mashed it out with his shoe, and put a breath mint in his mouth. I wasn't going to let this be a deal breaker—unfortunately, everyone smokes in Thailand. (Breath mints are an excellent addition to anyone's little sex tool kit.)

He came in a little closer, and I said, "Are you free?" Ooopsie— that was not the right phrasing.

"You want go with me?" he said.

"Yes," I replied.

"You pay bar. Not free," he told me with an indignant frown.

I laughed and corrected myself—"You are AVAILABLE?"

"Yes," he said.

"Now?" I asked. He nodded and smiled, swishing the breath mints around more rapidly.

"What do you like to do?" I inquired of the boy as if I was online or something. Damn it—another wrong question. Phytoon was going to kick my butt—I'm striking out! Deep breath, start over. Remember now, I'm the paying client—he's here to please me. You tell him what you want to do, and he agrees to it or not. Thus began my confusion over who was the sex worker and who was the client. It seemed I wanted to make him happy—to please HIM. Although it was a noble thought, it was confusing the guy.

He starts back at me, "What YOU want?"

This time I got it right. "I want kiss you," I told him, remembering to keep the sentences short and simple and in the present tense, maybe leaving out the prepositions. He gave me a definitive nod and smile. I leaned in to kiss him like one would try a sample of the pistachio ice cream. He gave me a nice freebie kiss. Soft, wet lips and gentle tongue. Excellent! I was all flush with excitement, if you know what I mean, standing across from this beautiful young man with rosy lips, black hair, brown eyes, and gorgeous, thick eyebrows

42

that almost met in the middle. He was clearly not pure Thai—some Malaysian or Cambodian blood, I was guessing.

Just then, one of the other boys came running out of the bar on a mission for something and swooped in past us. "DAY-ARH, you got good one. Handsome!" He grabbed my hard dick through my pants. Wow—was it that obvious? Day-Arh was unfazed by this drive-by groping.

I was now flying on the dopamine and adrenaline that a man gets when he's got a live one on the line. I was ready to pick him up and carry him to the bar.

But I continued feeling him out a bit: "You like to get fucked?" You'd think I would have learned—I was still trying to think about what would please him. Being the professional he was, he turned it around and asked me the more appropriate question: "You want fuck me?" I smiled and nodded. I couldn't contain my glee about negotiating something that over the course of my life I've spent thousands of hours stuck in the mystery of will he/won't he.

I confirmed for him: "Yes, I want fuck you, okay?"

"Yes, you fuck me," he said and held his smiling gaze up at me.

"Okay, I fuck you." I had to say it one more time just to amuse myself at how easy this was. After all this deliberation, I was beginning to think my time was up and I should now pay my money and go home.

I asked how much and he said 1,000 baht, which is about $35. I agreed and we basically moved on to the checkout counter. All the boys sat around the bar watching as I pulled out my wallet and thumbed through the notes as the bespectacled king's emotionless face looked at me from the bills.

Then came the extras . . . oh yes, the extras. . . it's the underground, nothing is written, and so you don't get a contract, receipt, warranty, and waiver to sign like you would in America.

Day-Arh said to me, "You have loom?"

"No, I don't have room. We go your place."

"No. Loom cost 200 baht." I was not aware of this detail. I started to back away from the bar and put my wallet away to think for a moment . . . hmmm. Could I bring him back to the hotel room with Darren next to us? Uh, not a good idea. I would have to go to *his* place—I assumed that's where we'd go anyway.

I got assertive. "You say 1,000. I pay 1,000. No more."

They all started squawking. "Loom 200, loom 200." Nope, sorry. And I started to walk away, thinking I'd been burned by the system again—no Ping-Pong pussy, no Day-Ahr.

Day-Ahr followed me out to the street and grabbed my hand, blinked his big girlish eyelashes pleadingly, and said, "You pay 800 to ME and pay bar 200."

"Total 1,000 for everything?" I asked.

"Yes. 1,000 total."

Okay. Good. I went to the bar, he said a few things to his comrades to quiet them down, and I handed the bartender a 1,000-baht note. They gave Day-Ahr 800 and kept the 200. Day-Ahr led me off down the street.

The momentary stress of that transaction began to fade as I focused on the back of Day-Ahr walking a few paces ahead of me. Everyone on the street knew what we were up to, and it felt like all eyes were watching us . . . not in disapproval so much as curiosity and material for the gossip session later on. I may very well have been the only client for anyone that day.

On the way to the room, I found out a little more information about him. He was in school and lived with his boyfriend in Phuket. And in fact, the next morning I saw him drive by on the back of a motorbike holding fast to another young Thai man who I assumed was his boyfriend. He said his boyfriend knew that he was a money boy and had given his approval.

I couldn't help notice what a cute butt Day-Ahr had as he led me up the steps to the "loom." He didn't really look like a sex worker American-style, but the jeans he wore were undoubtedly chosen for the way they presented his ass, his shirttail riding just slightly above the round mass. We went up three flights of a very rundown concrete building with only one tube of fluorescent lighting overhead and two

44

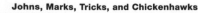

Johns, Marks, Tricks, and Chickenhawks

mattresses on the floor amid piles of clothes. It was clearly the crash pad of several guys . . . friends, he said, who loaned him the place for an hour. The building itself was crumbling. The apartment had no running water—just a toilet down the hall with a bucket of murky water used to spoon into the toilet—which was nothing more than a porcelain hole in the floor.

I was thinking that maybe it would have been better to bring him to the hotel and hope that Darren was knocked out on sleep meds, but I opted out of that idea, and we settled in on the dirty mattresses, undressing each other and kissing. I couldn't decide whether I wanted the light on or off. Making love under a fluorescent shop light was not exactly appealing; then again, the visuals of Day-Ahr were half the joy. We did a little lights-off and a little lights-on. I discovered to my delight that he had hairy legs and forearms and a little patch of hair in the middle of his chest—something very unusual in Thai men.

The rest of what happened with this beautiful young man is probably more interesting to me than you. He did deliver the goods as promised on the street. He was a great kisser and very easy to fuck . . . a professional. Interestingly, at first he wanted to only have sex facing me—I think that may be part of the unwritten code of safety: never turn your back on a client. But after a while he trusted me and didn't insist on this.

We wrestled back and forth with who was the client and who was the sex worker. I kept trying to do things that would please him, and he would lose his erection. When I let him please me, he would get turned on. So after a while I just stuck to my role as a paying customer. (FYI: We had safe sex—no fluids were exchanged, no one got sick, and no one got hurt.)

Seeing Day-Ahr lying spread out before me, both of us smiling in the darkness, his body inviting and sensual as Thailand itself, I felt privileged that he shared himself with me. His beautiful body and his attention for an hour and a half cost me so little money. For him it was good money, an honest living (one could eat in restaurants for a week in Thailand for $35). For me it was money well spent, a chance

45

to see into a world that is so shrouded in mystery and laced with shame. In the words of Justin Bond at the end of the film *Shortbus*, "Your demon is your best friend . . . and we all get it in the end."

Not being Day-Ahr's first, I'm certain that he would forget about me in some days or weeks. I could never say the same.

DAVID GILMORE is a graphic designer, filmmaker, photographer, and massage therapist living an unsustainably lean life in the desert southwest. He was born behind the "Orange curtain" of California. His dad was an art teacher and his mom was a paralegal. As a teen, he was shuttled off to southwest Florida where he languished, taking up serial masturbation to fend off boredom. As a young man he escaped to New York where he worked for the United Nations entertaining sexpot dignitaries protected by diplomatic immunity in the men's rooms of the General Assembly building, and occasionally doing some sound engineering. He returned to California in 1988 where he created and hosted Outright Radio, which aired on Public Radio International on over 100 stations nationwide from 1997 to 2005 and received the Edward R. Murrow Award for excellence in broadcast journalism in 2004. The show was funded by the Corporation for Public Broadcasting. David is the author of the tragicomedy memoir *HomoSteading at the Nineteenth Parallel—One Man's Adventures Building His Nightmare Dream House on the Big Island of Hawaii*, available on Amazon. He once lived in Germany. He has no formal education, no shame about anything, and no deep abiding faith in God, but he believes in the power of loving touch. He enjoys singing in orchestral choruses, taking photographs, and cooking. He loves his bicycle almost as much as his camera. He is an avid blogger and loves a good happy hour.

ELEGY FOR TONY KING

R.J. Martín Jr.

I was there the night Tony King became a pimp. I was there the night people's lives started spinning out of control and shooting in different directions like a star exploding. It was in the downstairs room of my mother's house on Forty-third Avenue in San Francisco, but it all started when we began selling weed to Tony's cousins in Oakland.

In the summer of America's bicentennial year, there were only three black families in our neighborhood. Irish-Catholics dominated the area, with subpopulations of Italians and Irish-Mexicans. "Green-beaners," we called them.

One of these black families had a son, Tony, who was our age. Tony was tall and lanky with a slow way of moving and talking that hinted at his family's roots in the South. His tawny skin and hazel eyes let you know that his ancestry was mixed, but it was so far back that Tony didn't know the details. He was between two worlds living in this white neighborhood. We called him "Tony," but in Oakland, where the rest of his family lived, he was known as "Tee" or "Green Eyes." Tony and I had both been asked to leave St. Ignatius High School and were in our final year at the public high school in our district.

In San Francisco, prostitution took place in brothels that were controlled by organized crime, or on the streets—completely un-controlled—where maniacal transgenders, despairing addicts, and the deeply disturbed roamed the avenues of the Tenderloin with nobody to tell them what to do, to protect them, or to love them for who they were.

Across the Bay Bridge it was different. The Pimp Game was a way of life for hundreds, if not thousands, of people. Oakland, California, in the glory days of American pimps, in a fortress of American pimping, was one of the places where the icon of the American pimp was forged. Oakland had the largest prostitution trade in all of California and the city was overrun with pimps. The infrastructure was perfect—plenty of freeway access, cheap motels, and an embattled police force struggling to maintain integrity as Oakland scored, year after bloody year, the distinction of having the highest murder rate in the country.

On the border between Oakland and Berkeley was the California Hotel: 500 rooms, a ballroom, and a nightclub—a gathering place for black people who had some measure of success, or at least a little money to toss around on Saturday night. The California Hotel was also ground zero for the Pimp Game. The girls paraded up and down San Pablo Avenue soliciting the cars that passed by . . . hot pants, miniskirts, Afro hairdos, and hats as big as manhole covers, while the pimps gathered in the hotel bar, drinking fruity multicolored beverages with tiny American flags in them. It was our country's 200th birthday.

When we first started going down there, we rode over in my mother's Volkswagen. We went about once a week to drop a package with Tony's cousins. Tony and his cousins were enamored with the Oakland pimps, who all seemed to be vying for the most fur, the longest coat, or the most outrageous ride. While smoking a joint in my mother's car and watching the Game unfold, one of the cousins might say in reverential tones, "There go MacDuff!" or "L'il Kenny!"

One night one of their role models passed close to the car, and I asked him if he wanted to smoke a joint. The guy laughed, but he sidled up and took a hit. When he saw what quality stuff we had, he asked for a sample. We gave him a baggie with a small amount of marijuana in it. When we saw him the next time, a couple of weeks later, I told Tony, "Go talk to him! Ask him if he wants some weed."

One thing led to another, and Tony King became the weed connection for these pimps in Oakland. More importantly, he let us know he was learning the Pimp Game.

At some point Tony made a decision that it was more important to him to be a successful pimp than anything else. He took a big step, one that his cousins were unwilling to make, and dropped out of school. He asked us to call him "Tee" instead of "Tony," and his speech became peppered with peculiar adages like "Pimpin's as easy as breathin' air" and "A ho without instruction is headed for destruction." One night after one of our soirees, crossing the Bay Bridge from Oakland to San Francisco, with the city lights twinkling against a moonless sky, I asked him about it.

"So Tony . . . I mean *Tee* . . . when ya' gonna start pimping?"

"I don't know, man; I'm still learning the rules."

"Rules? Like what rules?"

"I can't be talkin' 'bout that man, it's part of showing respect for the Game."

This, I could understand.

Back then, there was an honor and dignity in crime. A social hierarchy in which you could have a place. You would earn your place through the mastery of a certain set of skills. When you learned them, you were a part of something larger than yourself. As a safecracker, an extortionist, a grifter, a thief, or even a pimp, you would share a social network that included colorful people: raconteurs and roustabouts, call girls and street corner prostitutes, people who carried guns and people who carried little phone books with lists of numbers. Camaraderie and opportunity came through the social network. My friends and I had already begun internships in various avenues of crime. I interned with scammers, learning the three-card monte, the Brown Cow, the Murphy, and the Gypsy Twist. The first lesson in all these arrangements was to "respect the game" and not share trade secrets outside of the community.

"C'mon Tony . . . Tee! You never would have met those guys if it wasn't for me. I called them over the first time, that first night."

"Yeah, I guess I could tell you some of it."

"It's just between you and me, Tony."

"Yeah . . . well, there's a gentleman-like agreement that are rules of the Game."

"Okay . . ."

"If a pimp or girl don't understand the rules and laws, then they in violation, or what they call 'outta pocket' or 'bitch being outta pocket.' Every girl is supposed to have a pimp. Every pimp's supposed to give her a quota to earn and not let her come home until she earns it. And the pimp takes all the money."

"All of it?"

"That's right. What he does is pay all her expenses—her food, rent, medical bills, outfits, everything. And he protects her territory. A girl don't want to go down and start working somebody else's corner. When you start to do that, you start to be in violation of the Game. And when you in violation of the Game they all gonna come down on you. Another thing is that a girl gets to pick any pimp she wants. They call it 'choosing' or 're-choosing.' If a girl finds a better pimp than the one she has, she gives him a wad of cash she's kept from the first pimp, sort of like a, a . . . what they call it when a girl gets married?"

"A dowry?"

"That's right, a dowry. Then the new pimp goes to the old pimp and the old pimp is supposed to let her go. That's the rule. A guy who is in the Game will say, 'Look, man, your woman chose me. I want to pick up her clothes.' It's like a ritual, picking up the clothes."

"That's deep. So, Tony, how you gonna get started?"

"That's the thing man, there's only two ways to get started. Either you 'knock'—like, pull some other man's girl—or you got to turn somebody out."

"What's that mean, 'turn somebody out'?"

"It means you introduce her to the whole lifestyle."

"But how do you get her to do it?"

"That's enough, man; I done told you too much already."

We made plans to turn out Tony's steady girlfriend, Tricia, a cheery, copper-colored girl who Tony had romanced in Oakland. I knew Tricia. Tony had brought her around a couple of times, and she had shown the whole gang how to do the Latin Hustle and the Bump.

A couple of weeks later, Tony came by my mother's house with Tricia. All the houses in the neighborhood had the same architectural scheme: two stories, the top floor with a kitchen, bedrooms, and living room, and the ground floor with a garage and the "downstairs room," which was probably designed as a family room but was used throughout the neighborhood for teenage intrigue. We were having a party in the downstairs room. Earth, Wind & Fire and KC and the Sunshine Band on the stereo; everybody dancing, smoking dope, drinking malt liquor, and having a good time. Occasionally a couple might drift off to the basement or the back yard to be alone. Somebody put the "Theme From Soul Train" on the record player and we formed a *Soul Train* line, boys and girls on either side, everyone strutting, dancing down the middle in consecutive order, imitating the dancers we saw every Saturday morning on the TV show. When it was Tony and Tricia's turn to go down the line, they started out as robots—as if an unseen puppeteer was moving their arms and legs for them. The gang started shouting encouragement. Then, on some invisible cue, Tony and Tricia faced each other and launched into a complex routine that culminated with Tony sliding down the length of the line on his knees while the room roared in appreciation. After they went down the line, Tony took Tricia's hand and they moved away from the dance and sat down on the couch. He put his arm around her and said, "You know what, Dave's a little drunk. He wants to go out in the basement with you. He's never been with a girl before, you know what I mean? I told him to give me an ounce of weed and I'd ask you."

Tricia looked at him kind of cross-eyed and said, "What you talking 'bout, Tee? I ain't doin' nothin' like that!"

He kept at it: "Well, you know, it's only Dave. It's not a big deal. I could sell that weed and we could use the money. We could go do

The Street

51

something, go out to dinner, go buy you a dress or something like that. You take the money. You keep it! I don't want it. You can go buy yourself something with it. Don't nobody have to know, Tricia . . ."

After a few minutes of this, and Tony staring intently with his green eyes, this girl said, "Well, okay, it's only Dave. I know Dave. He's not a bad guy. Okay, I'll do it."

When Dave and Tricia came out of the basement, we were kind of giggling, elbowing each other. And I remember Tony getting very serious and saying, "Man, cut that shit out."

He talked with her. He hugged her. He kissed her. He showed her a lot of love, and I think he was applying the lessons he learned in his apprenticeship. I understood later that prostituting is like what killers say about killing: Once you've done it the first time, it's easy to do it again. Later that night, after Dave came out and Tony and Tricia were plenty high, another guy gave Tony some money and sneaked off into the basement with Tricia.

Tony became a player. He got chosen by a white woman named Luanne and became an "elevated" pimp. Luanne was older and made serious money. Tony got his own apartment in Oakland and didn't come to our parties anymore.

Several months after the party at my mother's house, I went to Tony's apartment to deliver some coke—which we were all using now—and I saw Tricia. She gave me a cool stare and didn't say hello. Tony told her to leave the room, and we sat down and started talking. Lying in the corner was a pile of blankets with a shock of blonde hair and a hand with four purple fingernails sticking out. Soon, we heard crashing and banging, stuff being tossed around in the back room. Tony said, "Tricia, come here." The banging stopped but she didn't come out. He yelled at the top of his voice, "Bitch, get your ass in here right fucking now!" The pile of blankets in the corner moved, and I heard a groan. Trisha came into the room, over to the couch where we were sitting, and Tony got up and launched a backhand slap at her, which she narrowly avoided by leaning back. Veins were popping out of Tony's forehead and he started to move around the table.

52

"Tony, whoa . . . Tony!"

"Man, this bitch know she outta pocket."

"Hey, let's take care of our business. I gotta get back to the city."

I said it in a nonchalant way, no concern for Tricia or judgment about Tony's tactics. Tricia was still standing there with a vacant stare on her face, but her anger had deflated like a balloon. Tony said, "Tricia, get your ass out of here."

I think Tony felt bad about dropping out of school and he wanted to show me that he had done it—become a real pimp. This breaking down of a person's constitution was now part of his business. Once you can get a person so they have no sense of self-worth left, then the only thing that they can do is believe in you, or believe in the Game. They start to associate their own self-esteem with the person who took it from them.

This is why, in Oakland, prostitutes wanted to make their pimps the best pimp. To have the wildest hat, the biggest Cadillac, the shiniest shoes, the longest coat. They lived vicariously through the very person who victimized them.

Many years later, I was living on Broadway in San Francisco and working as a barker. I would stand in front of the Condor nightclub screaming things like "Movin' and groovin', slippin and slidin', humping and grunting, bumpin' and grindin', hog-style, dog-style, in and out, roundabout, up and down and all around. The biggest! The best! The one that made Broadway famous. Right here! Right now! It's shoooooowtime!"

The trade in North Beach was nothing like Oakland, or even the Tenderloin for that matter. There was a Chinese brothel across the street and several working women who strolled the tourist-crowded streets making themselves unnoticeable except to potential customers.

People thought that because I was a barker for a strip club, I was also a pimp. They were always asking me to get them "a hooker." After a while, I asked a one of the girls if she would kick back something if I corralled customers. Soon I had some extra money coming in. After a couple of weeks, a diseased-looking Chinese man in a ratty business suit came over and said that I could send customers to the Sam Wong Hotel across the street. I made $50 a night plus tips for barking and maybe another $50 from tips provided by prostitutes for whom I had set up dates. In the cesspool of strip clubs and single-room occupancy hotels of 1980s Broadway, this made me a millionaire. I reported to the Condor at seven each night, worked my shift there, and then stayed up until sunrise. In the wintertime, when days were short, I never saw the sun at all.

Eventually, I got chosen. Her name was Angie. She worked at the massage parlor across the street, which wasn't a massage parlor at all. I liked Angie. She was a cute, fun-loving Filipina with hair black and shiny like a crow's wing, soft pliant eyes to match, and a small compact body with curves in all the right places.

One night she stopped by my doorway at the Condor and said, "Why don't you come by my job tonight?"

"Okay, I'll do that."

"Come and get my key, then you can just go to my room. I've got food and everything there. You can get yourself something to eat and I'll be there in a few hours."

"Okay."

I was about to go back into my barker routine and she said, "Oh, by the way, take this home for me." She hands me an envelope, which I can feel is full of cash. Not a lot, but she had maybe $400 in there.

So she handed me this money, and I said, "Sure."

After work, at 2 AM, I went to my room, got changed, went down the street to Angie's room at the Golden Eagle Hotel, and let myself in. Later, she made it home.

We sat down and started chatting while she got out a couple of balloons, a bent spoon, and some matches. I said to her, "Oh, by the way, I put your money in the nightstand."

"Oh, no. You can keep it. It's for you."

I became the pimp who couldn't shoot straight. Angie started living in my room, which was a little better equipped than hers was. Every night she came home with some money and gave it to me. I knew the Game but I just couldn't play it. I didn't care if she brought home $100 or $500. I spent it all on heroin and dinners in Chinatown and North Beach restaurants. The money felt somehow dirty to me, and I got rid of it as quickly as I could.

This went on for about a month. My dope habit became an "oil burner." One day, I was sleeping, Angie was gone, and this black guy showed up at my door. I had seen him around. He was a street-corner skel; an alcoholic. This bum said to me, "Look here, man, let me talk to you for a minute."

"What?"

"Look, man. Angie, she re-chose. She's choosing me. She want to be with me now. I hope you don't have no problem with none of this. I just wanted to come to you man-to-man and let you know what time it is."

As dignified as he was trying to be, and with my understanding of the Game, I knew I should have said to him, "Fine. That's fine. She can go." But I was so strung out and disgusted by that time, I said, "You want Angie's shit? Fuck you, motherfucker. Why don't you try to take it." I grabbed a butter knife that we used in the room and held it out in front of me.

"You got to respect the Game, man."

"Fuck that shit."

He just stood there with a look of mock-pity in his eyes, and then he turned and started back down the hallway. As he was walking away he said, "The Game will come back and bite you in the ass . . . it always does"

I took a deep breath, put the knife down, stepped back, and said, "Okay, here. Come and get this shit." He came back in and started putting her stuff into a plastic garbage bag that he pulled out of his pocket. In went black panties, halter-tops, skin cream, Top Ramen noodles, used syringes, and the only book she owned, the Holy Bible.

As he was leaving I said, "Hey man, do you know a guy named Tony King? A pimp?"

"No, I don't know no Tony King. And this ain't no pimp thing, me and Angie got a love relationship."

"Okay . . . I understand."

Twenty years later I wasn't the same person I had been on Broadway or back on Forty-third Avenue. I had a job as an English teacher in the county jail. After I went back to school, working in the jail seemed like a logical path. The people who ran the program there thought I would make a good role model for inmate students. But being there made me sad. Every morning I checked my class roster to see if there was someone I knew from the streets, but it rarely happened. Being in the jail made me think about Tony King, what had become of him, if he had gone straight, died of AIDS, or went to prison; it haunted me.

I knew a few deputies from the old days. One of them now had a desk job and access to the master database, the one with pictures and info about everyone who had done time in San Francisco. On my lunch break, I went by his desk.

"Can you see if there is a Tony King in there?"

The computer clicked. "Tony King? Do you mean Anthony King? Antone? A.J. King?"

"Is there one with Thirty-second Avenue as an address?"

Even though Tony had an apartment the last time I saw him, I figured he might have gone home, or at least used his parents' address if he got popped in San Francisco. Suddenly, there he was. The last mug shot was from 1997, and Tony looked like a cadaver. Same piercing green eyes, now tinged with sadness, his Natural now an oily mess of Jheri curls, as was the fashion at that time, and his face gaunt, sickly, lined with age. He was wearing a sweat-stained T-shirt that looked like a rag draped over his shoulders. At the bottom of his mug shot was "Section 11350," which referred to the Health and Safety Code for possession of a controlled substance.

Crack cocaine shattered the Pimp Game. Pale white nuggets enslaved a generation and killed the Mack-Daddy Pimp dead in his tracks. Pimps lost all control, and when they did, disorder trickled down to the girls. Tricks were able to get sex for a small piece of the new California gold instead of a market-driven price. Prostitutes eventually stopped reporting to pimps and instead went directly to drug peddlers. The "crack-ho" and the "toss-up" were born while the pimp died an ignominious death to be sadly reborn through pale imitators, wannabe rappers, pretenders to the throne. Those that might have kept the Game alive are gone—prison, overdose, disease, fatality, and in some pathetic cases like my own, rehabilitation . . . a death knell for the Golden Age of American pimping.

"Friend of yours?" said the deputy.

"Yes, he was my friend."

Something about the way I said it gave the deputy pause, and he looked up at me from the screen. I wanted to tell him how Tony went to Catholic school and was good at math, that his father owned an electrical contracting company, that he played on the basketball team and how he taught us all to dance like we were black. Just then, I heard someone come into the room behind me and the deputy swiftly closed out the screen, and that was the last I saw of my good friend, my schoolyard buddy, my crime partner.

I was there the night Tony King became a pimp. I wish I could have been there when the Game started to devour him.

RICHARD JAMES MARTIN JR., the son of a fighter pilot, was born on Barksdale Air Force Base in Bossier City, Louisiana. When his father died in a plane crash in 1956, Richard and his mother moved to New York City, where his mother worked as an X-ray technician and later a medical office administrator. When Richard was seven years old, they relocated to San Francisco, where he was educated in the parochial school system. Growing up, he worked as an actor with the American Conservatory Theater and learned to play the guitar, joining the musician's union at age 18. Several years later, Richard became a barker at San Francisco's infamous Condor nightclub, the first venue in the United States to feature topless, and later, bottomless entertainment. This led to a period of employment in North Beach sex clubs and with the criminal organizations that thrived there. After a twenty-year battle with heroin addiction, and facing a lengthy prison sentence, Richard entered treatment in 1996 and from there launched a career in nonprofit administration. In 2004, the Mayor of San Francisco presented Richard with a certificate of honor, recognizing the impact his work has had on the city. In that year, Richard also graduated San Francisco State University with a degree in English. His stories, poems, and journalism have appeared in numerous anthologies, magazines, newspapers, and literary publications. He now holds a master's degree in creative writing from San Francisco State University, and he works as a grant writer and as an English teacher in correctional settings and public high schools. Richard has been a foster parent to over thirty children and is a cat enthusiast who dreams of publishing a story in *Cat Fancy* magazine.

THE TRICK POLICE

Anne Hanavan

I thought so little of myself I just accepted the unacceptable. The
number of rapes and robberies I endured by tricks over the years are
countless. I never once reported an abusive trick to the cops. I just
chalked it all up as part of the game, shoved the feelings deep down
under bundles and bundles of dope, and kept it moving.

The cops I dealt with were not like the ones you might see on a
Law & Order episode. No way were any of them going to waste any
manpower on tracking down the dumb fuck who raped me in a stair-
well on Fourteenth and Second after I willingly brought the motherfucker into the building with the intention to fuck him. Granted, the
encounter was to be conducted as a business transaction, not as
me being forced to have sex with him while he held a knife to my
side the entire time he fucked me from behind while pushing my face
down against the filthy staircase beneath me. I can still taste the filth
in my mouth whenever I think of that day. Do you really think a cop is
going to give a shit about some guy who punched me in the face and
demanded his money back because he couldn't come? I don't think
any of the cops I ran into could have cared less. The lowest of the low
were the cowards who pretend to be cops under cover threatening to
bust me if I didn't give them a blow job. This happened to me every
now and again. Sometimes I submitted, and sometimes I called them
on their bluff. If they looked like they might get violent, I would usually submit.

This one fat fuck picked me up in this disheveled black Skylark. I don't know who looked worse, the car or the pathetic loser at the wheel. The car was rusted out with worn-out tires; its front bumper was literally being held up on one side by a wire cord. The moron behind the wheel had a mop of scraggly blond ringlets sitting on top of this swollen, oil-slicked-head with pinkish pockmarks peppering his cheeks. He looked like the type of guy who'd have a film of sweat on his brow in the middle of a snowstorm.

He circled the Stroll three times before he pulled over, and I jumped right in. I was only focused on the dope I could buy with the measly twenty bucks that I was hoping to get out of this guy.

"Goin' out?" I asked.

"You know it," he answered.

"Cool. What are ya interested in?"

"Whatever you got."

"I got a lot . . . depends on what you want." I knew this guy was going to be difficult. Sometimes tricks and hookers play a semantics game. No one wants to be the first to really flat-out say what they want. Everyone is afraid the other might be law enforcement. I sized this guy up and determined he was too fat and stupid to be a cop.

"Depends on what it's gonna run me." Now this I could believe. He could barely afford a replacement bulb on this hunk of junk he was riding in—I gave in.

"Blow job, $20. Straight, $30. Half and half, $40 . . . unless we hit the hotel—that's extra."

"Sounds fair."

As we drove to this little side street down by the ConEd building over at the end of Fourteenth Street, he made stupid chitchat. Where am I from? Why did I move to New York City in the first place? Does my family know where I am? All the wrong shit to ask a hooker who works the streets. Be smart enough to keep it light. Current events, weather. Stay away from personal questions. I already hated this guy.

We pulled over, he shuts the car off, and the bullshit started.

"Listen, sweetheart."

Sweetheart? This guy is a complete idiot.

"I'm a cop," he said

"You're a cop?"

"Yes, I am a cop. We can do this two ways: I can take you in to the station, or we can work something out between the two of us."

I was on one hand trying not to laugh in his face, but at the same time I was so enraged that I was so fucking far away from the Stroll and would have to walk all the way back to Eleventh and Second to catch a real trick. I couldn't believe my fucking luck. I knew I should have never jumped into this hoopty piece-of-shit car.

"Work something out? Work it out h-how?" I asked in a slightly exaggerated fearful tone.

"I think you know how," he said as he glanced at the crotch of the eight-year-old pair of ill-fitting jeans he most likely picked up at Sears.

Oh my God, he is totally serious. Mind you, I am a tall gal, but in my days as junkie whore I weighed in at 105 if I was lucky. This guy was HUGE in every way. His head was huge, his hands were huge, and it looked as if he had a huge basketball stuck under his frayed green sweatshirt, but I still didn't get the violent vibe from him.

"Look, you got two choices here." He was starting to raise his voice now. "You give me head or I take you to jail. I am serious."

I stared into his face then slowly lowered my eyes to the fly of his Sears specials, counted to three in my head, then slowly lifted my gaze to his and said: "You know what? I'll take jail. Yeah . . . I will definitely take jail."

"Don't fuck around with me, girl. I am serious." He was yelling now. I had no idea his face could have gotten any more red than it had been, but it was quickly turning fuchsia. "I will take your ass in."

"Take it in. I am not sucking your dick. I want to go to jail . . . Y'know what? I am fucking exhausted. Jail would do me good right about now. I got no fucking home. I'm fucking starving. If you lock me up, I got a place to get some sleep, get me something to eat . . . before ya know I'm out."

"I am starting the car and taking you to jail. We can do this another way," he said, trying to reason with me.

"I am stickin' with jail."

As he turned the ignition key all you could hear was loud clicking, clanking sound . . . *errr, errr, errr , errr* . . . His car wouldn't fuckin' start. His eyes were staring at the staring wheel with such intensity, as if he could will it to start, but it just kept making this horrible noise every time he turned the key.

"How do you expect to take me to jail?" I yelled. He looked over at me not a saying a word.

I started to crack up. "You better call your partner, Mr. Policeman— if your radio still works! Were you hiding it? Under your shirt?"

I unlocked the luckily manual lock on the door and jumped out.

"Where's your backup now?" I screamed as I slammed the door. As I started to run down the street, I turned and yelled, "You ain't no fucking cop, but you sure are a fucking PIG!"

ANNE HANAVAN was born and raised in Buffalo, New York. As soon as she graduated from high school in 1985, Anne moved to New York City. She started stripping at the Pussy Cat Lounge, did a few stints in some brothels, and, because of major dysfunction brought on by a huge heroin habit, she hit the strolls of the Lower East Side and stayed there for just under a decade. After kicking the habit eleven years ago, Anne started making experimental sexually explicit videos in which the artist aggressively confronts her past. Hanavan continues to take steps toward self-absolution by writing, taking the reader inside her head to see, from her perspective, her experiences of street walking, tricking, rape, robberies, jail, and the many people she interacted with along the way. She is also the lead singer for the art/punk band Transgendered Jesus.

Johns, Marks, Tricks, and Chickenhawks

CHERRY LOVE

Anonymous

Cherry Love was not her real name. I don't know her real name. She
was painfully thin and very dark black. So black she was almost blue.
She looked like a skeleton with a dark tarp stretched too tight over
it. Her mouth smelled like an open manhole cover. The few teeth
that remained were ragged, crooked, noirish nightmares. Her feet
were puffy, flaky, red, and raw, and they smelled like spoiled Chilean
sea bass. She wore a tattered baseball cap with silver lettering that
read FOXY, tiny white terry cloth shorts, and a dirty T-shirt with
silver lettering that read FOXY. Apparently, Cherry was foxy, and she
wanted to make sure the world knew it.

She liked my scar. As calmly as I could in my hazy pre-migraine
hysteria, with the lights popping all around my eyeballs, I asked
Cherry if she had a room to which we could retire. She asked me if I
wanted a date. I happily accepted. I tried breathing easy, tried to control the lights while we checked into the no-tell motel, where even
the roaches know your name. I signed the registration card "Mr. and
Mrs. Freud." I thought Sigmund would have liked that. The stench
smacked you right upside the head, a cheeky combination of moldy
bologna and old *eau de rancid sex*. The sheets looked as if they had
been used as a tourniquet during the Spanish-American War. Splat-
tered on one wall was a substance that resembled dried brain. Even
the bed bugs had bed bugs. Bad fuzzy Latin American porno was on
the television. At least I think it was. There was much fuzzy Spanish

63

moaning, and lots of what looked like Spanish penetration going on, but I was quite fuzzy myself, so it's hard to really be sure.

Cherry was fidgety as a jitterbug. Just watching her jim-jam around the room was making my brain throb. She was bound and determined to get her twenty bucks up front. I tried pushing her around a little, but she was wiry. And when I did, the lights bursting in my retinas shot through my cerebellum, and I crash-landed on my knees. Cherry swore on her dead mama she'd be right back, so I gave her the twenty. My bull desperately needed milking, and my bucket was bone-dry, so I coughed up the cash. She dashed. And as soon as she was gone, I knew I'd never see her again.

"Oh shit! Oh shit!!! Oh SHIIIIIIIIIIIIIIIIIIIIIITTTTT!!!" Looking at myself in the crusty mirror of my fetid no-tell motel room, the lights drowning me in a shattering bright white, my tell-tale heart pounding like a TNT metronome, I could barely recognize myself. When the pain put its giant thumb on the base of my skull, pushed the bottom of my brain in, I kicked the wall as hard as I could. My foot went right through it, and you could see the river outside. Then I punched my thigh over and over until I could feel a welt rise like a pain pancake. Through the migraine light show, I grabbed a shard of jagged glass and slashed three gashes in my bicep. The red blood trickled down my white skin, and when I could focus on that for a moment, the pain abated. I was in control for just a second. But the pain is clever and it will not be denied. It rerouted itself, attacking even harder at the flanks, and driving me down to the ground, making me beg for someone, anyone to stop it.

Cherry burst in like a skinny black cat that just caught a big fat mouse. "Hey, honey, Cherry Love is in the house. You know Cherry Love duz upon otherz like they would dooz upon her. You ax anybody. Cherry Love shoot straight." The straight-shooting Cherry Love laid out her equipment with the precision of an alchemist. Lit a candle. Dumped the white powder into the spoon. Laid the spike on the table. Wrapped a long thin brown strip of plastic stretch tubing tight around her arm. "Ah hope ta fuck ah kin fin' ma a vein. Ah hat me a c'llapsedded vein." She put the spoon over the flame and slowly the powder melted, boiled, bubbled, toiled, and troubled.

"Mutherfucker usetta hit me wiff a coathangah. Whapwhapwhap." Cherry paused to point out a hideous disfigurement on her inner thigh. "Ah coul'n't figgah out how he finded the same 'xact spot ever damn tahm. Whapwhapwhap." She drew the clear liquid meticulously through the filter of a cigarette and into the spike. Today, kids, Mr. Wizard is going to teach you how to shoot heroin. "Den one day he shavedded me bald. Cherry Love had her some fine ass hair, you could ax ennybody, an' he shavedded me bald. So I walk the fuck out. Leff my jams, my stereo, my mama's dishes, jus' walkedded the fuck out. An the mutherfucker come afta my ass. 'You comin' wit me. You my bitch.' 'I ain't nobody's bitch.' An' he grabs my ass, so I pulls out my piece an' I pops a cap in dat mutherfucker's ass. Kablam! Right in the ass. Kablam! Mutherfucker took all de way off . . . Tell you what though . . . I loved 'at mutherfucker."

As the lights scorched into my ache, Cherry Love searched for a vein like a gold miner hunting for the mother lode with a pinprick pick in the stinking desert. She thumped at her bicep with two bony fingers. She knocked on that arm until a vein finally dragged its raggedy ass out of bed and answered the door. On her other arm where the bicep met the forearm, a festering septic tank of a sore squatted squalidly, and my stomach flipped like a sick-fuck flapjack. She placed the spike on the barely pulsing vein. Plunged it in. Slowly pumped the junk into her hungry arm. She untied, and suddenly the sweetness was sweeping through Cherry Love. Her head lolligagged back like a bobbing-head doll in the back of an old Chevy. Her eyes drifted into the sunset, and she strolled off down Easy Street. Cherry Love was into her nod.

I stripped her down, slapped on a cockhat, and, praying to the pain god, poured raw molten sex into my bucket like there was no tomorrow. And the more she screamed, the harder I hurt until her skinny little corpse body was wracked. She cried for her daddy. She begged her daddy not to stop. Begged her daddy to do it harder. She wanted the pain. And I wanted to give it to her. It felt so good to make someone else suffer. I am not proud of violating Cherry Love, but I could not stop myself. I just wanted to be a man. The lights rocket-red-glared, and Ms. Love was screaming and I was screaming and the pain saturated the no-tell motel room, until I let myself go and came at the same time, and I shook like I was attached to an industrial strength paint mixer. And then the lights were gone. And that sweet skinny little junkie clutched herself next to me, shivering and sobbing. And as I stared at her, I saw myself lying there.

And then I c'llapsedded on the floor.

JUST TITS

Puma Perl

I had to shit on someone to make this money! shrieked Lani. ***I need*** *you to get me off! Now!*

Lani had translucent skin and tiny, spidery veins. Usually, I could find a place to hit her, but she'd done some serious damage on a recent coke run, and her reedy voice was getting on my nerves. When I'd first let her stay at my squat, it had worked for me—she tricked and bought me a couple of bags a day in return for the use of my place and my help in getting her a hit. Recently, she'd become more of a pain in the ass than she was worth.

Just as I thought I had it, she twitched and blew the shot. *Give me yours,* she begged, *I'll go out and make more money. I got a Con Edison regular gets off at four.* The fact was that I needed a bag of dope to go with the coke she'd brought, or I'd be even sicker, which didn't mean I didn't have eyes to do it anyway. She continued pleading for the coke until I finally threw it on the table and stormed out the door. *Take the fucking thing, but don't expect any help from me,* I yelled over my shoulder, as I ran down the five flights, ignoring her cursing. Nobody in the building gave a fuck; most of them were squatters like me. I knew if I got rid of Lani I'd have to make some more money to supplement what I received from welfare and a couple of half-assed sugar daddies; I was barely holding on to them because I couldn't stand being touched anymore. For some reason, these guys had some lingering love for me, maybe because they'd known me when I was a kid with wide eyes and the best ass on the strip.

I was broke, junk sick, and getting sicker; I wandered up to Seventh Street, where I still knew a couple of dope fiends who were doing slightly better than I was, and who might turn me on. When I got to the corner of Avenue B, I saw Sandi running down the street in a purple bathrobe. *Come on,* she said, *the spot's gonna close. Then we gotta go to the West Side, I have a trick for you.*

I didn't know why Sandi was suddenly my fairy godmother and I didn't care. We copped, got off, and were smoking her Newport Lights when she turned and gave me a critical once-over. *Look, all this guy likes is tits and I don't have any and you do, so I'll bring you over there. But we gotta clean you up. How did you let yourself become such a mess?* I didn't bother to argue. My hair was three different colors, and I'd accidentally cut it into a weird mullet; I was dressed in striped seersucker pants I'd found in the garbage and a stained orange Boy's Club T-shirt. My broken nails were peeling black and purple polish. I hadn't yet turned 30 and my skin and body were still pretty good, so an instant makeover was not out of the question.

An hour later, I was heading to the West Side wearing a pound of makeup, three tube tops, fishnet tights, and one of Sandi's ponytails. I actually didn't look bad. Sandi had changed from her bathrobe to one of the men's undershirts she wore as a dress. She was so skinny it didn't matter what she wore; she always looked like a hot, slutty 12-year-old.

The guy's name was Drew, and he was a fat, spoiled, depressed suburban kid with delusions of becoming a filmmaker. His only roadblocks were sloth, laziness, and a total lack of either talent or motivation. His parents had bought him a loft-like place on Sixth Avenue either to encourage his ambitions or so they wouldn't have to look at his pimply, pouting face. I think he even had cleaning ladies and cooks, courtesy of a worried grandmother.

How are you, Drew-Drew? Sandi asked brightly. *I've been too depressed to leave the house. I was supposed to meet my trainer and I blew him off.*

Do you want some soy chips? I later learned that he was constantly on expensive food and exercise plans, which he never followed. *Got any beer?* asked Sandi, and he took out some imported crap, and then casually remarked, *Might as well get rid of the munchies before I go back to my Zen macrobiotic diet,* and removed about five boxes of Godiva chocolates and pirouette cookies, and a couple of bags of M&M's. Finally, he noticed me. *She's the one you told me about?* he mumbled, reaching back into the fridge and pulling out a six-pack of Pepsi. *She's perfect for you!* chirped Sandi, surreptitiously shoving beer bottles into her tote bag. I studied the back of the Godiva box so I could locate mocha-filled chocolate and avoid jelly. Jelly was too much like food.

Drew pulled out two envelopes, handed one to me and one to Sandi. I also had to throw Sandi something, but that was okay with me; she had come through, big-time. We got down to business, which consisted of me pulling down tube top number one and sitting next to him on the leather couch while he guzzled soda, stuffed his face with candy, and pulled on my tits. He never looked at me or addressed me in any way. After about twenty minutes of being milked like a cow, he clamped his mouth on my left nipple, sucked like a starving infant, whimpered, and came in his pants. My tit was stained with chocolate nougat and I didn't want to ruin Sandi's tube top, but she didn't seem to care. She'd been leafing through his piles of *Architectural Digest* and *Gourmet*, waiting for him to finish so we could spend our earnings.

Sandi had told me that he tired of girls really quickly, but he might be good for a few more sessions. He gave me his card—Blowfish Productions, with a drawing of a fish face that looked exactly like his—and told me I could call him in two weeks. At a hundred dollars a pop, each tit was earning an easy fifty, and I was plenty willing to go by his rules.

I saw Blowfish, as I privately called him, three more times. He repeated the scenario exactly the same way, but at the end of the last session he suddenly started yelling at me, accusing me of eating the last mocha-filled Godiva chocolate and throwing empty Pepsi cans at me as I fled. I wound up running into the hallway half naked, and I realized I'd left my halter top inside. The important thing was that I had my C note, so I rummaged through my bag and found a bandana and a leather collar and managed to construct some sort of covering. Luckily, it was hot that day.

When I told Sandi about it, she said that was his way of letting you know he was done with you, but if I waited about six months and used a different name, he might pretend not to remember me. There was no chance of his actually forgetting, since each pair of tits was embedded into his genetic makeup. I called him several months later, but he'd changed his number.

Eventually, I got clean and out of the life, and I came to realize that I was actually a frustrated artist. Not knowing what else to with days that had been spent chasing drugs and money, I wandered into an orientation for something called *The Artist's Way*. We broke into small groups, called "clusters," and, guided by a series of prompts and exercises, shared our longing to create. We were encouraged to exchange contact information, and the particularly whiny, obese, pimply, slightly familiar-looking guy immediately gave me his card.

Blowfish Productions.

I didn't know whether he recognized me without my tits showing, but I raced out of there as quickly as I did the day he threw the Pepsi cans at me. I had all my clothes on this time, and even though I was a lacking a crisp C note, I finally grasped the fact that fat little rich boy tricks no longer had any control over me. I had an urge to go back and kick his ass, but I figured that sooner or later I'd kick all their asses—art kills!

PUMA PERL is a former narcotics enthusiast, which means everything was once for sale, including her soul. Her parents were blacklisted by Joe McCarthy, and she was taught never to sign anything. In response, she has disclosed most of her intimate secrets onstage. But she didn't sign her name. Today she is a writer, poet, performance artist, curator, and a founding member of DDAY Productions, which throws monthly poetry/performance events at the Yippie Museum Cafe. She is the author of the award-winning chapbook *Belinda and Her Friends* and the full-length poetry collection *knuckle tattoos*, both published by Erbacce Press. Her newest venture is Puma Perl's Punk Pandemonium, which launched at the Bowery Electric Map Room in 2012. She loves photography and rock and roll.

CHINESE HANDCUFF

Jesus Acevedo

"Behind closed doors" is a phrase which usually refers to sexual activity within the confines of a bedroom. However, it has been a more common saying in the bar where I was once employed—the confines of the "out of order" bathroom in the back of the establishment.

"Zeus! You wanna finish this?" said my friend who was fucking the girl that was currently giving me head. She stopped what she was doing with her upper half, turned around, and said to him, "I would give you head instead but with the amount of drugs you've taken I just might overdose from your load." Overdosing from trying to swallow an entire civilization all at once sounds likes the definition of the human condition. She was a philosophy major at Columbia with a minor in erotic literature. Go figure.

There are tales of the whore with the golden heart, but her heart was ripped to shreds long ago and in place of it was one of pyrite. It was made from all the false promises and cheap gifts received throughout the years from men who somehow managed to pump blood into their system without that organ at all.

Knock! Knock! "Hey, fellas, your dealer is here!" yelled Stan over the horrible mainstream music that was blaring from the speaker. Someone that was being manufactured as the next thing by some marketing "experts" who were trained to put out the product like Ford did with cars. Britney Spears's larynx was being cleaned out by her Out-of-Sync boyfriend again. And the tunes she was belting

72

out were better than ever. I wonder what is the equivalent to sound waves in regard to the amount of miles that passes when an oil change is due. She was subjecting herself at the time to the torture of being a virgin. Her lips are always chapped nowadays. Anyhow, better call the factory, for she may be injured—"Justin" case.

"Are you guys in there with what's-her-face? Dude, you should only feed the elephants when the circus is in town," said Stan, and he started to laugh hysterically. Cybil stopped her uptown activity with me once again and belted out, "Fuck you, Stan! Speaking of trunks, you don't have much of one yourself!" as saliva sprayed from her mouth and onto my penis. I imagined raindrops falling on it as I shut my eyes tight to escape the boredom of such pleasant nonsense.

My buddy Frank pulled out of Cybil and went to meet the dealer. "Lock the door," he calmly stated while pointing to Cybil's backside. "Always make sure she has an orgasm as well as you. Otherwise, she'll remember that you were only after your own physical high and that she was unencumbered by her lack of one," he would always tell me.

I pulled out of her mouth and told her to turn around. Unfortunately, I was so tweaked out that I wasn't able to keep an erection long enough to put on a condom. When that usually happens, I have to think of more sick and twisted sexual innuendos to ensure proper blood flow. Cybil knew exactly what I was going through because too much time had elapsed. She spit in her hand and began to rub my shaft. As soon as the blood flow began to irrigate its way down my cock, she grabbed it and began to push it inside her rectum. It was about as tight as the Suez Canal. Or a 17-year-old cheerleader who was considered the football team's mascot and not because of what she wore. But although not very tight, the mere act of doing so was enough for my body to be excited, and apparently she loved it as well. However, I noticed her rubbing herself with her left hand. A mutual exchange of orgasms by any means possible, I guess.

When I noticed that she was approaching an orgasm, I began to thrust myself in deeper and more violently, and, like a geyser at Yellowstone Park, exploded the semen that were fooled into believing

73

they were on their way for an egg. Nine more times of such activity and that would be enough sperm to repopulate the earth. God only knows how many planets I've destroyed.

"I was going to tell you to pull out before you come," said Cybil.

"Why didn't you?" I asked.

"I was too busy trying to make myself come," she replied. "Sex is such a lonely activity even when someone else is partaking in it with you."

Knock! Knock! "Zeus. Cybil. We're heading out. Nobody else is coming tonight." The last words made Cybil and I laugh like two hyenas in on a joke that no other animal seems to be in on. We cleaned ourselves up and exited the bathroom. Everyone in the bar was busy talking about nothing and lying around drinking with people they usually would try to avoid in a different setting. They had no idea what three of us had just been involved in; after all, it was "behind closed doors."

JESUS ACEVEDO JR. was born in Brooklyn on July 18, 1973, and was raised in the South Bronx. He later lived above an abortion clinic where his stepfather was security. Many of the protestors who attempted to block the entrance actually taught at his high school. Jesus and his stepfather would dump water out of their living room window on the seventh floor onto the protestors below, then run downstairs to get the teenage girls to their scheduled appointments. Cartoons never stood a chance those Saturday afternoons. One protestor later failed Jesus in biology for being unable to dissect frog or pig fetuses because they looked too much like human fetuses. He was afraid if he got a girl pregnant, then there was a two-thirds chance he might be the father of either Kermit the Frog or a pork chop. Jesus also does standup comedy throughout New York City as newyorkjesus.

Johns, Marks, Tricks, and Chickenhawks

I HAVE THE LOVE OF GOD

Violet N. Frost

I was a runaway. I ran away cuz I felt like my parents didn't care or love or appreciate me. Getting attention from men was very easy. I was 12 or 13 and very physically mature for my age. I was hanging out in Easton, Pennsylvania, at a place called Lighthouse, strolling up and down the street—you know, showcasing myself, handing out my number. I was hanging out with a group of girls, and some guys said, "You look better than them." And one of the guys said, "You could be a model, you're so pretty." That made me feel so good because I felt so bad about myself. I had lots of pictures taken. I'd wear an orange wig, a pink wig. Basically, I was screaming for attention.

So I was hanging out in the parking lot, drinking Hennessy, which was my devil and my best friend. I left with some guy. I'm a little fuzzy what happened next, but I woke up in a parking lot, beat up bad. I think I was raped or I was just really promiscuous. My stomach started hurting, I couldn't move. I called 911, I had pelvic inflammatory disease. I probably had it for a while. Thank God I got to the hospital on time because I would have died. There were many nights like this.

After the PID incident I came home, but I left after a week. I'd been on the streets; I'd been selling drugs, stealing and stripping. I crossed that line—I didn't want to listen to authority. So I went to a place called My Fair Lady in Elizabeth. I walked right in and talked to the guy. He didn't ask for ID. He said I was beautiful, I could be a model.

So I was excited. I had to drink to get up and dance. It was nerve-wracking. I didn't know how to dance in their style. I was wild and crazy and free with myself. I started buying outfits. I started dancing at Mermaids in Queens and the Warehouse in the Bronx. I was high all the time with weed and Hennessy. Living on the edge waiting to die.

Eventually, I met a client who was a really nice guy. He was my favorite client. Not just because he always gave me too much money, but because I could tell he was a really nice guy. Tall, dark, and handsome. He was a computer genius. He was black and really nice. Too nice. He had lots of empathy for dancers; he always spent a lot of money. He was my customer, then he was my friend. After I knew him a year as a friend, I moved in with him and we became family. One night I was drinking too much—I drank to black out—and I was assaulted. I woke up in a hotel. Sean—that's not his real name; if I use his real name he'd beat me up, ha-ha—he made me stop drinking. I was drinking cuz of my issues. My never-ending issues. Drinking was just my escape. I was violated at such a young age. Before being adopted, I was violated the first time when I was five. I could have been younger. A friend of my biological mom. He was wrong, of course, but my mom was the first. She had abused me in every way possible before I was even five. I still remember the abuse until this day. My bio dad was in jail the whole time. I used to have nightmares. I'm old enough to repress them now. I've forgiven her because I'm a Christian, so I've never confronted her. I'm afraid I might have too many bad feelings—I don't wanna open that can of worms.

The incident at the hotel was multiple parties, lots of guys. When I'd black out from drinking, my knuckles would be bruised. Afterward, people would say, "You were punching cars, walls, doors." I was always an aggressive person, so no one tried to recruit or pimp me. I've taken beatings since I came of age, so I'm used to being abused. I'm cordial and polite and friendly, but if you cross me I can be as fierce and real and tough as anybody. After the hotel, I couldn't dance. I'd been violated, I didn't want to be showcased. I was at a club, some guy grabbed my butt, I wasn't even dancing, so I said,

"Don't disrespect me." He broke a bottle over my head. Outside I went to pull out my twenty-two to shoot him, and he was gone. I had a thing for guns at that time. Not sure if I wanted the power or the protection more. Boy, am I glad I never had to use that thing. Some things you just can't take back.

I was such an angry person back then. I was so angry all of the time. A few months after the last hotel incident and after a few months of denial, I found out I was pregnant. I was 17. The father was someone who violated me. I wanted it to be someone else. I had had a termination before. I kept thinking, *Why didn't I get checked out?* I was in such denial. I had no intention of having another termination. Up until the day my daughter was born, I'd been living under an alias, so my whole life was a lie. I started telling my friends who I was, that I was not some 25-year-old fly girl. I was already so old because of everything I went through. I wanted to believe the father was someone I'd been going out with six months earlier. I didn't want to face the fact that I was gang-raped and left for dead. The test in testimony was coming.

After six or seven months, postpartum and PTSD kicked in; I couldn't take care of myself, I had wasted all my money on clothes and whatever. I tried to go home but I'd been on the street so long I couldn't follow all those rules. I wanted to do right by my kid, but I was on the verge of a nervous breakdown, so I decided to give my baby up for adoption. At first it felt like, *Wow, I'm free.* Then I was like, *I want my baby back.* Something led me to New York. I just got on the train without any plan; I just wanted a new life. I found people to help me, got my GED, got some anger management, counseling, and parenting classes. Then I started working with young women to help them cuz they could relate to me, and I could relate to them. Some of these young women who survived being sold by their parents, snatched while going to school, and the worst kinds of abuse. The agency was helping me to develop character. God led me to this place for a reason. My healing was starting to develop. I was realizing that everything that I had went through had served its purpose in those that I was helping. It allowed me to have compassion and empathy. An advocate was born. I was reborn in New York.

It's weird I woke up one day and I thought I wanted to be closer to God. I remembered when I was five and going through foster homes I would ask God what I had done to deserve this. I always called on God when I was a child, but when I started to go through the abuse, I felt like he left me. I don't mean the footprints-in-the-sand story either. I couldn't understand why he would leave me to go through so much. I would even ask myself often, *What kind of love is this?* One of my closest friends who was like my sister started sharing Scriptures. I mean, people had talked to me about God for years, but she actually took me to church one day. I actually thought the church would burn down upon my arrival. My initial thoughts were, *Why do people say, "amen" and, "father this, father that"?* I couldn't understand. After the service, which was ironically about forgiveness, my feelings changed. I realized that being in a church wasn't all that bad. I could actually do it again. I also realized that God put me through my hell of a life so I could learn and help other people. If nothing else, I could say that I am an incredibly strong person.

Last year I was in trouble. I was being forced to do the majority of the workload for my departments. Forced to work unpaid overtime and just treated horribly. The anger came back. It was abuse all over again, but this time I was not completely powerless. My boss, who wasn't the smart grape of the bunch, was driving me insane. The union failed to back me, and that left me in a tight spot. I honestly felt like I had no choice but to leave. I left because I felt like it wasn't worth it to risk the life of my newborn. Maybe that decision was a bit rushed, but I was so depressed and angry that I just wanted out. Instead of going on disability, I just quit. No money, no unemployment—just my faith. Instead of looking for a new job, I was looking for a church. I was looking for a church home. I would walk the streets looking for the right church. I had even found a church next to my favorite restaurant, and I went up the stairs, but when I got to the door I got cold feet. I couldn't do it. One day, I was probably seven months pregnant and hot, I was walking past a church with raucous music that was so fun and upbeat. I walked in and said, "What do I have to do to join?" They took me in and that was that. I later learned that my new church had recently relocated and that they were the church that I had cold feet at months prior. Talk about destiny.

I had a baby nine months ago, and my church took care of everything: crib, diapers, food, clothes, everything. Especially, prayers. I finally learned how to pray and why people say "amen" a lot. I am so thankful for my church family and the close friends who were keeping me off the ledge all those years. The love of God is something one can only hope to experience. It used to be that physical things were my God, but all that's gone and I could care less. Because I have the love of God now.

VIOLET N. FROST lives in Cincinnati, Ohio, with her two young daughters. Though she is very passionate about the arts and helping others, she thinks being a mother is the greatest gift that anyone could be granted. In her spare time, she enjoys research, writing, reading, volunteering, and photography.

CRIME AND SELF-PUNISHMENT

Chuck Willman

I ignored the rule of staying away from strangers, relying on their
kindness for affection and adventure like an addict craves a fix.

I made up my own rules when mother was drunk by nightfall,
and father traveled Monday through Friday on business.

Already a Two-Legged Amusement Park for the neighborhood boys,
I decided to become a "pro"—turning my first trick at 13,

accepting a ride to a park from a man three times my age and size,
    who
wanted me to do a striptease before fucking my ass accustomed
    only

to the dicks of other boys in the back seat of his Cadillac Eldorado.
He covered my whimpering mouth with his dirty hand, wiped the

shit and blood off his stout cock with my underwear, tossed two
    twenties
at me, and told me I could've made more had I not stained his
    leather seats.

Constipated for two days, I still felt like a golden trophy, and all for
twenty minutes "work" that beat a paper route or mowing lawns
    any day.

Johns, Marks, Tricks, and Chickenhawks

It wasn't just the money I was after. I wanted to fall like
a cat from a roof, see if I could land on my feet, get up,

shake my cute ass, and be ready for more. I did it, and I felt
    omnipotent.
But my own tests have always been the hardest to pass.

I hawked myself through suburban streets at night, behind adult
bookstores and parking lots of cheap motels, anyplace where

lonely men sought resuscitation from their boring wives, or secret
    lives.
This lanky, gawky teen during the day transformed into a prancing
    piece

with a price tag after dark, tossing out blond hair, blue eyes, and a
    perpetual
boner like chum, feeding on greasy seed like a good boy, in one
    hungry gulp;

• • •

A boy selling affection and youth, a powerful commodity and big
    bargaining chip
well-worth bartering for if you played your part without screwing
    up your lines.

Lonely men lined up to pay for a discretionary lay. I gladly became
    their plaything:
flexible, reliable, accommodating, my fake names gurgled in the dark.

At 21 I was *called* to Los Angeles, like a million runaways with
    unrealistic
dreams arriving in the City of Illusions, disguising desperation as
    ego or eccentricity.

Living on a corner of Santa Monica Boulevard—the beginning of
    Hustler's Mile—

I was daring with nothing to lose, taking my chances to play in the
    major leagues.

I walked my beat, batting my baby-blues, and bouncing my
    bubble-butt,
watching and waiting as the same sedans secretly shopped for
    satisfaction.

I sold my only real skills in the back seats of cars, or trash-filled
    alleys
where strays and rodents scurried, wagging my numb cock like a
    flag,

then marking myself down—a Bargain Basement Whore—just to
    stay
competitive and stocked with cocaine and Aqua Net—staples in
    the '80s,

looking exactly like everyone else while pretending to be
    dangerously unique:
spiked hair and tight clothes, wrists wrapped in crucifixes and
    cock-rings.

A Fortune 500 CEO scheduled me weekly for a while, whisking me
    to a
high-rise hotel in a black limo just to watch him dance on the coffee
    table

while he wore his fat wife's negligees and panties. All I had to do
    was cheer
him on, stuff *his* cash in the panties, and pretend to masturbate for
    an hour.

I was returned to *my corner* where his discreet driver handed me an
    envelope
stuffed with $500 each time, and his card with our next
    appointment.

Johns, Marks, Tricks, and Chickenhawks

The drugs and booze I thought were required for an "on call" career
    did me in.
Besides, hustling at age 27 was more like 100 in *whore years*.

Strung-out, wrung-out, desolate, exhausted, I crawled into rehab
    before it was cool
for a six-week rest, addicted to anything I could find to erase
    everything I knew.

Finally admitting I was gay to my family, my sanctimonious mother
    swore she
would not discuss *my secret* until I confessed to a priest. I didn't have
    the heart

• • •

to tell her my best customers had been Men of the Cloth—priests I
    had knelt
for, though never in prayer—having *my* collection plate filled for a
    change.

With only two suitcases, I bolted out of L.A. weeks later, relieved I
    had survived;
ready to reinvent myself again with a brand-new life and new identity.

Needing some support, I found a therapist and psychiatrist who
    immediately
deciphered my secret codes, finally diagnosing and treating my
    bipolar disorder,

and convincing me to test for HIV. Three days later, in a sterile
    clinic, as a caring
counselor tried to console me, the only word I heard was: POSITIVE—

Guilty as charged—sentenced to death without a date to mark off
    on my cell's wall.
Twenty-three years later I linger on, proof, I suppose, that life goes
    on after

our crimes and self-punishment; that we can be rescued in
   unexpected ways
despite being our own worst enemies.

CHUCK WILLMAN was born in Boulder, Colorado, raised all over the United States, and now lives in Las Vegas. He's a self-taught writer, though he attended Indiana University. He loves painting, hiking naked in the desert, and hanging out with his partner of twenty-four years and their dog. He's had poems in *Assaracus: A Journal of Gay Poetry, A&U Magazine* (including *A&U's Art & Understanding: 20th Anniversary Anthology,* from Black Lawrence Press), and *Nurturing Paws* (Whispering Angel Books). His erotica has been published in *Cruising* and is forthcoming in *Big Man on Campus* (both from Cleis Press), and other stories have appeared in *FirstHand, Manscape,* and *Guys* magazines (under the pseudonym Ethan Cox). He can be contacted via e-mail at pozchuck@live.com.

2
The Dungeon

SWEATER FETISH

Alíthea Howe

Fetishists know what they want. That's what I like about them. Well,
one of the things.

Too many clients just say, "Dominate me," which is so vague it may as
well be gibberish. You may as well ask me to flugle you; I'd have about
as much of an idea of what to do. Not so with fetishists. They know
what they want, how they want it, and they'll tell you straight out.

"I want you lying on your stomach with your knees at an eighty-
degree angle so that I can lick your feet, stare at your ass, and jerk off
all at the same time." Not much room for creativity, but you know
what you're getting into. There's a fetish for pretty much anything.
Name an object, a scenario, odds are good that anything you can
think of has at least one website devoted to porn about it. Feet, latex,
giants, farting, mommies, daddies, Nazis, pretending to be a puppy,
pretending to be a horse, being covered in undigested, partially digested, or completely digested food. I once read about a guy who
got off on pretending to be a turkey being roasted for Thanksgiving
dinner. If that's not specific, I don't know what is.

I knew all this. I could pull this list, and much more, off the top
of my head for years now. I may not have seen it all, but I was pretty
sure I'd heard it all.

That is until our manager, her voice high, unsure, confused, said,
"Coraline, can you do sweater fetish?"

Now, I am no stranger to the wide world of kink. At the age of six I proudly told my friends, "A sadist is someone who likes to hurt people!" By the age of 20 I was dating someone known for having tried and enjoyed everything in the book. I'd taken classes, I'd gone to kink events, I'd been a dominatrix for a year now. Trust me, I did my homework. In my years of study, "sweater fetish" had never come up. But a mark of a good dominatrix is one who's willing to give it the old college try, and I was keen to learn so I took the session.

He was cute, which was the second weirdest thing about him. He was thin, pale, nerdy in a hot way. Just the way I like 'em. He lit up when I walked in. He looked right at my face and said, "Wow. Perfect."

In fact, he only looked at my face, which was odd enough to notice. Every other client would take a moment to look you over, even if it's just that quick flick of the eyes down and up the body that guys can usually hide when you're not looking for it. But his eyes stayed on mine. It kind of threw me off. I don't remember what I was wearing, but I know that it wasn't much. One of the joys of sex work is the lax dress code, and in the middle of a New York August, one wants to wear as little as possible. I feel confident in saying that I have a nice body. I'm young, I'm slim, and, although I have the breasts of a 12-year-old, I've been told by a number of people that the sight of my ass could kill a man if I angled it right. I'll admit, I expected at least a little appreciation. Nevertheless, my client was unfazed by my scantily-cladness. Still smiling, he reached into one of three shopping bags from a nearby vintage store and handed me a butter-yellow angora sweater and a long, thick navy-blue tube of knitted wool. Something I could only imagine being called a sweater skirt. I have never seen anything like this before or since, and I still wonder if he had happened on it that day by lucky chance or if he carried it around with him all the time just in case he got the itch.

I went back into the office to change. The yellow angora was high-necked, and the skirt reached from my waist to the floor. I had gone from nearly naked to a member of some Amish knitting cult. As I walked back to the office door, I caught the eye of another girl. Her head turned slowly up at me from her computer, eyes already asking me, *No, really, what the fuck?*

But out loud she asked me, "What is this, grandma fetish?"

"Weirder," I replied. "Sweater fetish."

And everyone looked at me like I had gone insane.

I'd like to take a quick moment to point out that the idea of fetishizing a grandmother raised only a sardonic eyebrow, but the idea of being turned on by throat-to-ankle knitted wool was met with unmitigated shock and confusion.

I returned to find that he had changed, too. He was wearing a sweater, not surprisingly. What was surprising was that he was wearing about four of them. The first he wore in the usual fashion. The second he wore upside down so that his legs were in its sleeves. I surmised by the sleeves dangling from the head hole between his legs that he had at least two other sweaters wrapped around his junk. Interesting. Most people would have laughed or gasped or just stared in shock, and I can't say that I would blame them. But this was not my reaction. My reaction was more the kind one would have when learning an odd local custom of a foreign country one was visiting. It seemed strange, I didn't understand it, but, hell, when in Rome . . . This had also given me vital information about where this session was going. Fetishes usually revolve around sight, smell, touch, and breaking some kind of taboo. He had covered every available inch of both my skin and his skin in knitwear. So I had a pretty good idea of what this fetish was about.

Already he was as happy as a pig in shit. His smile was wide, eyes alight with anticipation, his spiky black hair already starting to dampen with sweat. He'd only listed nipple play, tease and denial, and ass-smothering as his other interests, but you'd be surprised how long you can stretch that out.

I cuffed him to the St. Andrew's cross and gently glided my angora across his face. I actually saw his glasses fog up. I ran my hands down his wool-covered chest, and he moaned in pleasure. I slid my hands up under his pullover, and he cried out when I pinched his nipples.

I'll be honest: This wasn't just fun, this wasn't just ridiculous (though it was plenty of both)—for a reaction junkie like me, this was actually pretty damn hot.

Not only that, it was easy. It was so fucking easy. Because having a fetish is like having a sex button. One push and you've got an instant erection. I don't know how this man survived through winter. I don't know how he didn't spend four months out of the year walking into walls and struggling to hide a permanent erection. So a little pinch here, a grind there, the soft brush of sweater-covered flesh against his skin, and he was near orgasmic. He actually said, between moans, "My God, how many marriage proposals do you get a week?"

And I almost asked him out right then and there.

But I didn't. I'm a professional.

So then he said, "I forgot to mention it before, but I really like public humiliation, so if you want to bring in some other girls . . ."

He didn't have to finish his sentence.

I was on it.

I brought every girl I could find. Because *everyone* had to see this. If other people hadn't seen it, I might one day lose faith and think this was all some crazy-ass dream. But not now. Now I had witnesses.

So after everyone had pointed and laughed and *had their minds totally blown*, I uncuffed him and laid him down on the bed. Sweat was pouring off him by now, and I was a little worried about his hydration levels. But we were on a roll and there was no time for a water break. Besides, there was ass-smothering to do.

Ass-smothering is often a dicey proposition because, underwear or no, you're still putting your genitals on a stranger's face and hoping that he won't get creepy about it. Everyone has different levels of comfort, and I'll admit to being on the prudish end of the sex-worker scale. I'll never be a stripper because the idea of giving just anyone a lap dance skeeves the hell out of me.

I was fine with ass-smothering *as long as the client didn't move.* A lot of them didn't. A lot of them got it. They were there to have their

Johns, Marks, Tricks, and Chickenhawks

breath controlled by my ass, no more, no less. But one guy out of every ten would try to move his face around or, gross upon gross, lick my panties as if he could get me off and I might not notice or mind. And then I would want to vomit on him and punch him in the crotch repeatedly. Assuming that wasn't something he'd asked for.

But I didn't. I'm a professional.

But with this guy, I had half an inch of wholesome, sweatery goodness between my ass and his face, so I couldn't care less how much he moved. I may as well have been wearing goose down granny panties. So I just let him go hog wild.

Now, obviously, he couldn't jerk off through the woolen mass between his legs, so he got off by humping the floor and letting friction and his cock cardigan do their sweet funky. So he's on the ground, writhing against the floor, and I'm pressing my angora-covered tits against his face, pinching his nipples, and saying all manner of obscene things to him, his frantic pumping building to its inevitable conclusion.

And that's when my boss walked in.

Yeah.

This happens more often than clients would like to think. There are lots of doors. They're usually closed. They can't be locked, for security reasons. Sometimes you think a room is empty when it is, quite awkwardly, not. It's a French farce in the making.

Working in a dungeon you learn rather quickly how to silently open a door and close it in one smooth motion, should the need suddenly arise. My boss was great at this. He'd owned the dungeon for five years, he ought to be.

But our orgiastic display of sweaters and floor humping was enough to stop him cold.

He stood stunned for a moment, hand still on the knob, dark eyes dazed and staring. I gave a quick wave, which seemed to break his trance, and he quickly, eyes still staring, stepped back into the hallway and closed the door.

My client, lost in his wooly heaven, was none the wiser.

91

When the session was over we cleaned ourselves up and exchanged cards, and I walked him to the door. I cleaned the room and walked into the hall to see my boss, cigarette dangling from his lips, eyes still glazed with confusion. I walked past him and he found his voice, only to say to me, "What in the Sam Hill?"

That moment summed up, in a nutshell, one of my favorite things about being a dominatrix. You can never see so much, or grow so jaded, that the world of sex, in its infinite variety, will not be able to throw you a curveball from time to time. The more you see the more you know that you can never have seen it all.

ALITHEA HOWE is a classically trained actor with a BFA from NYU who takes her clothes off in bars. Her mother is a costume designer and her father was a set/lighting designer who now is an event planner. As a dominatrix and burlesque performer, she is known for extreme geekiness and epic debauchery. She has worked as a theatre techie, phone sex operator, theatre concessions manager, costume designer, ticket bitch (ticket seller for Off-Broadway shows), fetish model, secretary, go-go dancer, English tutor, professional vagina (gynecological teaching assistant), art model, and burlesque producer. She has three blogs and performs under the stage name of Miss Mary Cyn. She enjoys sword fighting, painting, pole-dancing, sewing, writing, and watching ridiculous amounts of TV and movies.

ELIE

Melissa Febos

Corporal sessions are named for their distinguishing element: cor-
poral punishment. These sessions may or may not include sensual
aspects, roleplay, crossdressing (i.e., feminization or forced feminization), and even switching—where the domme takes a turn at being
submissive—but they always include a hearty dose of violence. In
retrospect, the word "corporal" connotes beatings: flogging, whipping, slapping, spanking, kicking, paddling, and so on, although the
term is also used to describe sessions of a more precise violence, like
Elie's. It seems odd now, but I can't remember the word "torture"
being used very often, though that's what it is.

By the time I arrived in midtown for my session, club goers with
their leather clothes, hair products, and sunglasses had already replaced the office grunts and tourists. Women with blown-out highlights shivered outside the twenty-four-hour deli, smoking and
casting sidelong glances at their reflections in the windows. At this
early hour, the garment district still showed life, but by the time I
left it would be a wasteland of locked storefront grates and concrete
broken only by steaming manholes and the whiz of cars.

Elie could easily have blended into the early evening demographic,
with his combed black hair and Mediterranean complexion. His
jacket was leather, designer; his Gauloises ever present, though as a
Frenchman he would never do anything so crass as wear sunglasses
after dark. He was early that night, as I would come to expect from

93

him, and I hung back beside the newspaper stand outside the deli while he rang the buzzer and was let in. He pinched his cigarette and sucked it down to the filter before ringing the bell, shoulders hunched and shifting his gaze around the street, behaving exactly the way I had trained myself not to behave while buying drugs.

I waited a minute or two and then followed him inside. Knowing the session would require dexterity, I decided to forgo the elbow-length gloves that I usually wore on nights I was using. In the bathroom, I waited until the angry red spot inside my elbow stopped beading with blood before smearing makeup over it. I had missed the shot slightly, and my elbow went numb and tingly as the cocaine seeped through the tiny blood vessels under my skin.

The beautiful thing about heroin is that it eradicates fear. It's hard to know how much of it you suffer from until you experience total freedom from it. Most of the buzzing, the anxiety, the ticker tape that streamed ceaselessly through my mind was motored by fear. What's going to happen, how can I control it, what can go wrong, what has already gone wrong, how can I fix it, what if I can't fix it, what if I'm not good enough, what if nobody else is, what if there is no use in anything, and so on, ad infinitum. Heroin pulls the plug on that. Imagine the quiet! The paradox of narcotics is that while they allow you to experience the present moment painlessly, the plug is still pulled, and so you are numb to it; nothing sinks in. The joy of the high never lasts longer than your drugs. It can make you feel as if everything is okay, but it can't make it true. While the bliss of a heroin high has a lot in common with the sense of well-being that years of meditation can give you, narcotic serenity is spiritually toxic. It's Sweet'n Low, fucking a prostitute, cheating on anything (except maybe your taxes); it makes life less tolerable, not more.

So take the empty palate that heroin makes of your consciousness, and splatter it with mania. Cocaine is drive. I've witnessed the mania of bipolar people, and the first thing that always strikes me is how identical it is to a cocaine high. It is grandiose, marveling, indiscriminate, tireless, and then suspicious, paranoid, angry, psychotic, debilitated. Heroin subtracts all the ugly parts. That's why I shot speedballs. The feeling of both well-being and ecstatic mania flooding your bloodstream is unparalleled. I become so agitated even writing about it, years after the last time I experienced it, that I have to make cup after cup of tea and start praying that the phone will ring. There is a retroactive fear that is slow to wane.

Though I had watched a number of Lena and Autumn's corporal sessions, which were heavy on verbal humiliation and torture, I had still been nervous to take them myself, and I found it difficult to imagine punishment coming as naturally to me as it seemed it did to them. But everything feels natural when you're high.

"He's in Med 3," Jordan told me as I walked into the office. "And he booked both you and Camille."

"Camille? Excellent. Is his stuff—"

"It's on your box."

I carried my box into the dressing room and dug through the black garbage bag on top of it until I found the aprons. Shiny and black, Elie's butcher aprons were straight out of a horror movie. They reached our shins and were adorned with wide pockets at the hips. Elie couldn't session without them. He once ran out of the dungeon in a tantrum because they had been lost somewhere in the rubble of the office supply closet. I hung one around my neck and cinched it tight around the waist of my zippered white nurse dress. Walking up to my reflection, I reached into my locker and pulled out a tube of lipstick. Adding a coat, I smacked my lips together, leaned in to check out my eyes, and stepped back to make sure my arm didn't look like it had a botched fake tan. Assured, I grabbed another apron and headed into the smaller dressing room to see if Camille was there.

Though Camille had only been hired a few months before me, it was difficult to imagine her doing anything else. With endless legs and a faint twang of Jersey in her gossamer voice, she collected vintage lingerie and already had one of the largest wardrobes in the house, full of genuine nurse, schoolmarm, and military uniforms. She had a dancer's body, not only in proportion, but also in that mesmerizing agility that never becomes tiresome to look at. She smoked Benson & Hedges, cut her hamburgers with a fork and knife, and was the only domme I had met who was an admitted submissive, though never with her clients at the dungeon. Hers was the only affected girliness I've ever encountered that I didn't find insufferable. She lounged around the dungeon reading BDSM-themed books, from intellectual highbrow to pictorial how-to, and she was always asking if she could practice some new bondage technique on you.

"Ooohhhh! Isn't that beautiful!" she'd coo after you were trussed on the rug with your arms bent like wings behind you.

"Ready, Freddy?" I threw the apron at her. She sighed and crinkled her smooth, white forehead.

"He really is quite perverted, isn't he, Justine?"

"Oh, quite."

"I'm really looking forward to this." Camille had some connection to London, a parent who lived there, or had lived there. It was enough to justify the accent that sometimes crept into her speech, apparently—and something else that only on her person did I not find pathetic and irritating. She stared dreamily at her own reflection and made an imperceptible adjustment to the nurse cap on her coiffed head. "It's from the '60s," she sighed. "I got it on eBay."

We made certain to walk heavily down the hallway, knowing how the click-clack of heels frightened the Frenchman, in a good way.

"Hello, darling," I greeted him. He stood in the largest of the three medical rooms, flicking his cigarette ash into the sink beside the steel cabinet that held most of our scopes, probes, pinchers, and other instruments that looked as cruel as they sounded. I saw that he had removed a pinwheel (like flatware with a tiny wheel at the end decorated with spikes) and some long-handled clamps and laid them on the stand beside the adjustable table.

"Oh! You are so beautiful, just as I remembered." His voice, thick with his native French, trembled slightly, as did his hands. He stepped forward and then back, sucking vigorously on the lit cigarette.

"Of course we are. Now come say hello," I demanded. He scurried forward and kissed both of my cheeks, then Camille's.

"Are you due for some punishment?" Camille asked him. While thorough and enthusiastic in her techniques, Camille didn't like to talk much in her sessions, and I could see that it made her nervous.

"I am." He looked so forlorn and said it with such dismay that had I not been buffered by the drugs, I would have stumbled over my next words.

"Well then, it's time for you to put your apron on and let us worry about the next few hours; they are not your concern." It was with a kind of relief that he then stripped off his tailored suit and folded it neatly on the stool beside him.

I have always known what people want from me. This skill played a large part in my success as a dominatrix. That is essentially the job description: Know what your client wants, and indulge or deny as prescribed. Of course, it's a more delicate operation than it sounds. And being high didn't hurt, as the quieter your own mind can be, the better it is to hear theirs. I could already see Elie's craving for maternal reassurance; he wanted to be told exactly what to do, albeit within specifications, not all spoken. A tall order and a common one.

He let us tie his own black apron around his slender waist and guide him into the chair, which we reclined, and we firmly tied his feet to the stirrups, his hands behind the headrest. It is too taxing to maintain strict character for the duration of a four-hour session. You end up slipping in and out of character ("out of character" not being yourself, but rather a low-gear version of your domme persona), revving up at the client's cue, and giving him a rest when necessary. This improvisation requires a close attention to subtle tonal shifts in his responses and facial expressions. There is never anything so obvious as an "Okay, let's get back to business, ladies." Many new dommes sour their business by being overzealous, and not knowing how to discern when enough is enough. And so, after a slow crescendo that began with bondage (fishing line skillfully knotted around his nipples and strung to the great mobile lamp overhead), and ended with "fire and ice" (cigarettes and cubes from the kitchen freezer), we settled down into easy conversation and the slow process of emptying his bladder into a glass jar with a catheter.

"Now, here you're going to feel some pressure as it perforates the bladder." Elie moaned and squeezed his eyes shut. "There we go. Not so bad, was it?" I smiled down at him in perfect nursey condescension. He shook his head childishly. I left Camille holding the jar to go fix again in the bathroom.

On my return, a conversation ensued in which we learned of his deathly fear of water, due to an episode of maternal negligence at the shore during his childhood.

"Oh, yes, I remember the fear of death vividly; even now I do. I have tried many times to swim, and every time it returns to me, just as it was that day when I was a boy. I cannot even take baths. It's very sad, I know."

Even at this early stage in my domme career I knew that nothing ever gets said carelessly in session. Camille knew the same. After she pierced his nipples while I held Saran Wrap over his face, we fed him a Dixie cup of water and stepped into the hallway.

"I have an idea," she whispered.

We found a large plastic tub in the closet where the cleaning supplies were kept. While she released him from the chair and blindfolded him, I filled it with cold water from the shower in the neighboring bathroom (the green bathroom—also where I had been fixing). Leaving it on the floor of the shower, I returned to Med 3. Elie was now standing, naked, still trembling slightly, though now it was probably less nerves and more adrenaline from the pain he'd just withstood. Hardened tears of wax, and their paths down his chest, clung to his goose-pimpled skin, his swollen nipples. He reached his arms out gently and Camille guided them behind his back to tie his wrists together.

"Where are you taking me?" he asked.

"That's not for you to worry about, now is it?" I said. "It wouldn't do any good anyway, would it?"

He shook his head. We cautiously led him down the hallway and into the bathroom.

"It's cold in here, Mistress."

"You need to shut up now, darling. Nobody's wants to hear a whiner, do they?"

He shook his blindfolded head.

"Now you get down on your knees for us." Camille pressed on his shoulders from behind. In her heels, she was taller than him by two inches. He sank to the floor, trembling more violently now. I inched the tub closer to the edge of the shower, until it was just below him, waist high. He whimpered. Crouched on either side of him, Camille and I each placed a hand on the back of his shoulders and his head. We silently counted together—one, two, three—and plunged his head into the bucket. The jolt that went through Elie's body was first one of sheer physical shock, as if he were being electrocuted. Then the terror shook him. A flash of something crossed Camille's face—the ripple of wind on a lake's surface—as he arched his back and bucked under our hands, but her expression resumed its placidity as her eyes met mine and said, *Now?* I nodded. We lightened our grip and his head popped up, mouth gasping fishlike, water streaming down his cheeks into it. After a few noisy mouthfuls of air, Camille's and my eyes met again—one, two, three—and we pushed him back under the water. This time, bubbles streamed up behind his ears, and we could hear his submerged screams.

His legs slid backward, bare knees slipping on the wet tile. We had planned to do three dunks, but we could tell we wouldn't be able to hold him down another round. We released him again, and after a few ragged gasps his body crumpled over and he let out a mournful moan. The three of us sat on the floor, damp and shivering. Camille and I rubbed slow circles on Elie's trembling back. Eventually we realized that he was weeping. Slow, wracking sobs, like fever chills,

99

shook him for a long time. When they finally slowed, he pulled my hand under his body and pressed his mouth against it. At first he kissed my palm, wetting it with tears and mucus. Then I could feel his mouth moving, but it wasn't until he looked up that I could hear him saying, "Thank you, thank you, thank you."

Years later, during my first therapy session, I had to explain to my therapist what a dominatrix was.

"So, would you consider yourself a sadist?" she asked me, not a trace of judgment in her tone. I laughed. Of course I didn't; the suggestion was absurd. I could barely watch someone get beaten on television, let alone on the street; I hid my eyes and plugged my ears when rabid dogs were shot in movies.

But didn't I enjoy hurting people? Sometimes. But not simply for the sake of their physical pain. I couldn't fathom hurting someone who didn't want it, but how many people get to experience the moral loophole of hurting someone who wants to be hurt? I don't know what it means that I enjoyed it, or what percent of the population would, if given the opportunity. But for someone so bent on mastering her given conditions, on inventing herself and her world in opposition to convention, it was an act of supreme defiance. As I had crouched on that bathroom floor, held that man's head beneath the water, I experienced a kind of transcendence. It was that utter alienation from self, a loosening of the glue that made my reality whole. It felt both horrific and triumphant.

MELISSA FEBOS is the daughter of a sea captain and a Buddhist psychotherapist. She was first employed as a chambermaid, and subsequently worked as a boatyard hand, babysitter, and dishwasher at a slew of seafood restaurants, despite the fact that she is a lifelong vegetarian and probably the only person raised on Cape Cod who has never tasted lobster. Despite this luminous résumé, the things she has spent most of her time doing, and the only things she has ever been arguably qualified to do, are writing, reading, and talking (a little) about books. At 15, she dropped out

Johns, Marks, Tricks, and Chickenhawks

of high school and home-schooled herself for a year. At 16, she moved to Boston and waited tables while taking night classes at Harvard. After moving to New York in 1999, she graduated from the New School University, spent four years working as a professional dominatrix, and received an MFA in writing from Sarah Lawrence College. She has now lived in Brooklyn for over a decade.

KICKING GUYS
IN THE BALLS FOR MONEY

Jill Morley

I don't think I'll ever understand why a guy would want to get kicked in the nuts. Much less, pay $50 to watch a video of a girl kicking another guy in the nuts. But this wasn't for me to judge or understand.

After all, I was broke and it was Christmastime. A time to extend goodwill and open your mind to the way other people receive joy. Did I mention I was broke?

I agreed to do the video to pay a vet bill for my dog and to buy Christmas presents for my family. I had already given up my dreams of acting and any kind of mainstream fame by this point, so the thought of this video being discovered years later didn't faze me. In fact, it was a bit of a fuck-you to those dreams. This was the '90s. I never would have guessed that fifteen years later, women would get their own TV shows by taking it up the ass on camera. But I digress.

Even though it was Christmas Eve, I knew I could rope Alicia into doing this with me. Like me, she is a freelance writer who lives a soft-core life with a spicy edge. She was at the bottom of her bank account too, which is usually where that spicy edge comes into play. I knew Alicia had friends who were dominatrices, so she would be walking into this with way more knowledge and understanding than me.

While other women my age were going to midnight Mass with their families and then joyfully going home and unwrapping presents, I would be disseminating a different kind of package. No, I had never done this kind of thing, and it was way before I had a black belt in tae kwon do or seven amateur fights as a boxer, but whoever asked me to do this must have sensed a tinge of violence in the fabric of my being.

The director, Gerard, was a short, wiry guy with beady eyes and an annoyingly thick French accent. I heard he often starred in his own films, much like Woody Allen or Mel Gibson. He was nasty when he was directing us: "Why are you eating? You will ruin your dress! Fix your hair, you look like a troll!" If you ever for a second wanted to kick a guy in the balls, it would be this guy.

Gerard didn't want a run-of-the-mill latex-corset-clad-women-kicking-guys-in-the-balls video. So trite and overdone! The scene was to be an all-girl cocktail party. As an auteur, this is what Gerard "saw"—his vision.

We were to wear elegant cocktail dresses and heels. A fresh take on the genre. In a burst of creativity, he said he wanted us to move "in slow motion throughout the whole piece," which of course never happened—so typical of a director whose idea works better in his head than in actuality.

It was a catered affair where any man who wandered in or was brought in by one of the girls was to be severely trampled. Yes, trampling is a "thing"—it's the term for literally walking all over a man, preferably in sharp heels.

I guess he wanted us to look like "regular" women instead of powerful dominatrices so that the fantasy would be more accessible. Like: *This could happen to you!*

There were other women in the loft—dancers, singers, performance artists also living in the East Village and also looking for fast cash. They had less *cajones* than we kickers, hired to be "spectators" instead. I suspect they didn't have the stomach to do what we were about to do. Instead, they were just supposed to sit around, eat, drink, and let the guys suck on their shoes. They got paid much less. I didn't see the point. We were spending Christmas Eve with these wingnuts. Why not get an extra $200 to kick them? What's the big deal? I was about to find out.

Besides Alicia and me, there was another mistress, a real one. Her name was Delilah. A cascade of red hair massaged her back, and a killer Jessica Rabbit body packed itself into five feet, three inches of woman (five-nine with heels). Delilah was going to do the hardcore stuff. The cock-and-ball torture. That is the clinical name for it. Insiders call it "CBT."

I'd first heard the acronym over the phone when Teka, the casting director/producer/director of photography/craft-service director, was discussing the scenario. After scanning her website where pictures of strangled genitalia appeared next to shoes being sucked, I realized that this whole thing might be a bit more than I bargained for. I told Teka that I would not be in any scenes with naked men and I would not do CBT. She told me that all I'd have to do was trample and humiliate; Delilah would do the CBT. What a fucking relief.

Gerard told me that I was to begin the scene by pulling a guy named Harry into the room by his hair and have him lick all the girls' shoes. Harry was a doughy, pale character with a not-meant-to-be-ironic '70s gay man moustache. Apparently he was blind in one eye, because there was a spooky white film covering it. He had scars on his legs and arms. Harry boasted while we were preparing to shoot that this was his twenty-eighth video. I imagine in the CBT video world, he was a famous character actor. I waited for Gerard to yell "action" before I even touched this wreck of a man's greasy hair and pulled him in. He immediately started licking the girls' shoes. It was disgusting. Harry was really ingesting the dust and dirt on the bottom of their shoes. Ew. Then Gerard wanted Alicia and me to pretend the guy was a rug and trample him. Before the camera started rolling, I asked Harry if he had ever been punctured by a heel before. He said that one time a girl slipped, fell, and separated one of his ribs, but that was it.

He told me to go for it.

On camera, Alicia and I made small talk—silly chatter reminiscent of the dialogue you hear in John Waters's old stuff or Andy Warhol's films.

"Is this a bargain rug?" Alicia asked me.

"I don't know yet if it's a bargain, let's see," I replied.

I helped her up onto Harry's belly and chest. "This rug is uneven," she said.

"Then I don't think it's much of a bargain," I said. "Maybe I'll bring it back."

"Did you keep the receipt?" she asked.

"I have it somewhere," I said, feigning to look for a receipt in my dress with no pockets.

Definitely not the kind of dialogue that moves a scene forward, but Gerard seemed to love our indie sensibility.

Alicia reached for my hand and helped me onto his body, and I unsteadily walked on him while continuing this inane chatter.

I was nervous about putting my full weight on him, but he seemed to be fine. Harry was a good actor. Very still. Like a real rug.

"Make sure that rug keeps his eyes closed so he doesn't look up your skirts," a spectator said. Harry closed his eyes and opened them again, his milky white orb glistening under the lights.

Alicia got very into her role and shouted, "What a perverted rug you have!" She dug one of her heels into his crotch. Harry cried out in muffled pain.

I was shocked at her . . . choice, but decided to go with it.

I screamed, "I've got a peeping rug on my hands!"

The scene went on and on and on like this. So did several others. In fact, the only thing that varied was that after a while they made us take off his shirt. This was especially gruesome because we were forced to see the welts, bruises, and heel marks we had made.

Then came Delilah's part. First, she brought in her own slave, stripped him, smacked him, kicked him, bitch-slapped him, and talked to him like a dog. Eventually, she made him take off his underwear and smacked his C and B around with some killer six-inch stiletto thigh-highs. By this time, my eyes had consumed way more than they could digest.

I went to a corner of the loft and smoked a cigarette out the window with another spectator who was nauseated. Snowflakes had just started falling, and I thought about how a few years earlier I go-go danced in Jersey on Christmas Eve, made $600, and spent it all on holiday gifts. It felt amazing to have that kind of money. But it was the kind of money that needed to leave my hands as soon as I made it. It's hard to save that kind of money. This kind of money. Some people call it dirty money, but I don't want to judge.

"Time for the finale, the *pièce de résistance*! Jill, get your nose out of the window," Gerard barked. This time, Gerard was to "act" with us. He was going to be a janitor, wandering in sweeping, and we were to notice him, get pissed, take off his clothes, except for his underwear, and kick him really hard in the groin.

By this time, we really had the bad acting down.

"How dare you show your pig face while we are present!" a spectator improvised. Delilah's face swelled with rage, and she let Gerard have it! I could see the production assistants peeking at the monitor and grimacing as Teka zoomed in and out of Delilah's thigh-high stilettos kicking Gerard's junk.

Then came my turn. It was very clear to me that I didn't want to go anywhere near his cock. Not a molecule of my being. Not near that thing. I tried to kick the inside part of his legs instead of the actual package, and I slowed down on contact.

"Cut!" Gerard said. He turned to me and said, "Your acting is terrible! You must kick harder! I can take severe pain!"

So Gerard didn't know this, but a few years earlier I was a real actress who had a stage show in the East Village that I had written. I was fortunate to have gotten great reviews from all the papers, including *The New York Times*, and we were packing the houses. I was getting interviewed on talk shows, featured in magazine shows, flown to Hollywood to possibly make the show into a feature film. The show was set to go Off-Broadway with a big budget, but the week before opening night the producers hadn't come up with the money and they pulled the plug on the production before we even opened. Hollywood also lost interest. It was one of those life-defining moments that I try to escape by doing fucked-up things like this. After that,

I quit acting and was trying to find myself as a writer. I thought I didn't' care anymore. It came as a surprise when Gerard's critique of my acting made my jaws clench tight, cheeks flush red, and temperature rise.

"Camera's rolling," Teka announced. Gerard barked on his hands and knees in a table-top position, "Action!" I repeated in my mind, *Your acting is terreeeble!* and let one fly. If his balls were a football, I would have kicked a field goal.

"AAAAAAAHHHHHHHHH!!!!" he cried.

Alicia, Delilah, and I continued to kick, walk, and stomp all over him until Teka ran out of tape. At the end of the shoot, Gerard, holding an ice pack to his crotch, placed three crisp, virgin $100 bills in my hand along with a candy cane.

My toes were in excruciating pain from my shoes, I was sweaty from all the kicking, and I wound up having nightmares about the whole ordeal.

I never did that kind of thing again. I didn't enjoy the experience or the aftermath. I'm still a fairly perverted, twisted person even after untwisting so many things. But I'm grateful that I'm at a point in my life where I know that kicking guys in the balls is not in my wheelhouse.

The fact is, after all my escapades, today my love life is very vanilla. My husband and I mostly have sex in the missionary position and our safe word is "Don't fuck me in the bunghole." More importantly, I can look at him in his underwear and the thought of kicking him in the balls never crosses my mind. Well . . .

JILL MORLEY's mom was a housewife and her dad was a check salesman, who used to take her with him on his suburban sales calls along with a yo-yo. He would entrance young moms with his good looks, charisma, and yo-yo tricks. He was the top salesman in the nation for his company. Jill has lived in New York City, the Hamptons, Martha's Vineyard, Fish Creek, Wisconsin, and, currently, Los Angeles. She has worked as perfume sprayer at Lord and Taylor's, chamber maid, tennis pro, cater waiter, critically acclaimed actress, New Jersey go-go girl, topless dancer, exotic dance instructor, playwright, decorator of a gay fetish bar for a night called "Pork," film director, producer, boxing coach, videographer, video editor, performance artist, and second-rate actress. For the last six years, she has been a licensed amateur boxer. She has had seven fights, and she won most of them. She is also a writer/filmmaker living in Los Angeles with her husband, Gary, and two dogs, but her heart remains in NYC. Her play, *True Confessions of a Go-Go Girl*, was published in *Women Playwrights: Best Plays of 1998*. Besides having monologues and short stories published in several anthologies, articles in *The Village Voice*, the *New York Press* and *Bust Magazine*, Jill has produced radio documentaries for NPR's *This American Life* and has made two feature documentary films, *Stripped*, which aired on the Sundance Channel, and *Fight Like a Girl*, which is soon to be released. She is currently looking for her next adventure.

Johns, Marks, Tricks, and Chickenhawks

SLAVE TRANSFORMATION

Din Torturslave

OVERTURE

[Buzz] Ringing the doorbell . . .

I remember it was two steps down. I had to enter a front door, take the two steps down, and there was a buzzer on the right side. Or was it the left side. Or was it another place where you had to walk more than two steps down. Places get blurred when you are horny.

I was standing outside the door and waiting for the door to open, waiting to enter into a world where I could get sexual satisfaction. In my imagination, the sexual satisfaction I wanted to have was as a male slave. My domina would greet me, and I would get what I wanted from her and leave satisfied. That was how I envisaged my dream, and that was what I had been chasing.

[Buzz] Ringing a second time . . .

I got slightly nervous. Would anybody pass by and see me? Would I be recognized? Could the world see that I was a male slave waiting for his domina? The thought actually just made me more exited, and I pictured slaves in bondage waiting to be used by their dominas. No. I wanted to keep my sexuality private, and I pulled up my coat collar and kept looking at the door. It seemed to be the right address. I was surely at the right place, and soon the door would open and I could take steps into the world of dominance. Steps into a world where my fantasy would become reality.

In my fantasy, I had a dream of serving a domina, being her slave and knowing that she would give me the sexual pleasure I craved. I had seen an abundance of photos with girls dominating men. If I were to enter that world, I wanted a domina as close to my fantasy as possible. After searching for a while in various forums, I found her. Imagine a cartoon figure come alive. Tall and dressed in black leather, with big firm breasts, long dark hair, and legs in high black stilettos. Her round bottom and long arms would force me into her sexual power, and my dreams would become alive. She was the one I wanted. Let us call her "U."

[Buzz] A third ring . . .

My mind wandered back to U. A small advertisement, a phone number, and an address, and I had taken my first three steps toward my role as a male slave.

It is fair to call U a professional dominatrix. She greeted me in a room that looked like a medieval torture chamber. It was exactly as I had pictured it in my dream. It filled me with a warm sensation, an expectation driven by my horny state of mind. I was prepared to live everything in my fantasy.

U was kind, accommodating, and understanding. I had imagined that she would be stern and utterly demanding; however, things started on a much more equal level, similar to an experience when visiting a doctor or consultant.

Most important, I was told, was to be open. To explain exactly what I expected and what I wanted. U looked at me with the same polite smile you find from a doctor who only wants to make you feel better. It was reassuring and, naturally, she was right: If I wanted to fulfill my sexual fantasies as a male slave, I either had to say what I wanted or find someone who could read my mind. She was there to fulfill as many of my fantasies that she could. It was all possible within the limits we both set up, and I only had to pay. It was much more straightforward than I imagined.

U asked detailed questions, but it was not easy to explain what I wanted in great detail. But U had experience, and a few stammering sentences from me soon became the basis for a script she could follow. In the end, it all sounded like I what I had in mind, and I was excited and ready to experience my role as a slave.

Steps behind the door . . . door opens

My remembrances about U vanished, and I was back. I got ready to enter the doorway. I looked up, and in front of me was the total opposite to U. The woman who opened the door was short and had blond hair, small tits with protruding nipples and hips like a boy. She was dressed in a short black corset, which didn't cover more than only a part of her body. She had short stockings and shoes with heels. Her eyes, gray-green, focused straight on me and had that no-nonsense approach you find in a woman who knows exactly what she wants, or, rather, what she doesn't want. I froze. I didn't know whether to enter or what to do. She took a step back and pointed to an adjoining room. Like a puppet I immediately walked into the room, the door closing behind me. I was confused and I had no idea what was going on. For a second I ran through the address in my head, but I was sure I had come to the correct location. Who was this woman who opened the door, and why did she have that firm and determined look? My mind started to wander again.

With U, we had a firm plan we followed. After a couple of visits, she began to remember, or she had probably made clever notes, about my likes and dislikes. She used my erect penis as a measure of how horny I was. When she tried out new things on me, it was easy to see if my penis remained erect. She closely followed my plan, and I could give her new ideas and enhance existing tricks she used to get me more and more horny. It was a perfect fulfillment of my dreams as a slave. We even had it down to the last practical details: I knew how much time she had reserved for me, how much she wanted for her services, and how long until my reward came—my orgasm. After a short shower or just a wipe with a towel, and I was soon dressed and on my way out again. She was the fulfillment of the dream I had about a domina. And I was the slave, of course. That is, I told her what

111

I liked and she did what she could to turn my fantasies into reality inside the framework we agreed on. It was only a question of expanding the framework and for me to expand my fantasy. It was the ideal relationship a male slave could have with his domina, at least according to my imagination. She kept me horny throughout the whole time and found inventive ways to give me a final ejaculation.

"Get your clothes off and come with me!"

Her sharp and rather deep voice hit me like a hammer. It sounded out of place with her small delicate body and only enforced my first impression of a very determined and stern personality. I started to undress immediately.

I remember when I came to U and we had exchanged a few pleasant words about weather or traffic, and she asked me to go to a room and get undressed. I went to the room alone and undressed, folding my clothes together and getting excited about what was going to happen. U knew what I liked, and often I would tell her how I liked it to start. Oftentimes, I brought some leather gear that I had seen in bondage photos, and I became even more exited while getting dressed and preparing for what would come. U often gave me compliments, and I felt calm and secure with her. She would do what we agreed to do and she would not step over any boundaries. In fact, we had a sweet so-called safe word I could use in case she occasionally went too far. Being her slave was a tender and wonderful experience because I could live my dreams and she was the one to help me do that.

"Crawl into the bathroom in front of the toilet bowl."

I don't remember how I got on my knees and how far it was to the toilet. I was still confused and began to remember I had not said a word to her. I noticed I was horny, with an erect penis, and for a moment I was back thinking about U.

During our search for new ways U could treat me as her slave, I gave her ideas from the BDSM magazines I had read, photos I had seen, and the combination of those images I created in my fantasy.

I was with U to be her slave, and she did a tremendous job to be the domina I wanted. Often there was teasing, and there would be punishment if the jobs were not done to her standard, but in general we had both agreed that the punishment should be within my limits. Yes, it would involve some pain, but it was a controlled pain carefully administered by U—a few slaps with her hand, a soft whip, or the occasional squeeze to my groin. I was constantly reminded I was her slave, and I enjoyed this domination. I knew how long we had agreed to, and I knew in the end I would get an orgasm. It was predictable, but I enjoyed it immensely.

"Masturbate your sperm out now!"

She stood very close to me and looked me straight in the eyes. She was talking straight business, and I was never in doubt of her intention. My semen should shoot out as fast as possible, straight into the toilet bowl. I grabbed my erect penis and started to pull it like mad.

I thought, *This was how U did it when I had bought extra time and she wanted me to shoot my load of semen twice.* We discussed several ways I would enjoy masturbating, and U demanded one way and I had to obey. Afterward she would caress me and let me get horny again, either by fondling her big breasts or, in some cases, I could lick her latex outfit or she would talk dirty to me. It was all what I wanted, and it was a great way of trying out my fantasy.

Maybe it was those thoughts about U or a combination of my being horny and slightly overwhelmed by the situation that made me ejaculate into the toilet bowl. It felt good and I immediately relaxed, and very shortly thereafter I was ready to stand up and leave the place. It was the end of the story for me. A rather quick and unexpected end, but I had what I always wanted. I had my final orgasm, and my mind was getting back to practical things in my everyday life again. For me, being a slave was a state I was in when I was horny. And only when I was horny. Yes, U could get me horny again, but I knew there would be a second time and I was in a way looking forward to that moment. We followed the plan and, in the end, I could leave this world of dominance and go out to the busy world of work and other chores. What was the plan now, I wondered? I was hesitant.

"Wipe your dick and crawl after me!"

Something strange was beginning to happen. I had lost my desire to play any sexual game. Before, after my orgasm, or after I had my ejaculation, the game had ended. I had reached the goal and in my mind I was ready to leave the premises. That was how it was with U, and I could not imagine it being different in any way.

I came to this new place more or less by chance. U had cancelled due to some unforeseen circumstances and I was horny, and I had heard about another place where there might be a domina. To me, a domina was a professional who would listen to what I wanted, talk me through the scenarios, find a way to give me the satisfaction I wanted, get paid, and, after the amount of time agreed to, send me out on the street again. Needless to say, it would all be done in a pleasing and sincere atmosphere. After the treatment, the domina would do her utmost for me to return again. That was how I felt it should be, and that was how my fantasy worked in my mind.

But the skinny little blond domina had no intention of letting me go. She pulled the chord and flushed the toilet bowl. She walked out of the toilet without any expression and into a room next door. I crawled after her as quickly as I could.

I do not remember much about the room. It might have been farther away from the toilet. It might have been dark, with furniture or maybe just the bare walls. For certain there was a couch. She sat down on the edge of it, spread her legs, and looked me straight in the eyes.

"Lick me. Very softly."

I think my first desire to be a male slave popped up in my mind when I first licked a girl. I gave head, as one says. The feeling that I could give someone pleasure without thinking of myself was a big turn-on. I had done it a few times with U, and she said she had enjoyed it. Actually I never really found out, because we had a rather long plan

114

of various things we needed to do when I was her slave. Licking was only one thing, and U would pay close attention to me and to her watch. After all, she was not there to get pleasure all the time. I had paid her to get the pleasure I wanted. That was also why I returned to her, and she was fully aware of that. She used to say it was a great game, and my reward was the final orgasm. I was allowed to ejaculate, and U would decide when and where.

The hard floor brought me back again. I crawled very close to her little body. I saw her finely shaped pussy right in the centre of her narrow hips. It was shaved, and her lips were larger than I would have expected from such a small body. She tasted slightly salty, and I knew she had not washed after she had pissed. My tongue started to work its way around her. I did not touch her with my hands, and I carefully moved my lips around her soft lips. She let out a small sigh and leaned back. I looked up and I could see that she had closed her eyes. It was impossible for me to say how long I was licking her, but it seemed like forever. Obviously she had endless time and was in no hurry. I began to feel that I was not there for my own pleasure and that she was using me as a licking machine. A tool she could use for her own pleasure. I began to get horny and desperately wanted to touch my erect penis. However, I did not dare. I was also concentrating on licking her satisfactorily and long enough, not wanting to disappoint her. I wanted to prove to her that I could lick her the way she wanted and not only as I wanted. It had to be done based on her premises.

Suddenly her legs squeezed hard around my head and a strong shiver ran through her body. Her hand grabbed my hair and forcefully pulled my head back. That was undoubtedly an intense orgasm. I felt proud. Proud that I could give her an orgasm and that I could lick her how she wanted. It was a small victory, and I felt as if I had passed a barrier into something new. *What would be next?* I thought. Maybe a reward of some kind or, well, I had no idea.

Suddenly she stood up and walked to a closet in the other end of the room. She pulled out a small glass and placed it on the floor in front of me.

"Masturbate into the glass!"

She looked at me and left the room, closing the door. I could hear her footsteps as she walked away.

I must admit I was horny from licking her, so my penis was erect and I started to fondle it. I began to imagine what would be her next step. Obviously I had to get my sperm in the glass, so she would know that I had done what she wanted. There was no way I could fake an orgasm, and my semen in the glass would be the evidence she was looking for.

U had once asked me to masturbate into a glass and poured the sperm into my mouth. It was humiliating, but I also enjoyed it. The taste was salty and the consistency rather creamy. U had done it quickly, so I was still horny and could easily swallow it. U had other ideas about my sperm, and I often told her about the fantasies I had about it, not the least inspired by various pornographic materials. U knew that I was open to her suggestions as well, as long as they were within the limits we had agreed to. For me, being a slave with U was all in a secure, predictable world, and that was how I felt it must be to live out my male slave fantasies. When I was horny, I was a slave, and when I was not horny, I didn't even think about being a slave. Reading about similar experiences from other men, I felt that was pretty close to how a relationship between customers visiting a professional domina should be. It was, after all, a game, and both parties needed to play their roles to perfection. A domina cannot work with a male slave who cannot express his wishes, and the male slave will surely find another domina if he is not satisfied. It's based on standard market principles, and, mostly, the customer is always right.

I do not know how I could ejaculate, but suddenly I did, and the semen dripped into the glass. I was lucky, for at that same moment she was standing in the door, her eyes fixed to the glass. She came over to me, reached down, and took the glass from the floor. Like a magician, in a flash she exchanged the glass filled with semen with a clean glass from her other hand. She must have brought the glass with her when she left the room.

"Do it again!"

She stood in front of me with that ice-cold look in her eyes. Reluctantly I glanced up. I must have looked bewildered, confused, or even slightly tired. How she would interpret my begging-dog eyes, I had no idea. For the first time I wanted to say something to her, but she turned around and went out of the door, closing it firmly behind her.

I was certainly not horny. It hurt to remain on my knees, and I was getting stressed and upset at the same time. How on earth could I get more sperm out of my limp penis?

I wanted to get up, go to the other room, and get my clothes, get dressed, and leave. This was not how I had previously experienced being a slave. Nothing was going as I had imagined. None of my fantasies were fulfilled, and my domina so obviously uninterested in what I wanted, least of all asking anything about me. I tried to imagine the great moments with U, but my mind could not concentrate and I felt totally out of place. My penis was totally flaccid and my mind was at best confused.

Suddenly the door opened and she came into the room. She looked at the empty glass, and I lowered my eyes immediately. For the first time I had not done exactly as she demanded. Undoubtedly she was disappointed and angry, but she said not a word. I looked up and she spat straight in my face. I do not remember my reaction, but before I could think she leaned over me and started to piss straight in my face. It was not a long stream of urine, but enough to hit my face and to run down to my mouth. She turned around and left the room.

I licked my mouth. The urine tasted strong and slightly bitter. This was her way of saying that I was a useless slave and that she despised me. It was a humiliating punishment and I felt in a strange way embarrassed. It was as if I had promised her something and I had failed. It began to dawn on me that by arriving at her door and entering into her house, I had instinctively agreed to be under her control. It was a far cry from how I was greeted when I came to U. There had been a few occasions when U had a fellow domina open the door for me. She had been well informed, and within the first minutes I was in my role as a slave. U's colleague did her best to follow my fantasy. But this was totally different from anything I had ever experienced or dreamed about before. I was, in other words, out of my comfort zone.

Practically unnoticed, my mind concentrated on my situation. I felt a strange new sensation. Something warm filled me from the inside. I was definitely not in control here. She had not even once asked me what my fantasy was. She had done nothing to accommodate any of my needs. Most surprisingly, she had not even once asked me what made me horny. Whatever my sexuality was, it was of no importance to her. I was a tool she could use for her own pleasure, and whatever pleasure I would get had no importance whatsoever. Here was a true domina and a woman in full control of herself and the situation. She followed her own desire and used a male slave for her own pleasure. Yes, I had read about these cases where the man was treated like the ancient slaves, but I could not in any way fathom what was exciting about such a relationship. In my mind I saw men dressed as housemaids, running around cleaning the house and in the end allowed to masturbate on the floor. No matter what scenario I remembered it always involved some pitiful man looking rather ridiculous to me. No, that was not the how I imagined being a slave to a woman. I was slowly beginning to see that the way I had thought of being a male slave to a domina was not like the situation I was in now.

When I was with U, I was in command. She was my domina, but she followed my requests and did her best to give me an experience. Now I was left in a new and unknown situation where sexuality was something very different from what normally got me horny.

To my surprise, my penis slowly became erect. I was licking her spit and urine, and in a strange way I felt close to her. I had given her an orgasm with my mouth and tasted her pussy, and now I tasted something from her mouth and bladder. I began to feel the joy of being used. I began to feel that I was only there to give her pleasure. In an indescribable way, I was proud that she allowed me in. It filled me with a strong joy that she had not closed the door on me.

Naturally, she had no idea who I was, and I could see she wanted to test me before I could even begin to dream of being her slave.

When I was a slave, I was always horny. In my everyday life I did not think about my time as a slave with U; only when I was in the so-called right mood, I would get horny and I would seek out U to make an appointment. My sexuality was closely connected to being horny.

I was now about to change drastically, and a hidden world in me was about to be revealed. I could feel the pleasure of serving and giving. I was not in control any more, and my domina would use me as a human tool. I would be something she could literally pull out when she needed it and leave it after use. My mind was focused on this new situation and, surprisingly to me, I managed to get a third orgasm. A few drops of semen fell into the glass, and my penis was immediately flaccid again. To masturbate was usually a pleasure, but here it was a punishment, and my penis was aching.

A strange new joy began to fill me. I was now concentrating on serving, and my everyday life stayed away from my mind. I was still a slave, and I did not want to leave the room. I had fulfilled my tests and, even if I was punished for not masturbating fast enough, I had triumphed. The third ejaculation was the evidence. I had done my duty. I was like a boy scout climbing to the highest tree and returning safely.

After a short time she entered the room, looked down at the glass with the few drops of semen, and for the first time a slight contented line began to form around her mouth. In my ecstatic state I interpreted it as a little smile; however, it was likely just a kind nod of approval.

"Get dressed and come back next week."
Inelegantly, I stood up and tried to mumble something, but she had already turned around and left the room. My knees cracked at every step, and I nearly fainted. I was utterly exhausted, and with the greatest effort I got dressed and found my way out. The cold wind and the darkness of the evening forced me back to reality. I

must have been with her at least three hours. Slowly I started to walk my way home.

In my mind I tried to reconstruct the whole event and to come to terms with the feelings and emotions I had inside myself. It was a shock to realize that I had never been a real devoted slave, that all my time with U it was me who was in control. In a way, I had passed a test I would never have even taken with U. She would never have treated me like the little blond domina did. Now, things had changed. My orgasms were not the pinnacle of my sexuality. They were now not what I had gone to a domina to experience. I did not need to be horny to be a slave. Or rather, to be a real slave, I needed not be horny. I had always been rather proud of my penis. It was slightly bigger than average. However, that had no importance anymore. All that centered on my penis with U, I could forget now. A new world as a slave was about to begin. Needless to say, I fell asleep that evening with my mind turned to a fully new direction.

Editor's note: This story came to us from Mistress Zanne, a "Danish pro domme sex worker" who indicated that she had collected "Slave Transformation" from one of her slave/clients. Below is the response she sent in reply to our request for a bio.

Here is the bio that the slave came up with:

Mistress
I was born on a small North German island way before the Gulf War and was raised among cows, larks, and boring neighbors. All were seemingly normal and could not have foreseen that the lanky lad would be a devoted slave. School passed quickly and when I finally got rid of the boring books, I took the ferry to the mainland. I managed to get some kind of university degree in injection-molding engineering. How, I have no idea. No wonder I needed sensible hobbies like sex, drugs, and rock and roll to survive. Loved to change cold plastic for hot meat. Believe it or not, but I gained money, age, and gray hair and forced myself into books; however, the words were a far cry from the grass-fed cows and the larks. I can easily fit into the

gray mold of mass population; however, in the darkness of the desire lurks something far deeper. Nevertheless, it did not frustrate me, but did leave me without a wife and ugly, demanding kids. Might have had enough with family from childhood. Now spending most of the time looking back in wonder at the sexual experiences. What a harvest for the old folks' home!

GEORGE: THE TRICK NOBODY HAS SEX WITH— LIVES WITH: MOTHER

Jennifer Blowdryer

Vincent something, that was the name of my George. Every girl who has hustled for a minute has a George—the guy who lives with his mother, doesn't really want flat-out sex, and is doggedly loyal. He's kind of your friend, except that you wouldn't really hang out with him if there wasn't any incentive. Somehow life has made you just that little bit more interesting than George, or maybe just more commercial. He's chosen female hustlers over, say, firemen, as his accessible public figures. It's true that firemen don't really have to talk to anybody. Their mystique is so plainly not for hire.

I was an inept hustler, and I still get slaughtered in business on the regular, but there was a time I was just so damn broke that my call girl friends were wracking their collective brains trying to help me make ends meet. A friend suggested I work at Paradise Lost, a dungeon in the Chelsea area. I was youngish, late 20s, and had black clothing, zero dollars. I suited up as best I could and showed up to meet Walter promptly at 11 AM.

I worry that I am undersexed. I had no fantasies about reporting to work at an S&M parlor. I had entertained the fantasy that I could get work as a waitress at this place called El Sombrero, or The Hat, but after dressing just like the other waitresses—dyed black hair, hoop earrings, black skirt, crisp top—and pestering them for weeks, I failed my initial run-through. No Spanish, no finesse. My friendly, wincing style didn't convey success to the management.

122

This working at Paradise Lost turned out to be a two-day affair, at least more successful than my one day as an assistant stylist, but frankly I sucked. I got picked by a client once, a Caucasian fellow with a gray beard, the kind that signals nerdish intellectualism in the middle-aged. I ran a vibrator along his penis, as he instructed. I gamely spanked him.

"I'd like to come back some time, and dominate you," he gently suggested, looking in my eyes with, yes, a twinkle.

Loser, I thought to myself. *He can tell I'm not a sadist. God, I'm such a loser.* I'm really best at things that don't pay, like reading and listening to music. Spoken word. Finishing other people's sentences for them.

"Okay," I said phonily. I knew I wasn't coming back; he was offering to dominate me as a kind of poor man's consolation prize.

The same day a mistress there—Leda, she sometimes calls herself—had me come into the room where she was working.

"Give me that, dog!" she barked at me.

What, what? I thought, flustered at being called a dog. It was some gadget. She had a man tied mostly upside down, his butt sticking out in the air. Ropes, rubber, suspension—Leda was displaying about ten winnerish skills at once, and the guy radiated happiness. For God's sake, I am no fast learner but this was clearly not a skill one took up on a lark. You don't get to be 28 and decide to be an opera singer or a car mechanic either. Of course, nobody gives you hundreds an hour for something you can't do.

I tried to interview Walter, the owner of the dungeon. His father was supposed to be something giant like the CEO of Kmart. Well, relatively giant. The poor guy carried methadone around in a briefcase. The misuse of briefcases is always touching. His parrot squawked constantly. I tried to interview him, thinking maybe I could turn my episode productive, but he mainly bitched that they shouldn't be playing loud heavy metal in fetish clubs. Scintillating. Quite a journalistic get.

But anyway—and the Georges of the world are never the first story you tell—but anyway, I did meet Vince while I was lounging around on the dungeon couch, waiting to get picked. So let me introduce you to our mild situationship. Wait, first I'm going to fix myself a snack, look at my toenails. Okay, now I'm back.

George, a.k.a. Vincent

Vincent hung around Paradise Lost looking to barter chores for a whipping. Your average George is somewhat broke, or acts broke, in a less-than-attractive way. The kind of person who queries, "Who had the ice tea?" after the diner check arrives. Nonetheless, my type can hardly poke holes in their working universe because Georges all work at slightly-better-than-crap jobs whereas I, I the opinionated, am debt-ridden.

What Vincent did for the dungeon, among other things, was make these gadgety electricity conductors, nipple clamps attached to a wire to zap a paying masochist with a non-lethal shock during play (oh, don't get me started about the newish use of the word "play"—"breath play" being my favorite annoying phrase). He could wire up little things like that, and had—gasp!—a car. In New York City, having a car puts you way ahead of the pack, manipulation-wise.

I chatted with Vincent while I was sitting around the waiting room of the dungeon, crossing and uncrossing my legs, chatty as always. He had a toupee, wire-rim glasses, a not-too-strong chin. He was talky, though nobody ever remembered a thing he said. Or maybe that is just me. I don't remember a thing he said. Like any low-level user, I caught the gist. The gist being the car, and willingness to attend events.

Nowadays, in the early twenty-first century, I hardly promote myself at all, but this was the late '80s, the era of the Lower East Side flyer. I was singing with a band, a couple of equally carless technocrats who brought a physics-level skill to their instrumentation, but they had no wheels, and really, who can afford a car in New York City? I believe I was making them labor under the self-serving moniker the Jennifer Blowdryer Experience, and one of our shows was coming up. I had made a small flyer for the occasion, and I handed one to Vincent.

Everybody in the neighborhood was handing each other flyers, and hardly anybody was going to the events listed on the flyer. If you didn't watch us do a reading, screech in front of a soundtrack wearing a small black dress, or perform the North American folk ritual of live music with percussion and string instruments backing us up, or at least not overly interfering with our canned spontaneity, then what was the point? If nobody saw us do these things, we might not be on the move. Peers meanly sensed this, and fiercely avoided confirming anybody else's idea of themselves as any type of, well, "special."

But Vincent, a true George, came to my little event. It was at a venue lamely called CB's Gallery, adjacent to the once-vital filth pit of CBGB's, the terra cotta warriors tourist reference of New York City, a rock club that shone for two and a half odd years circa the late 1970s and lived on in the memories of out-of-towners forever after.

Vince not only showed up, he cozied up to the front of the stage and took several photos of me alternately crooning and bellowing. The photos weren't bad. Well, to hand it to Vincent, they were good, really, but one thing really stood out. You could see all my cavity work, my now-dated mercury fillings, a row of them on either side of my lower mouth. Vincent had also brought me a present. A typical one for a George.

It was . . . a box of dental supplies, neatly arranged! Dental floss, miniature bottles of Listerine, a couple of toothbrushes. It wasn't so much of a subtle hint as a display of available booty. Vincent's job was to take photographs of dental work; he had a hook-up. I was and am no gold digger, in the end. I'm always happy to get the booty of a George or an unloving relative. Bring me the gift package you got with your cosmetics purchase, the home repair kit from Job Lot, the swag from a convention—I will take it! I will keep it! I might make a couple of small jokes at your expense, but of course who does that ultimately reflect on? Well, both of us, to be honest.

Vincent drove me and my musicians from point A to point B a couple of times, and he recorded me from the television when I was on Channel J. On Channel J (or the Sex Channel, as it used to be known), I read one of my essays out loud—spoken word, they call it nowadays—while ridiculously attired in a red negligee. A bit of a bottom feeder myself, I was making $100 for supplying the seven minutes of content these cable shows needed to spend the other twenty-three minutes in wild ads ("970 PEEE—the extra E is for extra pee!" one proclaimed). I read from a chapbook as "970 TWAT" ran on the lower part of the screen, right around my torso. Oh dear, years of college right out the window!

I was a peroxide blonde with pillowy lips that belied my cerebral, borderline-asexual nature, and nobody cared except for Vince, my toady of the month, who obediently supplied me lasting evidence of this time-specific low-rent hustle. He brought me the VHS recording. Terrific.

I don't have the psychic energy of a true top. A good mistress is a microcosm of a cult leader. Yep, you're in charge but you've got this squishy passive person on your hands, and without a true messianic fervor, it will work your last nerve. At some point, some point soon, I would brush off old Vincent, who did indeed live with his mother in Queens. If Georges don't live with their mothers, they at least seem like they do.

"The secret is, I never really broke from my mother," a friend told me recently. It was not really a secret.

I ran into my George, Vince, at some small theme reading in a bar, a couple of years later. A new mini-survivalist performer must have told him about the non-paying engagement I was barely participating in, but she was not to have Vincent either. At his side was a new Russian fiancée. Good-looking, calculating eyes. His mother, alas, had died, and God bless her, the Russian woman, she of the third-world imperative and first-world looks, was movin' on in. I idly wondered if she would torture him, like he liked. I sort of hoped so. I didn't really hate him, after all. He just made me a little bit uneasy.

JENNIFER BLOWDRYER's mother, at the age of 55, was a peace corps volunteer on the Ivory Coast, and now, at age 87, is active as a returned Peace Corps volunteer. Due to her background, gender, and being born in 1925, she didn't get to exercise her considerable potential much outside of raising Jennifer with a moral compass. Jennifer's father was a French teacher at URI and continues to write and publish poetry at age 86. Jennifer's lived in Minnesota, Rhode Island, Paris, Berkeley, Oakland, San Francisco, and New York City. She has worked as a Kelly Girl and at a swing club; has filmed one porn movie; has been an adjunct professor, lap-dance-parlor cashier, and DJ; a not-great go-go dancer at the Baby Doll Lounge, file clerk at Columbia University, shop girl at the Come Again erotic boutique; freelance writer for *Penthouse*, *Hustler*, the *New York Press*, *Maximumrocknroll*, *Downtown,* and *New York Howl;* book writer at Last Gasp, Piranha Press/DC Comics, and Manic D Press; ineptly turning tricks now and then, producing and MC-ing Smut Fests in various cities and countries, and being an air and breakfast hostess. Her passion is hanging out, meeting the new so-called colorful people, stopping in at squats like the Hot Mess squat in Oakland, collecting oral stories from good talkers, and working with the Jennifer Blowdryer Band as lyricist and singer. She'd love to place a song with one of the ballsy new young woman front people out there, as she is so glad the insipid vamp thing is played out. She doesn't feel older divas should have to sing vapid love songs either. Jennifer's books are *Modern English: A Trendy Slang Dictionary* (Last Gasp, 1985), *White Trash Debutante* (Galhattan Press, 1997), *The Laziest Secretary in the World* (Piranha Press, 1990, later reissued by Zeitgeist Press), and *Good Advice for Young Trendy People of All Ages* (Manic D Press, 2005). She's contributed to anthologies, including *How Dirty Girls Get Clean*, *It's So You*, and *The Outlaw Bible of American Poetry.*

RICE

AP

He had asked me to meet him in Times Square wearing only a skirt,
shirt, and heels. No bra, no underwear, no coat, no umbrella. The day
before I had been 3,000 miles from here, sleeping in my high school
bed and remembering the years before I would be habituated to these
kinds of requests. Today, though, I was shivering in a light New York
drizzle. He called at seven, as I had predicted he would, and booked
two hours, from nine to eleven that morning. I told him that I would
need a shower, that the dungeon would be open at eleven. He told
me that I wouldn't need a shower, and we would play at my apartment. This was not the moment to negotiate.

I got to Times Square and waited under a shallow overhang to try
and keep as dry as possible. It was the kind of drizzle that felt like
a prickling mist, and there was little protection. Despite knowing
he would be there at nine on the dot, I arrived closer to eight forty,
ready to spend twenty minutes or more, cold and waiting. I wanted
to be early. I wanted to prove I could be good for him again and that
I deserved his affection and adoration. Despite not having a shower
and still being jet-lagged, I wanted to prove that I could be perfect
for him. Despite holding onto the self-righteous insistence that I had
done nothing wrong, I wanted to prove that I was sorry that we had
fought at all.

At nine he texted that he was standing on the uncovered triangle in
the center of the area. I walked quickly, a glow betraying my shivers,

128

a smile betraying my collected exterior. I was still angry, still hurt, but I had still had missed him terribly in a way which troubled my grasp of professionalism.

When I met him, he stood just far enough from me that his umbrella, cocked back, provided me no comfort. Gooseflesh rose unapologetically on my arms and legs. My teeth made the only noise between us.

"Hi." It was so banal.

"Hi," I whispered back.

"You look beautiful." I smiled again, still shaking. He held the umbrella back, and the humiliation he was inflicting was not lost on me. I stood in the center of the Times Square triangle, cold and beholden. At his unspoken request, I stood in the rain; a T-shirt and a miniskirt my only cover from the damp.

"Do you want the umbrella?"

I nodded, arms crossed. He did not move, and I shivered harder.

"Should we go home?"

I nodded again, waiting for him to move first. I could see the gears turning in his head as he debated his next move.

I imagined I looked pathetic to him. I shivered, rubbing my legs together and finding little warmth. Finally he tilted the umbrella forward, and I took a half step toward him, despite still feeling layers of frustration with myself in the strength of my desire for closeness.

We walked in the train, my arms still crossed, trying to rub some warmth into my body. We made small talk about the trip, about school, about the impending collapse of the euro in a way that felt cruelly easy. I shivered on the train.

When I was with him in public, I gauged how close I was sitting. While I always want to show him affection, he was always carrying the mantle of plausible deniability when we were together. If anyone saw us I could always be a former intern, a friend's or boss's daughter, a reporter for a hedge fund rag without a readership.

When we got to my apartment, the atmosphere changed immediately. When I say that he was dominant, I mean that you could read it on him. He embodied it the same way you could describe him as tall, brown-haired, or Texan. And while I unapologetically uphold the "professional" part of professional submissive, I always reacted in the latter half in his presence. Every inch of me that was truly submissive purred like an anxiously waiting car anticipating its owner's next joy ride.

"Put something pretty on for me." He smacked my ass as I ran up the stairs. It felt affectionate and playful in a way that also felt false. I wondered what he had planned, what I might fall into if I relaxed.

Nonetheless, I immediately began peeling off wet layers before I reached the top of the stairs. I had recently bought an electric blue sheer lingerie set, and I was excited to christen it with him. I had bought it for the anonymous client I always shopped for, and at the same time, I had pictured him while in the dressing room.

I was also thrilled that he had given me a task. Though he often gave me challenges rife with pause and flickers of self-doubt, right now I could look pretty for him. I could look beautiful for him. I was startled by my own happiness at this request.

But when I descended the stairs, I almost cried walking into the living room. He sat calmly on an ottoman, arms on his knees, waiting for me. Spread out in a circle on the floor was a pile of cold, dry rice. I knew exactly what would happen next, and it made me stop in my tracks, tear up, and whimper out the most pleading of "nos." But we both knew that "no" was not a safe word.

He nodded. This would be my punishment.

"Kneel, baby."

I took the longest breath, took his extended hands, and slowly lowered myself onto the rice. It dug into my skin. I shifted down, letting it press coldly into the delicate flesh of my knees and shins, feeling it slice and mangle. I wined and whimpered, but all he did was let me settle.

We stared at each other for a long minute. I could only hear my breath and my heart. And then he slapped me hard across the face.

"Now, why did you do it?"

I took a moment to recover. I knew exactly what he was asking, but

I didn't know what to say. I stretched my neck slightly, regrouping. And I apparently took too long, as he slapped me again.

"I don't know." We both knew it was a lie.

He slapped me again, harder. "Yes, you do. Tell me why."

He was holding his anger coldly. If I didn't know consciously that I had wanted this, and if I didn't know that he knew how much I wanted this, exactly this, I would have been reminded of my college boyfriend, the one who used to punch me when he was annoyed with something I had said.

I paused. He wanted to know about the first Tuesday of my trip home. On the first Tuesday he had told me he wanted a picture. I had been instructed to buy the largest dildo I could find and send him a picture of me fucking myself with it. Lying in bed, already hurt and angry at him, I asked if he would pay for it. It was a simple request, and one that any provider would have made. I was not asking him to compensate me for my time or for the picture, but simply to cover the one thing he asked me to buy. I felt justified and self-righteous taking this stand.

And it had spurred our first real fight. We yelled, both angry and stewing on separate coasts. I had made him feel like just a client when we both knew that he was many, many things to me, and I to him.

"Tell me why."

"Because I'm stupid," I finally said.

He paused, his hand coming across my face hard. "No, you're not." I could see him getting frustrated. "You are a beautiful." He reached around and pressed my legs and knees into the rice, causing me to scream out. "Smart." Every time he said a kind word, he pushed down again, shifting my legs enough to make the rice shift and cut more into the skin. "Strong woman." Again. "And you are not stupid." He moved forward and for a fleeting moment I thought he would kiss me. Instead he pushed down, grinding my legs over the kernels.

I felt tears come to my eyes, threatening to break forward. I took a resolute breath and stared at him, fighting the tears until they were gone. My breath was strong, angry, and deliberate. I was fuming.

"You don't want to tell me why you did it?"

"No."

I had been so angry that Tuesday morning that I had debated, for the first time, ignoring him altogether.

The first Monday I was home we had bantered about what he would do for ten days without me. I suggested things like letters or requests for permission to come, all things I would have gladly given him.

I had called him as requested four times that day, each time masturbating and moaning into his voicemail. I had spent the entire day sneaking off to call him, getting wetter each time I heard his voice on the machine. On the last call he had answered, and sitting alone in my mother's car in a crowded Target parking lot, I came for him. Unpaid, three thousand miles away, and I felt just as vulnerable to him as I did kneeling at his feet.

"Do you want to stand up? I'll give you a break if you want it."

I nodded, and he leaned down so I could put my hands on his shoulders, his hands going to my hips. He brushed off blood-touched rice as I stood, rubbing my knees softly. It was at that moment I realized that I had fucked up, and I started to giggle through drying tears. I couldn't hold back a wide smile as I fought the tears that would inevitably come. While kneeling, the rice had settled into grooves of numbed skin. I would, in a moment, kneel back down and revisit the worst moments of the pain. I felt a tear streak down my cheek and off my jaw as I tried to stop laughing with the realization that I had just made the pain worse.

"So you figured it—"

I nodded before he could finish.

"Aww. My poor baby." He took my hand and squeezed it, his thumb caressing the skin, smiling up at me. "Kneel, baby."

I nodded and didn't bother to hesitate before I got back onto my knees, crying out, trying to stem the tears.

"You think you can do ten more minutes down there?"

I nodded, confident and taking long breaths. I had no doubt that I could do it if he asked.

"You think you could do twenty?"

I paused, my mouth opening slightly. He began to laugh.

"And we found a chink in her armor." I closed my eyes, my lips curling into a soft smile. "Would you do it if I asked?"

My mind went through the idea. It would hurt tremendously. Worse, though, would be the marks. I would have to be more careful for clients, and I loathed going into a session with cuts or scars from someone else. It felt deeply unprofessional, and not at all the fantasy I wanted to offer. I owed it to my other clients to not get large, avoidable gashes from my own play. As much as I wanted them, I still needed to be pristine.

But if he asked me to stay down for twenty minutes, I would have to. I nodded.

"You would stay down there until you passed out if I asked you to." I nodded.

"You're going to kill yourself with that iron will of yours if you're not careful." I cracked the slightest of smiles. "But that's why you're the best. And that's why you're mine."

I felt the rice grind into new, tender grooves and I winced, which always comes off as a snarl.

"But that's why I'm here," he said. "To take care of you, make sure you don't kill yourself." I looked up at him, mascara smeared, blood dotting my legs and the white, perfect rice. "You know I'll always take care of you, baby."

I thought about nodding but couldn't. I could only stare him in the eyes, hoping all the complex layers that I felt but couldn't articulate could just be felt.

His hand came across my face again, harder this time, and I felt my ear buzz. I rubbed my ear into my shoulder, trying to make it stop.

"Too hard?" he said, his hand going to cup my face.

I nodded, "My ear is buzzing."

He stroked my face softly.

"Tell me, baby."

I looked up at him. On Monday, in our early banter, before I left a single voicemail for him, before I gave him a suggestion on how to fill ten days without his girl, he had said he might simply replace me. I was wounded and pouted in my high school bedroom. We had been playing, but that was one joke I couldn't hear him say. The nature of our relationship meant that we could each walk away when we wanted. We would simply have to stop calling or responding and this would be done, neither of us would have any standing or recourse. But I was confident he knew that I would not have done that.

On that day, every time I called him, I put the words further and further from my mind. How could he replace me?

I had always known I was his prostitute, a provider, but there was no way he could replace me.

A few hours later, after I came for him, I spoke with another provider, another professional submissive who had almost seen a new client that day. I told her about some of my phone-based encounters. She had waxed on about her disappointment that a new client hadn't come through, tinged in anger that he had simply never confirmed. As she often did, she asked if I had ever seen him. I had been working more consistently and longer, and so many of her inquiries had cycled through my ad and screening at some point.

I felt achingly empty when she said his name. He had, in fact, tried to replace me. Even if it was just a fleeting thought, it had been strong enough of a suggestion for him to contact another provider. He had made me feel disposable, and I had wanted to make him feel disposable as well. At that moment, I felt like just his whore, and I wanted him to feel like just my client.

"Tell me why you did it." He pulled his hand back and I flinched, whimpering. He lowered his hand, waiting. He raised it again at my silence, and I broke.

"You said you would replace me." I turned away. I couldn't even meet his eyes.

He paused. "I said that after you asked for the money."

I shook my head, turning to stare him in the eyes. "No, you didn't.

You said it before." I was louder, angry that he had forgotten the moment when I had broken.

Feeling precariously close to tears, I opted not to tell him I knew he had almost seen someone else. I was a professional and it was his right. I had no place to tell him not to do it. He had paid my rate, treated me with love and affection, and owed me nothing, least of all some bastard sense of monogamy. However, it had still hurt desperately. Nonetheless, I had told her that I had seen him, that he had been an amazing client, and that I would think anyone who saw him was lucky.

"I did, huh?"

I nodded. He took my hands and told me to stand. I sat on his lap, smeared with dried tears cloaked in makeup and blood.

"I'm not replacing you, baby."

I sat on his lap and put my arms around him. He felt good to lean against. I didn't know if he was married, where he lived, or what his hobbies were, but this would remain one of the most intimate moments I have had with another person.

He fucked me after that, taking me crying and exhausted. We curled up together, and I nestled into the cavern that his body, which was over a foot taller than mine, created for me. When there were fifteen minutes left in the session, he redressed diligently. There was passing small talk about an article I had read in *The Economist* that week. He would leave the money in the living room, and I would reassemble the house after he left.

When he left, he kissed me again. "I'll always take care of you."

I nodded and held on to him for a long time before walking him to the door.

He paid me almost twice my two-hour rate. The scars from the rice would last for weeks, and I would opt never to tell him about the other provider. Despite not being a masochist, I would press the healing cuts sometimes just to think about kneeling before him, and the deep shards of pain would make me smile.

135

The Dungeon

AP is a queer, femme, bi-coastal sex worker and community organizer. As a community organizer, she supports community and capacity building, creates educational programming, and develops advocacy strategy. As a sex worker, she has worked as a dominatrix, a submissive, and an escort, and dabbled in some of the most boring cam work to date. In this role she has given business advice, troubleshot non-monogamy, fallen in love, and commented on a father's wedding toast. She holds a master's degree in international affairs and lives in Brooklyn, New York. She enjoys good tea and bad horror movies.

I FELL IN LOVE WITH A CLIENT ONCE

Kitty Stryker

It was completely unexpected. I have generally been good with emo-tional boundaries, having been in non-monogamous relationships for years. I knew how to keep people as close or as distant as I needed to. It was part of what made me a good sex worker. Or so I thought.

I remember the session. He had sent me a long e-mail detailing this crazy scene that really weirded me out, and I was nervous about it. Particularly as a pro-domme, I tended to make it clear that I would do as much or as little as I wanted, but I still wanted to satisfy some of the client's needs. This one wanted me to spit in his face, to restrain him in a variety of intense ways as I humiliated him, things I didn't tend to do with my lovers at home. I worried we wouldn't click well during the session, but I was determined to try.

I walked into the dungeon, and he was so attractive I couldn't believe it. Only a few years older than me, hot, *and* submissive? It seemed like a dream. I gathered myself together, determined to offer a dominant experience that would be sexy for us both, and then just walk away. I tied him up and called him all manner of humiliating things and found myself turned on by how he reacted, by the way he writhed for me. I found myself relaxed, comfortable, enjoying myself even more than usual. When he left, I stopped myself from asking him out for a drink, and I took the train back home, confused, but figuring I wouldn't see him again.

He wrote back the next day wanting to book another session that week. I agreed and instantly felt butterflies in my stomach.

I felt so unprofessional, so unsteady. There was a forum for sex workers, and I posted there, asking if any of the girls had ever felt that kind of attraction to their clients before. Some had, some hadn't, and all sorts of advice was offered to me to help me work out what to do. Ultimately I was asked the important question: Could I afford to lose him as a client? I thought about it, my heart asking if I could afford to not take a chance. Was this a real-life *Pretty Woman* thing? I didn't want to be so cliché, but there was chemistry swirling.

We had another session, and it was both incredibly sexy and absolutely hilarious. I tripped over my heels and we giggled about it, an intimacy developing between us. Two hours later, as we snuggled for some aftercare, I decided to go for it and ask him if he wanted to go to a fetish market with me, as he had commented on his lack of kinky clothes. He accepted, and we made plans.

I immediately panicked and asked my girlfriend to come with me to keep me from making a mistake and maybe let me know if I was being ridiculous and misreading him. Together we browsed stalls filled with kinky toys and pinstriped clothes, trying things on and trying toys out. There was an ease to our interactions, a comfortable friendliness, and my girlfriend said to me that she thought he liked me too (I seem to recall she was okay with him, but not overly fond). So I did the suave thing before we parted ways and said teasingly, "You know . . . if you let me do what I want, you wouldn't have to pay me anymore."

He grinned.

And so we began dating. We went to his first sex party, my girl-friend, my new boyfriend, and I, and proceeded to have fun dancing, making out, and watching the various goings-on. Early into the morning we left the party, exhausted, and he invited us to his flat to rest. He was in media, an exciting job that allowed him to live on his own in Soho, so we took him up on his offer and fell asleep, all snuggled together. I thought I was in heaven, sandwiched between these two sexy people. I found myself thinking that this might be the beginning of something long-lasting.

He was so kinky. I loved the challenge and all the things we did and tried. I made him nose hooks and mouth hooks, wrapped him in cling film and duct tape, spat in his mouth and pissed on him in the shower. We went to dark places together, him and me. But it was more than sex for me—we hung out and watched movies, went grocery shopping. I was so in love with him, and I thought he loved me back, two perverts who had found each other, a crazy sex worker love story.

I encouraged him to go to Burning Man, to meet my friends and communities in the hope he would find acceptance. We'd go to pubs, sex shops, and bookstores, holding hands and talking about politics and psychology. I fell deeper in love, so thankful to meet someone who didn't mind my work, who I didn't have to explain it to, who seemingly accepted me. We went to kinky clubs, slow dancing to electronica and kissing like we couldn't stop.

It all seemed so perfect. And it was, for a few months. This is the thing, right: He was a lovely guy, and a great boyfriend. Except for the ways in which he wasn't—but isn't that like most relationships?

There were hints that the fairytale was unraveling, but I ignored them. The desire he had to be enhanced in some way when we did kink, for example, I chalked up to his shame around his desires, and let it slide. He was embarrassed telling his friends how we met, so I was always a writer to them, my sex worker self put into the closet, if I met them at all. My friends knew and loved him. It didn't matter to them that he was originally a john, but he never seemed to notice that. Family was out of the question. It was hard, because I wondered if he was ashamed of me, when I was so proud of my job, happy to have met a great guy at work like any other girl. I felt frustrated sometimes, trapped into pretending to be someone I wasn't, but I loved him and respected him, so I kept quiet, even when friends of his said things about prostitution that made me uncomfortable. There were other indicators: The relationship was open, but he went on dates with monogamous girls, something that made me feel jealous and unstable. We'd fight, then fuck and make up, over and over again.

The truth is, we both realized that the sex work had created a rushed intimacy. We knew so much about each other's desires but so little about what made the other tick. Our sex became kinkier and darker, our fantasies more dangerous and tense in an attempt to make up for the chasm between us. I felt less inclined to do other sex work and spent my free time trying to understand what was going wrong, what I could do right. I worried I was losing him, but I told myself that I was being paranoid, that I had heard so many times that sex workers couldn't be in relationships that I believed it.

After a particularly difficult night before I flew home for a few months, we drove to the airport in silence. I was panicked about leaving the country, leaving him. I was sure everything was about to fall apart, and while I knew I was digging my own grave I wanted reassurance that he cared, that we had something special. I was in tears as he gave me three CDs. I spent the flight analyzing each song, reassuring myself that the music suggested he was confused, too, but we loved each other, that we would find a way. It had been only five months and yet I felt like I had found my soul mate. I slept fitfully.

When I landed I discovered an e-mail asking for space. He felt like we were struggling too much. I agreed. I could see that we needed some time for things to calm, for me to realize he did love me, that things would be okay. I started journaling every day to work out what needed to happen for our relationship to get back on track. I vowed not to sleep with anyone else, professionally or otherwise, while I reflected on us.

Three days later he was dating someone new, someone I had introduced him to. They moved in together. They broke up. He hadn't planned on fixing our relationship, he was just putting off the inevitable. I knew that our relationship was dead by then, and I mourned it. I felt like someone had ripped my heart out, my trust, and burned it in front of me. I railed at my friends. I fell apart.

I tried to heal, in time. We tried to be friends, meeting for coffee. But I was furious, and hurt, and not ready. I felt like he had betrayed me, that he had shunned me for my work. It was one of the most heartbreaking experiences I had ever had, and I cursed myself every day for losing control, for letting myself blur the boundaries between client and sex worker. A year later and I still hadn't recovered. Two years and I still struggled seeing his picture. Even now, I'll come across his profile somewhere or other and I'll feel sick to my stomach.

There was a party I went to, about a year and a half after the breakup. He was dating someone else, a woman who was in some of my communities. She and I ran into each other—she, probably on something; I, sick with the flu and somewhat delirious. Flopping onto a chair and draping her legs on me, she told me how thankful she was that he had met me, that he was so self-aware and open thanks to me. I realized that I had taught him how to be sexually confident in his kinks, that I had helped him become the ideal lover. I felt like I was going to throw up. I felt like love was something that would screw me over, every time, that all I could ever be as a sex worker was training wheels for a "real" relationship. Never had I been hit so hard with the irony that while the service I provided was invaluable to his well-being, that society ensured my well-being was ignored while claiming to want to protect me.

I cut him out of my life after that for a while. And, for the most part, I'm glad.

But I think, years later, that he left raw wounds that still affect me today, even in my current relationship, because I was hurt far more than I was angry, and that vulnerability can be dangerous in my profession. I still worry on some days that as a sex worker I will only ever be the girlfriend experience and never the girlfriend. I have never gotten close to a client like that again, and I doubt I ever will. There is a part of me that is still traumatized and miserable about the whole thing. It was one of the hardest lessons in boundaries, trust, and honesty I have ever had. And yet it was the Cinderella story brought to life—*Pretty Woman* in real time.

He seems happy now. I doubt he ever thinks of me, and I feel silly for thinking of him, for him still affecting me. I wonder if it ever mattered to him how much he hurt me by keeping me as his secret lover. I wonder how things might have been different if there wasn't this stigma about sex workers and clients, if he hadn't felt he had to hide me away, if he hadn't been ashamed of being a client. I wonder if he might've been able to see me as his white-picket-fence girl after all.

I guess I'll never know.

When they talk about trauma in sex work, they tend to mean being beaten and raped on the job, a daily reality for many sex workers worldwide. As an indoor sex worker with a lot of privilege and no arrests, I haven't experienced that kind of violence. I'm lucky in that way—while I live under the shadow of physical or sexual violence (more from the police than the clients), I've really only experienced various forms of emotional abuse, usually from people who felt they had the right because my choice to be an out prostitute was, apparently, consenting to constant public scrutiny.

So I got off easy, really, when it comes to trauma and sex work, and I want to acknowledge that—and yet even as a privileged sex worker, I do feel scarred. I think of how I tore my own relationship apart with my internalized whorephobia. I think of how the stigma of sex workers not being people can affect relationships and the people in them. I think of the way I have worried I would have to choose between a job that gives me autonomy and agency or having a partner (something I no longer stress over, having experience to the contrary).

Writing this, I'm pretty sure I know what the response will be. "Hookers can't afford to love," "He was just using you for sex," "You don't deserve a relationship anyway," "If you don't like it, quit your job." And that's exactly the problem—people feel very entitled to mistreat sex workers like me every day, like we're not people with hopes, families, loves, and losses. On the other side, people feel like it's okay to say that clients are ugly old men who want to treat women badly and that sex workers need protection from them—but clients are different across the board. Even now, I don't think he entered the relationship to hurt me. I don't think I went into things expecting to fall so hard, either.

Our relationship was not a political statement—it was just a girl loving a boy who didn't love her as much. The trauma had already been done before I ever met him, by a society that told me I was worthless because of my job.

If I am one of the lucky ones, imagine the stigma, shaming, and cruelty rained down on those more marginalized that I am.

KITTY STRYKER was born in Massachusetts, but her heart is torn between San Francisco and London. Founder of the Ladies High Tea and Pornography Society, co-founder of Consent Culture, and co-producer of live sex show Cum & Glitter, Kitty blends sexuality and activism on a regular basis. A sex clown, a hard femme, and a steam-punk courtesan, her work and wanderlust takes her all over the world. She writes for *Good Vibrations* and the *Huffington Post,* and her writing has appeared in anthologies such as *Hot and Heavy: Fierce Fat Girls on Life, Love, and Fashion* and *Stretched: Erotic Fiction That Fondles the Imagination.*

THE TOOTH FETISHIST

Alice Atlass

Men pay me to beat, humiliate, tease, and torture them. They beg to be kicked in the balls while I wear stilettos or black pleather fuck-me boots. They want to be whipped with a riding crop or hit with a ruler until their asses turn the shade of a fire engine or a well-broiled lobster. They rarely use "safe" words—"vanilla," "red," or the more obvious "mercy" and "stop." Some men want "small penis humiliation" and to hear I have written with implements more impressive than their peckers. Perhaps they should consider gender reassignment surgery? After all it's easier to "dig a hole" than "build a pole." I asked a fellow member of the tribe whether his "mohel made a mistake and cut off more than his foreskin." For providing these services, they place lovely crisp bills from the ATM in my all-too-eager hands. I had discovered my inner dominatrix while working bachelor parties. My favorite part of the night had been spanking the bachelor and best man. I could have wailed on those interchangeable assholes all night. The pimp who ran the stripping service had christened me Allie, but when I was "hired" at the dungeon, which involved no more than showing up so the owner, Madame Medusa, a Jamaican immigrant, could see I really looked as good as my pictures, I decided I needed a new name and settled on Summer. I like the irony of being called a sweet, whimsical name in a dark, smoky place where men pay to be urinated on and suspended from the ceiling. I've always been drawn to pseudonyms and the magic and mystery of being someone else.

144

Geographically, the dungeon is only a couple blocks from the World Trade Center. I find it impossible not to think about 9/11 when walking the streets of the financial district. I imagine the pandemonium of that day—people running every which way in a panic as airplanes flew into the buildings, trapping employees inside. Those unable to escape exposed to smoke curling all around them. No exit. Trapped on the upper floors. Standing on ledges and jumping to their deaths. The long weary walks the survivors took uptown and across the Brooklyn Bridge, women holding their heels, going barefoot, and the way the blue sky went gray with ash that stayed for days and days. Nearly a decade later, it's a chaotic construction site, where tourists come to gawk and take photographs. Floating around in a dissociative state, my body is present, my mind shut off. The majority of the time I am detached, barely aware of the events unfolding around me.

From time to time, truly shocking moments yank me back. A filthy man meanders in wanting his nipples pinched with clothes pins while he wears one of the adult diapers the dungeon stores in a black bin labeled Infantilism. He rubs himself frantically, his hardness straining the Depends. Or the one who looks homeless and shows up with a cage full of vermin. I wonder whether he caught the rats himself (lots lurked around the nearby C train station), but before I have the opportunity to ask, he releases them. One dashes dangerously close to my red stilettos. I scream and jump up on the futon. In moments like these I wonder, *What the hell happened to my life? I am a Jewish girl from Westchester. I had a bat mitzvah! I have an Ivy League education. This is so fucking fucked up! What the fuck?!*

The dungeon is like a meat market crossed with a sorority house. When not playing dress up, the mistresses sit around, chain smoking cigarettes, eating takeout, e-mailing potential customers, and watching DVDs for seven, eight, nine, even ten hours. Madame Medusa loosely enforces her no-drinking-or-smoking-up-during-business-hours policy, being that she is the in-house dealer and has an affinity for her own product. I have little interest in weed and prefer the seemingly never-ending supply of Adderall Mistress Harmony procures from Slave Scott, a podiatrist with a foot fetish. You could leave with $600 or with nothing. All sessions paid the same whether it was foot worship, which is easy and only entails letting some pathetic schmuck rub your feet and maybe kiss them, or whether it involved fantasy wrestling with Octavio, who wants his head pressed firmly between your thighs in a "scissor" hold. Since Medusa takes a 60/40 cut of every session, in her favor, I contemplate starting a freelancer's union for dommes in which we would be entitled to benefits, a 401(k), and an hourly wage. Sometimes I wonder what Medusa does when tax time comes round. It's no secret she doesn't report her income. None of us do. I have elaborate daydreams about ratting her out to the feds and INS and watching as she is led away in her own handcuffs to a detention center or internment camp.

When I do get money, it doesn't stay there long, what with the need for rent, my cell phone, Fancy Feast, and Fresh Step. Forget the student loans. They're on permanent deferral. In my mind, sex currency is superior to a check earned at a straight job be it Walmart or some truly heinous vocation like a meter maid. There is more risk involved in sex work, the revealing of oneself, removing clothes, and standing exposed before a stranger. Setting boundaries without a uniform—an ID badge or green barista's—is a unique challenge. Pretending to like him, playing the seductress who never seduces. Endeavoring to empty a wallet without penetration. You tell them, "Show me how you touch yourself. Show me what feels good." You want and wait for one moment to give way to the next, for the hour to fast-forward and be done, done, done. To finger the bills—twenties, fifties, sometimes hundreds.

You tell yourself this money is all that matters and you marvel each time you escape unscathed. At the dungeon there is often live entertainment as each mistress vies to be the center of attention. The place is a magnet for bitches with axis-II diagnoses. Nine out of ten don't give any thought to having photos—face shots, no less—on Medusa's website. They lavish in the attention and posing sexily for the camera. When my turn comes, I cover my face with a heart-shaped black paddle or my hair, or I have Mistress Harmony zoom in and snap my legs and ass.

Medusa snarls when she sees the shots and shakes her head of thick, spirally dreads. In her thick accent she says, "Them guys go on the site to see girls who show their faces. They gonna think yours is fucked up. Girl, you won't make no money." Meaning she wouldn't make any money. It was a risk I was willing to take. Much like online dating, everyone lies on their profile. Mistress Sophia claims she is a "cute college co-ed studying nursing," her proof the white nurse's outfit she scored at a day-after Halloween sale. The dark-haired, multi-pierced "student" is functionally illiterate and closer to 30 than 20. Several times a week, she takes out the collection of dildos and strap-ons from their plastic container beneath the futon and runs around the room wildly waving them in everyone's face, finally pretending to fuck Mistress Ophelia, a sub, with one.

We are technically not allowed to use strap-ons in session. It is against the law and considered prostitution. Dungeons have been busted for it. However we are told to do it for "regulars," like Cuddly Bear Brian, an extremely overweight white guy who stinks and likes to cuddle after taking it in the ass.

The laws are fascinating. Although it's legal to participate in and film a pornographic film, it's illegal to have sex in exchange for money. Or in this case, put a dildo in someone's ass for money. But you can do "dildo worship," wherein you wear a strap-on and the man kneels down and appreciates the visual of a chick with a dick. He is also welcome to insert objects into his own ass. This is legit. But where's the fun in it? We wait around for a degenerate to arrive and Madame Medusa to settle him in a session room. We quickly spray on perfume and slip on heels to parade in one at a time for a meet-and-greet. Madame Medusa tells us, "Two minutes tops. You don't be giving him no freebie. You be in and out." The trick is to make him choose you, to stand out, when he is at times meeting as many as ten other girls.

The pedophiles always go for Katie, a strawberry blond who has an A cup. At 21, with no hips or ass, Katie looks closer to 12. In tight, short black leather dresses and platforms, she could be a poster child for efforts to stop child sex trafficking. She sleeps at the dungeon most nights since her boyfriend held her at gunpoint. Several black and Asian girls are usually available, and no amount of red lipstick can defeat them if the client wants to be beaten by a Nubian or has a Chinese foot-binding fantasy. Also stiff competition is Mistress Scarlet owing to the mammoth breasts she has to tame and squeeze into a corset. Well versed in contemporary literature, she favors Camus and Nabokov, and she also enjoys reading about "children kept in captivity" on Wikipedia, particularly the Elisabeth Fritzl case. When she masturbates to porn, she gets off by fantasizing the actors are related. She says it makes her orgasms much more intense if she envisions a brother and sister doing the deed.

Unlike most of the mistresses, I do not sub or switch. I shudder at the thought of some perv tying me up, having a half hour or an hour to put his hands on me, while I wait for salvation in a "five-minute knock." While I enjoy "tease and denial"—tying them up and flaunting my body, the pink pussy they will never have—I will not make myself vulnerable. At one of the monthly fetish parties, I had gotten pulled into a "group" session where some guy in his 60s or 70s wanted to play a song called "Funky, Funky, Butt, Cheeks." I was happy to dance and pretend to be into his stupid song. But when I felt his hand smack my ass, my mouth froze and I wanted to scream.

In order to feed myself and my cat, I post ads about "Jewish girls gone wild—you bring the horseradish and I'll crack the whip!" and "Confess your secrets to a sexy school girl," on Craigslist and *The Village Voice*'s Backpage.com. When my ads aren't getting flagged, going through the responses is tedious. While the XYers are all looking for free sex, to me sex work means no sex and minimal work for an obscenely large sum of money. I find myself coming up against my and the men's difference in definitions time and again, a seemingly insurmountable wall. My comfort with the sex business only goes as far as creating the illusion of sex, and yet words do not describe my desire for tax-free dollars. If only I can reconcile the exchange of green for a man's carnal pleasure.

The e-mail responses are endless and arrive at all hours. I learn the BDSM community is an international one with members as close as ten blocks away and as far as Kolkata, India, where Rajiv, who is dying to be my "toilet slave," resides. If only I would accept him, he could move in with me in only "3 moths." Another cyber-stranger wants to be objectified and treated like "complete property," transformed into a sissy maid, a rubber doll, a piece of furniture, a pony, or a dog. A man in Staten Island asks for "financial domination" and wants a woman to add to the deed to his house then threaten to take it away. He balks when I say I need to consult my attorney first. Ted from Wisconsin sends his travel itinerary, along with dates, hotels where he will be staying, and references, names, and phone numbers of previous women he has been with who will most likely remember him for his "oral and salsa dancing skills." Despite the statistic that 85 percent of people have HPV, everyone claims to be "D&D free." All the men are "in great shape" and "very stable and normal outside the bedroom."

At some point I develop an unhealthy obsession with Christian Loubotins and finding a man with a foot fetish to buy the $900 shoes for me. I wonder if prior to the recession this might have been easier. I learn Collarme.com is not a place to earn revenue but is reserved for lifestyle BSDMers. I am told of a club called Paddles where lifestylers often go to get naked and spank one another. In a way, I am like a drug dealer who doesn't use her own product. And yet there is certainly sadism in me. I am prone to fantasies about maiming and torturing ex-boyfriends, setting them on fire. I envision acid burning the face of the ex-fiancé. Since I am not intent on bringing my ideation to fruition, I seek male substitutes to punish and take me on endless shopping sprees—handing me credit cards with no limits. I am limitless inside and cannot actually be fulfilled. No amount of shoes are likely to do it, no Louis Vuitton bag. It's doubtful I could ever feel satisfied, but I'd sure like to try. Medusa bursts into our

149

little area, barking, "There be a guy in ten minutes." She looks at us, lying around—listless, lazy girls—and shakes her head. She needs us to be mean, moneymaking machines. "Get up. It be the Tooth."

Mistress Sophia groans, "Not that fucker again."

"He comes here, too?" Mistress Oksana asks, her blue eyes widening with what looks like concern—and is that fear? It's her first day at Medusa's, but she says she's been in the scene for a while and worked at the Underground Playground and Salome's Salon before it got busted for using strap-ons.

"Relax, he likes to session with newbies," Mistress Scarlett says knowingly. "I'm not even getting dressed. Tell me, Medusa, did he not ask whose new here?"

Medusa lights up a Newport. The air is already so thick with smoke my eyes are tearing. "He wanna meet Summer." Suddenly all eyes are on me.

You'd think I had been bestowed some honor like captain of the cheerleading squad or nominated for prom queen. Katie, who's been quite vocal that she is saving up for her own place, looks particularly annoyed, and I know they will be talking about me as soon as I leave the room. Mistress Mona Lisa, who hails from South Africa, had tipped me off, earlier in the week. "Summer," she'd said, "if I were you I would watch my back." While I appreciate her looking out for me, I'm not intimidated by Katie, who's lost countless phones in the time I've known her and will go out for cigarettes and not return for days. She is the type of girl who would be late to her own catfight or forget about it altogether. The others aren't any better.

Ignoring Katie's and her comrades' glares, I head to the bathroom, where I reapply my signature red lipstick and accentuate my eyes with black liner and mascara. I manipulate a black push-up bra and silky red corset to give the appearance I have way more cleavage than I actually do, refasten my black garter belt to the fishnet thigh-highs I'm already wearing, and step into and zip up my boots. I look in the mirror and am pleased with my appearance. I look hot! I'd want to session with me! I consider for a second why they call him the Tooth and hope he isn't into some crazy vampire fetish; I'm well aware HIV can be transmitted through biting and neither want to bite nor be bitten by one of these disgusting creeps.

I follow Medusa to the session room where he is waiting. "You know the drill: Go in, meet him, come out." I nod obediently and knock on the door. I tell myself he can't be as bad as that cop who asked to have his own Taser used on him.

"Come in," a voice says, and I step inside. She has put him in the largest of the session rooms. The velvet curtains are drawn, and a single candle has been lit.

"Hi," I say, "I'm Mistress Summer." He is younger and slimmer than most of the men who come in. If he had the right haircut and wore a Brooks Brothers button-down, he could pass himself off as one of the finance clones who roam Wall Street in packs, clutching fresh copies of *The Economist*, sucking on cigarettes and boasting loudly about their bonuses. However, he lacks their bravado. I notice he is trembling. He takes me in.

"You are very beautiful, Mistress."

"Thank you," I respond.

"How long have you been working here?" he asks.

"About a month," I say.

"Are you a student?"

"Yes," I say. It's obviously what he wants to hear.

"What are you studying?" he asks, and I become nervous, painfully aware of the time, wanting to sneak a peek at my wristwatch and wondering if I can do so without him noticing.

Medusa knocks on the door and opens it simultaneously. "You want her?" she asks. "Mistress Summer make you real happy. She meet your needs." Usually she seals the deal without us in the room, but she's particularly aggressive around the first of the month when rent is due.

"Summer," she barks, "go on and get a pair of them rubber gloves. And a bucket." A bucket? I groan inwardly and pray Tooth isn't an anal guy or looking for an enema. Unfortunately the dungeon offers

151

"medical play." My first session had been with Oliver, a tall, aging Asian. A chance encounter in the school nurse's office thirtysomething years earlier with high school cheerleaders Blair and Clair had changed his life forever. Oliver had asked that I examine his "boy parts" much like the girls had done, all the while giggling and ridiculing him. His finale had been inserting a thermometer into the shaft of his penis. I retrieve a pair of yellow surgical gloves from the supply closet and a bucket from under the sink and tell myself the Tooth can't be as bad as Oliver.

When I return, the Tooth is naked, his clothes neatly hanging in the closet. I must look surprised because he says, "I don't want to get blood on them." Blood?! He unzips a red-and-black New York Sports Club gym bag and begins withdrawing all the dental tools of my nightmares: silver instruments with pointy ends, one with a small, shiny mirror attached to it, and several that look like pliers a plumber might use to repair a leaky faucet.

I am six years old again and awaking from general anesthesia in the pediatric dentist's chair. There is a green mask covering my nose and mouth. I am all alone, and I begin to cry. My mother appears, and I hear muffled words being exchanged. The dentist in his sterile scrubs says, "She's too young. I can't give her anymore." He needs to finish the procedure with me wide awake. An hour had lapsed owing to a patient in the waiting room having a heart attack and the dentist tending to him. I'd slept through the cardiac arrest, the attempts to resuscitate him, and the ambulance that had arrived to whisk him off. The drill began whirling loudly. It smelled like burning metal, and I screamed. I heard my mother lie and make pleading promises: "I'll let you get your ears pierced if you just stop crying!" I wouldn't have to wait to the previously agreed-upon age of 13 when I would have my bat mitzvah.

I reach up, now, to touch the diamond studs in my ears. Reassured they are still there I ask the Tooth, "What do you want?"

152

He opens his mouth, using his fingers to stretch the sides as wide as they will go. Like a jack-o'-lantern, he is missing numerous teeth on

Johns, Marks, Tricks, and Chickenhawks

the top and bottom. He uses his right index finger to point out what I believe is called a canine tooth. "You're going to extract this one."

"Like hell I am!"

He walks over to the closet, reaches into the pocket of his blue jeans, and pulls out a few fifties. He turns and tries to hand them to me, but I am not expecting it and simply watch as the bills flutter to the floor. My gaze goes back and forth between the money and the tools, unsure what to do. I remember retrieving dollar bills from under my pillow and how the accompanying notes from the Tooth Fairy congratulating me on my lost baby teeth were scripted in handwriting suspiciously similar to the Chanukah Fairy.

"You're not the Tooth Fairy," I point out. I realize I sound like a little kid telling the Santa Claus at the mall he's not the real Santa Claus. I clarify: "I mean you can't just go around paying people to pull your teeth out. I mean, you pay dentists for that, and it gets billed to insurance if you have it, but like the whole reason you go to a dentist is because you actually need to have a tooth pulled because it's infected or whatever but usually they do a root canal first, right? Have you been to a dentist?"

He looks annoyed. "I don't need a dentist."

"Maybe you do," I say. "They have that number on TV—1-800-DENTIST. I've never called it but you could try. And if you have insurance, you could ask them for a list of providers. I just can't imagine you wouldn't need antibiotics if you have a tooth pulled without anesthesia. Didn't you get an infection last time?"

He smiles, and I feel slightly ill when I see the missing teeth. "Today you are my dentist, Mistress Summer."

"I don't think so," I mutter under my breath. I wonder why he can't have a "normal" fetish and want a spanking or ball busting like our other clientele. I mean, who the hell does this guy think he is coming in here with these dental tools expecting me to pull his teeth out?

I've learned that a lot of the guys who come here were abused as children by family members or religious figures—priests or rabbis. Perhaps he was molested by the family dentist? I wonder where he

153

The Dungeon

got the dental tools and if they are available for purchase online or if he broke into a dentist's office to steal them. I wonder whether he will want a release after the tooth is pulled. Is this going to excite him and turn him on?

He picks the fifties up off the floor and adds an additional hundred-dollar bill. He holds the money out to me. I sigh and I take it. I guess everyone has their price, and at that moment mine is $300. He removes a thin plastic tube and a bottle of mouthwash from the gym bag. It's the whitening kind, and the bottle brags that its contents "prevent tooth decay" along with "strengthening and restoring enamel." I cannot fathom what difference it makes if his are yellowing and stained or the picture-perfect, porcelain variety you'd find in an advertisement for veneers. My mother saved all my baby teeth. I wonder what he does with his.

The Tooth expertly puts one end of the tube in his mouth and lets the other end hang into the bucket. He lies down on the couch, like a therapy patient, and hands me a pair of pliers. He tilts his head back and opens his mouth wide, gesturing to the one he wants taken out. I can feel my heart racing as I pull on the rubber gloves. I grip the tooth with the pliers. I have little upper-arm strength to begin with, and my destitution has made a gym membership and the prospect of lifting weights rather unrealistic.

I try to wiggle the tooth, but it is firmly implanted in his mouth. How the hell am I supposed to get this sucker out? I haven't had any proper training. I didn't go to dental school. I try pretending he is an ex. This usually works when I am paddling a guy's behind, but it is harder now with his face so close, his eyes anxiously searching mine. I'm beginning to get a headache. A couple Excedrin and a tumbler of scotch on the rocks would do the trick. Some Valium would also be nice, and I make a mental note to ask Harmony if she can convince Slave Scott to write a scrip.

"Do it harder!" he attempts to yell, but his words slur; it sounds like he has a speech impediment. He gestures with his fist a pulling action reminiscent of my fourth-grade class putting on *Excalibur*. I remember the terrible acting of my peers grunting and straining as they attempted to cajole an aluminum foil sword from a papier mâché stone until finally Ross Rosenblatt, who had been cast as Young Arthur, effortlessly withdrew it and our parents and teachers cheered. Somehow I doubted a secret lineage would be revealed to me should I succeed in pulling out this fool's tooth. It was highly unlikely I would take my rightful place in the monarchy and marry Prince William or at least his renegade redheaded younger brother.

"Why do you want this?" I ask in a voice so soft I am unsure if I've spoken aloud until I realize I've upset him.

"Don't ask me that! You're not a therapist!" the Tooth roars, sitting up.

The door swings open and Madame Medusa enters. Her eyes are bloodshot, her movements languid. I'm fairly certain she's been into her ganja supply again. "What be the problem, here?"

"She"—the Tooth points at me—"is NOT meeting my needs!"

"So sorry, Mister! Summer, she be one the newest girls and I don't think she be working out so good. Me be real sorry. Me know you like them new girls but last time you was here you had your session with Mistress Scarlett and you was real happy with her. She be the one with them big titties!" She holds out her hands to her bosom and squeezes, motioning and gesturing wildly. She nods her head, smiles, and winks at the Tooth. "Me send her in. She make you real happy!"

The Tooth pretends to think it over a moment before finally nodding. "I suppose that would be all right."

I follow Medusa out of the room. The smile has left her face. She looks livid and I wonder if she is going to hit me. "Me gonna get Scarlett. Get you things, you leave, and don't you never come back here."

"Are you paying me for the session?" I ask.

"Hell no I ain't! You don't do your job, you don't get paid. That's the way it works in America. Now get out of here. Me done looking at you." The way she pronounces the "you" sounds like an "oo" as if she is actually in pain from the mere sight of me.

I am being fired by an illegal immigrant from a job at a dungeon where I am seldom paid. There will be no severance wages, no exit interview, and no COBRA. I finger the $300 and am annoyed about the session money Medusa will now be giving to Scarlett who will saunter in to take my place. I imagine her cooing and exclaiming how good it is to see the Tooth again. She will meet his needs.

ALICE ATLASS is a nice Jewish girl who hails from Westchester. She has written about her misadventures seeking a sugar daddy to pay off her $100,000 in student loans and keep her and her felines in the life of luxury she believes they deserve.

DUPLICITY

Shawna Kenney

My second outcall was another cross-dresser. He was way out in the suburbs of Virginia, so Miranda charged him $300 for the hour. I arrived at a small townhouse where a short, well-dressed Latin man who looked strangely feminine opened the door. He invited me in with his broken English. Now I could see he was wearing a light-pink lip gloss and false eyelashes. I told him I'd be in the bathroom changing and ordered him to strip and wait on his knees, just as Miranda taught me, and just as I did with all of my clients. He just stared at me, standing in the middle of a plush, white square of carpet, surrounded by shelves of books and those enviable knickknacks of the well-traveled.

"Didn't you hear me? I said strip and get on your knees!" I knew Tony was listening at the door for the first few minutes, just to be sure everything went okay. If this jerk tried anything funny, his door would be knocked down in two seconds flat.

"P-p-please, Madam. I don't want to do that."

"I don't care what you WANT. I am the dominatrix and you'll do as I say!" I was on my period, and believe me, there's nothing scarier than a dominatrix with cramps. I must have sounded especially evil. Tears formed in his eyes.

"What's wrong?" I softened my tone. I didn't think he was dangerous anymore. Hopefully Tony got the same feeling.

"I just want to talk and be with you." The man offered me a seat on the couch.

"May I take off my shirt?" he asked timidly.

"Go ahead."

He unbuttoned his white shirt to reveal a white corset that looked like it had seen better days—and even then, it was probably still ugly. He stared at me, as if to ask, "Is this okay?" I nodded. He unbuttoned his pants. He had on the biggest grandma-looking underwear I'd ever seen. He looked down, ashamed.

"Does this o-o-offend you, Mistress?"

"No, why would it?"

He walked over to me and asked permission to lie on the couch, his head face up in my lap. I granted it, and we talked this way for the next two hours. I decided to test my third-year Spanish skills, and he was thrilled with my clumsy efforts. "*Digame en español*," I tell him. He told me he was a surgeon, originally from Argentina. His wife knows about his love for women's clothing but doesn't wish to see it. He speaks too quickly and I tell him to slow it down, laughing to myself as I wonder why we've never learned vocabulary like "cross-dresser," "submissive," or "you need to get some better underwear" in class. Whatever would *Profesora* Maria Helena think of how I'm implementing her lessons? I stroke his hair and tell him of the other men I've met like him, and he can't believe it.

"You mean, there are others?" The 50-year-old becomes a child, his brown eyes big with joy and wonder.

"Of course." I told him about the special closet at Miranda's dungeon, filled with furs, silky dresses, nighties, shoes, and wigs for our cross-dressers. He was in complete shock.

"I come from a country where it is very important to be macho. To be like me is a disgrace."

"You are not a disgrace. You are just you," I tell him. It sounds weak when I say it, but it seems to satisfy him. My friends always tell me I should be a therapist. That or a bartender. *How sad,* I thought, *to not be able to be yourself with your lover.* I wonder if his visit with me made him feel better or worse. Better for finding someone who understands, or worse and frustrated for doing this behind his wife's back, suppressing his urges around her. Maybe it's no worse than some of my friends not knowing "the real me" and what I've done in the past. People can be judgmental, so we have to keep our secrets.

We said pleasant goodbyes, and he told me he'd call the agency when he needed to talk again. The day was a lesson to me—every session was different because each person was different. "You are the dominatrix and you can do whatever you want." Miranda's words echoed in my head. True, but I could not continue to go through the motions of spanking and giving orders in the same way to every client. I had to pay attention and tailor each session to fit the person I was with. I had to get creative. Just like with school and life in general—I wanted to push myself to do the best I could.

About 25 percent of all clients ended up being outcalls. They brought me deeper into this world. They opened up worlds I'd never seen up close. I was going to the finest hotels in Washington. Marble staircases. Glass elevators. If I'd had a particularly hectic day and no time to eat a decent meal, I'd have the guys order room service in time for our session. Shrimp, cheesecake, salad. It was the first time I could look at expensive menus and order exactly what I wanted with no thought of price. In true white-trash fashion, I even ordered extra appetizers and desserts—food I knew I couldn't finish—and took it home with me for the next day. The client never seemed to care. Half the time it was on his company's credit card anyway. I also got to explore some of the nicest homes. Houses you'd see in magazines. I had never been so close to such extreme wealth. Many rich older people lived alone in huge mansions, with their pets as their only company. They just indulged their fantasies once in a while by paying someone like me. It was always riskier going to someone's house. I mean, who knew what they had planned? But I had Tony as backup, plus I liked meeting them in their own surroundings. Studying their books. Pianos.

Closets. Medicine cabinets. (Oh, the medicine cabinets! I never realized what a medicated society we lived in until I started this form of snooping!" Anal-itch cream, antifungal ointment, flush-free niacin. *What is that stuff?*) Anyway, I think most were just plain lonely. Maybe even bored with life.

I showed up at one guy's house on a beautiful summer afternoon. I don't know if he even knew what a dominatrix was or what, but he seemed extremely happy to see me. He introduced himself as Norman, welcomed me in, and asked me to please have a seat on the couch. He fixed me a glass of ice water at my request, then sat down and put his face in his hands.

"You don't have to get undressed or anything. I don't know why I called you people," he said.

"I wouldn't be getting undressed anyway, smart guy," I tried to explain to him. "I'm here to . . ." All of a sudden he was crying. Big tears rolled down from his eyes over his thin, aging hands.

"My wife died twelve years ago," he sobbed. "And I haven't been this close to a woman since."

His chest heaved, he was crying so hard by this time. I was completely stunned. I hadn't prepared for this.

He went on: "I don't know why I called. I just wanted to talk to somebody—a woman."

I thought maybe he was thinking I was a prostitute, so I clarified that he was not going to have sex with me. He sobbed harder. It wasn't what he wanted anyway. He really just wanted to talk. When I finally believed him, I put my hand on his back and smoothed over it back and forth, like my mom used to for me. His frail body shivered under the thin checkered shirt's cloth. He composed himself and stopped sobbing eventually, and then told me he was from Seattle but his daughter was attending school in D.C. When his wife died, his life ended. He was completely lost without her. He retired a year ago and moved to D.C. to be closer to his daughter. He was battling depression and wanted to try just about anything to get his life moving again. He told me he tried dating twice, but both times he felt so guilty about it. His wife was the love of his life and he didn't want anyone else. I had no psychiatric background, and being so young I had no experience with what he was going through, but I knew he had passion for this woman he shared his life with, and I was touched. I know I probably should've told him she'd want him to get on with his life and all those other things you're supposed to say, but to this day I know when I die I want someone to have loved me like that. I didn't know what to tell him, so I asked him questions about her, her likes and dislikes. I noticed a few antique cameras on display in a glass cabinet, and told him I was studying photography. He was so happy to take the cameras out and show me how they still worked. He pulled out photos of his wife and daughter, and I was sincere when I commented on how beautiful they both were. Our time ran over and my pager beeped. It was Miranda, calling to ask me if I was staying for another hour or what. If so, I'd have to charge him. I told him I had to go, and he happily paid the $100 for an extra half hour with me. (Miranda marked the price down like that if we were already "mid-session.") I couldn't believe this man was paying just for my company. Thoreau was right. The mass of men do lead lives of quiet desperation. He called the agency a few more times to see me, always ready with stories and sometimes lunch. We never did anything sexual or acted out fetishes or fantasies, and Miranda never knew he was any different from the "other freaks," as she called them. I ended up giving him my phone number and stopping by—for free—to check in on him from time to time. From every job I've ever had, no matter how miserable or insignificant, I've always walked away with at least one true friend. Norman was it for this one.

SHAWNA KENNEY is an American author and journalist. Shawna was born in Auburn, New York. She authored the memoir *I Was a Teenage Dominatrix* (Last Gasp) at the age of 29. The book developed an underground cult following, receiving a Firecracker Alternative Book Award in 2000, with translations published in Italy and the U.K. Kenney's personal essays appear in several anthologies, most notably *Without a Net: The Female Experience of Growing Up Working Class* (Seal Press) and *Pills, Thrills, Chills, and Heartache: Adventures in the First Person,* as well as *Ms.*, *Bust Magazine*, *Juxtapoz*, *The Florida Review,* and numerous anthologies.

Johns, Marks, Tricks, and Chickenhawks

TOPPING FROM THE BOTTOM

Lauri Shaw

When Clarissa agreed to join me and Mitchell on one of our "dates,"
I was surprised. I haven't spent time with her outside of work since
that strange night at the after-hours club when we walked in on her
boyfriend getting fucked by another guy. But she said she was definitely up for making an easy $500, and that was that. So here we are.

Mitchell has just run us through our usual routine. All of that was
fine. But after the steak house and the strip clubs, the moment of
truth arrives. Clarissa meekly follows me out of the cab. She tries for
a poker face and is nowhere near the mark.

I can always forge a certain brashness that will fool, if nobody else,
a stranger into thinking I have limitless confidence. Clarissa, on the
other hand, carries herself like a wet dishrag. Sometimes I'm embarrassed for her. Other times she just plain annoys me with that shit,
and then I feel funny about being seen with her. Hasn't she ever heard
of guilt by association? The minute one of these creeps figures out
what my hot buttons are, it'll be the beginning of the end.

Clarissa and I have chatted and gone over the scenario that I
expect. But she hasn't loosened up yet. She looks nervous. That, in
turn, makes me nervous.

Thankfully, Mitchell is totally oblivious to her uncertainty. His
drunken gait, a few paces ahead of us, is as obnoxious as the rest
of him. I whisper and gesture, trying to make light of his ridiculous

figure wobbling down the road. All I can get out of Clarissa is some tinny, nervous laughter.

We're about to go up into the same motel he took me to last time. A paper bag blows down the otherwise deserted block. The motel's cheap neon sign appears forlorn next to the dark windows of the office buildings.

I look my protégée up and down. The truth is, she has no fashion sense. She looks much better naked. Tonight she's wearing a hideous brown shirt with a fake leopard fur collar and matching cuffs. Her denim miniskirt is the wrong cut—her legs look skinny and her ass looks flat. Maybe there's something to those "bridge and tunnel" clichés after all. Worse, she's gone and cut her hair very short, making her penciled-in eyebrows stand right out. I swear, sometimes all I want to do is shake some sense into her. Why'd I pick her? Because there was no else I could ask.

In any case, I'm grateful for the company. At least now Mitchell is outnumbered. Now I just have to calm her down.

"This is kind of fun, right?" I say. "You've been having a good time so far. How 'bout that restaurant he took us to?"

I'm rewarded with a small smile. Clarissa liked her lobster.

"In another hour or so, we're each gonna be $500 richer," I say.

"I feel fine," she says. She's a terrible liar. "Just . . . Anthony wasn't too thrilled about me going out, you know?" She tries to laugh it off. It comes out hollow.

"Why do you care what he thinks?" She looks away, so I change the subject. "Babe. Listen, okay? You're one of the sexiest women in New York City," I tell her. "Men pay to see us naked. They actually pay! Do you know what kind of power we have over them? We're the ones in control here. All the time. Remember that."

I've heard this somewhere. I don't really believe it. But it seems to brighten Clarissa up a bit.

"He's an easy mark." I toss my hair over my shoulder and then touch her hand. "Follow my lead and we'll be out of here in no time."

"It's fine. Really. I trust you," Clarissa says.

I pat her on the back. "Good. Now let's go smack around a fat old loser and make some money."

Mitchell wanted us to arrive separately in the motel room. Why he asked for that is a mystery. The doorman certainly knows him and is well aware that he won't be staying for the whole night.

But when he opens the door, I see he's wearing a red silk bath-robe . . . and a leather mask over his face, à la *Pulp Fiction*. *Oh, good Lord* . . . I don't dare look at Clarissa. If I do, I know neither of us will be able to stop laughing. Instead, I stomp into the bedroom on my big leather boots. I drop six grams of Harlem coke on the nightstand. I flat out ignore Mitchell's ridiculous getup.

"I got two for me, two for you, and two for tonight. They were eighty apiece," I announce.

He nods. "So I'll give you an extra five hundred later."

"Not later. I want to settle up now, before we start dipping into each other's stash."

"Well, that takes the fun out of it," Mitchell whines. I'll bet he's scowling behind his mask.

"Did you hear me?" I bark, brandishing a riding crop. Clarissa gasps softly. We've already begun. I put my arm around Clarissa. "It would make my friend here feel much more comfortable if you paid us now. This being her first time and all."

"Okay, okay, babe. Whatever you want."

"Okay, *who?*" I hiss, taking a step closer to Mitchell.

"Okay . . . *Mistress.*" He takes out his wallet and puts two piles of money on the nightstand next to the coke. One pile for me and one for Clarissa. I count both piles, take what's mine, and pass Clarissa her money. Then I pick up my share of the coke and put it neatly into my handbag with the cash.

"What else can I do for my mistress?" Mitchell wheedles at me.

Oh, man. This shit is just too tempting sometimes. If I didn't know that Mitchell could easily overpower me whenever he wanted to, I might just unleash some of my real anger on him.

"Take off the stupid mask," I settle for. "I want to see your face while you're blushing and groveling."

Honestly, this "bring out the gimp" vibe is just giving me the willies. Clarissa stands in the corner like a mannequin while I strap Mitchell's leather restraints to his wrists and ankles.

"Come over here, Clarissa," I call. She obeys. I hand her the riding crop. "Tell our boy how lucky he is that he's got you to punish him tonight if he steps out of line."

Clarissa holds the crop nervously. She parrots me. "You're . . . really lucky . . ."

But she doesn't sound like she means it. And on the bed, Mitchell rolls his eyes.

"Give me a break," he complains.

Clarissa's lousy at this. I should have known. She's not believable. She stutters when she's supposed to improvise. Mitchell looks annoyed. He calls a time out and nods at me to take him out of the restraints.

"Let's try it this way. You've never been on top before, so I'm gonna teach you how to top me," he tells Clarissa.

She looks at the floor, then back up at him.

"When I come out of the bathroom, I want you to slap me in the face as hard as you can and yell at me that I've been a filthy, naughty boy. Simple. Think you can manage it?"

"Okay . . . sure," she agrees. She giggles. When he isn't looking, I kick her to shut her up. If she can't keep it together, I'm going to be stuck alone with him again. Mitchell goes into the bathroom and closes the door. I face Clarissa. "You can do this," I whisper.

She nods again. But she's still looking at the floor.

The first time Mitchell emerges from the doorway, Clarissa can't keep a straight face. She says the line, and her lips quiver into an embarrassed smile. When she smacks Mitchell, he stops and shakes his head.

"You call that a slap?" he asks her.

"I'm sorry," Clarissa says.

"No! Don't be sorry!" Mitchell erupts. Then he softens. "You're supposed to make *me* sorry."

She giggles, and then stops herself. "Sorry. I'm sorry," she repeats. "No . . . I mean . . ."

"We'll try it again, okay?" he directs.

The second time is no better. Clarissa just can't seem to bring herself to yell at Mitchell in a way that is plausible. And she doesn't hit hard enough for his liking.

"I give up. You're a born sub," he finally sighs. "Get back on the bottom or I'm sending you home."

"That was not the deal," I protest as I head for the nightstand. I snort a line of coke and light a cigarette. I blow smoke in Mitchell's direction.

"She has to earn her keep," Mitchell tells me. "Otherwise, what's the point of me having both of you here?" He turns to Clarissa. "Get on the bed."

"What's the safe word?" I ask.

"No safe words," he says.

"Mitchell, that's not the way we—"

"It's okay," Clarissa interrupts me. I want to scream at her, to grab her arm and drag her out of the room. I told my client that I don't bottom, and neither does Clarissa. If she's agreeing to change the rules, how long before he tries to switch those same rules up on me?

She quietly plants herself on the bed.

"Not that way. On your stomach, slut!" Mitchell orders.

"Hang on," I say to him. He either doesn't hear me or he's ignoring me.

"You like it," he croons, touching Clarissa with a whip he's just pulled off his belt. "Tell me you like it."

"I . . . like it," she says. I hear hesitance.

"Louder!" Mitchell flicks the whip hard against Clarissa's thigh. She winces. "I like it," she breathes, a little louder than the first time, and turns over.

"Yeah, you whore, of course you like it. You're a filthy little girl.

You're not supposed to like it when Daddy punishes you," Mitchell babbles as he buckles her into the restraints. "You like it—you *love* it—because you're a disgusting slut. Getting Daddy all worked up. Twitching your little ass in Daddy's face all the time, so he has no choice but to give you what you have to have."

I can't see her face right now.

"What are you waiting for?" Mitchell says to me.

I pick up the crop, and I smack Clarissa's ass with it. *Let's just get this over with. I want my money and I want to go home.* "Clarissa, you are a stupid slut," I say. It comes out sharp because I *am* actually upset with her. She's messed up the easy scene I'd planned, and now I have to try to fix it. Mitchell leers at me approvingly.

"I'm sorry . . ." Clarissa sounds like she means it.

"You *are* sorry. Look at you. You're a sorry little slave. You'll do anything the master says. But your mistress is the one you promised to listen to. You'd better beg me to have mercy," I say.

Maybe I can rein this bizarre power struggle back in where it belongs. "Has the slave shown us that she deserves mercy?" Mitchell interrupts.

To my horror, he fishes around in a small leather bag and pulls out a very large butt plug. We're talking gay-porn large. He yanks down her panties and slaps her ass. "I have a special treat for you," he says. When he pulls his hand away, I can see that he's left the beginnings of a palm print on her.

"Mitchell, time out," I say. He glares at me and covers the toy with lube.

"No time outs," he snaps. He leans in next to Clarissa's ear. "You'll take it and you'll like it," he says. "Understand?"

Clarissa turns her head and silently scrunches up her face. Mitchell slaps her ass again. "That's good, isn't it?" he snarls. When she doesn't answer him, he inserts the vile thing into her ass, a little at a time.

Clarissa whimpers. But she doesn't try to fight. What can she do? She's tied up. She's on her stomach.

"You like it. You like it. Answer me."

She whimpers again and tells him that she likes it in a voice that suggests that she believes that if she *doesn't* say what he wants, he might hurt her more than she's ever been hurt before.

I do a line. This is going much further than I wanted it to go.

"You fucking love this, bitch. You don't even deserve to feel this good," Mitchell chants, slipping the thing in and out of Clarissa, faster and faster.

It makes wet noises because of the lube—thank God he's at least used lube. I can't tell if he's hurting her more than he's humiliating her, or vice versa. Her pathetic apologies sound completely authentic. Her soft cries pull the cords to my own pain, the shit that sits just behind the curtain. I'm afraid I may become violently ill.

I want to stop him, but I'm scared to try. He seems to have forgotten I'm here, and I don't want to remind him of my presence. I've tried going the knight-in-shining-armor route before with disastrous consequences. Above all else, I'm glad it isn't me on that bed with a piece of plastic shoved up my ass. I don't want to be next.

Clarissa is the easiest mark I've ever met. She might as well have a "kick me" sign tattooed on her forehead for the world to see. I am looking at a person who has been pushed around to the point of resignation. She believes that this is just the way things are. The best thing she can strive for is the softest blow. And I brought her right through this door.

What the hell kind of person sells out a friend this way? My conscience hammers incessantly at me in little whispers. I do line after line of coke to blot it out. And I stand there, open-mouthed and useless, while Mitchell goes to town on Clarissa's ass, without her permission and against her will.

His breathing gets heavier until it reaches a crescendo. Clarissa, face down, continues to whimper and gasp until the moment Mitchell grunts, yanks the butt plug out of her, and drops it on the bed.

"Untie her," he wheezes. The expression on his face is a mixture of disgust and sexual relief. "We're done."

He lumbers off into the bathroom, and I dash to the side of the bed. My hands shake as I undo Clarissa's restraints. When she turns over and sits up, her face is streaked with mascara tracks and there's snot dripping from her nose.

"Clarissa, my God! I'm so sorry," I whisper. "I had no idea! He's never tried anything even close to that with me. Are you okay?"

"I'm fine." Her voice is calmer than I've ever heard it. Her eyes tell a different story. "Can we leave now?" she asks. She wipes her nose with the back of her hand.

"Oh, yeah. We're outta here," I say. "You sure you're all right?"

"I promised Anthony I wouldn't be late," she says.

LAURI SHAW was born in Queens and raised on Long Island, after which she misspent her youth as a Manhattan stripper. She grew disillusioned with sex work around the time Rudy Giuliani's "quality of life" laws were gutting the club scene as she knew it. Bright eyed and still a bit idealistic, Lauri put her clothes back on and attended audio school. It was there she learned the skills she'd acquired for stripping would absolutely qualify her to work in mainstream entertainment. Lauri's subsequent jobs have included stints as a recording studio manager, an L.A. music journalist, and a work-for-hire copywriter. Her hobbies include singing at blues jams, travelling, and animal rescue. For the past several years she has lived in London, England, where she recently achieved dual citizenship.

Johns, Marks, Tricks, and Chickenhawks

3

Mansions, Hotels, and Luxury Condominiums

DO YOU LOVE MOMMY?

David Henry Sterry

The beginning of the end comes innocently enough. Just a normal job on a normal day in the life of a normal 17-year-old boy hooker.

Tooling through a trendy tree-lined Pacific Palisades neighborhood chockablock with brown migrating workers mowing green lawns, pink children throwing red balls, and white women driving overpriced foreign automobiles, I have that wonderful sense of déjà vu all over again as I go from the seedy pit of Hollywood to the clean high-toned America of my youth.

I ring the bell. Split a second and that's how long it takes a postmodern June Cleaver to pull the door open too fast, say hello too hard, and lead me into her too-immaculate, too-decorated home.

She does look good for an old broad, except for all the cakey makeup. Brownish hair slicked back anorexic ballerina style, eyes drowning in pools of blue eye shadow. She's working a creamy calf-length sleeveless dress, plain white flats, and pearls. God love her, she put the pearls on for her chicken.

The kitchen is full of wallpaper choking on flowers. Linoleum rides the floor, Wedgwood watches from running boards, and a desert island sits arid with a butcher-block cutting board sinking in its middle. It's like a movie set of a perfect American home, with a housewife played by an actress who looks right for the role but is just a little too stiff.

173

"Did anyone see you come in?" There's a disturbing urgency in the lines fraying around the edges of her eyes and the veins popping on her neck.

Then she realizes how harsh she sounded, and she tries to pretend she's all casual and carefree. "Not that it matters, but you know how people talk."

This bundle of too-tightly-tied wires tries to smile. But there's no smile there. Her pupils start darting back and forth like someone who's about to flunk a lie detector test.

"And if anyone asks, maybe you could say you're a high school student who's here to help me organize my miniatures. I collect miniatures. Would you like to see them?"

My spider senses are tingling, but my pokerface is firmly in place. Maybe she's just a little nervous. Family's out of town, looking for a little fun. Maybe she's never had sex with anyone besides her painintheassbastardhusband. Maybe she just wants me to get nekked and tell her how hot she is.

Maybe.

"I'm sure people have better things to do than stare at my back door. But let's say they were walking the dog, people like to walk their dogs, well, I suppose they have to, but the point is they *could* see you and if they did, I just want us to be on the same page, you see what I mean?"

I follow my seven o'clock Monday trick to the Miniature Room, and as she finishes her monologue she opens a door revealing a room exploding with teenytiny miniatures: little geldings with no little balls; tiny Chinese potentates and French diplomats; gnomes, sprites, and fairies; a very small Dorothy Gale from Kansas with her ittybitty ruby slippers and her wee dog Toto; diminutive Bob's Big Boy, the Michelin Man, and the Sta-Puff Marshmallow Man; minute Benjamin Franklin, Genghis Khan, and even a mini–Marilyn Monroe, trying to hold her skirt down while the wind threatens to expose her panties for all eternity.

My seven o'clock Monday trick tries to smile again. She comes a little closer this time but still hasn't hit it.

Her failure brings me back to the here and now though. She wants me to admire her miniatures. This is what I must do.

"Wow . . . this is really . . . incredible."

I *say* "incredible" like it's a good thing, whereas I *mean* "incredible" like it's a very scary thing. Everything's all lined up too perfectly, there's too much of it, and it's way too small. The whole thing makes me want to run, not walk, as fast as I can away from this woman.

But I don't. I can't.

"Thank you very much. It's taken a long time to collect, as you can imagine, and I'm . . ."

Her mouth is open, but nothing's coming out of this pearly woman standing in front of her collection of three-inch animals, movie characters, and famous historical figures.

I can hear my pimp's voice in my head: If something seems weird it probably is.

But I can't say no to Mommy.

I don't know how yet.

"These miniatures are totally amazing."

I'm desperately trying to resuscitate my pearly Mommy trick, who stares at me, a plaster of Paris mask of a normal person fixed on her face. I don't know what to do. But I'm 100 percent sure I gotta do something. Try to start the sex? I'm afraid if I touch her she'll shatter into a million pieces. And where's my stinking money? This is getting ridiculous. I'm gonna have to talk to Mr. Hartley about this shit, cuz I need my money in plain sight when I walk in the door, no questions asked.

"And they're so . . . *small*," I say, trying desperately to fill in the silence.

As soon as she hears the word "small," Mommy comes back to life, like some perfect robot replica of a human that gets activated by flipping a switch on the back of her head.

"Yes, they're so small, aren't they? I love how small they all are. I'll show you my favorite," she says.

I still don't know her name, or what the hell she wants, and I still DO NOT HAVE MY MONEY UP FRONT. But at least she's not acting like the walking dead anymore. She picks up a miniature with a rose complexion and dark hair, dressed very Civil War. Vaguely resembles Scarlett O'Hara.

"It's Scarlett O'Hara. Don't you just love her?" She stares rapturously at the lifeless Scarlett O'Hara doll like it's a three-inch lover.

"Yeah, I loved how she made that dress out of the curtains . . ." Having noticed that the mini-Scarlett's wearing the curtain dress, I feel this might help move us along.

"Oh gosh," she says, "I love that scene where Mammy sews the dress, and she grumbles the whole time. Oh that Mammy, she's such a character . . . and Scarlet puts on the dress, and of course she looks fabulous, and she goes to see Rhett in prison, and pretends like everything's okay, but he sees right through her. Oh that Rhett, he's such a scallywag . . . and does he give her a tongue-lashing. See, the thing people don't realize is that they were always madly in love with each other, but never at the same time . . ."

And with that she clicks into some other time zone where crazed assassins lurk in every church tower, puts the little Scarlett carefully back in its place between President Abraham Lincoln and General Robert E. Lee, and ushers me out posthaste.

Suddenly the forecast has gone from mostly sunny to severe storm warnings. Her skeletal structure visibly stiffens, skin tightening and lips constricting. For a second I think it's me. I see her on the phone with Mr. Hartley, who calls Sunny, who chucks me back in the dumpster.

I need my money.

I need my money.

I need my money.

Mommy mutters under her breath as I pad down the hall after her. The only words I can make out are, "ashamed," "irresponsible," and "neglect." I'm sure I'm not supposed to respond. In fact, I'm sure she's not even aware she's vocalizing at this almost intelligible level.

She stops, turns suddenly, and tries to smile again. Again she fails. She looks down, regroups, and looks toward me, but not at me.

"My husband is not . . . with us . . ."

Euphemism for "dead," I'm assuming, although for all I know he could be away on a golf junket.

"I thought you should know. I mean, I didn't want you to think . . ."

Who the hell cares what I think? I'm the whore houseboy, remember? And she doesn't want me to think what? That she's immoral? Unfaithful? Or just out of her mind?

"He took his own life. After our son died . . ."

"Oh . . . I'm really . . . sorry." My affable mask melts, and I'm drenched in sad.

"We had a wonderful marriage. He was very handsome and attentive. My therapist said I should date again, that it would help me . . . get over the whole thing, so . . ."

I doubt this is the kind of date he had in mind.

"Everyone says I should sell the house, but I don't want to sell the house. I love this house . . . Would *you* sell the house?"

Now she's asking the boy hooker for real estate advice. "No, I think it's a great house. I thought that when I came in—I thought, 'This is a *great* house.'"

"It is, isn't it? That's what I'm gonna tell people. I'll just say, 'It's a great house . . .' My husband loved this house. He took his own life, did I tell you that?"

Yes, you did mention that.

"You'll have to forgive me, I've been very . . . forgetful lately. The fact is, he really never got over Braddy's passing. Braddy was our son . . . our only child. It was a terrible tragedy . . . his friend had been

177

drinking . . . Braddy wasn't drinking, the coroner confirmed that. He had no alcohol in his system, or very little alcohol. They ran head-on into a bus . . . Just like that—alive one second, dead the next. Makes you wonder, doesn't it?"

Yes, it certainly does.

"Yes, it certainly does," I say.

She looks at me like she's coming out of a coma, and for the first time I see who she was before all this shit happened: a beautiful wifemommy living large with the handsome husband, the cute kid, and the great house. Like my mom.

"You'll have to excuse me . . . I, uh, haven't been myself lately. . ."

Dead son. Husband offs himself. I want to take her in my arms, rock the hurt right out of her and tell her everything's gonna be okay.

But I can't. I don't know how yet.

A sincere "I'm sorry" is all I can muster.

What a couple of funked-up ducks we are, this ex-mom slash ex-wife and me, trying to get some love in the worst way.

"Thanks," she says.

She tries to smile again and this time it actually works. And when the smile finally does arrive it's very sweet, and drenched in sorrow, like cherries jubilee just about to be lit on fire.

BOY! screams the room Mommy leads me into: pennants, trophies, posters of ballplayers, old caramel-colored baseball mitt with scuffed ball sitting in it, pictures of a brown-haired dimply boy growing up cute: grade school, Little League team, camp friends, high-school-tuxed, and posing with a pretty young polyester plaid baby. There's a trophy exactly like one I had. It's so cool; it's just like my room.

But the longer I stand there the more wigged I get. We definitely have something in the woodshed here. This isn't a boy's room any-more. It's a museum of a boy's room. This room is dead.

"This is Braddy's room. His real name was Bradley, but when he was a baby he could only say Braddy, and I guess it just stuck. He wanted to go to UCLA; that was his dream. And he was a very good athlete. Golf, tennis, baseball. Are you an athlete?" she asks with great expectations.

Doesn't take a rocket surgeon to figure out the answer to that one. "Yes, I am."

"It was his friend Aaron . . . I never liked that boy; he was a very bad influence. I tried to tell Braddy, but he was stubborn, just like his dad. There was no alcohol found in Braddy. Or very little alcohol . . . very little alcohol . . ."

I want to get out of this dead boy's room.

I want to get paid.

I want.

"Would you . . . do me a favor?" She's filled with hesitation.

I still don't think she fully understands the nature of our transaction. That's what I'm here for. She give me money. I do her favors.

But first of course, she has to give me MONEY!

"Sure," I say.

"Uh . . . would you mind . . . uh . . . putting these on?"

Pearly Mommy pulls a Hawaiian shirt and khaki shorts from the closet. I see Braddy behind her on the wall in a blown-up framed picture, dressed in the same Hawaiian shirt and khaki shorts.

"This was his favorite outfit. We used to kid him that it was his uniform. I washed it and washed it afterward to get all . . . you know . . . the stains out. It wasn't easy, believe you me, but I've always said if you want something bad enough and you're willing to work at it, you can accomplish anything. Don't you think?"

"Definitely . . ." I manage to mumble.

Mommy hands me Braddy's Hawaiian shirt and khaki shorts.

"You don't mind, do you?"

No, no, no, I can't, let's have a cup of tea or something and talk about getting you some professional help.

"No problem, that's cool . . ."

"Cool? Isn't that marvelous? That was Braddy's favorite word. He had a wonderful vocabulary, but every other word out of his mouth was 'cool.' I'm just gonna go freshen up while you change. Would you like some cookies and milk?" she asks, like Oedipus's mother in pearls.

"Cookies and milk? Cool." I'm laying it on thick, but trying not to milk the cookies too hard.

She giggles like a crazy 40-year-old schoolgirl and leaves me alone in her dead son's room.

A Civil War rages in my head. The North says put on the outfit, then get the money. The South says get the money, then put on the outfit. After several bloody skirmishes the South relents, and I put on the outfit. But if she doesn't come back in with my money, that's it, I don't give a damn, I am going, going, gone.

The clothes fit like they were made for me. I look in the mirror. I look at Braddy in the khakis and Hawaiian shirt. Then I look back in the mirror.

I have completely disappeared.

A flimsy blue negligee trimmed with black faux fur and red high heels walks through the door carrying a purple plate of brown cookies and a white glass of milk. Slimmy hips, pale belly, good gams nicely turned. Normally a sight like this would make my mojo corkscrew, but here, now, my heart plummets like the cable snapped, and I plunge fast, knowing there's a nasty crash coming and there's absolutely nothing I can do about it. Fevered hotsweats flash all over me, but I'm trying to keep this blank smile on my face, all the while wanting to scream, "Are you mad, woman? Go put some clothes on and check yourself into a clinic, where you can get some state-of-the-art mental health care!"

But I don't. I can't.

"My husband gave me this and I never got a chance to wear it. Do you like it?"

My mommy trick strikes what's supposed to be a tarty pose but ends up looking more like a mental patient than a sex baby.

"Have a cookie . . ."

She moves the plate of cookies toward me, and there it sits, half hidden under a cookie like an invitation to the gold miner's ball: my envelope.

Casually, oh-so-casually, I pick up the cookie over my envelope, take a bite out of it, then palm the sweet succor of my money into the back pocket of the dead Braddy's khakis. I'm a hundred bucks richer and suddenly I don't give a whatever about nothing. And the cookie's good. Moist. I like a moist cookie. I wash it down with the milk.

Envelope in hot pocket, cookie in cool belly, and devilmaycare upon my lips, I squint my eyes and make her into the hottyhot porno star baby of my loverstudguy movie.

"Why don't you come over and sit on the bed with Mommy, Braddy? You don't mind if I call you Braddy, do you?" She smiles like Mother Mary on acid from the bed covered by the blanket with the sports guys on it.

No, no, no, no, no, no.

"No," I say, "that's cool."

My trick mommy pats the bed next to her, the cue for Braddy to sit on the dead bed with his bereaved mother. Is it too late to give back the envelope and get the hell out? Yes, I believe it is. Just do what she wants and everything'll be fine, you'll get some ice cream, have a hang in 3D, and see if Sunny's got some sweet young baby for you to swing with.

When I sit on the bed, Mommy pulls me into her and starts rocking. I'm confused. Does she want me to get sexy with her? Does she want me to be her little boy? I can barely breathe, suffocated by all this Mommy, her sickly sweet perfume pounding on my temples.

She lies back on Braddy's bed and takes me with her. I end up embryonic, head on her chest. Then she guides my mouth to her breast, and it's clear dear dead Braddy is supposed to suckle on Mommy.

So I suck.

Mommy guides me up on top of her, between her legs, and her hips stiltingly do a spasmodic grind while she fumbles with my zipper.

I fish myself out. Fish being the operative word. As in cold and limp. Again, there are many things in life you can fake. An erection is not one of them. My eyes are clamped, because I don't want to see what's underneath me. So I position myself where I can get maximum rubbage, and with my eyes closed, I find the loverstudguy voice in my head:

"Oh baby . . . give it to me you nasty little baby . . . you love it, don't you, baby? Oh baby, baby, baby."

That gets the blood moving in the right direction, and suddenly I'm in, thank you, Jesus! And once I'm in, I'm in.

"Do you love Mommy, Braddy?"

She grabs my head and puts me right in her face.

It jolts me right out of my river and lands me smack-dab in the middle of this dead boy inside his mommy, who's got wet eyes I didn't even notice were crying, as she downloads her pain right into me.

I need to scream. I don't. I can't.

"I . . . I do . . . I lo . . . I lo . . . lo . . ."

The words just don't come out, no matter how much I push them.

"Do you love Mommy, Braddy?"

She asks again, voice cracking like a pane of dropped glass, wild eyes pleading with her dead son while she has sex with her boy whore.

Braddy's supposed to tell Mommy he loves her, but I can't get the words out of my mouth.

Until the need to please takes over.

"I love you, Mommy" somehow burbles out between my frozen lips.

She grabs my hips and starts pulling me into her heart.

So I shut my eyes, and in the dark I manage to get everything working again, and she starts making little sex sounds, so I'm thinking I'm earning my money at least.

Her body lurches, and I open my eyes just in time to see her lean her head over the side of the bed and unload a stream of sick onto the floor, the wave of vomit smell breaking all over me.

She pushes me off her like a mom lifting an automobile off her child who's trapped under the front tire. Then she bolts out of bed, and out the door.

I sit on the edge of the dead Braddy's bed, Mommy's secretions shining on me, and the smell of her sick cutting through me.

Careful not to step in the sick, I step out of Braddy's dead bed, shed his dead clothes, and slip back into my own. I touch the $100 bill. That's better. Normally I want my tip, and God knows I earned it, but today I feel like a diver surfacing too fast, my insides bending, and if I don't get out of here quick, I'm sure my brain's gonna explode.

I shoot like infected sperm out of Braddy's room. But I can't leave yet. I have to make sure she's okay. I tiptoe down the hall and peek in the bedroom. It's long-day's-journey-into-night dark in there. I hear a little mumbly snuffly sound.

"Uh . . . excuse me . . ." I say softly.

More mumbles and snuffles.

"Um . . . I was just wondering if you're . . . okay." Louder this time, poking my head further into the room.

Mumbles. Snuffles.

"Do you need . . . Are you all right?" I say so I know she'll hear me.

Her head snaps up.

"Do you want more money? Is that what you want? There's more money on the desk in the den, take whatever you want, but please, just go . . ." Her face is all puffy red mad like Lady Macbeth at the end when she's trying to get that damned spot out.

It's like looking at a wounded animal bleeding in the middle of the road. You have to stop the car and get out and help. Don't you?

"Are you sure you don't want—"

"Just go! *GO!*"

Her shriek curdles my blood, and I bolt down the hall. But even now, I need my money. That's how empty I am. So I jam into the den and open a fancy-looking box on the desk where a wad of cash stares at me. Gotta be five hundred bucks there. My first impulse is to clean her out. Hey, I earned it. But I can't. I take a fifty.

I feel like I earned it.

DAVID HENRY STERRY is the son of immigrants. One grandfather was a coalminer who died of black lung disease, the other a professional athlete and amateur pedophile. His father made explosives and his mother was a homemaker and then a leading educator for very, very young people. David was born in New Jersey and subsequently lived in Hueytown, Alabama; Virginia; Minnesota; Dallas, Texas; upstate New York; Portland, Oregon; Coxlodge, England; Brooklyn and Manhattan, New York; San Francisco, Hollywood, San Rafael, Echo Park, Silver Lake, and Venice, California; and Montclair, New Jersey. He has worked as a newspaper delivery specialist, a soda jerk, a babysitter, a building inspector, a marriage counselor, a limousine driver, a telephone solicitor, a sitcom actor, a TV spokesman for everyone from AT&T and Publishers Clearing House to Chia Pets, performed over 5,000 sets of standup comedy, and acted with everyone from Will Smith and Michael Caine to Zippy the Chimp. He has written screenplays for Disney, and he is an activist, a muckraker, a book doctor, and the author of thirteen books. He is a regular contributor to the Huffington Post, and his writing has appeared in many anthologies. He is a Henry Miller Award finalist. Every since he was a little kid, he's loved writing. He still loves writing. He likes to talk, loves studying people, enjoys laughing, watches way too much sports, goes to way too many movies, reads books incessantly, grows sunflowers, bakes brownies, plays very serious soccer and baseball, has not worn matching socks in two decades, is the proud owner of a Harley-Davidson, and adores swimming, music, and hanging out with his two girls.

BLUE LOVE

David Austin

> *Now is the winter of our discontent.*
> —Shakespeare, *Richard III*

Tonight was the night. I was sure of it as I walked to the Bank of America on Fourth and Second to withdraw the necessary funds to complete the transaction we had discussed at the office a few hours beforehand. I made sure to call her on the land line from JTF, no private numbers and no identities revealed. Had to be on the safe side, free from the prospect of gash cash coming back to haunt me later. Who knew where or what I'd be involved in three months from now? All I knew at that moment was that I had a suite reserved at the Affinia on Thirty-fourth Street adjacent from the Garden, $8,000 in bonuses from the beginning of tax season, and an itch I needed to scratch.

It was January, and I felt the need to give myself the Christmas present that nobody else saw fit to put under my plastic tree last month. The provider in question bore my sister's name, Alli (although oddly enough, she spelled it "Alley" on her Backpage profile), and her photos piqued my prurient interests. She bore all the marks of my usual victims—five-foot-five, 115 pounds, 34C breasts, slender and lean and mean-looking. Vaguely European and totally über-NYC hot with Jewish facial features, the type of girl who could crush your windpipe with the musculature shining through the skin of her thighs. The sly smile behind her lips as her pale bare ass gleamed from the light of her glamour shots sucked me in. I'd just broken up with a girl who'd put me through hell and high water and laughed as I crushed up enough Xanax and Vicodin to kill three bodybuilders and injected them into the bulging blue vein in my cock in the hopes that the cocktail would take me out quicker. Her last words to me were that she hoped I would finally croak so she wouldn't have to touch me again. If I couldn't have her or anyone else . . . I would buy her. It was payback time and I would pay plenty in order to get someone on their back.

It all seemed to go according to plan by the time I slid my bank card into the slot at the Bank of America ATM. The agreed-upon rate was $350 an hour, no frills and no pretend-girlfriend nonsense. This was a straight deal. My goal was to get at least two hours, the swelling and heaving in my scrotum assuring me that I could quite easily enjoy a second cup of coffee with no performance anxiety or doubts about being able to keep it up. It all seemed incredibly easy as I entered in my PIN and punched in the amount—$800. The extra $100 was to ensure a good time—if your provider senses a deadbeat, the tendency is to clam up in the face of financial inadequacy. Money makes the world go round, and we all have to work hard for the money, but does it really treat you right?

As I withdrew my cash and fit it neatly into my billfold (fourteen $50 notes and five twenties), I spotted something underneath the deposit slips. It seemed to have a human form, albeit an exaggerated one. Upon closer inspection, it was two bodies instead of one. I came in to examine and found a couple of some form, older and by sight African-American, sleeping uneasily in the bank lobby. Two down-and-outers seeking shelter from the beginnings of a New York cold front. Their wool caps pulled down over their ears and eyes, they had wrapped themselves in an oversize North Face down jacket and huddled together tight. Were they married? I spotted no rings on their fingers—considering the circumstances, perhaps they had pawned their rings to keep alive and put a meal in their bellies. Most of my colleagues were not known for their social altruism, but the sight before my eyes registered somewhere deep and cold within me. I went back to the ATM and withdrew an extra $100, paying little attention to the amount left in my account and even less on what the future may hold. Leaning softly over the couple, I snuck the bills into a clenched Nubian fist. Hopefully, it would go to something besides an addiction. Hopefully, it would help them somehow.

Upon leaving the bank en route to the Affinia, a wave of bitter sadness ran down my spine. The bullet of existential angst bullshit had scored a direct hit, freezing the nerves and curbing my enthusiasm stone dead. Here I was, the Bad Boy of finance, glowering in sales pitch websites behind a $100 haircut and a desk littered with the minutiae of death clown paraphernalia and shock art staring out into the lens behind me . . . and for the first (and probably not the last) time, resorting to paying a beautiful young woman to accompany me to a suite in one of the finest hotels in the city while two people who obviously had a strength inside of themselves and a love I could never imagine feeling were making a makeshift hovel out of a bank lobby. Their resolve brought my flop sweat and enthusiasm down. I was little more than a scared little boy who could never hope to feel the kind of love that drove two people to stick together for better or for worse. The only way I could ever hope for even a simulacrum of what those two had was to buy it . . . my currency could get me a taste of the warmth and comfort that only true, genuine love could provide—and that world would always remain closed from my end. As it all came crashing down during my cab ride, the bitter realization hit me that the life I had led was little more than a protracted pimp-whore con. While I envisioned myself a master of the universe, I was little more than another sucker standing in line to get played.

True to her word, Alley came to the Affinia an hour later. The first thing that struck me about her actual physical presence was that she was much shorter than the pictures had led me to believe. Instead of the buxom five-foot-five brunette with the blueberry muffin breasts, here was this munchkin with an accent to rival Nikita Khrushchev sitting on an easy chair before me counting out money like a Vegas loan shark. Odder still, she pulled out a counterfeit pen and checked the bills to make sure I hadn't thrown out money from the Bank of Canon. Satisfied, she shoved my hard-earned jack into her thigh-high boot and proceeded to remove her clothes.

What followed next was two and a half hours of pornographic excess by way of J. G. Ballard. She understood her role, and I barely knew mine—varieties of positions, orifices, and erogenous zones plundered and examined and caressed and prodded and cajoled into action by two actors thrown together at the last minute. Actions and caresses that had formerly teased and pleased more-willing partners registered as noble gestures of nothingness across the acreage of Alley's fresh flesh. Was nothing truly shocking anymore? Had most of her clientele seen her as some form of a replacement for reciprocation? As I mounted her in the missionary position, I looked into her face to try and get some sense of mutual benefit. Did she find the relative heft of my cock pleasurable? Had she gotten her rocks off? The vacant glare told me in no uncertain terms that my penis was nothing compared to the girth of my body, and I was causing more discomfort than pleasure. The deep sense of shame and pain nearly caused me to wilt as I drove myself deeper inside of her in some feeble attempt to impress. To her, I was little more than an easy $800 and the real pleasure was the deposit, not the withdrawal.

After what seemed like an endless charade of carnality, I finally blobbed off in my second rubber as she rubbed me out. Was I seemingly that infected that I couldn't take the rubber off for a hand job? No telling here, as Alley was strictly business all the way with her glasnost intonations and Cold War eyes. Judging by the way that she rushed to the bathroom to cleanse herself of my pig sweat, my amateur-hour enthusiasm was little more than a BFD. The "present to self" had turned out to be another lump of coal in my stocking. Merry Christmas and a Happy New Year indeed—now put this in your pipe and smoke it.

After an interminable amount of time in the bathroom, Alley came out fully clothed and ready to go to bed. Hers was a job well done if not well hung. A smile, the same smile that drew me in from her ad, had crept back across her face. She kissed me on the cheek and suggested I call her again sometime soon, a gesture I didn't know how to register. The door slammed and I checked my watch: 11:15 PM, nine more hours left on the room. I was hungry and tuckered out by what I convinced myself was some outstanding fucking. I pulled on some clothes and hit midtown in order to find some rotisserie chicken and fries and maybe, hopefully, somebody who gave a fuck.

DAVID AUSTIN was born and raised in Atlanta, Georgia, and attended Emory-Oxford University. He currently lives in Brooklyn with a panther and a walking disco ball. While not a writer by trade, Mr. Austin's work has appeared in *Deep Red*, *Ultra Violent*, *Sex & Guts*, and *The Wall Street Journal*, and at the Melbourne Fringe Festival. His interests include filmmaking, investments, theatrical production/presentation, working long hours crunching numbers, and playing drums.

THESE ARE A FEW
OF MY FAVORITE TRICKS

Xaviera Hollander

I had so many interesting and amazing clients. It's been forty years since I wrote *The Happy Hooker*, and after all these years, they still stick in my mind. There were a couple of brothers, from a very famous family—I think they're dead, but I'm not sure. Anyway, let's just say they came from a family that was famous for owning a big department store in midtown Manhattan. Apparently they came from a very restrictive Jewish family with a dominating mother, and the result was that the younger one became very sweet and, well, masochistic, so he required a dominant prostitute, which is why he picked me. I could do anything, and suddenly he became like putty in my hands . . . so to speak. But his brother, that was the older one, he was the big powerful man in the business. He was an extreme dominant, a really sadistic guy. So what he did to the girls was he would spank them really loud, really hard. In order to take away the pain, there was a kind of cream I could apply to the buttocks of the girls, who didn't want to hurt too much. It would increase the sounds and decrease the pain. So he thought he was making a hell of a lot of pain. He just made a lot of rattling sounds.

And then there was the very famous race car driver—he was total controlling freak; he had to have everything within the second he wanted it. And if he didn't, he would freak out. He was usually very drunk and then he felt sorry and would apologize to death. He was a pain in the ass, but I had some very nice times with him. Then there

190

was a very nice actor. He was a sweetheart, a darling hot lover, and a great, great guy. Burt Reynolds. I met him when I was in London, right after he became famous from that photo of him holding his cock in *Cosmopolitan*. He was actually a hell of a nice guy too. Quite a stud!

There were also women. I worked a number of times with CB and RS. They took a lot of white substances and ordered several girls up to their mansion; they had the most beautiful apartment! She was very masochistic, and it really hurt me to hurt her. I could beat up any man if I had to or tie him up and put him in bondage or something. But I really have trouble being nasty to a woman who had the milkiest white big breasts. To see her being really ripped to pieces or bound up was almost too much.

I will never forget the Golden Shower King. He didn't want them to just go *psssh*, *psssh*; he wanted the girls to make giant waterfalls, and he'd sprinkle it around himself. But I had to train the girls. I had to show them how to hold back. I would train them at my house with rubber sheets. *Psssh* and go, *psssh* and go, *psssh* and go . . . it was quite hysterical actually. They had to drink lots of beer. Now it makes me thirsty just to think about it!

I also had a client who just loved to wrestle. He was a big financial reporter. He predicted the entire stock market. Jewish guy . . . I don't know why they're all Jewish. Of course I'm Jewish too, maybe that's why, I don't know. Hs wife was always complaining, "I want a baby, I want a baby! Why can't you fuck me . . . I want you to come!" And then he finally confessed to her, "I really want to wrestle and you are just too sweet for me!" So he ended up at my house and we wrestled several times and he had no problem getting a big huge massive erection. So his wife found out—he obviously confessed to her—and then they paid me very, very handsomely to get him really excited wrestling. She would sit next to me and jump on top of him and fuck him until he came while I had his hands behind him. And that's how they made two babies.

One of my all-time favorite clients was a young fellow New Yorker. He actually lost his virginity to me at the age of 18 . . . a sweet boy

. . . a handsome boy. He was so beautiful and so innocent he never forgot the way I seduced him, and we're still in touch after all these years. To take someone's virginity is wonderful. Usually they are very appreciative. I did a lot of that in Puerto Rico. A boy's father would approach me about taking his son's virginity. "Okay, pop my son's cherry." Usually the boy would give a wimpy handshake, like a soft wet cloth. I would tell him to straighten up his back, look me in the eye, and give a proper handshake, like a man. Let's start with that, then the rest comes easy. One guy, oh God, he's the son of a friend of ours. He made such an issue about being a virgin. This was in Spain. And this kid came up, he was 16 years old, and he said, "I- I- I- I . . . Will I ever lose it? Young girls, they're too stupid." So his friend said, "Try Xaviera." So he got very drunk, he came home late, I got the knock at my door, and my then-husband John said, "What the fuck is it?" Well this is the kid's friend saying, "He's still a virgin." And then there was this kid waiting in his bedroom in his little white underpants. I said, "Look, you have to take your underpants off!" He said, "My mother never saw me naked!" I said, "But I am not your effing mother!" Then he said, "Oh my God! I think I have to barf!" I said, "Okay, go back, when you finish barfing and cleaning up, come back." So half an hour later, I started making love to my husband, there's a knock at the door, I open it, and this boy is standing there. So I asked him in. He's now naked in the bed with a massive erection. I tapped on it a little bit—I didn't even dare to touch it long as he's about ready to explode. I jump on top of him and with three strokes—bum . . . bum . . . bum . . . he comes and then he looks very disappointed. "Is that all there is? What's crazy about all this?" Honey, there's more where this comes from, and now he's got five children.

Many years ago I ran into Harry Belafonte in an elevator at the Waldorf-Astoria. We went riding up with other people, I recognized him, and he said, "You're the one that wrote *The Happy Hooker*, right?" I said, "Yeah, I'm having a little press party down here at the Waldorf." He says, "Do you have one with you; can I buy it?" I said, "Look, I'll give it to you." He said, "Can you dedicate it to me?" I said,

"Yes." I wrote, "The Bigger, the Blacker, the Better? Love Xaviera." And he wrote down, "Come and see me in suite so and so." And guess what, the bigger, the blacker, the better was true! Absolutely true. That's all for now; if any of you are ever in Amsterdam, come see me at my bed and breakfast.

XAVIERA HOLLANDER is the most famous madame of the world's oldest profession and the author of the legendary, groundbreaker book, *The Happy Hooker*. Her father was a well-known psychiatrist and later an internist/ medical doctor in his own hospital in Soerabaja. Her mother, Germaine, was a most beautiful tall and slender German-French top model who, after she married Xaviera's father, assisted him in his practice until she ended it after thirty years of marriage. Xaviera has lived in Amsterdam, London, Johannesburg, Toronto, New York, and Marbella, Spain. She worked for years as copy writer and assistant account executive for various major advertising agencies in Holland and Johannesburg. In New York, she became private secretary to the Dutch and, later, Belgian consulate before starting her career as happy hooker in 1970 and having the best, most fun bordello in Manhattan from 1970 to 1972. She was deported to Holland and now runs one of the top bed and breakfasts in Amsterdam. She is also a theater producer of English-language plays in Europe. She has written over more than a dozen dirty books and the occasional book of fiction, and she wrote a *Penthouse* magazine sex advice column for thirty-five years. In every era, there are just a handful of individuals who change the way we think or act. Xaviera Hollander did not invent sex: She was one of the leading spirits who brought it out of the closet.

HELLO BABYLON

Kirk Read

Let's go back in time to a pre-millennial moment—my gold rush, my bygone era, my nostalgia factory. In twenty years, I'll pat the heads of baby queers and witch pups and I'll say things were so much better then.

It was a golden era of Bay Area prostitution, a time of prosperity for outlaws—the likes of which hadn't been seen since the dusty mining camps and Barbary Coast brothels. It was 1999, somewhere between the dot-com boom and bust, a time when I could feel a month's rent through my pocket, riding down the elevator at the Hyatt.

Traveling businessmen were renting entire suites for absolutely no good reason at the Mark Hopkins, the W, the Marriott. Hookers should run the Chamber of Commerce, because we know these places.

Sometimes I don't do hotel calls if the workers are striking because I will not cross a picket. I tell my clients that. I need them to know that their rent boy is having a Norma Rae moment.

Back to 1999. A man from Boston called me from the Fairmont. It was his fortieth birthday and he'd spent $5,000 at Mr. S Leather, which is FAO Schwartz for perverts. When I arrived, he had the shit laid out on one of the queen-size beds—not just run-of-the-mill fetish shop gear, not the stage wear of heavy metal hair bands. Not Mötley Crüe. I'm talking Queensrÿche. Classy.

194

Johns, Marks, Tricks, and Chickenhawks

I'm talking cock cages and hoods, five types of handcuffs and a deerskin body bag with a zipper that moved like a duck through water, smooth.

This man wanted deliverance, and I am from the South, so I am qualified to give it to him.

He told me he was in the Bible business—a high-ranking, important man—not quite grand wizard, more of a machinery type. This man was the identified enemy, and he wanted love. I was with him for three days.

I filled every fancy cherrywood furniture surface with cheap candles from the Mission—tall glass candles in oversaturated hues, candles for every saint I could find. I called the front desk and asked for extra sheets and towels. I burned some sage and smudged that place the fuck down.

I tied him face down to a crucifix with four hundred feet of rope. I could have used more. I reached into the bedside drawer and held his Bible in my hands. I gave each butt cheek a whack, then went about my usual hotel ritual—something I do every time I'm in a hotel—I ripped out Leviticus, the Chronicles of Thou Shalt Not, page by page. I ripped out Romans and kept going until he was completely covered in a crumpled fine print blanket, until he was in an aboveground tomb. It took me an hour before I got to Revelations, and I knew by that point I felt better. I gave him a sip of water, then went to the lobby where I bummed a cigarette from the valet. I don't normally smoke but I was feeling it.

Outside the Fairmont, high above Nob Hill, there's an American flag—supersized—like the flags they break out at car dealerships on Memorial Day weekend. The wind was whipping around so hard that the edges were frayed. That's us: the whores and freaks and queers and witches and artists. The threadbare ridge where shit gets messy.

If you haven't read Revelations, you should. It's the only way to understand what's going on in the United States. People believe the epilogue. It's like William S. Burroughs did a twenty-page cut-up of

The Lord of the Rings. People wearing the mark of the beast (which these days is any corporate logo), killer angels and giants and dragons made of eyeballs and horses and horses and horses.

I'm from Virginia so I feel right at home in all this.

In the final pages of Revelations, God releases his wrath upon the Great Prostitute, who, naturally, gets blamed for everything by John the Revelator.

On the forehead of the Great Prostitute is written:

MYSTERY
BABYLON THE GREAT
THE MOTHER OF PROSTITUTES
AND OF THE ABOMINATIONS OF THE EARTH

Which is a great idea for a tattoo.

I went back inside the Fairmont, dug him out, and released him from four hundred feet of rope. I smoothed down his baby-fine tufts of hair and reached into my backpack. He got a scared look as I took out a plastic box then put my hand over his eyes.

I read to him from what Jesus says to the Church of Philadelphia: I know your deeds. See, I have placed before you an open door that no one can shut. I am coming soon. Hold on to what you have so that no one can take your crown.

In the box was a piece of an apple pie I'd made from scratch for Joseph Kramer, the architect of the Body Electric Massage School. The crust was made of dates, almonds, spelt, and seeds. I fed it to him slowly. He took tiny sips of water and sobbed. It was at that point I realized I hadn't noticed how green his eyes were.

KIRK READ was born in 1973 and raised in Lexington, Virginia. He got a BA from the University of Virginia and an MFA from San Francisco State University, and he is now working toward a nursing degree. He is the author of *How I Learned to Snap*, a memoir about being out in high school, which was named an Honor Book by the American Library Association. He was a phlebotomist and HIV counselor at St. James Infirmary, a free clinic for sex workers. He is the director of Army of Lovers, which produces literary and performance events in San Francisco, including "Formerly Known As," a festival of performance by male and trans sex workers. He has co-hosted the open mics *Smack Dab* with Larry-Bob Roberts and *K'vetsh* with Tara Jepsen. He has toured with Sister Spit and twice with the Sex Workers Art Show. For his solo shows *This Is the Thing* and *Computer Face*, the San Francisco Bay Guardian named him Best Performance Artist of 2012. After fourteen years of sex work and mostly unpaid artistic work in the city, he is currently living in a redwood forest, restoring a hillside with native plants. He is teaching himself plumbing, carpentry, roofing, and other worldly pursuits. He enjoys backpacking, karaoke, cheap beer, and psychedelics in the wilderness. He met his partner, writer and AIDS educator Ed Wolf, in 2001. They have two cats, Dewey and Frankie, named after troubled teenage girls in Southern literature.

DATING FOR DOLLARS

Jodi Sh. Doff

I pause at the doorway to the dining room of Lutèce, allowing ev-eryone in the room a good view. My deep purple spandex dress fits like a wet suit in the few places it bothers to cover. One arm bare and supple, the back cut low and the sides cut high. My nipples, straining against the material, manage to rise to the occasion of all the attention. The maître d' smiles and motions, across a sea of perfectly coiffed silver heads, for us to follow. The gentle murmur of polite conversation slows as all heads turn in concert. I hear the whisper of pearls across black velvet, the subtle intake of breath, and the click of my three-inch heels as polite conversation stops to watch me stroll across the room. The maître d', delighted by the reaction I provoke, takes his time as he walks me to the center before turning to direct us to a semi-private corner banquet. I feel the watery eyes of flaccid ruddy-cheeked men gaze surreptitiously, while the eyes of wives shoot arrows of disgust.

I enjoy these reactions immensely.

I don't belong here. My dress is too tight, my hair too short and too red, and my class too low. So I take pleasure in the fact that I am here. My date for the evening seems to feel only slightly uncomfortable in his conservative suit and foolish grin. Perhaps it's the simple gold wedding band he wears that causes him discomfort. Or maybe he wasn't prepared for the reaction my appearance here would create. Whatever it is, it's his problem now. He has already paid me my fee

198

for the evening, the $200 I would've made had I worked tonight in the topless club we met at.

I slip next to him on the brocade cushions of the banquet, our thighs touch, and I can feel the heat rise as his face colors slightly. His uneasiness excites me. We share several martinis before dinner, and he begins to relax, asking the questions they all do eventually.

"Do you like your work?" *Oh sure. When I was little I always imagined I'd grow up, be naked, and spend my time drinking cheap champagne with assholes.*

"Do you like being naked in front of strangers?" *See question number one.*

"Do you get turned on with everyone watching?" *If I was turned on do you think I would be charging you?*

"Does your family know?" *Sure they do. They brag over holiday dinners. They're thinking of including photos in the next family newsletter.*

"Have you ever done it with a woman?" *Have you?*

I tell him what he wants to hear and watch tiny beads of sweat begin to appear around his hairline. There is a moment of relief for him as the waiter comes for our order. I lean over to whisper in his ear, one hand resting between his legs, my breast rubbing against his arm.

"I don't know what I want. I'd like you make all the decisions tonight." I leave my arm, hand, and breast on him while he orders, feeling his erection growing.

"Thank you," I whisper as the waiter retreats, "I knew you could take care of me, Daddy." I let my hand brush across his cock as I lean back and fish the olive from my martini. He smiles and slips his hand between my legs as I suck the vodka off the olive. I cross my legs, trapping his hand, "Not here Daddy . . . after dinner."

We share a sumptuous dinner, watched by proper mature ladies whose glares he tries to avoid and the envious men whose eyes I catch intentionally and smile directly into while my hand tortures my date's erection beneath the linen tablecloth. The women feel self-righteous and upset, their balding overstuffed husbands thinking of the deflated breasts and dry pussies across the table from them and groaning in desperation. My date is straining for the release of orgasm. Everyone is right where I want them to be, and I am in my glory.

"Check," he calls, unable to stand the teasing another minute.

"And coffee, please," I add.

He pulls out his gold American Express card. This is what I have been waiting for all night, the *pièce de résistance*. He prepares to sign, but I need a moment more.

"Would you pour me the last of the Cristal? It's a sin to let good champagne go to waste." He reaches over for the bottle, giving me a clear view of the gold plastic card. It's just a matter of memorizing a short series of numbers: fifteen of them divided into three segments. I take one sip of the champagne and excuse myself to the ladies room.

I slip into a phone booth instead and drop in a dime. Smitty answers on the first ring; he's been waiting for my call.

"AmEx. Gold. Member since 1981." I reel off his name and the numbers off the card. "Gotta go, don't want to lose my momentum."

"You comin' home?"

"Later, he's still got some cash I have my eye on."

"Tomorrow then?"

"Tomorrow." Click.

The dried-up women and unhappy husbands watch me again as I walk the length of the dining room, back to the secluded corner where my Romeo of the moment waits. He's thinking about a hotel; I can see it on his face. The wedding ring makes it obvious he can't take me home with him.

I always look for the wedding ring. Wives make my life so much easier.

He doesn't even suggest my place. Saving me the trouble of coming up with a reason why we can't go there.

"Let's get a little blow and have some real fun before we settle in for the night. What d'ya think? Coke makes me really crazy." I let my body brush full against his. He's lost, he's helpless, he's mine. I hustle him into a cab and head thirty blocks downtown and two flights up to a dim and dirty cavernous space where I know everybody. Through a dark room with an old pool table and a couple of warped sticks into a darker room where the bar is. The liquor's cut-rate, the glasses are plastic, and the music is blaring.

Now he's the outsider, the one who doesn't belong. These are my people, and everyone here wants his money as badly as I do. But I have a leg up. Literally. I'm next to him on a threadbare corner couch; one leg sprawled across his lap snaking down between his legs, pressing against the ever-present erection. My hand inside his jacket plays with his nipple as Max the Mumbler wanders over with pockets full of cocaine. My Romeo pays for an eight ball, flashing his bankroll as he does.

The night crawlers and coke whores smell it in the air. Drifting nonchalantly closer, they slowly surround us, drawn by the scent of a sucker's money. We are the center of this universe as long as we have cocaine and money. He is loving it. He's never known people like this. The red light of the club gives it a surreal dangerous quality, but he feels safe with me. We share our coke with his new friends: Johnny Blue Eyes, a jewel thief wanted in five states; Franco, a Richard Gere look-a-like who will have sex with anyone for $100; Wella, recently released from an eight-year bid she did for dismembering a Japanese trick. Smilin' Dennis, Jack the Jew, Jimmy Bug Eyes . . . the more coke we have, the more friends we have. Romeo loves it. They talk to him as if he's one of them. He imagines that he's not just a daytime citizen anymore.

I sense I'm beginning to lose control. There are too many fingers trying to stick themselves in my pie, so I steer him over to one of the blackjack tables in the corner.

"I wanna play too," I pout. He peels off $100 for me and settles in to play cards.

"Oh, Vincent's here," I whisper in his ear, "his coke is so much better than Max's . . . Please, can I, Daddy? You'll see how good it is." I get an eight ball from Vincent, give Romeo half a gram, keep the remaining three grams for myself, and sit in for two hands of twenty-one, both of which I promptly lose.

"Too rich for my blood," I say as I push away from the table, stretching my body out against the thin plum of my dress. I let my hand drop into his lap and caress his cock, which has shriveled down to its original birth weight. I spend another twenty minutes feeding him coke and cocktails and rubbing his shoulders from behind, letting my breasts rub across the back of his head. He's losing like crazy. Everyone is happy. The house has some of his money, I have more of his money and most his coke, and he thinks he has me.

"I'm gonna shoot some pool with the Mouse out front. Come get me as soon as you're ready. Okay, Daddy?" He turns and takes one look at the Mouse, her breasts barely covered by the black strapless number she's wearing. They have a gravitational pull all their own. Her dark hair slides over them, caresses them. She slips her arm around me, and he looks as though he's going to pass out. We always get this reaction; we're an irresistible one-two punch. If I can't hurt them, she can. If she can't hurt them, I can, and there's damn few that can resist the combination of her dark voluptuousness and my pale outrageousness.

"Yeah, here, take some of this," he hands me his vial of coke. "I just want to get a little even here. Turn your friend on too."

"Oh, I was planning on turning her on. You ready for me to turn you on, Mouse?"

"Ready, J," she purrs. We turn. We kiss. Long and soft and warm.

"Don't keep us waiting too long." We walk away, my arm around the sharp curve of her waist, her hand on my big round ass.

Mouse and I enter the barely lit entranceway where the pool table is occupied by a couple of baby pimps. We couldn't play in these dresses even if the table were empty. The minute we would lean over to shoot, our respective breasts would roll out of our respective dresses and display themselves on the torn green felt. The thought of shooting pool never crossed either of our minds.

We keep strolling right on out the door, down the two flights, and into a cab headed east into the morning light. Me and the Mouse sit crosstown in another after-hours club drinking cheap vodka, sharing the coke, and laughing over Romeo's probable reaction when he discovers that we, as well as the coke and his money, are gone.

The game was fixed.

The whole evening was fixed.

He will always be just a daytime citizen. They will not let him back into the club the next night or any night unless he's with someone like me. His wedding band guarantees he won't go the police and risk having the wife find out.

Wedding bands are my insurance policy.

He will go home and tell outrageous stories about his wild night with a bad girl to his buddies over backyard barbecue, leaving out the embarrassing details. And when I get home sometime this afternoon, there'll be a new American Express card, exactly like his, waiting on my pillow.

JODI SH. DOFF, a.k.a. Scarlett Fever, has lived in four of the five boroughs in New York City. She started making her own money when she was 14. She's been a waitress, hostess, coat-check girl, and bartender. She flipped burgers, shucked lobsters, and sold seeds door-to-door. She pinched a twenty now and then from her father's wallet. She punched a time-clock for a few pre-Christmas seasons picking stock in a mail-order warehouse, spent a summer sleeping on an outdoor stage as security, and lasted one day in a factory spooling wire from big wooden spools to little wooden spools. She sold karate lessons. She panhandled. She filed. She answered phones. She shimmied and shook her way across various stages and behind sundry bars all around Times Square. She was a mall Santa for a week in 1978. She worked the lights at CBGB's for two weeks in 1979. She has written for *Bust Magazine, Penthouse, Playgirl, Tear,* and *Cosmopolitan;* her writing has been included in *Best American Erotica 1995*; *Bearing Life*; *Between the Sheets*; *Hos, Hookers, Call Girls, and Rent Boys* (Soft Skull, 2009); and *The Bust Guide to a New Girl Order.* She enjoys driving, by herself, with the music loud and no particular place to be; photographing urban decay and making visible and beautiful the invisible and mundane things we pass every day; anything that has to do with any critter—furred, feathered, two-legged, four-legged, no-legged, or winged—and she maintains three blogs: onlythejodi.com, dirtygirldiaries.com, and jshdoff.tumblr.com. And when she has time, she makes soup.

Johns, Marks, Tricks, and Chickenhawks

CAPTAIN SAVE-A-HO

Fiona Helmsey

I never know what to say when I'm asked if I knew anyone who died on September 11. It's a conflict that cuts right to the strange nature of sex work—the intimate anonymity, the intimate indifference. I could be standing in front of a client's name on the memorial wall at Ground Zero and never know it, as I never knew his last name or have long since forgotten it.

I'm pretty sure Stephen died on Sept. 11. He worked at Cantor Fitzgerald, a company located on the 101st through 105th floors of Tower 1. Six hundred and fifty-eight employees, most of the people in the company's offices that morning, died in the attacks. I was seeing Stephen two to three times a month through the outcall escort agency I worked for in New York City, and after August of 2001, I never saw him again.

I met Stephen at a bachelor party. I hated bachelor parties. I hated them because the elements that made them such a good time for the men in attendance—the randy women, the booze, the feeling of brotherhood—conspired to bring out something very ugly in them: bravado.

The bachelor party immediately got off to a bad start. A friend of the groom called the woman who I was doing the party with—a voluptuous Latina in a platinum blonde wig who went by the name Moet—"hefty," and she freaked out, storming off to find the friend of the groom who had set up the party, demanding an apology before she would perform. The party was held inside some kind of shipping/receiving warehouse in Manhattan, and I didn't know Moet at all. I had met her just minutes before outside the warehouse, and when she stormed off, I assumed she had left me. Standing there, all by myself, in a transparent slip dress and heels, I felt like carrion for a pack of hungry wolves.

"How much for a blow job?" one man barked.

"Will you let me snort coke off your ass?" asked another.

"You and the fat one—you eat her pussy?" inquired a third.

To make matters worse, I wasn't much of a dancer. I had tried stripping once, and hated it, finding my fit in sex work that was much more one-on-one, much less all-eyes-on-me. Though most of the other escorts at the agency liked doing bachelor parties because of the tips and party atmosphere, I avoided them, viewing them as frat parties for grown men. The only reason I had agreed to do this one was the soothing words of the phone girl: It was only a few guys, she'd sworn. Hastily organized. Not even a real bachelor party, more a last-minute nightcap on festivities. From their voices on the phone, they sounded so drunk she doubted they would be standing up. And Moet—bachelor parties were her forte. She was a pro.

From where I stood, Moet-less, flanked by a group of at least ten men and counting, all of whom stood upright and alert unless electing to sit in one of the circle of foldout chairs in the middle of the room—the phone girl's assurances had been a con job, tailored to placate my insecurities. The men had probably requested a white girl for the party, and I was the only one available. Though confident I could handle the situation, I felt vulnerable and extremely uncomfortable, the primary reasons I chose to avoid bachelor parties in the first place.

"Hey! I got an idea!" a man called out from behind a large desk in a corner of the room. "Let's all play strip poker!"

"Shut up, Steve!" a sweaty man in a suit jacket whined. Most of the men were clad in subtle variations of the same ensemble: pants and suit jackets that had probably appeared much nattier earlier in the evening. "Come sit on my lap, baby, and rub those titties all over me. I know you've got some great titties under that dress," the sweaty man beckoned, crooking his finger in a come-hither motion in my direction.

"That's not fair, Ray!" the man behind the desk scolded, standing up. He looked to be about 50, with a paunchy stomach and khaki pants worn high on his waist. He took off his suit jacket and draped it on the back of his chair dramatically, à la Demi Moore in *Striptease*. "Why should she be the only one who takes her clothes off?" he said, jiggling his big belly and unbuttoning his shirt to an imaginary beat.

"I don't know, Steve, maybe because she's a stripper?" a voice in the group growled.

The man with the large belly opened a drawer of the desk and gestured toward me. "We have our company poker night here," he said. He reached into the desk drawer and pulled out a basket filled with unopened card decks. "You know how to play?" he asked.

I shook my head no.

"I'll show ya," he answered with a wink, handing me an unopened deck. He lowered his voice, and I leaned in closer to hear him. "It's been a *loooooong* night, hon. We're just getting back from the casino, and I'm pretty sure the groom's puking in another room. Everyone here's nice, just wasted. Just do your thing, hon. These"—he indicted toward the cards—"should keep the heat off of you a little bit."

"Let's play STRIP POKER!" he yelled out, rolling his belly and wiggling his hips as he threw the card decks to the men in all directions. "I can't wait to see what you're working with, Hector!"

In light of Moet's MIA status, the man's gesture made me feel like I had an ally, though one could never be sure in this business. As the men grumbled to themselves and dodged the flying card decks, I moved to the center of the chair circle, ready to start my slow, drawn-out removal of garments. There was no music, so the men's obnoxious inquiries and demands would have to serve as my soundtrack. Suddenly, Moet burst back into the room, the groom, supported by the best man, following behind her.

"Come on now, Kenny," the best man slurred. "You have to apologize to this lovely lady! Look at those lips! She could suck the chrome off a bumper!" He had lipstick on both sides of his face and wobbled on his feet. His fly was partway unzipped, and I could make out the tartan plaid of his boxer shorts through the opening.

"I never said anything to her, Mike! I swear. It was all a misunderstanding," Kenny stammered. "I was asking for a Hefty bag, for the beer cans . . ."

"Well, she's ready to show us all a good time, but only if you say those two magic words. Otherwise, she's out of here, and it's going to be all your fault. Right, Moet?"

Moet appeared to be in much better spirits upon reentering the room, and she was wearing a man's tie around her neck, its knot perfectly aligned with the ample swell of her cleavage. Her spandex mini-dress looked to be at least three sizes too small and barely touched the tops of her meaty thighs. She marched over to Kenny, a slight man with feminine features and large glasses that threatened to overwhelm his face, and straddled his lap.

"Do I feel heavy to you, baby?" she purred, her large posterior extending far past his knees.

"No, baby, no! You feel just right!" Kenny exclaimed, his voice going up a few octaves as his small frame was engulfed by so much Moet.

The best man looked at me. "You gonna show us a good time, too, Courtney?"

I opened my mouth to speak with my best feigned enthusiasm, but the man with the large belly cut me off.

"I was kind of hoping Courtney and I could be alone, Mike."

Moet gyrated deeper into the lap of the man who had insulted her. The best man surveyed the room, his eyes stopping to linger on Moet. Based on her performance, he must have decided mine wouldn't be necessary.

"Alright Steve-o, she's yours, but you owe me. You can take her into that room in the back."

Another thing I didn't particularly enjoy about bachelor parties were these public negotiations of my services that didn't involve me.

I picked up my bag from a chair and waited for the man to lead me to the back room, but he just stood there, looking at me impatiently.

"What's the matter?" I asked.

"You're forgetting your cards, hon." He answered. "You want to learn, right?"

I looked over at Moet in an attempt to communicate to her where I was going, but I couldn't get her attention. She was bent over Kenny's chair as if doing a back bend, her arms on either side of his lap, and her breasts upside down in his face.

It was the one thing about the bachelor party the phone girl hadn't lied about.

Moet was a pro.

Stephen and I sat in the back room for the next hour and half playing strip poker for prudes. He didn't want me to take off anything beyond my bra and panties. All that left me to remove was my dress and shoes. He stayed in his boxer shorts.

"Thanks," I said, in acknowledgement of the diversion he'd tried to create in the other room. "But you didn't have to do that. I've done plenty of bachelor parties."

"I saw your eyes, Courtney," he said. "You looked like a deer in the headlights of life. Moet doesn't have that look." He ashed his cigarette into a plastic cup of beer. "I wouldn't have been able to live with myself. I can't get off on that. My name's Stephen, but I also have a superhero alter ego. They call me Captain-Save-A-Ho."

I laughed, even though he was calling me a ho.

All of the men at the bachelor party that night, except for the groom's best man, worked at Cantor Fitzgerald, in Tower 1 of the World Trade Center.

The phone girl told me that Stephen had called every night since the party to see if I was working. A few nights later, I was, and I was driven to his Brooklyn Heights brownstone. Five years before, he told me, he had split up with his wife, who was living on Long

Island with their teenage daughter. We went into his bedroom, and he reached into a dresser drawer and took out a small bag of white powder.

"I got this the other night at the casino. Bought it in the parking lot. I'm not really sure why," he said. "It's not my thing."

I cut a line of it on top of the table next to his bed. Its consistency was both soft and crunchy, like some kind of salt mixed with soap. I blew it behind the bed when he wasn't looking. I didn't have the heart to tell him it was fake.

We had sex, and his sweat rained down on me in salty droplets. His breathing quickly became labored.

"I wish you could have seen me in my prime, Courtney," he said. "Wait," he ran into another room and came back with a photo album. There were pictures of him from high school playing football, pictures from what looked to be a college frat party, making me think of the bachelor party at the warehouse. "After your forties, hon, it's all downhill," he said. "But it was a great ride."

As I was leaving, he tipped me a hundred dollars, then made an all-too-familiar request.

"Give me your phone number, hon. We can cut the agency right out of it," he said.

I'd been down that road a million times before and had learned the hard way that unless you had some kind of special line just for them, it never paid to give a client your phone number. It ended up abused, treated like a free phone sex line or a drunken confessional. So I compromised and gave Stephen my e-mail address, my first one ever. My mother had just bought me something she'd seen advertised on television, after she had bought one for herself first. Not a real computer, something called an i-Opener, similar to WebTV in that it was just the Internet, a keyboard, and a screen. Because my i-Opener had been a gift from my mom, it was registered through her account, and my e-mail address had one very small difference from hers: the number one.

As I wrote down my e-mail address for Stephen, I stressed the importance of remembering this digit.

"Don't forget the one," I said.

"No worries, hon," he replied.

He forgot the one, and e-mailed my mom.

As a sex worker, there are three questions you are asked constantly by clients. The first one is, "What's your real name?" Clients are obsessed with this question. If they can get you to tell them your real name, it makes them feel special, elevated. The relationship is still a paid one, but they now know you as anyone who is important to you in your other life does. The disclosure also negates what may be the most important veneer a sex worker has: their anonymity. It's a revelation that can be interpreted to imply "She either trusts me enough not to call out to her if I were to see her on the street, or she actually wants me to come up to her and say hello." The second question clients always ask is about the circumstances that led you to sex work—that is, what, in their minds, the circumstances were that led you astray, from good girl to bad. The third question is, "What gets you off sexually?" This is usually phrased, "Now tell me what you like."

I had never told Stephen my real name. It was nothing against him. I had told other clients my name in the past, but because Fiona came across as more exotic sounding than Courtney, in this time before the movie *Shrek* at least, to them it sounded like even more of a stripper name, and they never believed me. So I told Stephen that Courtney was my real name, that in spite of what he may have believed as Captain Save-A-Ho, there was nothing there to save me from—my private life and public life all blurred together as one. So when Stephen e-mailed my mother, he addressed the e-mail in part to Courtney.

My mother had gotten other e-mails meant for me since buying me the i-Opener, but nothing related to sex work, and, thankfully, Stephen hadn't written anything too revealing, just that he would like to see me again soon and had enjoyed our time together. My mother probably wouldn't have even thought the e-mail was meant

211

for me at all if Stephen hadn't addressed it not just to Courtney but to Courtney Love. He was being funny, but I was a big fan, and my mother knew this.

In January of 2002, I was living with my mom and using her i-Opener when I came across Stephen's e-mail, then six months old. My exit from New York City had happened hastily the previous December when I had lost my apartment in a perfect storm of Xanax addiction and unpaid rent. Clients come and go from your life, your life and theirs mixing in hour intervals and dollar allotments, and it occurred to me as I read Stephen's e-mail that I couldn't recall seeing him after August of the previous summer.

I wrote down his e-mail address, logged into my newly created Yahoo e-mail account, and wrote:

> Stephen—
>
> It's Courtney. Sorry I didn't get in touch sooner, but everything's just been so crazy the last few months. I can't imagine what it's been like for you. The loss of life is staggering. I don't want to say too much now, I'd rather wait for you to respond first, but I'm no longer in New York. Hopefully I'll be back soon. Just wanted to make sure you're okay and let you know I'm thinking about you.

Just as I was about to hit send, it occurred to me that my new e-mail address might cause some confusion. It contained my real name, Fiona, followed by some numbers that were relevant to my life. I'd been so adamant to Stephen about Courtney being my real name that I figured it warranted some kind of passing explanation.

> This is my new e-mail address. Fiona's my real name. I was just trying to keep some distance, you know?

I did make it back to New York, and in the summer of 2002, I found myself working for the same outcall escort agency I had worked for when I met Stephen. One night, my driver for the evening took me to meet a friend of his, another driver for the agency, between calls. I recognized the girl his friend was driving for the night immediately—the big breasts, the wide, shapely hips. The only thing different about her was the sable color of her wig. It was Moet.

"I remember you," she said, getting out of the car to smoke a cigarette and empty the sand from her shoes. Her driver had just picked her up from a call she had done at the beach. "We did that bachelor party together, and you ditched me."

"I didn't ditch you!" I said defensively. I had experienced the brunt end of other girls' reactions to imagined crimes in the past.

"Relax, mommy," she said. "You remembered where those guys worked, didn't you? That company, in the towers? What's your name again, mommy?"

"Courtney."

"People can say whatever they want about us, and what we do, Courtney, but those men, that night, they didn't have much time left. And maybe I'm crazy for even thinking like this, but that night, I know I showed them a good time, and they went home happy. Do you know what I mean, mommy? I gave them my all that night, and I feel good about that."

FIONA HELMSLEY is a Connecticut-based writer of creative nonfiction and poetry. Her father was an Irish-Nationalist who immigrated to New York from Dublin in the 1960s. He worked as a house painter and met her mother, who was thirteen years his junior, at a Northern Ireland Civil Rights Association meeting in the early 1970's. They left New York to raise Fiona and her siblings in Connecticut, where her dad continued to work as a house painter and her mother worked as a secretary. Her dad died when she was a junior in high school. By the time of his death, her parents had divorced. She's worked as an escort and an exotic dancer, and she spent a considerable amount of time working at a penthouse on Madison Avenue that billed its services as "fantasy/role-play." There was some role-playing involved, but its clientele were mostly wealthy Wall Streeters willing to spend exorbitant amounts for hand jobs. Fiona's a writer and has spent a lot of time working in book stores. She is obsessed with books and greatly enjoys being surrounded by them. She would like to die being crushed by a bookcase. She lived in New York City for almost a decade, exploring how the seedier half lives. She has also spent time in Berkeley and San Francisco, California. She likes big cities with storied histories, especially when it comes to art, literature, and civil unrest. She has learned to be skeptical whenever her boyfriend claims he's "just going out to play tennis." She loves to read, write, and take pictures of herself. She is a bit of a photo whore. If she has a great outfit on, she wants to share it. Her first obsession was a 1960s boy band the Monkees, and she has the scrapbook to prove it. She loves having information and memorabilia to chase after. Her writings can be found online on sites such as the Rumpus and Jezebel, and in various anthologies such as *How Dirty Girls Get Clean* and *Air in the Paragraph Line*. She also greatly enjoys physical activity and is an avid walker. She loves sexual intercourse, and it shows.

Johns, Marks, Tricks, and Chickenhawks

ICE CREAM

Hawk Kinkaid

I came back for my boots.

The streets were still slush coated from the city's first snowfall when I found myself standing outside Ice Cream's door clad in damp tennis shoes rather than my black thrift-store Harleys. This surprise visit was the last resort to a spate of unreturned phone calls and canceled sessions. I foolishly thought I might supplement picking up the boots with an hour of work to bankroll some of the holidays.

I stood on the stoop, watching the entire neighborhood indulge in blinking cheer. The tireless electric lines hummed, an occasional dollop of snow slipped off a roof, and faux descending icicles wrapped up the neighbors' homes like unintentional drool. I was already tired of the festive display. Ice Cream may as easily have grown tired of me. Or I might have been supplanted by someone who could feign greater surprise. Someone who could look more uncertain. Someone to whom this would again be new.

I just wanted my boots back.

I decided to wait five more minutes in the cold. It may seem futile, but a note tacked with spit on the door or jammed under the wind guard felt wrong, as if it would make me sound like I was a jilted lover or a neighborhood missionary. The note could have been brief like, *Stopped by to get my stuff. You weren't here. Call me. Happy holidays.* But I don't normally have that kind of self-control. Instead, I would easily risk writing *Ice Cream*—because that's what I called him—*what the fuck? I have been trying to reach you and get my boots back. Please tell me you cleaned them and that you didn't let some other guy use 'em. Fungal shit spreads. Hell, you can buy 'em off me if you want, but whatever you decide to do, please let me know. You looking to see me again?*

It was good money doing a session with Ice Cream. Mostly, I just stood around. For a few hundred an hour, standing seemed like a pretty sweet deal. And the last five minutes of jerking each other off? An adolescent finale reminiscent of my own early intimate suburban experiences and pretty light stuff compared to the energy required to fuck or flog or . . . You might consider it a pretty sweet deal.

Ice Cream was king of two-car garage-land. He touted a chain of popular ice cream shops and was the picture of what a lactose leader might look like: bloated, creamy, hairless skin, a pompous gait, and jolly belly-heavy laughter at jokes that were funny only because he found them funny. It was difficult to separate laughing at him from laughing with him. He was easy to like as a client. His place was a collection of museum-grade retro relics, and he had a penchant for the double-dairy-entendre: "Peaches and Cream," "Fudge Ripple," "Very Cherry," or the most provocative "Double Muffin Berry Split." Even his first phone call was simple, playful, and slightly shy as the topic veered from familiar ("Do you like men my age?") to the fantastic ("What do you like to do?").

During that conversation, I learned that he had overalls for me to wear but no boots that were my size. I should bring my own, he suggested as if it weren't a suggestion at all. The scenario was still unclear, but with more than a hundred kink clients under my belt, my range for shock and awe was comfortably set above kidnapping and below granny porn. Shy of asking me to let an octogenarian suck my dick, I tend to be good to go.

Or, in this case, goo.

Ice Cream's use of ice cream would have made sense. Even in the most complex of psychoanalytic babble, the introduction of what made this man much of his wealth into a sexual scenario would be both understandable and, frankly, tasty. I might have even relished some of my own gluttony to revel for an hour as someone's strawberry sundae. I was a fat kid. I always wrestled with my weight. I have a whole mouth of sweet teeth tempting me daily to my downfall. Accessorize with whipped cream, and it might have felt like some pedestrian schoolgirl's wet dream. I wasn't afraid of milk products because they seemed friendly to me. After all, it does a body good, no?

I can get milk, but the client had other ideas.

It was like cement that was still flaccid. He threw it at me like a grade-schooler sloppily slings snowballs. Each glob landed with a soft splatter. My shoulder. My thigh. My crotch, covered in a requisite pair of tighty-whities. My job was to stand there and egg him on to throw more, throw it harder. *Throw it, Ice Cream!* This turned him on.

I like to think I was who he wished he had been when younger boys did this to him at school. I like to think there was a rationale for the plastic tarps at my feet, the large cans of gray mixture that seemed mostly clay and water. I like to think there were discernible reasons for pleasure and that the man paying me to stand in his basement coaching bravado under a layer of cold mud wasn't purely random. I like to think some good would come from this other than another couple hundred bucks in my pocket for me and a money shot for him.

I think this often. I thought the same of the Pat Benatar fan that needed to be mugged outside his home, violently disrobed in his foyer, and fucked to the *Tropico* album. Or the client that watched me eat a $200 meal for the entire session. Or the one married guy who demanded I demand him to get on his knees and pray before plunging a crucifix dildo in his ass. I like to think there is sense to it.

When my overalls were covered and the couple of canisters he had prepared were empty, he finally whipped his dick out. At that point, I did as well, and the entire slopping exercise resulted in a teenage jerk-off session, sound-tracked by ongoing bravado about how Ice Cream can do it even with his minimal endowment. It's the accomplishment that we celebrated, only it was never clear what we had actually done.

After the fifth time, the one in which I forgot my boots, we never spoke again. Outside his door that night, I waited five more minutes. And five minutes after that. Once my feet began to tingle and the cold settled in under the jacket, it was time to leave the cookie-cutter wonderland's quiet glee.

I don't know why he never called again, and while it seems natural to make up some story to explain the sudden absence, I remember that there may be no sense in it at all and that I don't have to understand it to participate in it. It's my job, and at the end of the night, coming back for my boots may be a fruitless as finding the meaning in Ice Cream.

Born and raised in the Midwest, **HAWK KINKAID** is the founder and current president of HOOK (hookonline.org), the American-based harm reduction nonprofit project by, for, and about men in the sex industry started in 1997. In addition to the interactive experience, HOOK produces Rent University (rent-u.com), an education series for sex workers. Kinkaid is a former sex worker, current writer/spoken word artist, and lifelong harm-reduction activist (a.k.a. a big pile of ginger trouble). He participates at conferences internationally including the European Network on Male Prostitution, the Gay Men's Health Summit, and the National Harm Reduction Conference, as well as the first Southern Summit on Sex Work held this past December in Asheville, North Carolina.

Johns, Marks, Tricks, and Chickenhawks

TICKLE TORTURE

Justin Jones

His pudgy white hands grasp the edges of the stained fabric. "People are watching," the man says, snapping the curtain rings together. "The neighbors talk, you know." The drapes swing violently from side to side, so violently that they simultaneously knock Walter's Coke-bottle glasses to one side of his round face and blow a heavy scent of newspaper ink and cat urine across the room.

As my view of synthetic green lawns is instantly replaced by thick beige drapes, my arms jam against the fabric restraints at the sides of the twin hospital bed. I bite down hard on the knotted gag. I try to swallow, but there's no saliva. The walls of my throat are stuck together.

On the phone, Walter's voice had given the impression of a tall box-jawed army lieutenant. *Dangerous territory for a prostitute,* I thought as I whipped down the freeway from Axis Falls. I love it.

Walter turns toward a metal desk in the corner, "$500, $600, $650." With the precision of little red laser beams, my eyes follow the crisp bills as Walter slides them, one by one, beneath an antique brass desk clock.

Walter sits down on the bed. I crane my head toward him, half-hoping that if he is, in fact, a psycho killer, my mirrored shades will expose him to himself, and his reflection will keep him from slashing my chest open with the shiny letter opener over there next to the

219

money. I look around the room for something to focus on, besides fear. And there it is: a huge, portrait-style painting of a redheaded matriarch frowning down at us. Her stolid gaze takes away what little breath I've been managing to squeeze through the corners of his gag.

"That's my mother," says Walter as he slowly removes my sunglasses.

I shudder, wondering if I've gone too far this time, coming out to this fucked-up place. I yank against the wrist restraints.

Walter slowly pulls down the tiny zipper of my dress pants while glancing over the rest of the uniform. Not exactly a suit and tie, which was Walter's original request, but one button-down shirt, a silk olive long-sleever that I'd kept around in the unlikely event of a job interview.

"So, on a scale of one to ten," Walter asks as he removes the gag, "how ticklish are you?" The word ticklish dances light and playful—completely out of place in this suburban pre-crime scene.

"Let's see," I say through cracked, dry lips. "Probably an eight?"

"And do you laugh when you are tickled?"

"Yes," I say, or says "Jeff," trying to remember the last time I was tickled to the point of laughter. It may have been the time that Jeff's, er, Justin's uncle, came to visit when he was four. That was torture.

"How hard to you laugh?"

"Um, very hard?"

"Well, Jeff, as you know, this is a three hour session. If you can make it through all three hours, and if you are expressive enough for my liking," his white chins wobble on his face while he speaks, "the money is yours."

The possibilities! A car note AND Blue Shield bill! Paid before the late fees hit!

"Bwaaah!" My burst of laughter sends a fleck of dry spit up into the musty room.

"Maybe I'm a nine!" Walter removes my black dress socks, replaces them with thinner ones, and drags a feather across the bottoms of my feet.

"It's a science of sorts," says Walter the banker with a mad gleam in his eye. "It took me years to develop—many young boys like you."

"Please!" I cry for mercy between hysterical gasps.

"I like to observe the exact moment you lose sense of time and place. I like to play with that edge."

"Please!" I can barely hear Walter over my own howl. "Bwaaah ha ha ha!"

Walter stops tickling. He reaches up and wraps his soft warm hand around my penis, which immediately calms me, spiraling my brain-craze down to a crawl. Walter releases his grip, stares down at the rent boy.

The room falls eerily silent save for the ticking of the clock and creaking of the bedsprings. Blood pounds in my temples, down my arms, into my genitals. *Holy shit,* I think. *I've got major wood!*

"Looks like somebody wants more," says Walter, touching, stroking, bringing me slowly to the edge and holding me there, suspended in bucking, writhing hypersexuality.

"You like that?"

My eyes flutter back into their sockets. "Dude, I'm so close to spewing hot lava all over this fucking suburb, so close to seeding this entire Godforsaken neighborhood. I think I'm gonna . . ."

Walter stops, releases his hands. I open my eyes.

Walter's mother stares down like an Eastern Orthodox icon. WHAT ARE YOU DOING ON MY BED? I want this to be over NOW! I squeeze my eyes shut, think about the last porno I saw. Stop looking at me, lady! I zero in on the scene, the fantasy, the money shot from the opening sequence of *L.A. Tool and Die.* Must—will—self—to—orgasm. Need—release—from—this—

Walter stops all movement completely, shifts his focus back to my feet. "Arrgghh!" Fireworks explode in my head. Pleasure mixes with pain. Abstract biological urges swirl with an inexplicable desire to please this man and escape his mother. I yank against the fabric cuffs. Tears blur my vision. The room is liquid.

Walter releases my right restraint. My hand whips down, strokes three times, and the volcano erupts. My head falls to the left. I stare sideways at the money and the ticking clock. It's only been an hour.

"Hour two is bodywork," says Walter as he unshackles Jeff. "Ever given a massage?"

"Uh, yea," I say, sweaty and exhausted.

"Well, there's a bottle of lotion over there on the desk." Walter turns sideways on the hospital bed and awkwardly shimmy-strips down to white underpants. Then he plants himself face-down on the floor. "Okay," he says with one cheek pushed into the shag. "I'm ready."

Walter's flesh squishes out on either side like marshmallows in a s'more. I grab the yellow bottle with the Walgreen's sticker and pop the lid. I point it down toward his back and squeeze. Scented air blasts out, coating my nose and throat with perfumed chemicals. Then the yellow gunk spatters into the center of his back.

"Oh!" Walter squirms. "It's cold!" I rub my hands together, circling lotion into the top layer of his pasty white skin.

A bead of sweat falls from my forehead and lands in the center of Walter's back. I swirl it into the pattern. Then, starting in the center with two fingers, I trace small but firm circles, using the clock as a metronome—tick, tock, tick, tock. "Wow, you're really good at this," says Walter. "Are you sure you haven't done this before?"

Still high from the tickle, Walter's flesh turns into morphing shapes and colors before my eyes. I drill my elbows into the center of the atrophied muscles and then drag them down to the small of his back. This is, I think, without a doubt, the highest art. Artist: Jeff E. Popp. Palette: Walgreen's yellow. Canvas: a mountain of uncooked pizza dough named Walter Finkle.

222   **Has it been an hour yet? Having traced and retraced the words "I'm** bored" at least twenty times, I have artist block. Where do I go from here? Do I take off his panties? Flip him over onto his back? Isn't that what they do in the parlors? I look over at the clock, a face even more unforgiving than the mom. Twenty-seven minutes. How is this possible? I swear this clock is rigged! My eyes drop down toward the second hand. A miniature Walter pushes back the ticking wand, slowing time down to a crawl.

I look back down at the lump that is Walter. He hasn't moved in a while. Maybe he's sleeping. I stop moving and stare forward, numbly. Walter wiggles from side to side, wordlessly urging me to keep going.

With a deep breath, I take it from the top, retracing his steps and patterns from the initial greasy blast. After all, I think, all good compositions have a repetitive element. Only this time, the entire process takes less than five minutes! Still, it's not as fun as techno. I can't for the life of me reach the end of the second hour. I whimper a little before repeating the verse three more times, which lulls Walter into a comfortable half-snore.

I look up at the clock. Mini-Walter pushes against the rod with all of his might. But even he can't stop the Last. Excruciating. Second. From. Passing. Tick!

"Okay, Walter," I say quietly. "The second hour is up."

Walter rolls over groggily, his hair pointing straight up. "Yes, you're right," he says, glancing at the clock. "Thank you for watching the time. I could have stayed there all day."

"I enjoyed it too, Walter," I say, recalling the first artful five minutes. "Got sort of lost in the moment there."

"Okay, Jeff," says Walter, sitting Indian style in his saggy white underpants. "You're doing great. We're on hour three now. I want you to hold my breasts and squeeze them really hard."

"Okay," I say, hunching over. "Like this?"

"You're going to need to work much harder than that."

"Why couldn't this have been first?"

223

"Now tell me I'm stupid or something," says Walter, ignoring my whine. I look at down Walter curiously, grab his man-boobs. "Dumb fag," I say, twisting his flesh inward and upward. Walter's eyes light up.

"What the fuck is the matter with you?" I pull on the skin like salt-water taffy.

"More," says Walter.

I drag Walter across the room, wondering why the little man is not shrieking in pain. "Isn't there a machine for this?" I say. "My wrists are about to snap." When the two-car train finally pulls up to the edge of the hospital bed, I release my grip and look at the clock. Twenty-seven minutes. Walter's mini-mom digs her gold pumps into the steel casing of the clock frame. He looks closer. Yep, that's her, alright! She's pushing AGAINST the second hand, urging time FORWARD. Hey, she's on my side! She wants this to end as much as I do! Fueled by mini-mom's fire, I glance back up at the clock before finding and activating my inner sadist. "Who gave you permission to touch yourself, you pathetic little wretch?" I bark, slapping Walter across the face.

"Hey!" yells Walter, startling me out of my neo-Nazi trance. "No hitting."

"Oh, sorry," I say, shocked that a little pat on the cheek could possibly hurt more than a ten-foot mammary stretch. "You stupid fuck," I try again, grabbing his boobs, "gimme all your money!" Great, I think. Now I'm a mugger. I suck at this.

Walter rolls over and pumps vigorously for a half second before extracting his hand from his underpants. He lies back against the hospital bed, spent. Did he come? I lean beside the man, exhausted, watching as the second hand of the clock approaches the end of hour number three. Tick!

I pat my fat jeans pocket while marching through the thick brush of Walter's overgrown front yard. I've never felt so rich or so deserving. I am totally elemental now, using my body to earn my living, not manipulating people with a forced, girly smile.

"Relationship sales, e-commerce, there's always a new name for business, isn't there," I say as I hop into my Rav. "And it's always the same thing. Lies. Thank you, Walter, for giving me a glimpse of the truth. I will earn my own damned way out of poverty, thankyouverymuch."

As I pull slowly out of the cul-de-sac, I imagine that Walter moved into his mother's house and that she is now dead. I imagine that each big bay window is a set of eyeballs: the bridge club, members of the neighborhood watch. I imagine their eyes peering out at my green Rav just as they used to peer out at that strange little boy named Walter playing hopscotch and lurking in the shadows. I drive through the cookie-cutter homes, onto the freeway, back to the city, where being a freak is the rule, not the exception.

JUSTIN JONES is a California-based writer and multimedia artist whose stories have been published in several anthologies. He has performed as a spoken word artist in New York, San Francisco, Los Angeles, and beyond.

CAPTAIN OF INDUSTRY AND THE ULTIMATE TRANSSEXUAL

Anonymous

I only ever had sex with one chick whose dick was bigger than mine.
Her name was Antonello Holmes, and she was huge. I found her
online. She was operating out of Beverly Hills. She was a real lady.
I mean in the best sense of the word. She had this gorgeous apartment. All these Japanese prints, lots of mirrors on the wall. Velvet
everywhere. She was from South America I think. It's fascinating to
me how many of these transsexuals are from Latin American countries. They've got such a code of machismo; there's such a premium
put on being a man's man. I don't think it's a coincidence that that
culture produces so many incredible trannies. I've paid lots of trannies to have sex with me. One of the things I like about them is that
they try harder than any woman to be a woman. They have amazing
skills because they have access to the equipment 24/7. The problem
is, many chicks who call themselves transsexuals are just guys who
took some hormone shots and put a wig on. But not Antonello. She
was almost six feet tall, but she had really soft skin, and she was
dressed impeccably in this long Japanese dressing gown. It was kind
of funny: When I got into her apartment, I couldn't find my money. It
was weird. I was searching all my pockets. I felt embarrassed and like
a total idiot. But she was so nice. I mean, I could see from her perspective how if some guy came into her apartment and then claimed
he couldn't find his money, she would think that was weird. But she
was just as sweet as sweet could be. So I went back out to find my

money. I got into the elevator, and there it was. $250. Five $50 bills. Just lying there on the floor of the elevator. I couldn't believe it. It was like magic or something. In Beverly Hills of all places! So I went back in with the money, and we laughed together. She just could not have been any nicer. She had very soft breasts. I hate those rock-hard titties that some of these "girls" have. You could break your teeth on them, seriously. And very big nipples. I like that in a transsexual. She said she was not on hormones. I guess that was true because she got hard as a rock. As I said, she had a gigantic dick. I mean it was a monster. So many of these chicks with dicks who advertise online, they'll say they have ten inches. And that they're totally functional. What a joke. Most of them, their dicks look like sad little shriveled worms. They're pathetic. Not Antonello Holmes. She was the real deal. I asked her if I could sit on it. Her Moby-Dick that is. She said no, she could only do it if I was lying on my back. Which is okay with me. Moreover, I respected her for just saying exactly what she could and couldn't do. A total professional. I'll never forget looking in the mirror and watching that huge enormous thing start to go inside of me. It was so exciting to watch. Even now, just thinking about it, it gets me all excited. I swear I have masturbated while thinking about that over and over and over. I could barely take it. But she was very slow, very patient. She really worked with me until the whole thing was in there. It was such a great feeling, being so completely full. I have a high-stress, very demanding job. I'm what you'd call a captain of industry. It's up to me to make all the decisions. Decisions that affect people's lives. One of the things I like about being with someone like Antonello is that I don't have to make any decisions. She was in total control, and I was just along for the ride. I could let go of all that stress. And I actually had an orgasm with her inside me, without even touching myself. I still am not sure how the hell she did that. But she did. I tried to hook up with her a couple times afterward, but we were never quite able to work it out. I was doing some research online to see what other people said about her. I found something really interesting she wrote. Here it is:

227

"Be willing to honor your agreements with clients and if, for any reason, you doubt whether you can honor an agreement, don't make it in the first place. If a client is looking for a nine-inch top and you are a six-inch bottom don't agree to do the gig, pretending over the phone you are going to be able to fit the bill.

Most clients resent duplicity and cherish honesty in an escort.

Stick to your agreements about the duration of appointments. If you agreed to get together for an hour you should be ready to spend sixty minutes with your client. It is fine if he doesn't want the whole time but do not expect to hear from him if you 'get him off' quickly and rush him out the door in thirty minutes.

I would advise that one should examine the reasons for getting in the escort business. There are countless valid reasons, but if one enters the business out of financial desperation or as an attempt to escape something in life, it's probably not a good idea. Examine motives and establish some goals for what you wish to accomplish via this business.

Make a list of what you will and will not do, keep the list by the phone, and be honest in your communications. Determine your compatibility with a client by matching his activities with yours: If he wants X, and X is in your 'I would rather die than do that' list, tell him you don't do that. If he has to have that, it is best for him to find someone else than you to go through with a call and have an awkward time explaining why you won't do X after the client felt you would.

Check your comfort level. Not every client will look like your ideal guy. Don't be swayed by the beauty of the good-looking ones, and always look for something good in those clients to whom you are not so attracted. The average-looking guys usually have a lot going for them in other areas.

228

Develop a tough skin. As with any business, there will be customer satisfaction situations that cannot be resolved; on occasion some mean things will be said to you. Stay professional and honest, don't strike back with the same verbal abuse, and don't take a bad situation personally.

Be able to put work in a box at the end of the day and walk away from it. On the other hand, don't let a great call go to your head: You are there to offer a service, not to fall in love. Stay professional at all times.

Know when to quit. Look when to quit; look beyond this business and toward goals and growth needs.

As this is a business about taking care of the needs of others, be aware of your own needs for security and personal growth, and move into other areas when the time is right for you.

Most importantly, take vacations from this business. Go on a real date, take a trip, read a book, help someone in deep need. When you get back, you will enjoy and do a better job (they will notice it and enjoy it too), and always remember that what you are offering is a very comfortable convenience for people who appreciate time (the nice ones). Let the others go . . . somewhere else . . . (the nut cases) . . . they know where to go . . .

Thank you all, Ladies and Gentleman.

Antonello, wherever you are, I have a soft spot in my heart for your hard spot! And for what an amazing human being you are.

229

4

Cyberspace

"YOUR DICK IS SO SMALL, LOOK AT YOUR TINY LITTLE COCK!"

Alexandra Foxx

As a struggling doctoral student in my mid-20s, I was a little strapped for cash. Okay, wait . . . I am *still* strapped for cash, financially fucked and drowning in student debt. Some of my classmates work in retail, others work in bars, and, worse yet, some babysit. I did the whole retail thing . . . when I was 17. Fuck no, not again. Bars? Did it, sick of it. Babysitting? I find children to be a tad repulsive. When I stumbled upon an amateur webcam porn site, it seemed like the perfect way to put myself through school—and it was (still is!). At $2 to $3 per minute, I have been raking in a ton of extra cash. So, what does a webcam girl do exactly? Well, I normally put on a crazy wig and a pair of five-inch heels and ya know . . . rub one out. Sometimes I can see the client on the screen, sometimes I can't. I never do anything that I don't feel like doing, and I always respect myself while I'm on cam. So far, the only downside of my career as a part-time webcam slut has been an occasional sore pussy, but I can live with that. The money and the fabulous stories make it all worth it.

My favorite clients are always the ones that require very little effort on my part. Foot fetish guys are the best! What could be better than getting paid to put on a pair of panty hose and rub your own feet? I'll tell you what: sitting in a chair topless and screaming at a guy while you watch him jerk off. He would pay me to scream the following: "YOUR DICK IS SO SMALL! LOOK AT YOUR TINY

LITTLE COCK!" The great irony was that his dick was one of the largest dicks that I'd ever seen on cam. Oh, and I can't even tell you how much money I've been offered to do a sex show with my dog. Two words on that matter: FUCK. NO.

Sean is my all-time favorite client. Sean has been purchasing shows, services, and panties from me for almost a year. He's kind, VERY generous, and trapped in the military in a loveless marriage. Sean's dirty little secret is that he enjoys dressing up as a woman and being dominated. Due to his personal circumstances, it hasn't been possible for him to enjoy his fantasies in real life with somebody. Thank goodness for Sean (and for my bank account), he found me. Sometimes he comes during our shows, but often he doesn't. Sean is a typical sub: he loves being yelled at, told what to do, and dominated by a powerful woman. I enjoy screaming at men, telling them to shove random objects up their asses, and getting a nice monetary gift in exchange. The whole thing has been working beautifully. Recently, Sean requested that I put together a gift box for him. This gift box is currently in the works, and it will include a wig, a few pairs of my used panties (he hopes that they arrive damp), my old jewelry, some makeup, and one of my sex toys. I think he also requested a jar of my urine so that he could "mark himself as my slave," but we are still trying to figure out the details. By societal standards, Sean sounds like a fucking freak, doesn't he? Well, he sort of is, but he's also sensitive, interesting to chat with, and kind. In between webcam shows, I would chat with Sean online about non-sexual things. I would vent to him about schoolwork, and he would vent to me about his life. The strange thing was that I actually cared. I started seeing Sean as an actual human being, rather than just a fun way to pay my bills. Sean has insecurities, fears, and goals, just like I do, and sometimes I find solace in our brief conversations.

I enjoy leading this double life—it's my own "dirty little secret." I love being a sex worker, and I look forward to the day where I'm far enough along in my professional career that I can come out of the sex worker closet. Until then, I'll keep my head in the books and my tits on cam. As far as Sean, I'm still not sure if I'm going to send him a jar of urine, but I guess that's a decision for another day.

ALEXANDRA FOXX is a twentysomething-year-old doctoral student and proud webcam girl. She considers herself to be quite bright and can be obsessive when it comes to achieving her goals. When she's not on cam, she's usually buried in books, conducting research, doing yoga, or enjoying a stiff drink.

UNCONDITIONAL LOVE AT BECK'S

Anonymous

My whore ad evolved, or at least it changed, over the first few months of business. What started as a picture ad with the words "Hot Pierced Bicycle Boy, easygoing, vanilla to light bondage, either way I'm bound to please" gradually morphed into a text ad.

The picture ad came about from my first major motion picture release, *Luther's Tickle Dungeon*. As I'm sure you know from the Siskel and Ebert review, or *The Times*, I played a straight punk panhandler who gets picked up with the offer to make a little extra cigarette money doing a bondage photo shoot. Streetwise, the Punk is not totally gullible, and he verifies that the shoot isn't gay, saying, "It's not some gay thing, is it? 'Cause I'm str8 and I gotta girlfriend with a tight pussy." The photographer placates the punk, explaining that it's not gay and that he will just get tied up fully clothed. Unfortunately, the photographer is a sadist, and my punk persona gets stripped, tied up, and tickled, and somehow has a gay epiphany, getting a boner and coming with a dildo in his mouth. If you haven't seen this movie, you really must. It's a barrel of laughs with a climatic ending.

So playing off the fame of that first role, the producer created a whore ad for me. He took a photo from the film and added some text to it. In spite of the overwhelming response to the ad as the hordes of movie fans sought me out (a client or two a week is a horde, isn't it?), I barely made rent. My phone number changed, and so I had to change the ad. Lacking Photoshop skills, I shifted to text ads. Every

Sunday I'd let my creative juices flow dreaming up new headlines and wording for my ads in the *B.A.R.* And every Monday morning, I'd join the river of male sex workers in their weekly pilgrimage to the office of the *B.A.R.* I'd dumbly ask, "Is it okay to use the word 'orgasmic?'" and get turned down while somehow my peers would get ads run that said, "Suck my c#@k!" I'd excitedly expand the genre of whore ads with such ad writing breakthroughs as "Got milk? Pierced dude milks and squirts" or "If it doesn't get all over the place, it doesn't belong in your face?" And I quickly learned that humor doesn't work in the exciting world of adult advertising. My "got milk" campaign produced only two inquiries, both wanting to know if I was a lactating male. On the bright side, I never got sued by the Dairy Board or Carl's Jr. for borrowing their slogans.

An off-the-job orgasm catapulted me into the world of reiki and new age healing, and I delved into espousing the healing aspects of my work, thinking of myself as a sacred whore. My headlines evolved into "tend your inner garden" and eventually into "Unconditional Love." I emphasized orgasmic transcendence of stress, disease, and trauma to achieve deep inner peace.

As my ads changed, so did my clientele, honing into an older, more spiritual demographic, often including body electric types. One day I ended up answering a call for "Unconditional Love" at Beck's Motor Lodge, that temple of ecstatic worship in the Castro. My john was a guy from Reno, middle-aged, and a bit paunchy. We embraced and started kissing as I entered the temple door. We disrobed like monks eager to foray into the realm of God . . . Well, like homo monks, eager to taste each other's flesh . . . Well, more like one monk eager to taste flesh, and the other eager to make some money.

You might think that monks wouldn't do such things. But just the other day I was reading Tobias Schneebaum's *Wild Man*. One of our gay ancestors, Schneebaum was a blossoming artist and homosexual in the 1950s. His fame arose from his Fulbright-scholarship-sponsored journey to Peru, in which he disappeared into the jungle and lived with a tribe of cannibals. Schneebaum had a knack for cultural immersion into tribes in which men loved men as well as women. His monk adventure occurred in Burma when a Buddhist monk entered his room, stripped, and showed him God through carnal pleasures. A couple days later the monk returned with another monk, and they disrobed and took Schneebaum to see God once again. Schneebaum experienced mystical energies emanating from the monks and was sure they were doing powerful spiritual healing on him. When they left, he discovered his wallet was missing. So you see, monks can be both carnal and money-hungry as well as spiritually enlightening.

But getting back to RenoJohn and the Beck's Motor Temple, RenoJohn and I stood kissing, embracing, cocks growing Godward. Then he whispered in my ear, "Are you into anal?" Ever the people pleaser, I said yes, though at the time I was a bit naïve. My idea of "anal" was fucking, and, although I had a sense that "anal" could entail a lot more, I didn't really have a clue just how much more it could entail. You see, that was years ago, long before I discovered the joys of getting fucked, and much longer before I learned about shoving yogurt up my ass, only to shoot it out like twenty loads of cum. It was long before I had learned about putting beads, marbles, ice, or assorted vegetables up my ass. It was long before I bought daikon radishes from women pedaling their vegetables on the streets of Ladakh just so I could keep my tight hole open.

At the time, I wasn't even sure if the invitation "Are you into anal?" was going to mean my ass or his. But I'm a people pleaser, and on top of that I wanted to make money. The paunchy white guy paying me, though, he knew what to do, and he ran from my embrace and plopped back on the bed in a hurry. Before I could recite the five principles of reiki, he was on his back with his legs hiked up and a jar of Crisco open on the nightstand next to the coin box for activating the vibrating bed.

I hunkered down between his legs, squatting on my knees with a transcendent half smile on my lips. I was acting, of course. Being early on in my anal explorations, I was still a bit afraid of ass. This was long before I'd ever rimmed a guy. I was entirely scatophobic. At that point in my sexual evolution, the ass was something I blindly stuck my cock into, fully wrapped of course, when I happened to hook up with a bottom who demanded me to. The ass wasn't something I went around sticking my fingers into willy-nilly, nor did I particularly like to look at the hole out of which our shit springs.

But I knew enough to smile and affirm my client's wishes. He said, "Look over the side of the bed and grab a dildo and stick it in." I looked over the side of the bed and indeed saw a couple of dildos. They were huge. I'd never had anything like these up my ass, nor had I seen anyone like these up anyone else's ass. They were fat eight-to-ten-inchers, probably about two inches in diameter. They were bigger than any cock I'd ever seen, except maybe Andre the Giant, a straight guy I "danced" with at the Nob Hill Theatre. His cock was about as fat as a soda can, and one and a half times as long . . . soft! I'm not sure I ever saw it hard. He had an easy time making bank with a cock like that. He didn't even have to get hard. I imagine he didn't even have to do anything in private shows with his clients. I suspect most of the them wouldn't even have a clue what to do with a cock like that. Now there's a good skill-building workshop for you: "What to Do With a Monster Cock."

Most of the patrons there were pretty timid. I still remember being in the back room with a couple of patrons and other "dancers." One of my colleagues, Joe, a strapping young black guy who stood well over six feet tall, big-boned and broad, approached a petite Asian patron who sat on a side rail watching all of us "dancers" with big eyes. Joe sauntered up to the patron and took his hand, guiding it along Joe's smooth outer leg. The room filled with the air of excitement. The Asian guy froze, transfixed. You could tell he wanted it. He wanted man flesh. You could feel his excitement like that of a teenage virgin. You could hear his knees trembling and feel his balls filling in cumly anticipation. Joe led the neophyte's trembling hand along his belly, closer and closer to his meat. The Asian guy's eyes nearly popped out of his head like a premature ejaculation. Then suddenly he bolted. He just ran out the door, like a deer across a field.

Meanwhile, back in the temple of Beck's Motor Lodge, I didn't flee. The large dildos intimidated me, and RenoJohn's ass intimidated me. But dutifully, and stoically, I calmly continued being the best channel of Unconditional Love I could be. I donned some latex gloves for hygiene's sake—did I mention I was scatophobic? Then I picked up one of the mammoth dildos while my john greased his chute. It didn't look at all appealing to me . . . his rosebud. I mean, it was more like a lava tube than a rosebud, nestled between flabby mounds of flesh. To be honest, if anything, I have a fetish for skinny guys. I'm really more into twinks than bears. I've been known to cruise speed freaks and heroin addicts. So a lava tube nestled between white flabby mounds of ass did nothing for my libido except diminish it.

But I did the honorable thing. I'm a professional, after all. I smiled and slid the phallic hunk of jelly plastic into his gaping hole. "Oh yeahhhh . . ." he moaned, "that's hot . . ." And he looked into my eyes for validation. I returned his gaze. As his inner self trembled in ecstatic pleasure, plastic against prostate, my inner self trembled in a mixture of repulsion, shock, and amazement watching the rubber phallus dive between the flabs of his ass. I gingerly thrust the dildo in and out of his hole with my latex-enshrouded fingertips, trying to keep as much distance as possible between potential scat and my flesh. I didn't even really want to look down there for fear of seeing some scat. I smiled and murmured, "Uh . . . yeah, that's really hot."

After several minutes of sharing this ecstatic state—this Unconditional Love together—he wanted more. I suppose this is what the Buddhists mean by "desire." He said, "Now get the other dildo and stick it in." I started to pull the first dildo out of his lava shoot, and he said, "No, stick the other one in there along with it." I guess I must have already reached enlightenment because I could have easily overcome the desire to stick anything else up his ass. In fact, I was mastering non-attachment. I felt absolutely no attachment to his ass or the dildo; in fact I wanted as little attachment as possible with them. I wanted distance. Sitting on my legs, I stretched my ass even further back on the bed so that I had to arch my back forward and extend my arms as far as possible in front of me to just touch the dildo with my fingertips. I checked my latex gloves and pulled them up my wrists as tight as I could. I think I gained a half an inch in coverage. Then, to my dismay, the gloves slid back down as soon as I flexed my hands. I vowed to get longer gloves for my care bear kit. Maybe I could find the kind like vets use for artificial insemination.

My reverie into wrist protection ended as he gobbed his ass with more Crisco and I gingerly pushed the second dildo alongside the first monstrosity in his ass. I smiled. When in doubt, smile—that was my mantra for customer satisfaction. I used the very tips of my fingers to push the second dildo deeper. I wished I had longer fingernails to give me an extra few millimeters of advantage in the situation. I worried that the shit would hit the fan and bring the scene to an embarrassing gag-stop order that would undermine my smile. To top it off, I felt the latex gloves slowly disintegrating as the Crisco ate through them. I made a mental note to get polyethylene gloves next time—long ones. My amazement grew by the moment as the second dildo delved deeper into his ecstatic lava shoot. I was equally amazed and pleased that there were no signs of scat. "Oh yeah," he moaned, "that's hot." My cock lay limp between my legs. Whatever arousal it enjoyed from our passionate kissing had long since gone dissolved into anal amazement and scatological trepidation. I smiled as best I could and said, "Yeah, that's really hot." I didn't think I was executing my lines as well as I had in my film debut, but the fat man was still singing as his sphincter slid around the double penetrating dildos.

After several more moments of sharing this bliss together, his desire reared its fleshy jellified plastic head once again. And now I know why the Buddhists are so emphatic about overcoming desire. He said—and I. Kid. You. Not—"Now take those two out, and stick the big one in." My mind went into slow motion . . . stick . . . the . . . big . . . one . . . in . . . My mind tried to wrap itself around the concept of "big one" in this context. It was like a child's hand trying to grasp an elephant's dick. Here a guy had two dildos up his ass simultaneously. These dildos were bigger than 99 percent of men's cocks. And he wanted me to pull them out and stick a big one in! As my mind froze in a state of shock, he went on, "Yeah, it's by the bed." I pulled the two dildos out of his ass, thankful I didn't see any scat upon a very cursory inspection (but in fact I probably didn't look at them any more than I had to). I leaned over the side of the bed and spotted the "big dildo" hiding under the folds of the dust ruffle on a carpet that had no doubt seen all of this before.

The "big one" was the size of a horse cock, three to four inches in diameter and over a foot long. By the time I hoisted it back over the side of the bed, RenoJohn was lubed up and ready. I tried to pull my slowly disintegrating gloves a bit higher up my exposed wrists. Then I pushed the horse cock dildo slowly in. It moved steadily but slowly like an ocean liner into a headwind. My fingers fully extended, my smile of Unconditional Love on my face, I pushed onwards like Ahab after Moby-Dick. I handled the monster dildo like I might handle a mousetrap baited with Limburger cheese, except that I forced myself to keep my face and nose pointed forward.

The dildo ran aground and came to a halt about seven inches into the beached whale. "Oooooh, yeahhh," RenoJohn moaned, "that's really hot . . ." At a total loss for anything else to say, I said, "Oh yeah, that's hot." Sometimes it's good just to be a mirror when practicing Unconditional Love. I smiled and looked into his eyes, not that the eye contact really meant anything, mind you. It was just the safest place for me to look. I didn't dare look at the horrifying horse cock in his hole. In fact I didn't dare look anywhere near "down there" for fear of seeing scat. His body, far from twinkish, held little appeal for my eyes. I couldn't really close them or look at the wall for fear of appearing uninterested. And so I gazed into his eyes. Somehow I must have been convincing. The horse-hung dildo worked its magic and sated him like a good meditation, freeing him from further desire. He touched God. He shot his load.

I ran to the bathroom to wash every vestige of unholiness or essence of scat off my body. I blindly ran into the shower like a bee victim jumping into a lake seeking salvation. As I stood under the water, my eyes came into focus upon a horror scene. First of all, it was a motor lodge, so the bathroom was just plain skanky. That I could have handled. But as I turned around to get my back wet, I came face-to-face with his enema bag. I furiously coated myself with as much lather as possible. It was then I glanced to the towel rack. It was empty. I glanced downward. All the towels lay on the floor, and the hand cloths, daintily lying on top of the pile, wore brown streaks. I was beginning to think it wasn't such a good idea to come in here to clean up. I used more soap and carefully kept all parts of my body from touching ANYTHING in that bathroom. No clean towels available, I wiped the water off me with my hands. Shock, I tell you. I was in shock. It was not so much that the towels had brown streaks, but that he didn't hide them for goodness' sake. This was not the bathroom etiquette my mother taught me. I knew I'd have to take another shower when I got home.

I returned to the bed, where RenoJohn reclined in orgasmic bliss. The horse-hung dildo lay just outside his hole. He looked into my eyes and said, "You certainly live up to your ad, 'Unconditional Love.'" I murmured thanks as he handed me the $120 that would certify this as a religious experience for me. "If you ever get to Reno, look me up," he said.

"I will," I said, and went out the door, leaving the temple of Beck's Motor Lodge both a bit dirtier and a bit more enlightened than when I'd gone in. Soon after, I procured elbow-length gloves in preparation for future adventures in "Unconditional Love."

POSTSCRIPT

It wasn't until I wrote this and read it aloud at an open mic that I realized that I actually did give him Unconditional Love. Unconditional

Love is acknowledging the divine in someone or something even when we don't see it or understand it. By looking in his eyes and holding space, I transcended my judgments and honored his pleasures. Eye contact is a powerful transmission of honoring someone's presence in the world.

I "HEART" STEVE, FOR $2,500

Candye Kane

We spoke on the phone almost twice a week—he, with his cute
Southern drawl and me with my sultry, hushed phone-sex voice. I
filed and polished my nails in bright red as I listened to him tell me
about his wife and their sex life and issues. Our conversations started
with him whispering about all the things his wife refused him in bed
and inevitably ended with his loud moaning orgasm. I described
in juicy detail how I would submit immediately, whenever he demanded, and thank him for my spanking. Sometimes our conversations consisted of him telling me about an argument he had with his
wife, or his mother, or other women in his life. I was his plaything on
the phone for the hour or so that we spoke per week, and he paid $35
an hour for the privilege. He called the shots.

After our phone call, as was the practice at Personal Services, I
posed for a Polaroid photo per his specific requests. I wrote "I heart
Steve" on my belly or thigh in my signature cherries-in-the-snow lipstick. I posed sweetly in a French maid's uniform without panties.
I would simply smile and squeeze my 44Gs together. He said the
photos he received made him feel closer to me. He often said that I
looked like a younger version of his ex-wife.

Most of my other phone-sex clients were impersonal and sometimes even disturbed. I felt like a therapist giving advice to sad, lonely
people, but even with my thick skin I still felt uncomfortable with

245

some of the calls I encountered. One man was a priest who wanted to talk about how he would assault and rape me. He wanted me to scream like I was being stabbed in the stomach while he furiously stroked his cock. He would always climax when I was screaming my loudest scream. Another man was a submissive who wanted me to boss him around. I tried to be dominant, but I just wasn't very good at it. My co-worker Cindy, who wore ponytails in her Polaroids and looked like she was 12, told him to put his cock in the window sill and let the window slam down on it. She had us all come in the room and listen on speaker-phone because that was part of this man's fantasy—for us to hear him and berate him while being humiliated. It was sometimes hard for me to keep my "laissez-faire-trying-to-make-a-buck" attitude when I thought about just how plain mean the world could be. I could never be that cruel to someone, even if it was their fantasy.

I really looked forward to my weekly calls from Steve. He was so normal compared to the other callers I dealt with. He felt like a safe friend. He worked as an engineer and often called me from his private office. He rode horses and owned a couple of mustangs, which this city girl found fascinating. And he was a sci-fi enthusiast and collected comic books. He sent me a photo once to my P.O. box way before the Internet made it quick and easy. He had short brown hair and a neatly trimmed matching beard. He was handsome in a nice, honest, Midwestern way. He looked like he could be chubby, and he had kind eyes. Our strict phone-sex-job rules dictated that we weren't supposed to share our personal information with cus-tomers. But we'd been having phone sex for over a year now, and I wanted to see what he looked like. Our phone-sex boss kept Hitachi magic wand vibrators in all the drawers of the house at Clune Street. I admit there were times that I ended my conversation with Steve writhing around on the magic wand while telling him vivid, graphic stories about where I would wrap my full red lips and how my lovely, soft hands would touch his most vulnerable of places.

One day he called me in a very excited state. He was coming to a convention in Santa Ana, California, and he asked if I would meet him at his hotel for a "face-to-face." I hesitated. We could be fired from our jobs for sharing info with clients or doing private calls with them from our homes. And we were NEVER, under any circumstances, allowed to meet our clients. So, when Steve asked me to meet him for money, I said no, at first. I had never turned a trick before. I was just an 18-year-old phone-sex girl. Sure, I gave it away nightly for nothing to my favorite Hollywood rock and roller with the pompadour and tattoos. And there was my French Maserati mechanic lover with the great biceps. Then there was that super-cute witty writer who wrote me up in the *L.A. Weekly* all the time—but to sell it to a stranger for money seemed like a brand-new concept. I hadn't even posed nude yet for my first magazine. I was a novice. I would eventually appear in over 150 magazines with names like *Velvet Talks*, *Juggs*, and *Floppers*, but to meet a stranger in a hotel room for sex/money?

Then he offered me $2,500.

I was a teenage mom with a two-year-old son, living in my parents' abusive home. Twenty-five hundred dollars would be enough for me to find a new place of our own and pay the first and last months' rent. I jumped at the chance.

I explained to Steve that we really had to keep this hush-hush or I would be fired. He could never tell any of the other girls at Personal Services that we had met. I told him he had to pay me in crisp $100 bills BEFORE he was allowed to touch me. He promised to keep the secret and agreed to my terms. He would be staying at the Sheraton, and we would meet in the lobby at noon after he was finished with his morning meetings. There was no e-mail or texting then—no easy cell phone access—just the agreement that I would be there at noon on April 27 wearing a white dress with white industrial bra, white stockings, a garter belt, and white stiletto heels.

As the day grew closer, I grew more apprehensive. What if he tried to kill me when we were in the room together? Steve didn't seem like the murderous type on the phone, but I didn't really know the guy. What if he had another man in the room and they raped me? I didn't know what to do. There was no one I could tell about this meeting.

Cyberspace

The only people who might not judge me would be my phone-sex colleagues, and any one of them might snitch to the boss out of spite.

April 27 arrived, and I drove my Dodge Dart Swinger to the hotel holding tightly to the steering wheel with my sweaty palms. I was waxed, blow-dried, manicured, spit-shined, and polished. Dressed just as my dial-up daddy had requested—the tight white polyester dress accentuating my California tan and my full red-lipsticked lips. I looked sexy as hell even if, inside, I was scared to death.

I sat in the lobby, perched at the end of a brown leather chair with my knees pressed tightly together. I didn't want anyone else in this hotel to know I was a hooker, even if I was just a high-priced beginner. There were all kinds of men milling around with placards pinned to their pocket protectors. Hello! My name is Larry sat next to me in the next chair, reading *The Wall Street Journal*. I looked around the lobby nervously, hoping I would get a chance to see Steve first before he saw me. Maybe if I didn't like what I saw, I could chicken out and run away. I could hide out in the ladies room until he left. If I could get a good look at him first, I could change my mind entirely if he looked suspicious or was with someone else. Then suddenly I felt a hand on my shoulder. I turned around and looked into the eyes of my first trick. He was super-nervous too and had perspiration on his forehead. "Hi, Candye . . ." he stammered. "Let's go up to the room."

We walked to the elevator side by side, in silence. Neither one of us spoke, lest we reveal to any eavesdroppers that we were meeting for the very first time. We stepped out of the elevator on the tenth floor. I tried to break the ice. "How's the convention been going? Are you having fun?" He fumbled clumsily for his room key and slid it in the key slot of room 1028 without answering.

Once in the hotel room, Steve went into the bathroom immediately. "The money is there for you next to the television," he hollered through the closed bathroom door. I stepped across the brown shag carpeting and opened the fat envelope, carefully fingering the twenty-five crisp $100 bills. I put them in my wallet and stood leaning against the desk waiting for Steve. I was so happy to have that money in my pocketbook. I went into actress mode. I was gonna give Steve the time of his life.

He came out of the bathroom with his pressed white business shirt unbuttoned and his pants off. He wore white Fruit of the Loom nut-huggers. He didn't look at all like the bossy daddy who wanted to throw me down and give me a spanking. He looked like a scared and nervous teenage boy. "I have something to show you," I said and asked him to have a seat on the bed. He leaned against the headboard. I stood in front of the bed fully clad in my virgin whites and started rubbing myself between my legs. "*Mmmm*, seeing you in person makes me so hot, Steve," I purred. "Take out your throbbing dick and stroke it for me while I show you my gigantic breasts."

Steve moaned and did as he was told, pumping furiously and not taking his eyes off of me.

I slowly unzipped my skin-tight dress, careful to linger as long as possible on every inch of my own body with my long red nails. I was enjoying this opportunity to tease my captive audience and I found it fairly easy. I rubbed my own nipples as I stepped out of the dress, revealing my vintage Sears catalog 44GG bra and my garter belt. "I am so attracted to you, Steve," I lied. "You make me so wet down there." I dipped my finger. "Would you like a taste?" I asked as I sauntered closer and offered him my finger. Steve sucked my finger hungrily for a minute, and I stepped back. "Not so fast, cowboy," I said. "Let me show you what I can do." I gracefully slid my hands in, lifting my heavy right breast out of the tight constraints of this medieval torture bra. Steve groaned loudly and kept sliding his hands up and down like an obedient oil rig. My right breast is bigger and heavier than the other, and I struggled to bring it up to my face. I rubbed my pretty face all over my own breast and said, "Ohhh, Steve, wouldn't you just love for me to come over there and rub my big breasts all over you?" I placed my nipple in my mouth and sucked and smacked my lips between each sexy word and sound. Next, I pulled out the left one and repeated the action—rubbing them on my face, watching him carefully through my half-closed bedroom eyes, tantalizing and seducing him—cooing and moaning between each action. "I'm gonna wrap my huge tits around your hardness right now, Steve, and make you squirt all over my pretty face." I slid closer to him and bent down to make good on my promise. All of a sudden, before I even touched him with my hands or my breasts, Steve came in his hand with a loud unexpected groan.

Both of us stood there in shocked disbelief for a minute. I went to the bathroom to get him a hot towel, but he started wiping the sheets hastily on his crotch and said, "You have to get out of here. My wife will be back with her mother any minute!" He jumped up from the bed and ran into the bathroom. He closed the door in a panic. "Thanks for coming! Talk soon."

I heard the sound of the shower as I gathered up my clothing, slipping easily back into my dress and high heels. Smiling with smug satisfaction, I stuffed my money deeper into the bottom of my purse as I sauntered down the long hallway to the elevator. I couldn't believe I had made so much money in such a short amount of time. If hooking was this easy, I didn't know why on earth I had waited so long before trying it.

The elevator bell rang and the doors opened, revealing two ladies who stepped out as I entered. The younger woman was a 40-ish brunette, and the women beside her wore a gray, fresh beauty salon set. I knew immediately that this was Steve's wife and mother-in-law. They chatted happily as they walked toward room 1028. Unbeknownst to them, their respective husband and son-in-law had just cum into his own palm while staring at my naked tits. Truth is truly stranger than fiction.

In the following weeks, with my sudden financial windfall, I moved into my own little house behind a pizza parlor in Eagle Rock. My toddler son and I had to share a bedroom, but it was our own house—just the two of us. I still had a long drive to Marina Del Rey, where I continued to work at the phone-sex company and Steve continued to be my loyal customer for many years. He kept our tryst a secret and I kept my job. A win-win situation.

After my experience with Steve, I turned about ten more tricks in my brief career as a prostitute. None of my tricks were ever as quick, easy, or lucrative as that very first one. I quickly found that when it came to physical contact with someone for money, it was way harder than it seemed. I was an okay actress from a distance—or even one-on-one with a co-star in an X-rated film. But sex with the man who owns the liquor store, or sex with an anonymous stranger, assigned to me through an escort service, proved to be much more of a challenge.

Phone sex was a much easier vocation—one in which I could detach easily and retain my anonymity. As I became more successful as a nude model and ultimately became the monthly advice columnist for *Gent* magazine, I didn't need to turn tricks anymore. I started to go on live stripping tours, making hundreds of dollars a day just posing for Polaroids on my fans' laps, without having to go all the way.

One night, twenty years later, I am playing a musical engagement with my blues band in Oklahoma City. After the show, as I sit at the table signing CDs and chatting to fans, I see a familiar face in the line. I can't place it, but I know I have met this gentleman somewhere before. He makes his way to the front of the line, purchases a CD, and asks me for my autograph. "How shall I sign it?" I ask pleasantly. In a sexy Southern drawl that I recognize immediately, he says: "Thanks for the great night at the Sheraton in Santa Ana so many years ago." I look up at my old friend with a sly smile as I sign his CD with my long red nails. It was still the easiest money I have ever made, but now I'm the one calling all the shots. And I do it without ever shedding a stitch!

CANDYE KANE is an American singer, songwriter, and performer best known in the blues and jazz genre. Her mom was a mentally unstable workaholic who taught her to shoplift at the same time she enrolled Candye in Sears charm school so she could steal a set of flatware and know the difference between the salad and dinner fork. Her bio dad was in Chino state prison. Her stepdad was a body-painting hippie who worked as a layout artist for Adams Film World and other porn mags. He also worked as a teamster driving a laundry truck to make ends meet. She has lived in East L.A., Venice Beach, and Encinitas. She has been a switchboard operator, phone sex girl, porn star, topless model, songwriter, and blues singer. She tours the world 250 days a year performing her original songs of empowerment and triumph. She is a cancer fighter, having been diagnosed in 2008 with neuroendocrine pancreatic cancer. She has been nominated for seven national blues awards, started the first N.O.W chapter at her college, and performed for the presidents of France and Italy at the French embassy in Rome, as well as the Hookers Ball in San Francisco and thousands of blues joints and festivals all over the world. Her songs have been performed or used on television and in movies like *The Chris Isaak Show* and *Hidden Palms.* Her passion is music and writing, and she is always working on songs in various stages of development. She has recorded eleven internationally released CDs, and has been included in *The Rolling Stone Jazz & Blues Album Guide*; *Elwood's Blues,* by Dan Aykroyd; *The Blueshound Guide to Blues*; *Allmusic*; and other blues books and periodicals. She has performed at the NY Fringe Festival in a stage play about her life. She is addicted to Facebook and LU French cookies with the milk chocolate school boy on the top of the cookie. She continues to fight cancer while working full time as a blues diva. Music heals and she takes hundreds of people with her on a journey of strength and courage through the words of her songs, like "I'm the Toughest Girl Alive." She has raised two grown sons and lives alone in her beach house in Oceanside.

Johns, Marks, Tricks, and Chickenhawks

MY HOBBY IS
FUCKING WHORES IN THE ASS

Buster Butt

It's not like I'm proud of it. I don't go around at my high school re-union saying, "Yeah, I got a great job at a startup, I just ran a marathon, and I love fucking whores in the ass. And what have you been up to?"

I do think it's kind of sick. It's not like I'm in therapy or anything. I have a really nice girlfriend. I always have a really nice girlfriend. They're always smart but not stuck-up. They always come from nice families. They're always in great shape. Usually they're runners with slamming bodies. High achievers with low self-esteem. Sometimes I wonder what Mom and Dad would think if they knew I liked to fuck whores in the ass. They would probably want me to go to therapy. I wonder what my girlfriend would think if she knew I like to fuck whores in the ass. We've been going out about six months. I can tell she's getting sick of me. Actually, I'm kind of getting sick of her too. When I asked my girlfriend if I could fuck her in the ass—of course I didn't say it like that, I said it in a chick-friendly way, like, "I love you and I'm so turned on by your butt I'd like to make love to you there"—she looked at me like I'd asked her if her mom would blow me. I don't know why I even keep asking. Every girlfriend I've ever had said no. And I've asked every single one.

So I have to ask myself, *Why do I like it so much?* Well, first of all there's porn. I was raised on porn. These chicks in porn, they all seem to love anal. Some of them even love double anal. And these are very hot girls. Sometimes they even squirt when they're getting fucked in the ass. I don't know if you've ever seen this, but it's like watching fireworks when you're a kid. Plus, it's dirty. It's perverted. It's forbidden. All that stuff. I guess that's human nature, right? The more you're not supposed to do something, the more you want to do it. It makes me feel dangerous and nasty and hot when I do it. That I'm not some vanilla, white-bread white boy. Plus, when it comes right down to it, it feels really good. When you go in, it makes your cock look so big. I suppose that's kind of obvious when you say it. I mean, that's just physics or whatever. But when you're doing it, at the time, it's totally intense. I can't get enough of looking down and feeling so dominant and in control and gigantic when I see my cock inside some girl's tight little ass. It is just that good.

Bunny was the first girl I ever fucked in the ass. I was 18. I found her online. I was nervous. I went to her hotel. It was a Holiday Inn Express. The whole thing was exciting. Hunting her down online and then finding her ad. In fact, looking through all the ads was weirdly hot. I guess I never really thought about how many chicks are hookers. Whores. Prostitutes. Whatever. And every single one of them will fuck me if I give them enough money. I find that kind of mind-boggling actually. And some of them look like girls out of a porno. After I was looking awhile, I started thinking, *These girls all have moms and dads. I wonder what would happen if one of their dads was trolling through the Internet looking for some professional nookie and found his precious daughter with her tits hanging out and her pussy flapping around on the information superhighway. What would he think? Would he think he failed as a dad?* I mean, seriously, if I ever have a daughter, I'm definitely gonna tell her that she shouldn't be a hooker. I mean, not that there's anything wrong with hookers, per se. I probably had sex with about fifty hookers now and most of them are pretty nice people. Of course, there are some who are assholes. And some of them are totally drugged out. And some of them have that weirdly like, vacant look, like there's nobody home. And also, there's chicks pretending to be prostitutes who are actually thieves. But I think if you took fifty lawyers, you'd probably find about the same ratio of drug addicts and thieves in that group. Maybe even more.

Bunny was super nice. Her room, on the other hand, was a filthy pigsty. There were clothes, fast food containers, makeup, and long strings of condom packages everywhere. But her personal hygiene was excellent. She smelled awesomely nice. She answered the door in this red bra with these matching red panties. It was possibly the hottest thing I ever saw in my life. I still fantasize about that some-times when I jerk off. It was like walking into my own porn movie. She's little. That's what I was looking for. In her ad it said B*kdo*r E*tr*es W*lcum. It took me a while to figure out that E*tr*es was "Entries." They do that so if the cops are ever doing word searches, it'll mess up the search engines. I swear, most hookers are pretty good business people. I mean just in terms of getting around the police and attracting customers. I swear some of them are better than the marketing people at this startup I work for. But a lot of the times these hookers, even though they're making a lot of money, they seem like they're broke. There's this whole circuit that they travel. Atlanta, Dallas, Phoenix, L.A., San Francisco, Chicago, New York. A few of them let me know when they're coming into town.

Bunny has a really nice smile. I still see her every chance I get. But she told me that she's semi-retired the last time I saw her. She only sees a few people. That actually made me feel good. That I was one of the people she kept seeing. I don't know why, but the fact that this whore really likes me, I took a lot of weird pride in that. And then I start thinking, *Damn what would a shrink think of that?!* She told me it would be $150 for an hour of straight half-and-half. Which is a blowjob and sex. But I said I wanted the backdoor entry. She said that would be $250. But I only had budgeted for $200. That was true. That's all the money I had on me. She was really cool about it. She said she would do it for $200. She's charged me that ever since. But now I bring her a nice tip. Like $20 or $30. So we started doing it. She seemed really into the sex. I mean, she was wet and everything. Of course, I knew she was probably faking it. But it's funny, when Bunny was acting like she was really into it, I actually started believing that she was really into it. That she liked having sex with me, even though I was giving her money. Who knows whether she really liked it? But it's like that part of your brain turns off. While the other part of your brain gets turned on. You kind of know something can't be really true, but you believe it is you want to bad enough. And believe me, I really wanted to believe that she was into it. First while I was fucking her pussy she put one finger in her ass, then two fingers, and she was kind of like massaging me through the skin between her ass and her pussy. It was like getting a blow job while you were getting fucked. I never felt anything like it. Seriously, it blew my mind. And then when she asked if I was ready to fuck her in the ass, just hearing those words, it got me so revved up. Actually, that's another thing I use to jerk off with sometimes. A lot of times I use the whole sequence, of her answering the door, then turning around and asking me, and then her coming. Or pretending to come. Or whatever.

So she took me out of her pussy, and she put me right at the tip of her ass. She kind of wiggled all around me. Like she was opening up her ass little by little. She was holding my dick at the base. I was crazy hard. Just like a massive steel girder. And then she just sucked me right in her ass. I thought I was going to cum, but I stopped myself. It was like she kind of got comfortable with me inside her ass. Then she started moving back toward me. She told me not to move. And when I was finally in, like I said, it was so tight. I never felt anything that tight. And my cock really did look like it belonged to a giant porn star: Buck Naked. Then she started fingering herself, I mean really aggressively stroking her bishop, and squeezing really hard on my dick with her ass while she was moving up and down, harder and harder and faster and faster; I couldn't believe she was taking all that all the way up inside her, it was spectacular. She started telling me she was going to come, and she was making all these crazy noises like she was coming in a porno movie. And that made me come like crazy. I was shouting, screaming, and everything. Which I never did before.

It was seriously one of the most awesome and excellent things that's happened to me my whole life. I'm not kidding.

Bunny was really sweet afterward. She got me this hot washcloth and put it on my dick. It felt crazy good. I wished I had brought more money so I could give it her. I felt bad that I didn't. I told her that, and she told me not to worry about it. But the next time, I brought her a tip.

The thing is, though, it is kind of like a drug, I guess. It's never been as good as it was that first time. It's like I'm always trying to chase that mythical ass-fucking-virgin high I had. And it's never ever quite as good. Not even with Bunny. I think, well, maybe I just feel nostalgia, like it's kind of myth now how great it was that first time. Don't get me wrong, it's always good. Although some whores just sort of lay there and you can tell they're clock watchers. They can't wait for you to be done and get the hell out. Which is a turn-off. I can understand why. But it's still a turn-off. I try to fuck those girls as long as I can in the ass. I guess it seems kind of fucked-up when I say it like that. I can understand how that would seem fucked-up if you said it to a therapist. Or your mom. Or the hooker's dad. Sometimes I think, *Well maybe if I wasn't so obsessed with fucking whores in the ass I'd be able to find somebody I could stand to be with for longer than a few months.* I mean, theoretically I would like to have a wife and a couple of kids. But I'm not really into talking about everything and figuring everything out and doing all the shit you don't want to do, and your kids end up hating you, and you resent them because you can't hang out with your buds at the bar, and your wife wants you to take her out on a date on Friday night, but you can't say, "Listen honey, I'm going out to fuck a whore in the ass, see you in a couple of hours, Love you, sweetie!" I don't think I'm a pervert. But definitely don't think I'm normal either.

Cyberspace

FLAMED BY LANCE
& PROTECTED BY WILLY

Felicity Hodgeman

Lance is my two o'clock. As I drive to meet him, I offer up my stan-dard supplication: *Please God, please God, please God, don't let him be a cop.* This is the only thing I worry about. I have no one to call to pay my bail so I can be home in time to meet my little boy's bus. The day is white hot. I'm thankful for the air conditioning in my truck, otherwise my careful makeup would melt off my face. At stop lights I examine my thighs and knees and double-check that I didn't miss any spots when I shaved. I am wearing a short red skirt, thin white halter, and platform sandals. I aim for sexy over trashy with no idea if I ever succeed.

We meet in the parking lot of a strip mall across the highway from a motel and greet each other through driver's side windows.

"Hi baby. What do you think?" I smile and hope I look sincere.

I've e-mailed photos of myself so he will recognize me; I recognize him by where he has parked—away from all the other cars belonging to shoppers—and by his air of expectation.

"Let's go across the street," he replies.

Lance is a married guy who wants to get laid. I don't care enough anymore to wonder about the wives at home. I've got enough problems of my own without trying to analyze strangers' marriages. He has slick black hair and oily skin, and he looks like a businessman. The jut of his chin reminds me of my mother's second husband, who was illiterate but believed he was better than everyone else because he was Italian.

We drive across the street and I wait while he gets us a room. This is a short-stay motel: doors open into cramped rooms with wilted beds and televisions turned to porn channels. I can smell the disinfectant—I can always smell it—and I try not to think about other girls' leftover pubic hair.

"What would you like, baby?" I say gently.

He takes off my halter. He unhooks his fancy office pants. I reach inside his white briefs: limp. He'd signed all of his e-mails as "HARD Lance." I guess that was his wishful thinking. I stroke and squeeze and coax him into an erection. I'm in character: The Girl Who Thinks You're an Amazingly Hot Stud. I smile at him in the mirror where he's watching us. I'm naked and on top, and I allow myself one moment to appreciate my arched back and the curve of my ass.

"Oh yes. God, you're so big. Oh! That feels so good, do you like it, baby? Yeah, baby. Yes, yes, yes." When he takes a turn on top, I reach around to finger his ass and feel the folds of his hemorrhoids. I close my eyes and compose my speech to the Academy.

After we fuck, we lie side by side on the bed, looking at our reflections in the mirror on the ceiling. I listen to him talk about the beauty of Argentinian women. I'm not Argentinian. I'm ready to be done: I want to wash this date off me and shift into mommy role.

Driving home, counting the bills he'd left folded on top of the television, I realize I've been shortchanged. This has never happened to me before, and I call him as I navigate the highway on-ramp. He ticks off an accounting that includes the room fee. I don't pay for the room, ever, but okay. There's nothing I can do about it now. I can't chase him down and I won't call him back. He certainly will not receive the thank-you e-mail I usually send.

At home, I shower, and even though the bathroom needs to be cleaned, I'm glad to be washed. I wonder what my son will want to do this afternoon. Ride bikes? Play basketball?

I get into my safe clothes: red sweatpants and a white thermal shirt with stretched-out sleeves. It doesn't matter that it's August. I have built a house of cards and I want at least to be comfortable in the event of a collapse. I check my e-mails and the usual websites: Craigslist and Backpage. I check a site that reviews Long Island working girls.

Then I see it: Lance has posted a cruel review, full of lies. "Velvet Zoë is fat, and ugly. Handled my cock like a baseball bat. I fucked her in the ass and made her scream: Please fuck me like the pig I am!"

Nerve endings recoil from my fingers and toes. I can't breathe. I stand, walk upstairs. His words are branded on my brain. I don't cry. *Why did he bother going through with our appointment? If he thought I was fat and ugly, why didn't he cancel while we were still in the parking lot?*

I cancel my six o'clock with a new client, William. I'm not feeling well, I explain, and apologize. He thanks me for letting him know.

I stay home with my family and watch television even though this is a lie, now, too. Alcohol and my cozy clothes hold me in: I'm a brittle husk on the verge of disintegration. Looking at the television, I wonder if it's time for me to start looking for a regular job.

The next morning there is an e-mail from William: *Can we reschedule? Just for a drink?* A snake of anger and hurt is slithering around in my belly. But there are bills to pay. I reply via e-mail: *Just for a drink. Yes.*

There is some comfort in the familiar routine: nylons, short skirt, makeup, perfume. I usually like to bring something lacey to wear. I try to offer erogenous experiences and not just live porn. This time, though, I don't crush any piece of lingerie into my purse.

We meet at a hotel bar: I approach his back. Is he watching for me in the mirror? Probably. Of course. He is a big man. His thighs and buttocks spill over the edges of his seat. I place my hand flat on his back and slide onto the tall stool beside him.

"Hi, how are you?"

I drink red wine. I'd prefer shots of tequila, but I will have to drive home eventually. The alcohol hits me quickly because I've been fasting since Lance's remarks.

William tells me he read the review. This doesn't surprise me; quite a few of my clients find me through that site.

"I understood why you cancelled," he said. "I thought, *This is a real person! This hurt her!*"

I laugh. "Are most of the girls you meet not real?"

He tells me about Russian women he's met who arrive high, who fall asleep and still expect payment.

I shake my head. "This is a job. I wouldn't expect to show up in an office and fall asleep and still get paid."

I do accompany William up to his room. I apologize for my lack of lingerie.

"I'm so sorry those other girls didn't treat you right. But it's a win for me."

We lie naked next to each other on the bed, and I reach below his belly and find him hard, unlike "HARD" Lance. It's easy to give him a blowjob: He's not big enough to hit the back of my throat. He is vocal in his enjoyment. After I've dressed he presses cash into my hand and hugs me goodbye. I drive home pleased, my faith in my ability to fellate restored.

William always books lovely hotel rooms, where he will stay even after I have left. Clean rooms with thick comforters and pillows like heaven are a delicious departure: usually I spend afternoon hours working in grimy bleach-smelling short-stay motels, where the beds are stacked sandwiches of frail mattresses, stained sheets, scratchy blankets, and slippery coverlets. It's fun to listen to William talk about how wonderful and beautiful I am, even though I know he's mistaken. He believes the things he says because he doesn't know me. He requests weekly 6 PM dates and takes me out to dinner. I figure our meetings into my budget.

"Not a clock-watcher." That's how I advertise myself. So I often spend more than an hour with William. At first I think I am talking and staying just because he wants me to. I want to be good at this, possibly the Best, and that means giving my clients What They Want.

I give him the easy nickname, "Willy," instead of "Baby," which is what everyone else gets. He calls me Zoë and even though I want to tell him my real name, there never seems to be a right time.

Before I understand what's happening, the lines blur. Willy reveals his flesh and his life to me. He's married to a woman twenty years his senior. She lost interest in sex when she hit menopause. Willy did not. They had a Discussion and now that have an Arrangement: He packs a bag on the weekends and stays in hotels and Does What He Needs to Do. I am looking up at the popcorn ceiling while he is talking and touching me. I can feel his fingers, and my body responds. My limbic lobe is silent.

"*Mmm*, that feels nice," I almost whisper, slithering my hips towards him.

Willy is a great big man, so it's always me on top. It's him lying back while I service him. It's me riding the wave of his belly and his orgasm with a blue lace teddy still on, shoved to one side of my crotch. Work feels less like acting with Willy because I like him: He's nice to me and I want him to feel good. I feel terrible about his marriage and grateful that he thinks well of me. He never takes very long to come, so getting him off is never a task, the way it is with some men. If he doesn't go down on me, then I masturbate. Almost all of my clients have watched me get myself off, and I've grown to love an audience. My orgasms are reliable and easy and completely disconnected from my emotions.

When we're not talking or fucking, when Willy's not working, he's busy trying to destroy Lance. This is his Mission, and he has taken it on with gusto. He's discovered that Lance is the owner of the review website. He's contacted the ISP. I only half-listen when he describes the progress he's making. I've moved on and tucked that particular pain away in the back of my brain, alongside other scabbed wounds. I never could think of the correct response when the woman I believed was my best friend didn't invite me to her wedding, or when my angry husband told me I couldn't have grocery money anymore, or when my sister told me, "I wouldn't piss on you if you fell off the earth in a ball of flames." Okay. Okay, okay. In the scope of my universe, Lance's review doesn't really matter. I stay away from that site, and there are enough other clients that I am able to believe he was just a singular asshole. It matters to Willy, though, so I profess gratitude.

What I am grateful for, and what catches me entirely off guard, is that this man seems to actually give a shit about the entire chaotic train wreck that is my life. I don't understand this, when all I want to do is avoid or deny or run away from the whole mess. I don't feel smart enough to puzzle it all out.

It's Saturday at the Marriott. My family believes I am tending bar, but I am here with Willy. I lie on the big bed on my stomach while he sits naked at a desk using his laptop. He wants to show me something online. My head on my crossed arms is level with Willy's chair. I glimpse a hole where his penis should be. The fat around his groin has asexualized him. *Mind bleach, mind bleach, mind bleach*, I pray. But now I know: that at a certain weight, in certain positions, some men turn into temporary eunuchs. I'm sorry about the things I am learning about men: that they will cheat on their wives and they will leave shit smeared on the toilet seat. I never wanted to know these things.

A huge part of my job is overlooking ugly facts. I especially overlook my own ugliness. Every day I run away from my own family and husband and life and fuck men I'll never see again. I carefully ignore the fact that I have more sympathy for strangers whose names and faces I will forget, than for myself; that I show more tenderness to a client like Willy than to my own husband.

It becomes easy to break my own rules and talk to Willy.

"I want to leave my husband . . . he shouts at the kids and he's always angry and tired. I want to go back to college. Actually no, all I really want is to make jewelry and sell it from booths at craft fairs. I want to live alone with my kids and my dog in a cottage in the woods, where we can eat meals at the table together and no one has to walk on eggshells. Is that so much to ask?"

Willy hugs me. "How did I get so lucky?" He has said this to me before.

263

I laugh and roll my eyes. "You're delusional."

But even I like the person Willy likes. Zoë seems to be smart, beautiful, and charming.

I'm shopping at Toys"R"Us. It pleases me to finish holiday shopping before September. My celly rings and I don't recognize the number. "Dates" don't get my number without first providing their own; this is my feeble attempt to keep this gig organized. I wedge a bright yellow Tonka truck against my hip and say, "Hello?"

"Is this Zoë?"

"Who is this?"

"I'm calling about your ad," he says.

I don't have an ad running right now.

I hang up and I finish my shopping and check out. As I drive, I make a mental list. *Flag the ad. Call Craigslist.* Mike, one of my sweet regulars, calls me: "There's a fake ad with your picture on Craigslist. I knew it was bullshit. I flagged it for you."

"Oh, thank you, baby." *Always be gracious.*

At home, I leave the colorful plastic bags full of toys in the back of my truck and rush inside to check the online bulletin board.

Lance has posted an advertisement, with a photo of me and my phone number. *Fuck, why didn't I change my number?* It's ridiculous and obviously fake because the text is unflattering: "Come see the shit stains in my underwear." Again, the breathlessness, the heat in my cheeks, the ringing in my ears, the fist in my stomach. *Fucking, fucking bastard!* This time I do cry, which helps me convince the Craigslist staff, who repeatedly explain that they're an operation of two people and they can't just remove the posting, that I really am an innocent party.

I call my cell phone provider and change the number, and then call Willy and let him know what's happened. He has already seen the ad and flagged it. I consider returning the call of the fellow who responded to the ad. *Really? You want to meet a girl with dirty underwear?*

Willy increases his campaign to close Lance's website down. He tells me about calls to lawyers and claims he's made that the owner of the website is harassing one of his family members, and I ask if maybe he should just let it go.

"No, it's a matter of principle now."

I don't understand what the principle is, but I don't question him. And my gratitude is no longer desultory. He really is good to me, and I really am glad.

I say, "If anything happens between you and your wife, I've got dibs." I don't mean it. We are too different. I wish I could mean it, though. It would be nice to imagine that I could arrange a life with someone who knows my secrets, with a man who thinks he is Lucky to be with me.

It's already dark when I arrive at the Holiday Inn even though it's only 6 PM. As I get out of the truck, I notice that the leaves are changing already.

I click through the clean tiled lobby and pretend that I am Someone Important. The dog hair and dirt that accumulates in the corners of my living room doesn't exist here. The air is not freighted with friction and disappointments. For a few hours, I don't have to protect my son or save my daughter. I can ignore the way I've destroyed the neat suburban life I was supposed to be having. I can use the soap and the towels in the bathroom and know that someone else will clean up my mess.

Tonight I stay with Willy until nine thirty. He knows how I feel about the money, especially from him, now: uncomfortable. So he presses it, folded, into my hand at the last possible moment, as he hugs me goodbye at the door of his hotel room.

Tonight this doesn't happen, and panic sets in as I ride down in the quiet elevator.

What the fuck? I need that money. What does he think this is? Oh, fuck, how am I going to straighten this out, now? Now he probably thinks he never has to pay me again. There is no quiet in my brain. I think about the car insurance, the cell phone bill, the truck payment. *Jesus. Does he think because I let him go down on me, now he doesn't have to pay me?*

The stream of thoughts begins to splinter into little creeks: *I . . . what the . . . goddamn . . . he better . . .*

Oh fuck. Okay . . . I have to run an ad tomorrow. Whoever responds, I'm going to have to see them. I hate the brick of desperation settling into my belly.

I'm through the vestibule, out into the sharp blue night. It's cold. I jam my hands in my pockets and feel the doubled-up cash.

Oh.

I laugh as I slide into my truck.

Clients start appearing everywhere: at the playground where my son and I are flying kites and in the bagel store where I'm buying coffee. They send me texts: "I saw you running with your dog today." It's disconcerting, and I worry about somehow being discovered in the overlap. On top of that, the constant arguing with my husband flattens me. At last I am able to be completely silent at home, but it feels more like defeat than the triumph I'd imagined. I realize that my resignation is only inches from a coffin. I begin to understand that leaving is no longer a choice. I've been telling my husband for years how much I hate Long Island. I've signed leases on other apartments far away and then panicked at the last minute and lost deposits. *Why not try one more time?* I have nothing left to lose.

Willy and I eat dinner at a Mexican restaurant before we return to his hotel room. We shower together after sex, and I dress to return home.

"Why don't you just leave him?" Willy's remark is offhand. I am standing in front of an empty bureau, facing a mirror, pushing my earring through my earlobe.

Why don't I just leave him? The loop of excuses tumbles forth: *I don't have enough money. I certainly don't have enough money to survive on Long Island . . . I don't quite trust my income . . . If I move far away from my husband, to a less-expensive area, how will our son see his father? If I move far away from my husband, I'll be the bad guy.*

I'll be the bad guy? Who am I kidding? I already am the bad guy. I don't deserve to be happy.

Willy is flipping through news channels on the television. Maybe he doesn't think his question requires an answer.

I don't deserve to be happy? Whoa. That feels like a Big New Thought.

I am like an amoeba: I have no hard edges. If I ever did know who I was, I don't know. Wife, Mother, Barmaid, Student, Secretary: I ruined all of those roles. This is all I have now, and unless I want to do this forever, I had better figure out what the hell is next.

"I don't know . . . Am I seeing you on Monday?"

I sneak away, pretending to visit an old school friend for a weekend. Instead I drive to my childhood town and sign a lease on a two-bedroom apartment and sleep there alone on an air mattress for two days. I sit in silence on the top stair and I am giddy with the terrible, wonderful thing I am doing. It is so nice to take a full breath. I hadn't understood how long I'd been gasping.

Willy helps me the next week. We drive three hours with a hundred-dollar mattress from the Salvation Army store in the back of his truck. He stocks my refrigerator. He buys me a microwave and a laptop and pays my car insurance. My gratitude blooms when I realize that I am the one who is Lucky. I can't see any watery mirage of myself, waving from the future; but hopefully I will resemble the funny, smart, graceful girl that Willy believes in.

FELICITY HODGEMAN was born on Long Island and raised herself between there and various New England locations. Her parents collected divorces (five between the two of them), which she then used as an excuse for her inability to commit to anyone. Her mom wanted to be a single mother to children without opinions and her father expected the children to obey without question, even when that included doing things that children should not have been doing. She has moved over thirty times and is highly resistant to unpacking her storage unit. She has not paid rent since 1999. She's been a recreation therapist, a barmaid, a secretary, a grant writer, a reading tutor, and a wholesale fish delivery driver. Currently, she is busy having a happy childhood. She likes to run and dance and practice yoga, and get messy making jewelry and paper bowls. She's trying to let go of grief. When she's not staring at a computer screen or crouched over her journal, she can be found hammering jewelry. She is interested in authentic dialogue about the sex industry. Her proudest accomplishment is surviving. This is her first published piece.

THE PERSON I WANTED TO BE

Melissa Petro

The Big Book of Alcoholics Anonymous describes the fellowship as "people who normally would not mix." That's a good way of describing James and me. I was 27 years old, a grad student, bored and curious—just like my ad said. James was in his mid-30s, a little too old and far too normal. He was not the kind of guy who'd approach me in another situation, at least that's what I thought when I saw him. Then again, James and I would never meet in any situation other than this.

I was a Craigslist call girl. James was my first. I had gotten the idea from a friend. "There are ads," she said, "placed by men, looking for"— she raised an eyebrow—"*company*."

That night I got online. It was just as she'd described: SWM seeks non pro, GFE, a little fun. FS. DATY. BBBJ. A lady that speaks GREEK, possibly, a road of possibilities, a chance encounter, no strings attached. For 200 roses, 300 reasons, a generous donation, a happy ending. You can start any day that you like.

On the now-shuttered adult services section of Craigslist—to the left and below where you'd rent an apartment or sell a couch—you could find ads, written in their own coded language, from men and women and everything in between, all of them after one thing: the simple exchange of money for sex.

It was just what I needed. Working full time as a research assistant at a hospital, I struggled to make ends meet. I was single for the first time in adulthood. Besides my ex, who'd been my high school sweetheart, I'd only slept with a handful of people. I shocked us both by calling off the engagement. I was not ready to start a family. I didn't want to grow up. In the weeks and months after our breakup, I slept with anyone who'd have me—most of my male classmates and some of the women—until I'd alienated many of the people who had once been my friends. I was guilt-ridden. I was alone.

It was a Tuesday night after class, and I'd had three or four drinks at the bar. It was one of those nights where no matter how much I drank, I couldn't get drunk. No one would talk to me either; I went home alone, pitiful and unsafe in my own skin. But not twenty minutes later, I found myself in a yellow cab traveling south down the West Side Highway, on my way to meet a man who called himself James.

How I got to James is something of a blur. I remember answering James's ad, getting directions, getting dressed, hailing a cab. I had his phone number and address written on a scrap of paper I held in my hand. I remember the cab stopping at an intersection, our green light, and two bright white lights—headlights—coming straight at me.

When the other car made impact, we spun. The taxi was facing the opposite direction when it finally stopped. I can still remember the quiet, the pause.

The paramedics said, "Don't move." But I wasn't hurt. I scanned my body as if it were someone else's, but I felt nothing.

"Really," I told them, "I'm not hurt. Not one bump or scratch." The driver lay slumped over the steering wheel.

"Do you have anyone to call?" the paramedic asked. I shook my head. "No family? No friends?"

I looked down at the scrap of paper still in my hand. I called James.

When James arrived, I saw that he was not bad-looking. Irish American, deep blue eyes. He was not my type, exactly—he had a beer gut and was wearing a Red Sox sweatshirt and a matching baseball hat—but he was a normal guy. As James helped me fill out the police report, I couldn't stop laughing. I felt giddy. I had just survived a near-fatal accident without so much as a scratch. This was so surreal.

"She'll feel it," one paramedic said to the other, "when the vodka wears off."

Back at James's place, I made myself comfortable. His home was nice in a Crate & Barrel sort of way. I sat down on his micro suede sectional and slipped off my heels. From the kitchen, he offered me wine. I asked him what he did for a living.

"I own a sports bar on the Upper East Side."

"You're not having one?" I asked, as he reappeared with one glass.

"I don't drink."

"You own a bar and you don't drink?"

"It's complicated," he said.

Whatever, I thought. *Enough with the small talk.* I drained the glass and returned it to its coaster. As soon as he sat next to me, I straddled his lap. *This is fun, I told myself. This is no big deal.*

Sex for money is not the same as casual sex. When you're getting paid by someone, you become his employee. I didn't understand this at the time. I set up two dates with another man and met James later that week. I sold the "girlfriend experience," or GFE for short. GFE meant the encounter would feel like a "real" date. I'd show affection for the guy and act as if I were attracted to him. After a drink or two, we'd end up at my place or his. There'd be kissing, petting, cuddling, oral sex, sex.

Normal being what I wanted, normal was what I sold. I began attaching a picture to my e-mail. The picture was taken by my mother a few Christmases back. I'm sitting at my computer, wearing a sweater, a knitted scarf wrapped around my neck. It looked like an author's photo.

In the beginning, I scheduled dates for evenings when I didn't have class. I made the arrangements days ahead of time, e-mailing back and forth multiple times before we'd actually meet. At the time, I might have told you I was screening my clients. The truth is that the e-mails were foreplay. It was part of the thrill. I liked meeting new people. I liked seeing new places. I liked being in apartments nicer than mine. I liked seeing the insides of fancy hotels. I liked getting dressed up. I liked making lots of money, fast. Most of all, I liked having sex. I was aroused by the fantasy of getting paid to do all this. Becoming someone else's fantasy really turned me on.

In my eyes, I was a non-pro—not a professional, not a prostitute. I was different, I thought. I was educated. I was not drug-addicted. I was no victim of trafficking. I didn't have a pimp. I was doing it by choice. I didn't know what I was doing, and I didn't want to know. This wasn't my *career*. I wasn't a *whore*.

"You know," James said one night when we were done, "you don't have to do all that you do." He meant, I understood, my giving a blow job without a condom. "Most girls don't," he said, and then hesitated. "Or they'll charge more."

I'd never given a blow job with a condom, but, having been to the dentist, I knew that latex tasted gross. I said as much to James. "Besides," I went on, "it's safe, right? I don't let you come in my mouth, and if you did, I'd just spit it out."

James looked at me like I was nuts, like he felt sorry for me or like maybe he wanted to help. But he knew he had tried to help enough.

James told me all the time that what I was doing was wrong. He'd say, "You're a good girl, Melissa," and, "Shit, Melissa, you gotta stop." A part of him meant it: the part of him that put potpourri in a little jar next to the sink in the bathroom. The part that had hung the plaque in the hall decorated with geese that read, Bless this house. Part of him felt guilty, ashamed: the part of him that would always offer me the ride home that I'd always refuse.

Then there was the other part of James, the part that contacted me like clockwork nearly every night an hour before he got off work, cryptic texts that would inevitably lead to my coming over, if I didn't already have "plans." This part of him was excited by the very things that brought him shame. I understood it well. It was the part of James I knew best, maybe the only part of him I ever really met. "We can't do this again," he'd say every time just as soon as we'd finished. He'd say, "We gotta stop." And "You gotta stop; this isn't right." He'd make me promise I wasn't doing it with anybody else and so I would, even though we both knew it was a lie.

The fact that there was a "good" part of me—a part of myself that I was proud of, a self-esteem still salvageable—just as there was still a good part in him is what made me appealing to James, which made it all the worse. He was destroying that part of me, he understood, just as he was destroying that part in himself.

Refresh, refresh, refresh. After less than a month I'd started trawling for dates during the daytime at my desk at the hospital. The hospital where I worked had spyware; I didn't care. After just one month of selling sex online, I had already accumulated a literal pile of money—tax-free, in cash—that I kept it in a desk drawer at home. I'd take it out some nights and I'd count it just for fun.

I started squeezing more than one date in a night. I was meeting men before and after class. If the offer was sweet enough, I'd skip class altogether. I spent all my free time sitting at my computer, posting ads, responding to ads, e-mailing back and forth. I became less interested in getting to know them ahead of time and more interested in making it happen, as quickly as possible, so I could get on to the next. Every encounter, I got a little charge. Night after night in the same dress, the same ad, the same scenario—two and a half months into it, it was becoming harder and harder to bill myself as "non-pro." I was crossing boundaries I hadn't even known existed.

I once met a guy who said you can buy anything on Craigslist. He was talking about collectible antique furniture, but I thought it was so funny I wrote it down. You know, ironic. He said it as we took the back stairs up to the fourteenth floor of the granite building where he worked on Fifth Avenue, where in his corner office I gave him a blow job for $200, the city lit up behind him like a Broadway set. When he finished, he opened the top drawer of his desk and brought out an antiseptic towelette, as if he did this all the time, as if I were contagious. I didn't write that part down, but I remember.

Every man I had sex with for money, all the strangers that I met—when it comes to memory, you have no choice what you remember and what you forget. I could tell you the good parts: the nice guys I met, like James, and the fancy restaurants. I could describe the interiors of every luxurious hotel. I could tell you all about the time I was flown to Paris with a man I'd met just the week before. We stayed at the Four Seasons and ate $800 meals. I could tell you the price of the meal, but I can't tell you I enjoyed it. Hell is getting everything you want—everything you think you need and more than what you even asked for—and not enjoying any of it. Getting everything you think will make you happy and still feeling nothing at all.

The longer I sold sex, the less I was the person I wanted to be. After three months of prostitution, I felt raggedy, used-up. I was anxious and afraid. Condoms broke. People stiffed me. The only way to deal with these things, I thought, was to pretend they didn't happen. Trading sex for money, I changed.

James changed too. He began asking me to do things that I wouldn't do—anal sex, sex without a condom—wanting to take bigger and bigger risks. Alternately, he would e-mail me on Thanksgiving, wishing me a happy holiday. He would ask me out on dates. He was a good person—we both were—but we did not know how to be good to each other. We were using each other to get high. I wanted real relationships. For me, prostitution had made that impossible. As much as I wanted to trust James, I could not. The first night we met, when the police asked, he said his name was Chris. But how could I trust anyone? I couldn't trust myself.

No one forced me to have sex for money, and no one could have compelled me to stop. But when the pain became great enough, I became willing. Today, I don't believe in accidents. I believe things happen for a reason. I haven't seen James since I stopped selling sex, months before I stopped drinking and long before I became a teacher. But that is another story entirely.

273

Cyberspace

MELISSA PETRO has written for Salon, the Daily Beast, the Huffington Post, Jezebel, xoJane, *Bitch* magazine, the Frisky, the Fix, Rumpus.net, and elsewhere. She holds an MFA in creative nonfiction and teaches memoir writing for the Gotham Writers' Workshop and the Red Umbrella Project, an organization that provides direct services to individuals with experience in the sex trades.

Johns, Marks, Tricks, and Chickenhawks

THE MAN I GAVE A HAND JOB TO IN WEST HOLLYWOOD WILL SURELY BLOW HIS BRAINS OUT BEFORE I SEE HIM AGAIN

Antonia Crane

We dated for six months. It was the second anniversary of my mom's death.

"I'm done," Adam said and slammed down the phone. His Bill Hicks mug rolled around the floor of my car while I drove in circles. Our afternoon sex CD blasted on repeat: Dead Weather, Elliot Smith, Radiohead. I clutched the steering wheel and eyed the charm bracelet he'd brought back from Ireland. The oval Celtic knots carved into silver beads and the dancing girl holding her fist in the air, I figured, promised steak dinners and wedding dresses, expensive hair products, and a Bellagio suite in Vegas where we'd cuddle under million-count sheets. The charm bracelet meant cozy mornings in his Craftsman house on the hill, where I would soon live with him and his three orange cats. Underneath his comedy act was nails and glass. He never wanted to spend the entire night with me, so I acquired a taste for panic and filled in the blanks. He couldn't mean *done* done. I called him again. Voicemail. Mom was gone, and so was he.

I wanted a different ending. I e-mailed him. I drove by his house. When I saw his black Kia parked in the driveway, I hyperventilated and put my head between my legs, then rolled down my window and spat on the sidewalk. Pedestrians watched me nervously, so I stared intently on a billboard advertisement for a Brazilian blowout.

I texted him: *I miss you.*

275

He replied: *I don't want to engage.*

Even though texting is engaging. Asshole. I asked yogafied hipsters in line at Nature Mart why he didn't love me. "He's just not that into you," they said, their feathered earrings quivering.

Amazon delivered books on grief and love addiction and wheat grass diets. *Men Are From Mars, Women Are From Venus* appeared in my mailbox. After nearly twenty years of stripping, I was classically trained to let men slide over me and wash away. But Adam stuck. He had taken me to shows and dinners. We'd held hands in the rain. "You melt the numb," I told him. I mailed him chicory coffee from New Orleans and got a spray tan. I let my hair fall in greasy, tangled strands. My fingernails grew until they bent in half and ripped off. I stopped showering. I knew he would bang the first girl he bumped into, and photos of them smirking would be plastered all over the Internet any second. I watched Comedy Central and searched for signs of her in his gestures.

For one, he's not a pacer onstage. And he was pacing. He liked to fester in his own hostile juices, stand his ground or sit perched on a tall, wooden stool. But he was perky. His new girl put pep in his step. While I mouthed his jokes, I imagined plucking his heart from his chest and chewing on the soft parts he never showed me. If the stringy bits got stuck in my teeth, I'd toss them under his avocado tree and call the neighborhood dogs to finish the job. I'd watch with wet lips while dogs sucked the tender juice, smear *I'm done* on the sidewalk in his blood. I'd stab his car tire with a steel cleaver, leave the blade in to make my point. Instead, I tossed the charm bracelet in the trashcan at EZ Lube and gave the saddest man in West Hollywood a hand job for a couple greenbacks.

I wasn't in the mood. But when I'm not in the mood, my sensual massage clients can't get enough of me. Whenever I'm broke and need the cash, I wait by the phone for clients to book appointments, but there's nothing but crickets. When I'm anxious and lonely, my phone rings nonstop. My dentist called to confirm my root canal appointment. AT&T called to upgrade my cable to the gold package.

My clients sensed my suffering and wanted to splash around in it for a fifty-minute hour, pulled by the tide of my self-pity.

Billy, my client, lived in an ugly apartment complex on a street known for ritzy breakfast joints and valet parking. On his block, waxy magnolia trees and Spanish bungalows wore their hundred-year-old yellow paint like a Christmas doily. Nearly out of massage oil and half an hour late, I showed up and parked at a meter.

A tall, slim white guy in khaki shorts waved from a balcony where ivy dripped over the ledge. Wine glass in hand, he buzzed me in, then met me in the lobby. He could've been anywhere between 25 and 45, blond and freckled. Nothing like Adam, who was tan with electric olive eyes and soft, chubby fingers. "Do you want to ride the elevator or take the stairs?" Billy asked. I looked down at my shoes. They were over six inches high.

"Elevator." The button lit up when he pushed it. We waited a couple more minutes.

"The stairs are faster," he said. The elevator arrived. We stepped inside. I've been to many apartment buildings like Billy's in Los Angeles, with too many smells from too many kitchens: eggs and Rice-A-Roni. Coffee and moldy tortillas. Billy's apartment was at the end of a hall that had a window overlooking an empty concrete court-yard. It was big for one person, twice the size of my one-bedroom in Silverlake. I put my purse on a glass table. He leaned into me. He tucked his head in the space between my chin and collarbone. His hair was soft and fine. Nothing like Adam's tangled brown curls I loved to pull. Billy's breath was warm wine. He'd moved into my skin, like he belonged there.

"Do you live alone?" I asked. He didn't move. He rocked slightly. I touched his clean neck.

"I have a daughter," he said.

"Where is she?"

"Albuquerque." His eyes were light blue marbles with blond lashes. I hoped he couldn't tell I hadn't showered.

"Is that where you're from?" This was the easy chatter of the heavy-hearted; the cheerful smokescreen hiding the fact that I didn't want to be there but was too sad not to be. At least half of him didn't want me there either. Cheering crowd noises echoed from the next room.

"I'm from New York," he said.

"Why'd you move to L.A.?" He stood up straight and picked up a glass that still had red wine in it. He drank the rest.

"I got a job on a horrible reality TV show." He watched me remove my jacket and throw it on the table next to my purse and keys, then he handed me some twenties, which I counted casually and shoved into my purse. Two hundred.

More wine glasses occupied tidy white surfaces, all with puddles of dried red blood at the bottom. Computer screens glowed and blinked. Next to a bookcase, the New York Giants played on a widescreen TV. Billy hugged me. Like I was the last human on Earth. Then he led me down a slim hallway where elegant black-and-white photos adorned the walls. "Did you take these?" I asked.

"These two." He pointed to a picture of a woman on a beach with black hair blowing in the wind behind her as she stared out ahead; the other one was of the ocean, titled *Catalina*. They were framed tastefully and moved together like a symphony.

"Is that what you do?"

"Not anymore." He'd accepted the reality TV show paycheck but what he really wanted to do was take moody photographs. It was the collective, soul-sucking L.A. tragedy.

A television lit the room where he took me. He wasn't a candle man. The younger guys aren't into candles. He was probably under 40. His bed was huge with soft, white Egyptian sheets, a neat, blond wooden bed frame, a white comforter, and expensive feather pillows to cushion the blow of profound disappointment. My faded blue bedding still smelled like Adam: patchouli and Nicorette gum.

Billy watched me undress. He took off his pants and kept on wrinkled white boxers. Then he fell backwards on the bed, where I massaged his back, then his cock, but no matter what I did, I couldn't get him hard. "Been drinking?" I asked. He wanted to eat my pussy, so I let him for a couple minutes while the huge TV submitted sounds of a baseball game, its bluster of horns and muffled cheers.

I worried that I tasted like Depo-Provera, the birth control I'd been taking for two months. He looked up and said, "You just got sad. What happened?"

"I went on birth control for someone I'm not with anymore. It makes me bleed black and I hope you can't taste it."

"I just want you here," Billy said. I wanted to ask him why. But the question was too personal. This was the first time he'd met me. He'd never know my real name. I massaged him with the last of my oil and lay my whole body on top of his. I ran my greasy fingers through his soft hair. My lips touched his earlobe. "It's okay," I whispered.

"It happens to everyone in L.A."

ANTONIA CRANE is the only person from Humboldt County who doesn't smoke weed. She comes from a family of lawyers and paralegals, carpenters and beekeepers, basically hillbillies with college degrees. The men in her family build their own homes, restore boats, and do their own plumbing. The women in her family are over-achieving, award-winning public speakers and past valedictorians who never cook anything from a box or a can. Antonia's first job was acting in commercials in Bombay, India, when she was a lost and rebellious Rotary exchange student at age 15. Later, she delivered balloons to kids in hospitals dressed as Miss Piggy, but she has also cleaned houses for swimsuit models and personally assisted Hollywood types. She has catered, bartended, and dressed as a sexy Santa for a surf company's Christmas party. She migrated to San Francisco in the '90s, where she sang karaoke at the Mint on Market Street and was chosen to front the punk band Dirt Box for many years. A rebel rouser, she was part of the union effort that resulted in SEIU Local 790: The Exotic Dancers Alliance, and she stripped her way through both Mills College and Antioch University. Her writing has appeared in *The Heroin Chronicles* (edited by Jerry Stahl), the Rumpus, *The Los Angeles Review*, *Black Clock*, *Slake*, *PANK*, *ZYZZYVA*, and elsewhere. She teaches photography to high school students and creative writing to incarcerated teenagers in Los Angeles.

She's writing a memoir about the sex industry and her mother's illness, SPENT. She loves teaching and long-distance running and is convinced that God lives at the top of Griffith Park mountain. More than anything, she wants to make a living writing stories that will impact lives, stories that are not allowed to be told by women, and stories that echo in the bones and heart.

Johns, Marks, Tricks, and Chickenhawks

DIRTY TRICKS & HAPPY ENDINGS

Dominick

Early in 2004, I embarked on a career as a full-time escort in New York *City. Calls took me all over the greater metropolitan area, four of five bor-oughs, the suburbs of Long Island, Westchester County, Northern New Jersey, and Connecticut. I marketed myself as a bisexual Italian stud—a "packin' Long Island Guido." It was a fantasy I felt capable of fulfilling, at least for an hour at a time. Though I received some calls from women and married couples, the vast majority of the calls I took were from men—young, old, gay, bi, down-low, closeted, partnered, married, travelers in hotels, and locals.*

I was pushing 40 when I started escorting. I felt like an old bull in a stable full of bucks. I told myself I'd succeed because there were too many boys trying to do a man's job—and to a large extent, that proved to be true. My experience and business acumen trumped their fleeting glow. I knew my appeal in New York's vast meat market and honed my pitch accordingly. I made my terms clear. I listened to my clients, even when they themselves were barely able to express their desires. I kept a spreadsheet to manage logistics (rate, location, preferences) and a diary to record my impressions. I showed up on time, unlike some younger guys who'd keep clients waiting. Most impor-tantly, I delivered the goods, unlike some of the sketchier hustlers, or certain porn stars, who would flex and pose while watching the clock.

What follow are accounts culled from my diaries—two highlights, and one of the low points of my career. You'll note various references to screen names—it was not long ago that AOL was a robust social network and online platform. I advertised using nothing more than a suggestive AOL profile, and I sat in the "NYC Companions" chat room to make contact with prospective clients.

Today, what I most vividly recall of my immersion in sex work isn't the war story, or the occasional sexual rapture—nor is it the grind, nor the twilight shift, nor the clouded conscience, nor the cash validation—it's a feeling of weary fulfillment from a good job done well. I did the world some good in those days, or at least I did no harm. How many men can say the same of how they earned their living during the same period? You derivatives traders? You scam artists? You war profiteers? You vulture capitalists? I provided intimate touch and a sincere measure of love to my clients, even the nightmares. Hell, the Bible instructs us to "Love thy Neighbor," so I did, one at a time, for an hour or two at a time. So along with these glimpses into my former self, I offer the reader that one pure biblical injunction, modified to suit my heart: Love whoever you can, however you can, whenever you can, whatever the circumstances, whatever the range and accuracy of your love gun. Don't let anyone else's preconceptions of how to love keep you from firing.

- **Client Name: Adam / Location: Ulster, NY**
  Date: February 2004

I was initially suspicious about this guy, as it sounded too good to be true. A young guy, who lives in his own house upstate, laying out so much green to bring up New York City hustlers? But I'd gotten an IM from a certain "XxXHungCubano" who vouched for him. Apparently, the guy had asked him to recruit hung white tops. XxXHungCubano told me that this guy was a regular, a good guy who likes to have different types of big dick and muscle. I contacted him, and he proposed I come up on the train right away for an overnight.

Adam picks me up at the train station in a huge white vintage Cadillac El Dorado. He takes me back to a simple, comfortable house in a nice neighborhood, where he lives with five cats. He has this bachelor existence in the house his parents raised him in. It's genteel and well maintained and frozen in time. There's a quaint country charm,

282

and a lot of Nixon memorabilia—his dad clearly loved that man. Adam has done little to change the décor of the house, so the overall vibe is being on a sitcom stage set.

We get to know each other with a little chat, and then watch a little TV together, while Adam smokes from a bong. One of the programs we watch is *Forensic Files* on the Discovery Channel; he expresses an intense fascination with the methods of forensic investigators. I must have been getting a little secondhand pot paranoia, because I start to ruminate that maybe he had done away with his parents, and that story about them moving to Delray Beach was a cover-up. But I soon got over it. After the chat and TV, he proposes we shower. I'm all for that, since I suspect I stink like an animal at this point, after the long train ride in a stuffy car.

I'm offered a fresh towel and a new bar of soap. I undress and lay my clothes out on a laundry rack Adam has provided. He approaches to assess the goods. He's a boyish 27, by no means unattractive, with a frat boy vibe and a country-strong but doughy physique—the result of eating too much comfort food in diners.

I come out of the shower, and we get it started. Adam's submissive side comes out—he likes to be put on his knees, force-fed cock, and he likes his "pussy" teased. I don't like referring to the anus as a "pussy," so I substitute my favorite endearment, "fuckhole." I get very verbal with him, whispering my demands to him: "Take that cock down your throat, you dick whore. Open your mouth, so I can spit in it and get it all slick for my cock. I'm gonna grab you by your neck and skull-fuck you. You want that? Huh, pussy boy? Beg me for it." He loves it.

We take it up to the bedroom. Adam's a demanding and ener-getic submissive, goading me into ever-more dominant behavior. Now and then one of the cats comes into the room and swipes at me while I, the provider, am fucking the cat's provider. What can I do? I joke that I didn't know it was going to be a three-way, and I pet the cat while fucking away. I come, as instructed, into his open mouth. He's kneeling on the floor and spills his own little seed puddle onto the carpet. The next morning, he wakes up hungry for more. He comes again on the carpet. I have a feeling that carpet sees lots of action.

We head out for a delicious country breakfast of steak and eggs. Adam tells me over breakfast he was the town alderman for a term, the youngest ever elected. He ran on the Republican slate. He works as an undertaker in the town's funeral home. We stop at the Target—they're having a sale on Brawny paper towels—and then he drops me off at the Amtrak station.

....

EPILOGUE:

Since this first meeting back in 2004, I have seen Adam at least once a month, sometimes upstate, and sometimes in the city. I've gotten to know him and find him a kind and likable person, if a bit of a stoner. His political views have evolved considerably since I've known him. He lives in a small town, which has its advantages and its limitations. One of which is he's just not finding any dick up there. He also dwells in the realm of the aged, dying, and dead. He drives around his depressed hometown in his vintage Caddy waiting for calls that someone else has kicked off—a country grim reaper. So it's no small wonder that he likes a vigorous life-affirming fuck every now and then. So that's where I come in, and it's been my pleasure.

- **Client Name: "Revolutions" / Location: Hester Street, Lower East Side Date: May 2004**

His AOL screen name is "MuscleJuicer," and he is an implausibly hot bodybuilder. He starts chatting me up from out of the blue, proposing we work together. He has a three-hour call on the Lower East Side. We set up an appointment.

I get to the building—it's an assisted-living facility for the disabled. MuscleJuicer had told me that I'd need ID to sign in (I'd normally leave my ID at home). I don't see any money on the table. A bad sign, but I'm seduced by the possibility of a big payoff. Three-hour calls don't come along every day.

284

The john, "Revolutions," is a sweaty, heavyset man and an advanced fisting bottom. MuscleJuicer is running late, he says, so we should get started. He's honking up big lines of coke and even has me put coke up his ass. This should have been a big red flag to me, but my morbid fascination kicked in. While being fisted, he likes you to turn your hand around inside his ass. Hence his screen name. (Okay, whatever, butt puppet . . .)

Revolution's lying on the kitchen table. It's wobbly under his weight, he's got his big ass launched upward, and I'm giving him an earnest fisting, with accompanying dirty talk. This despite the unappealing site of his gaping, slick, inflamed, bloody hole, and the rolls of flesh he has to peer over to make eye contact. Now MuscleJuicer calls to say he'd been in a taxi accident and isn't going to make it. This is getting sketchy—I still haven't seen any money. I'm beginning to doubt MuscleJuicer's very existence. I've been there long enough. I tell Revolutions that if he wants to see me get off, he needs to produce some cash. He anxiously cadges together a stack of bills— a couple of twenties with a bunch of fives underneath. Not nearly enough. He says he has to go to the ATM for the rest. So I gather up his wallet and his coke and march him out the door.

Sure enough, when he gets to the ATM, he says he it won't dispense cash "for some reason." I call him out as a scam artist on public assistance who made up MuscleJuicer to lure me here. I'm about to take off with his wallet and his coke. So confronted, this strung-out, clumsy oaf starts fumbling with something in his pocket. He sprays a can of mace at me.

I'm running up Essex Street with red, swelling, irritated eyes. I throw his coke vials down the sewer and run all the way home. This guy has my info—I signed in at the building. I have his ID, Social Security card, benefits card, library card. The camera at that ATM likely has some interesting footage. I call to tell him I'm turning his wallet over to the police. He says it was a big misunderstanding. I leave his wallet at the nearest precinct, taking the money, leaving in its stead a card from Alcoholics Anonymous, with the twelve steps on one side and the serenity prayer on the other. The officer takes my name and number. I don't know whether this guy's going to keep his cool and just be relieved to get his wallet back. Minutes later, I'm home and hoping this whole sorry episode is over.

The phone rings—it's the police. Damn, I am trapped in the plot of a mediocre crime drama! The officer would like my address. I don't give it to her and she understands, but I am unnerved. I detect a note of falseness in her tone. I wonder what Revolutions has told her. I'm counting on him being short on credibility, owing to the fact that he's strung out on coke. I decide to get out of my apartment. I shower and dress and make my way downstairs.

A squad car idles in front of the building. In a panic, I run to the back and jump the fence into a community garden on Twelfth Street. Adrenalin's rushing, and I scramble to my employer's car, which luckily I have parked right on Twelfth. Once in the car, relief floods in. It's 3 AM and I start work at seven thirty that morning. It's clear I won't get any sleep; adrenalin is coursing through my body. So I go to Florent. Luckily, Andy, a very cute guy I know, is working the overnight shift there. I lay out the whole sordid episode over eggs and boudin noir.

EPILOGUE:

Some weeks later I have a heated online exchange with both Muscle-Juicer (who I never did meet) and Revolutions. MuscleJuicer is mad at me for "trying to rob his client," and I'm mad at him for setting me up on a bad scene and then bailing. We hash out our differences. The episode was a spiritual bottoming out for Revolution, who soon after got off drugs, apologized, and gave me a money order for what he owed me.

MuscleJuicer makes vague claims of knowing me, and having mutual friends. It's creepy and frustrating that while he seems to know me, I could not know him. He's careful to maintain his anonymity—I only ever contacted him via e-mail and chat, I don't even have his phone number. I was dumb to accept the call under these circumstances.

Was MuscleJuicer an invention of Revolutions or a down-low hooker who recruited me and it just went really wrong? I stopped caring once I get paid.

- **Client Name: "Cherry" / Location: My place**
  Date: April–December 2005

I don't remember his name, or even his screen name. I'm not sure at this point I ever got it. So I'll call him "Cherry" for reasons that shall become clear. He initially contacted me via IM, and, after negotiating a price and a time, came over to my East Village studio. He was younger than me by about fifteen years, lean, of average height and very fine features. He'd graduated from college the prior year and was working at an interactive marketing shop near Union Square. Since this was his lunch break and it took a while to walk over to my place, we didn't have too much time.

It was immediately apparent that Cherry had little or no experience with gay sex. He was nervous and shy but had willed himself into taking this step with a measure of fortitude. I undressed him—he was a sight to behold. He had a lean, perfectly formed, nearly hairless body, like a Greek *kouros*. He had close-cropped hair and a halo of innocence that made horns sprout from my forehead. I made some gentle advances on him in an attempt to put him at ease, but his rare and fine beauty made me feel like a big clumsy brute.

Cherry was determined to get fucked. He had the tightest little ass this side of adulthood. I asked him if he was sure he wanted to do this, that my goods were not exactly a "starter set." That usually got a laugh, but he was resolute. Clearly, there was no going back for this young man. After a great deal of lube, much coaxing, and many stoic grimaces, I managed to push in. And after about ninety seconds, he shot off. He showered quickly and dressed back into in his new-looking Banana Republic work attire, and was off, back to work. He seemed embarrassed about his performance, so seeking to reassure him, I told him he got a gold star for effort. He gave me a brave smile.

June 24, 2005:

I thought I'd never see Cherry again, but he called. This session went pretty much like the first, but he was a bit more relaxed, a little more game. I tried to lick his pretty ass, but his legs snapped shut so quickly, I nearly lost an ear. So I went through the same steps—lube, push, grimace, repeat; this time he lasted a bit longer, like four minutes. Progress!

September 21, 2005:

Cherry's back at my door! Still reserved, but a little less so. Still a little rigid under me, with his courageous grimace and that glazed stoic expression he gets in his eyes. A thought struck me—was Cherry damaged goods? Was this an attempt on his part to work through a past molestation? I experienced a true ethical crisis—maybe this is wrong? Still waters run deep and all. My dilemma had no effect on my cock however, which was rock solid inside his little ass. We made it to about ten minutes, after which Cherry sat at my kitchen table and ate the sandwich he'd brought with him in a lunch bag. I gave him some lemonade. He talked a little about his job, where he had started just before he first came to see me. He has some gay colleagues, and they were beginning to seek each other out and socialize. He's coming out of his shell!

December 15, 2005:

Cherry called me from his company's holiday party, which was held at Gotham Bar & Grill, a large, noisy venue. I could barely hear him over the din, and he sounded like he'd had a few cocktails. I thought I could hear him laughing with some friends or colleagues, who seemed to be egging him on. I yelled for him to come on over. This was unusual, since all of his past visits had been arranged well in advance and on his lunch break.

From the minute he walked in, Cherry looked like he was in an erotic trance. He pressed his whole being into me and gave me a passionate deep kiss—not our first kiss, but definitely the first with juice. He guided me as much as I guided him. It was astounding, and this time *I* was the one who had to hold back from coming too soon. I fucked that pretty little ass every which way, starting in our usual position, with Cherry on his back. Then he got on his hands and knees for doggie—a first! Before I went back in, I jammed my tongue into his little hole—no objections this time—and it was a taste of heaven. After a little doggie, we went into a sideways spoon-fuck, so I could kiss him with my musky tongue. Then the little fucker twirled himself back onto his back, at which point I picked him up, still impaled on my dick, and walked him over to the kitchen table. I really banged his hole out there, and he reached back, grabbed on to the warm steam pipe, and started fucking right back at me. Cherry the stoic, a possible victim of molestation, had transformed into a clamoring little butt monkey! At one point, I grabbed his head in both hands and forced him to look into my eyes while I found a stroke he liked. He looked back at me and gave me a consensual nod and the dirtiest little smirk. His climax triggered mine.

Through these four sessions, I had taken on the role of patient and encouraging teacher with Cherry, offering gold stars for each milestone. At first, I could hardly believe my good fortune that such an adorable young guy had crossed my threshold. But my enthusiasm was always tempered by an overbearing sense of responsibility, I had to convey the joy and the beauty of sex with every gesture, in every moment. After lesson four, as we lay there glued together by his wad, I realized my work was done. I said: "You just graduated." Cherry replied with one of his shy laughs.

....
EPILOGUE:

It proved to be true. I never heard from Cherry again, nor did I ever seek him out. All these years later, I like to picture Cherry having really raucous and funny sex, with boys who deserve him, with a wide smile replacing that tight grimace. I'd like Cherry to know that under other circumstances, I'd have paid him for a taste of his sweet heaven. So here's to Cherry, my star pupil and my favorite sweet, pulpy, tangy, juicy little drupe.

DOMINICK is a Brooklyn-born Italian. As an awkward, disconnected teen, his dream of being an American gigolo was sparked by Blondie's driving, siren theme song from that movie he was too young to see. He spent his 20s as the kept boy to an aristocratic British decorator of some renown. Sugar daddy in tow, Dominick traveled throughout Europe, visiting palaces and gardens, eating and drinking at the finest tables. In the wake of his sugar daddy's alcohol-fueled death, he was left a modest fortune that fueled his own addiction. In recovery, he embarked on a career as a full-time escort—an effort to redeem his gigolo illusion, and a shot at living out the questionable decade we now know as "the Noughties" underground. He kept a diary and an excel spreadsheet, and after a successful run, he retired from escorting to take a management position. Dominick now mines his experience at blog.rentboy.com for their audience of thirty thousand subscribers, offering escorts and clients alike advice on a wide range of topics. He's a frequent presence at the Red Umbrella Diaries, has appeared on Dan Savage's podcast, and is a guest contributor to Savage's beloved "Savage Love" column. He writes from his Hell's Kitchen co-op, which he shares with his very understanding boyfriend and a devious Abyssinian.

Johns, Marks, Tricks, and Chickenhawks

ANIMAL PLANET BOB

Lilycat

"He says he is calling us to work on a story for a children's book. He is just weird. I don't want to take the call. You want to talk to him?" asked one of my coworkers.

Seeing that we were working at a sex line, it was weird that he was calling us for that reason. I liked him and his weirdness, so I was willing to take his calls.

He was a regular customer, who went by the sex-caller fallback name of Bob. Even if the operators would give a different name off the credit cards of the callers as they hooked us up with them, when they got on the phone with us, so many of them used the name Bob. This Bob was very special and with a specific very odd request.

This is how a typical call with Bob would go down: He would have you choose to be an animal from a selection of animals: Mary Moose, Harriet Horse, Betty Bear, and another animal that I can no longer remember. Each of these animals would have a certain voice he wanted you to talk in: Mary Moose was a bit like Bullwinkle, but softer and sexier; Harriet Horse was a bit like Mr. Ed with nagging, but also softer and sexier; and Betty Bear was a bit like Marlene Dietrich on a really bad day with a bit of a growl.

He would have you describe how the animal looked and give details down to the claws and teeth. He would play the part of a tree, bush, or cactus, and have you talk about nibbling, clawing at, and eating him.

I figure this was the only way a very shy man, who could only use symbolism and metaphors to talk about sex and watched too much *Animal Planet*, could ask for a verbal blowjob. It was a bit sad; but since it was different from the normal "Oh God, baby, give it to me harder"–type chat we did constantly, and it was sort like acting in a cartoon, I personally liked talking to this Bob.

I did like talking to Bob, until the day the fantasy changed. One day he called and announced we would do things a bit different today. He was going to be himself, a human in this verbal fantasy telling.

"And I will be myself!" I said all excitedly thinking Bob had made a breakthrough and would actually ask for a real, literal human-on-human spoken word blow job.

"No, I want you to be Mary Moose," he replied.

Shit, I thought as I explained to him that we weren't allowed to talk about bestiality on the sex phone line.

He said that it wasn't going to be bestiality. But him being a human, me being an animal, and this being a phone sex line, I wasn't sure how it wouldn't go that way, but Bob had proved to be special, so I figured I would talk to him for a bit and see what he had in mind.

So we started off like normal, with me talking in the Mary Moose voice and describing how I looked, with the most attention given to the claws and teeth. Then Bob said what I hadn't expected or wanted to hear, "Now I want you to attack me, shred and eat me all up."

I was *so* not wanting to do a "when animals attack" violent role-play that I used my *Wild Kingdom* knowledge and explained that moose were herbivores and did not eat humans.

A bit disgruntled, he quickly told me just to be Betty Bear then.

So, I began again in the Betty Bear voice explaining in as many long details as I could think of what Betty Bear would look like to try to avoid talking about the mauling. Since there is only so much one can say about how a bear looks, eventually we got to the part where the attack would begin.

"I'm lying on the ground; you come and rip me with your claws," Bob said.

Still trying to avoid things, I explained that a bear wouldn't attack someone lying on the ground; the bear would think he was dead and leave him alone. Bob was so not happy with my knowledge of animal behavioral facts at this point that he said, "What if I came up and hit you in the face?!"

"Well, that would be mean and why would you hit a bear in the face—that is stupid." I tried to start a discussion on manners while in the woods, but Bob didn't want to talk about that. I had no choice—I began to tell him how I would rip at his flesh with my mighty claws and bite bits of him off with my sharp teeth. I had gotten to the part where I had ripped him open and was dinning on his insides when Bob stopped me.

"So, would it hurt?" he timidly asked.

"A bear eating your organs?" I stated, a bit startled by his question. "I guess it would hurt a little."

Bob thanked me, hung up, and never called back.

I hope Bob is out there somewhere, happy and living in the city, not the woods, and definitely not writing a children's book.

LILYCAT was born and raised in New Orleans and educated from kindergarten through college in Catholic schools, but she managed to transcend her God-almighty education. She is a people person . . . No, really, she loves to hear people's life stories . . . It is sort of her vice . . . Well, that and chocolate, booze, adult cartoons, and quality with Mr. Buzzy Happy Love. She often traps people into telling her their life stories on FCC Free Radio. She has stories in *Chemical Lust*, *Whipped*, *More 5 Minute Erotica*, *Surprise*, and *Hos, Hookers, Call Girls, and Rent Boys*, and other places.

Cyberspace

5
The Brothel

NO GIRLS ALLOWED
AT THE MUSTANG RANCH

Veronica Monet

I first heard about the Mustang Ranch, a brothel in Nevada, when I was about 17. I remember feeling curious and jealous. My boyfriend at the time cracked some joke about "the Ranch" to one of his friends, and my face burned with embarrassment because I didn't know what he was talking about. When I asked for details the information I got was pretty sketchy; this was forbidden territory: no girls allowed. I hated that feeling, because if a man could do something, so could a woman. After all, I had cut my teeth on toy trucks and cars, raised live snakes and lizards, target-practiced with all types of guns, and ridden dirt motorcycles. Suddenly, here was another male bastion I wanted to force my way into.

Years passed (more than I care to admit) and I became, in turn, a college graduate, a sober alcoholic/addict, a sex worker, and then a wife. But I still hadn't fulfilled my wish of going everywhere the boys go. I thought being a sex worker might solve some of my angst, but working in the sex industry just isn't the same as playing in it. The former is about pleasing others while the latter is about having it your way. I wanted to find out for myself. So when my husband asked, "What do you want for your birthday?" I didn't have to give it another thought.

Why hadn't I tried to fulfill this wish on my own? I once walked across the street from my apartment when I lived in the Tenderloin in San Francisco and knocked on the door to a massage parlor. A woman peered through a small crack she made with the door and asked what I wanted in a gruff voice. When I said I wanted a massage, she said, "We're closed." "What's the matter? Don't you see women?" I demanded. "Sure we do," she replied as she slammed the door in my face.

I called the Mustang Ranch in advance to see if they would accept female customers. There was no sense in driving all the way to Nevada just to get another door slammed in my face. It turned out that they only saw women with their male partners. My only solution was to get a male escort into "men-only country." It did get me in, but not necessarily with open arms.

We drove to Reno and then farther into the desert. It was dark and at first seemed very desolate, but we soon saw the famous Christmas lights I had heard about. Three plain one-story buildings stood in a row surrounded by chain link fences and decorated with those lights. The middle building sported a small sign proclaiming The World Famous Mustang Ranch, and my stomach got a little upset from nervousness and excitement.

My husband and I walked up to the building on the right called the Old Bridge Ranch. We rang the bell and the madam opened the door with a smile on her face. She stopped us before we went in to ask us what we wanted. I had an urge to say, "How about a haircut?" but I resisted the temptation and let my husband tell her we wanted to "party with a girl." The madam then welcomed us in and escorted us to a private room where we were asked to wait for the girls who would be willing to "party with a couple." I wondered why we didn't get to pick our girl from the traditional lineup. One of the women caught my eye. She was cute and reminded me of Shirley MacLaine in *Irma La Douce*. She also seemed very friendly and fun. But I still wanted to "shop," so we went off to the Original Mustang Ranch next door.

We rang the bell on the gate and this madam came to the door with something less than a smile. I saw the women start to form a lineup, but as we headed up the sidewalk to the door, they all scattered like they had seen a ghost. The madam suspiciously asked what we wanted. When we said sex, she quickly had a big security guard escort us into a room. I protested that I wanted to see the bar and pick a girl from the lineup, but this husky guard said they couldn't allow that since "non-working women" aren't allowed in the bar. At this point I wanted to go back home to San Francisco, where queers like me aren't treated like we have a disease. While we interviewed women in the private room, I was able to talk one of the women into getting me a water and giving me a tour of the bar after all. There wasn't that much to see, but it was the principle of it all. I wanted to be treated like one of the boys. And if I couldn't get a lineup like the guys do, just because some of the girls think that eating pussy is gross, at least I could walk through the joint like a real customer instead of getting shoved behind closed doors like some criminal. In the interest of continuing my shopping spree, we finished our interviews of the available women and headed to the third and last house.

The Mustang Ranch No. 2 didn't impress me. Most of the women weren't what I had in mind, and the reception was pretty cold. I got a couple sneers from some of the "working women" in all three of the houses. I'd say homophobia is alive and well in the desert. We eventually went back to the Old Bridge Ranch and picked the friendly girl whom I had noticed the first time around. She was available and talked me out of $400. I didn't know this at the time, but the house had microphones installed in all the girl's rooms so that management can eavesdrop on the financial negotiations (I hope this is all they listen to). After she took my money, she left the room to give the house its half and returned with a couple of non-alcoholic drinks for us.

She began the session by dancing seductively. I love that. Then she began to undress me. When she was finished, she jumped in the middle of us and laid back waiting for our "attack." We obliged enthusiastically. As the three of us worked our way through many of the positions three people can assume in bed together, my husband came, but I still wasn't quite there. When I complained, our hostess got a determined look on her face and pulled out a vibrator and a large double-headed dildo. I was lying on my back with my head in my

299

husband's lap, so I'm not sure exactly what she did to me with those implements. But I am sure the people having drinks in the front lobby heard me have a great time at least twice.

I stood up with shaky legs, and the three of us had a group shower. As we were dressing, I asked her how she liked working at the brothel. She said it was all right, but the house charged the girls for everything, including ten dollars for laundry! She "partied" and lived in this room for weeks at a time while the house restricted her comings and goings and guests. It started to sound like prison. I wanted to take her to a COYOTE (Call Off Your Old Tired Ethics, a San Francisco prostitutes' rights activist group) meeting and liberate her. I was sure I'd be even less welcome if management knew I was a member of COYOTE. As she escorted us to the door, she hugged us and patted our butts goodbye. I left satisfied and a little sad to think she was sharing so much of her earnings with the house.

My urge to rescue this woman was eventually replaced with an increased determination to continue my efforts to educate people about the abridgment of sex workers' rights. I also came away with the conviction that the service prostitutes offer is worth every penny charged. Being a customer for one evening gave me a deep appreciation for what a wonderful service prostitution is. I hope it will always be available legally and in settings that do not oppress, degrade, or shame the prostitute. Prostitutes should be revered and respected as the great healers, therapists, and entertainers they are.

Yes, working in the sex industry is different from being a customer: Yes it is. I couldn't believe how involved in the fantasy I became as a customer. I felt affection for the woman I just spent an hour with, even though I knew it was just business for her. I felt that she was special, and I had a hard time accepting that we were just another appointment to her. But it didn't make any difference in the end. If I had wanted emotional involvement, I would have placed a personal ad. I sought out a prostitute precisely because I didn't want to risk emotional involvement—and it was erotic, fun, exciting, and fulfilling. She was the one in charge of the hour we spent together. And that was great—to relax and turn everything over to a professional. It's delightful to pay for what you want and then let someone else orchestrate it for you. After all, we pay professionals to do what they are good at. And she, like me and all the other whores I know, is very good at what she does. That's why we get paid.

VERONICA MONET, ACS, CAM, was born in a small rural community in Eastern Oregon to parents who were members of a conservative Christian cult. She did not attend public school until she pursued and obtained her psychology degree at Oregon State University. Desiring to be an author at age eight, she entered a writing competition, which she did not win. However, her dream of being an author persisted and she freelanced many articles long before there were blogs. Although she spent seven years in corporate jobs after graduating from college, she eventually entered the sex industry as a high-end escort. Her career as an escort spanned fourteen years, during which she was also married with stepchildren. When she retired from escorting in 2004, she realized her childhood dream to become a published author when *Sex Secrets of Escorts* was published by Penguin. She has appeared on every national network as well as CNN, A&E, FOX, WE, the Playboy Channel, and in *The New York Times.* Today, she has a private practice in Northern California assisting couples to rebirth their relationships. Find out more at TheShameFreeZone.com.

SID

LZ Hansen

"Lizzy, your eight o'clock is here. Room three. Hurry!" Ingrid yelled from the office.

I'd been lounging in the living room with the other women. I stubbed my cigarette out and pulled myself up from the couch.

"On my way up now!" I yelled back.

I had been prepared for Sidney Glick, a client of the house who favored domme sessions. We had never met. Ingrid had directed him to me as I was the only girl on schedule who didn't mind doing dominance sessions. I lunged up the stairs two at a time in my six-inch heels to the third floor. I knocked on the door and walked in, morphing into Mistress.

"Hello, Sidney," I began softly. "You'll call me Mistress. You will only look at me when I allow it." Sidney was a small unassuming gray-haired man in his 60s. He had developed a slight hunch from years of hard work, and frail bony arms hung loosely by his side. It was easier for him to look at the ground as his neck had stiffened, but he lifted his head with a strain, and his blue eyes smiled.

"Sidney, what can I do for you tonight?" That was my opening line. I tried my best to act sexy, superior, and as stern as I possibly could. I also wanted to obtain as much information as I could from Sid, so that I could turn myself into exactly what he wanted.

"I'd like it if you could use the cuffs to restrain my arms behind my back. I-I-I'd like to be b-b-b-blindfolded." His mouth watered, his eyes got glassy, and he rubbed his lips together.

"So you want me to restrain you?" I asked with some hesitation. "And blindfold you. Then what?"

"Well . . . if you c-c-could . . ."

I was not a professional domme. I was a whore. But when a client called requesting a light dominance session, there was no reason to send him away. I had been trained by a lifestyle domme years ago. She had given me a starter kit of corsets, whips, paddles, handcuffs, and enough education on how to give good humiliation, fantasy, and enemas. It was a welcome break in a day of fucking and sucking. I had done seven sessions yesterday; my body ached from staying in awkward positions for long periods. If I could make money and not fuck for an hour, I was thrilled.

Sid sat hands in his lap, and head bowed, on the edge of the bed.

"Talk to me," I ordered.

"Well um err . . . can I look at you, Mistress?" Sid stuttered.

"Yes." I smiled. I must stop smiling.

"Oh, you r-r-really are a pretty one, aren't you?"

I stood in my six-inch-heeled black-patent-leather thigh-high boots, my legs spread a foot apart. Hands fisted and resting on my cinched waist. I enjoyed the height; it made me confident in my role as a sadistic dominatrix. Looking down my nose at the old man in front of me, I began to feel extremely sexy.

"Go ahead, Sidney. Describe what would you like me to do today. What's your dream?"

"Well, I-I . . . I . . ." he said, looking away from me. Why was he so nervous? He got up and said matter-of-factly, "I want you to call me a filthy little Jew bastard!"

He looked directly into my eyes to see my reaction. I tried to have none, but I was certainly thrown off my cool demeanor momentarily. I could see his mouth starting to tremble. His small eyes glistened.

"Call me a filthy Jew pig. A good-for-nothing animal. That I should be gassed and slaughtered, thrown away with all the other filthy Jew pigs."

What the fuck!? . . . Wow! Okay. Now I was shocked.

Still, I tried not to show any reaction. I had learnt that clients often wanted to shock or upset a girl. That's part of their whole trip. The scenario they have created and mulled over for some time was so bottled up that they wanted a reaction, just like the pervs who flash their penises on the street. They want to shock. But I didn't think Sid was going through this to shock me. I believed he was simply describing what he wanted from our session.

"Get your clothes off!" I ordered through clenched teeth.

Sid got up from the edge of the bed. He slowly removed his clothes and folded his shirt and pants and put them on the chair. He was wearing a white undershirt and boxer shorts with black socks.

I nervously walked over to him, not quite sure how to begin our session; I would have to make it up as I went along, to improvise the whole show. But as I had done on my very first outcall, I slipped into an alter ego. Like my name, none of this was real; it was all made up. That realization somehow made me comfortable.

"Okay, PIG," I began. "You're a nasty little bastard, aren't you?"

Then there was silence. My mind raced. I felt red with nerves and embarrassment.

I leaned over just enough that Sid could see up my short skirt to my exposed buttocks, and I heard him inhale sharply. Once I knew he was watching me it gave me something to discipline him about.

"Who told you to look at my ass? Did you hear me, you little shit?" I yelled.

That sounded a bit weak. "Little shit" certainly wasn't severe enough. I leaned over and put down the paddle I was holding. While doing so I passed my unbuttoned cleavage under Sid's nose. When I saw him looking at my breasts, I grabbed the cuffs that were on the bed and yanked his arms behind his back.

Johns, Marks, Tricks, and Chickenhawks

"Who gave you permission to look at my breasts? You vile, pathetic piece of dirt." That's a little better. The word vile sounded good. I liked that word.

I yanked on his brittle arms and cuffed them.

Sid's head was bowed the entire time. I couldn't tell if he was aroused or not, but he seemed to enjoy my roughness. He was so old and frail. I didn't really enjoy treating a man of his age this way. It was way too easy to hurt him.

"Now say it . . . call me a filthy Jew pig," he whispered. His eyes focused on the floor.

I had done domme sessions before and at the client's request humiliated them, peed on them, tied them up, and whipped them till they bled. But the anti-Semitic names seemed so sick, it seemed so. . . demented.

"YOU DISGUSTING . . . FILTHY . . . Jew . . . PIG!" There, I said it. I said the whole sentence with conviction, but I lowered my tone when I said the word "Jew." I wondered if anyone heard me in the hall outside.

I took long strides around Sid, secretly admiring the way a few inches of skin showed between my boots and my leather miniskirt in the mirror opposite the bed. I was buying time before my next move.

I raised one leg onto the small nightstand so Sid could catch a glimpse of my crotch and my white girlish underwear.

"Do you want to get blindfolded, YOU FILTHY JEW . . . err . . . PIG?"

Again I tested the words. Okay, now I've said it twice.

"Yes p-p-please," Sid said, as eager as if I'd asked if he wanted a glass of lemonade.

I blindfolded Sid and looked at him as he stood in his white under-clothes. Where else could he fulfill this fantasy? It wasn't as though he could go home to his wife after a hard day's work and say, "Honey, let's play this little game . . . where I'm a dirty Jew fuck. And you're a Nazi bitch . . ." I smiled to myself at the thought.

305

That's why prostitutes exist. We actually serve a very necessary purpose. I had a vision of myself standing on a stage in Stockholm accepting a Nobel Peace Prize: "For my kind benevolent service in helping tricks . . . err . . . johns, umm . . . men, feel fulfilled, complete, and whole. Thank you, everyone who has made this day possible." I saw myself thanking my mother, my father, my aunt Millie. I began thinking of all the friends who I would thank, if I were ever in a position to accept an award. It's good to have these things prepared. But my parents would be listed just for appearance's sake, as they had nothing to do with my impending success.

The scene in my head made me giggle. Sid was blindfolded, so he couldn't see me entertaining myself. I made a mental note to tell my coworkers about my thoughts on prostitution being a noted, worthwhile humanitarian endeavor.

I got into doing exactly what Sid wanted. I told myself he was paying for a service, and I was going to give him the best humiliation I could. This was his dream. This was my job.

I took Sid's hand in mine, and guided him to the chair that I sat on. I told Sid to lie across my lap.

"Because you're a disobedient piece of garbage, and waste of my time, I need to teach you a lesson. You need a good hard spanking," I said through clenched teeth.

I felt his muscles tense as I tried to hold his weight on my lap. I could feel his body warmth. I looked at his bony buttocks through his striped boxers. The whole scene was becoming comical to me. To Sid, he was in the midst of his fantasy; being belittled, made fun off, and humiliated.

I needed to make sure a spanking was something he wanted without blowing the role I was playing.

"So, you bad disgusting piece of shit, do you want me to spank you?"

"Yes please," he said again. "But please don't leave any marks."

I felt awful hitting such an old and frail man with a paddle. It was used for serious spankings and stung like hell, so I started off with some light taps. He didn't seem to really feel them and whispered for me to spank harder, so I put some more muscle into it. It left a red patch on his skin, but he seemed to be enjoying it.

"More," he said, quietly.

"You're a piece of SHIT," I yelled. "And you deserve this punishment because—you're a JEW. A LOUSY STINKING JEW." Whew!

I watched Sid feel his way around the floor blindfolded. I couldn't help but like him. His manner and the way he spoke to me led me to believe he was a gentle, sweet, bright man. He had probably been a good father and provider for his family. I imagined a handful of grown children and even more grandchildren, and I was certain they loved and cared about him.

I hoped I was right.

I was an emotional person. I felt for other people; I often felt their pain. But the words, it was the words that I was being asked to say that were so . . . bizarre and revolting. I didn't confess to Sid that I was also a Jew. My mother's mother was a Brooklyn Jew who married a handsome Mexican. So my mother is a Jew, making me one too. I was bought up as a Protestant who did some time in a Catholic convent school as a child. So I'm a screwed-up, non-religious Jew. But the blood runs thick, I am a member of the tribe.

In England, we still hold World War II close. My father taught us to dislike Germans for what they did to us, to Europe and the Jews. This session bought about mixed feelings. Being told to call this small frail man such anti-Semitic names. Was I wrong in doing as I was told? Should I have refused the session?

I spanked Sid and rode around on his brittle, bony back. I tried my hardest to humiliate him by repeating the "filthy Jew" bit and slapping his bony ass with my crop.

"Sidney, come here, you pathetic, smelly, little scumbag Jew bitch." Wow! I was getting used to these words, and it surprised me to see how easily they came tumbling from my lips. It made me cringe. But I was honestly beginning to enjoy the freedom to say things that I had never dreamed of uttering.

"I know you're thinking about things you shouldn't be . . . because you're a dirty, FILTHY JEW . . . you cunt BITCH! I don't want you thinking about my breasts or my ass. Got it Jew? Bitch, filthy cunt JEWBOY!" Had I gone overboard? Was I hurting his feelings? Oh God, I hoped I hadn't gone too far with that last bit. I knelt down next to Sid so he could feel my presence and he could smell my faint perfume. I put my face right up to his and pulled his blindfold off.

His nostrils flared. His worn, pale blue eyes had a spark of fire in them. It was an intense moment as we sat nose to nose looking into each other's eyes. I saw so much behind those tired eyes. His life, a good life, fun, laughter, and love, but also pain, a deep buried pain that probably never surfaced. I was the only person on earth who knew his secret. A secret that he didn't even fully understand. I thought I'd gotten a glimpse into his soul for a split second.

He touched himself.

"I don't remember you asking permission to do that," I said calmly and quietly. "Now you Jew fuck, I'm forced to spank your unworthy filthy Jewboy ass!"

He began breathing a little harder. His penis was pushing against his underwear.

"Relieve yourself, you nasty Jew, because . . . I wouldn't ever dream of touching you, because . . . YOU'RE A FILTHY LITTLE JEW BASTARD!"

"Ahhh, yes, Mistress, yes . . ." Sid's eyes rolled back in his head.

"Slowly!" I yelled. "Now stop! You fuck!" This was fun . . .

"Please Mistress, please . . . I beg you . . ." I could see his tension building; his sexual excitement turned me on. The power.

"Say it . . ." Sid whispered.

"You disgust me because . . . YOU'RE A FILTHY FUCKING CUNT JEW . . ."

"Oooh Mis . . . tress . . . ahhhhh . . . ahhh . . . ahh . . . Sid slipped to his knees as he came, barely touching himself at all. The words had apparently been enough.

Just at that moment the bell rang, ending the hour. I stood up without saying a word. I went out to the bathroom at the end of the long dark hall, leaving Sid alone. It was good to get out of the stuffy, claustrophobic room.

Kiki, a petite, dark-skinned woman with a tough street demeanor, walked from her session next door to the bathroom with me. We hadn't talked before, and I was surprised when she spoke to me.

"How you like the old man?" she asked in her deep, raspy voice with a heavy Hispanic accent. Kiki squatted over the toilet bowl and peed.

"Fine, sweet old guy, I guess," I replied as pleasantly as possible. "A bit weird," I added.

"Yeah, but he easy," she said. "We could do with more of them Sidneys up in this bitch." Kiki wiped herself and flushed the toilet.

I looked into the mirror studying myself. I couldn't get Sid's face out of my head. His small hunched shoulders and tired eyes that held so much. I wondered if I'd ever see him again. I washed my hands.

As I walked down the darkened hall to room three, my mother's face flashed before me, making me shudder. She wasn't dead but still haunted me. I blinked her out of my head.

I took off the patent leather domme boots and slipped on my clear plastic platform stripper/whore shoes. I unsnapped the corset and exhaled, finally able to relax my abdomen and breathe easy again. I dressed back into my tight, cleavage-revealing hooker top and mini-skirt and started cleaning up the room. I tore off the top sheet on the double bed and straightened up the dresser. We hadn't used the bed except to sit on it, so there was no need to spray Lysol to get rid of the funky smell that was usual after a session. I put the dominance toys away—the whips, paddles, restraints, handcuffs, and blindfolds.

"Dear, I hope I can see you again," Sid said, interrupting the silence.

"Oh, I'd love to." I meant it.

He stepped into his pants. I watched him zip his fly and fasten his thin worn belt. What was with this man? He patted his back left pocket for his wallet. He slid the billfold out and carefully opened it.

309

The Brothel

His movements were so slow and deliberate. He selected two neatly folded $100 bills and five twenties. All the money was in order and facing the same way.

Ninety dollars would go to the house; the rest was mine. I thanked Sid, but I was strangely embarrassed at accepting the money.

I walked Sid down to the first floor.

"Good bye, dear," he said politely.

"Good bye, Sid, and thank you." I watched as he walked away with short, stiff, shuffling steps.

I headed out to the kitchen to clear my head and breathe a little.

I poured a glass of Diet Coke, which I never usually drank, and sat at the kitchen table. Summer sat opposite me painting her toenails.

I'd never met a client who had had such an impact on me. I'd seen men who I liked, and hated, but I was always able to put them into a part of my mind where I didn't think about them after their money was in my hand and they were out the door. That was the way I liked it. I didn't want clients living rent-free in my head. But Sidney, he had broken through my thick wall of protection, he'd touched me and I felt him. Maybe because I didn't understand him. I hoped those watery blue eyes wouldn't haunt me. I blinked him out of my head.

"Lizzy, honey, Jeff is here . . . your nine o'clock . . ." Ingrid yelled from the office.

"Be right there." I ran my hands through my hair, checked myself in the mirror hanging by the door, and went out to greet my nine o'clock.

Sid was fading already.

LZ HANSEN was raised in London, England, where she attended private boarding school. Having always rebelled against her middle-upper-class roots, she was inspired by the birth of punk rock in the late 1970s and its connection with New York City. Hansen collected anything to do with New York—films, photos of tenement buildings and Times Square—and was particularly fascinated with its seedier side. She packed her bags at 17 and left home for Manhattan. Having always had a gift of "the gab," she fell easily

Johns, Marks, Tricks, and Chickenhawks

into the fabulous downtown club scene and became a much sought-after stylist working on early MTV videos. Zoe (as she's known to her friends) lived in the Hotel Chelsea in the haunted "room one hundred" for years, all the while nurturing a growing heroin and cocaine habit. She entered the sex industry via a close friend who worked as a "hooker booker." Her speedball habit proved costly, one that no regular job could support. Zoe went on to work as an escort, street ho, brothel worker, jerk-off technician, and fetish clothing store owner named "Jezebella." She describes getting clean from drugs as being "sprinkled with the magic dust." In 1996, she'd had enough of the paranoia and insanity that comes along with cocaine psychosis, and she signed onto a methadone program, a move that would save her life. Zoe opened five different brothels and one massage studio in Manhattan, all of which would be highly successful. Having always had a love for writing, she began writing about her colorful life, addiction, and the sex industry. Her work has now appeared in numerous successful anthologies, online magazines, and blogs. She's cohosted and been a frequent guest at reading series in and around Manhattan.

THE MUMMY'S DICK

David Huberman

Dreaming and waking up abruptly, Ann was staring right at me with her deep blue eyes. I must have dozed off and images of a dream were escaping my consciousness. Suddenly she kissed me and said, "Did you see the Buddha while you were asleep?"

I looked up at the ceiling and didn't say anything for a while. "No, I don't think so." We were joined together comfortably in the middle of an old queen-size bed in a yellow-colored room. There was a small cable television, a chestnut cabinet, a closet, two chairs, and a phone, plus a refrigerator for water and our Tiger beer. On the right of me was an economical bathroom with the toilet under the shower and a sink. Frank Sinatra was singing in my head, "My type of town, Chicago is," and I thought of Pattaya instead. The armpit of Asia, and here I am, messed up. Ann kept on saying, "I want to see it." You could really detect the French in her. The hair, dirty blonde; lips, thin like a Frenchwoman's; and the eyes, blue but slanted and caught in a round Chinese face. I used to tell her, "Ann, you're Eurasian." But she would nod her head slowly back and forth and say, "No, I Thai girl."

The journey from New York was exhausting. Seventeen hours to Japan, hang around three hours for a connecting flight and then another six hours before landing at Suvarnabhumi Airport. Moreover, there was the bus to Pattaya, which was another hour and a half. But jet lag was the least of my problems. Even my 84-year-old Jewish mother had put her two cents in. "Who goes to Thailand in your condition? You should not go if I was you." Maybe my travel insurance would eventually have paid up if I would have canceled, but I wanted to go to the land of smiles no matter what state I was in. Slowly she was getting my pants off, then my briefs, searching for my illness. We had e-mailed each other before my journey, and I had told her about my mishap. Ann mentioned that an old *farang* movie was on Thai television about it, which didn't make any sense to me. I glanced down at the purple flower-print sarong she wore and then further to her feet that I always found enchanting. They were arousing with high arches, expensive red nail polish, no chipping on any of the toes, perfectly polished. You could eat peaches off them. I could only compare them to those of film sirens like Zsa Zsa Gabor or Joan Collins. Teasing me with my fetish, sometimes she would tangle her foot over my thigh, and slowly rub it, watching for the sexual energy that would shoot through my groin right to my eyes. What power she had over me at times, but thanks to the Buddha, there was compassion not to do it now.

Finally the underwear was off. Her eyes flared bright blue and that mixed face resembled a circus clown. She exclaimed, "Just like USA cinema. Very ancient, yes, I believe." Once again, I didn't get what Ann was saying.

"What are . . . ?"

She interrupted. "*The Mummy*, that's name of movie. He could not shit or fuck. Have too much rice paper on him; your dick is Mummy's dick."

I sighed. "I told you what happened. I was lonely; we met in a bar, one of thousands in New York City, and had a one-night stand, except the condom didn't work so well." Our eyes met, she looked deep into me.

"I know everything from your e-mail, I not mad at you, but you e-mail me weeks ago, you tell me *farang* woman not bathe, how can you be with dirty *farang*, she smell very bad. No wonder you have no power to be with her. Every Thai girl shower many times before having boom-boom. She no good. Very bad lady!"

"I know I know," I repeated. "Look, in a few days the bandage will be off, the warts have been burnt off, the open sores will be gone, and we can have good boom-boom again. I'll wear two condoms to make sure you don't get anything from me."

Ann kissed me on my forehead and smiled. "Danny, you go to Thailand many times. You butterfly, I bar girl. We go many years together, I know your ways. Sometimes you want other lady. Okay, you butterfly, but you good not cheap Charlie. I cannot go with you if you mess with dirty *farang* lady in America. I don't want to see you with Mummy's dick again."

I nodded my head. "You're right, she was drunk, didn't want to shower, snorted cocaine, smelled bad, and I still slept with her. In addition, this is what I got as a gift. No, you're right," I repeated. "For now on it's just you and . . ."

Ann interrupted my sentence. "You butterfly." She kissed me passionately. "Does it hurt you when we kiss?" she asked.

"Somewhat, but its pain I can deal with," I said.

"Good," she whispered. "It will remind you of your punishment. You will give me the five fingers of pleasure now. I smell good down there."

"Yes, you do." I whispered back.

Then we both laughed.

DAVID HUBERMAN was born in some nameless hospital in Manhattan; the reason it is nameless is that his mother doesn't remember, and he never asked her until recently. His father was a concentration camp survivor who came to the United States and became a waiter in a resort in the Catskill Mountains of New York State. He met David's mother there, who was a second-generation American Jew. They fell in love and got married, and he then became a cab driver for a few years, saved his money, and bought a baby-clothes store. From that store, he graduated to buying a NYC candy store, called the Luncheonette. Then he lost most of his money in the stock market, so they were always lower-middle-class people. Recently, David's sister found photos on the Internet of their father being liberated from the concentration camp. He grew up in the South Bronx as the only white person attending Taft High School at that time. He worked for the

Johns, Marks, Tricks, and Chickenhawks

post office for thirty years, and on the side became a flea market dealer on weekends. He also sold out-of-print books on the Internet for Amazon and eBay. When he was young, he liked smoking angel dust, but that hobby got him a few stays in some mental hospitals and a little jail time. On the application for the post office job, he told them the truth, but they hired him anyway. At the age of 31, he gave up all chemicals for fourteen years. His passions are old comics, toys, books, and robots, and people call his studio apartment in Queens "the Toy museum." He played a serial killer in a B-horror film called *Trail of Blood.* His writing has been published in *Tribes, The Unbearable Anthologies, The Outlaw Bible of American Poetry, The Best of Panic,* and many other magazines, anthologies, and chap books.

EL CAMPAMENTO

Sherrill Jaffe

I was caught off guard that year when summer rolled around and Wendy, my girlfriend, flew off to volunteer on a kibbutz. We'd spent every weekend that spring semester making out on the beer-drenched couch down in the basement of my fraternity house, and we'd done everything it was possible to do sexually—without actually going all the way—on her narrow dorm-room bed with its madras spread, for the year was 1964, a time when a respectable American girl needed to preserve her hymen intact for the day when she would need to present it in payment for a wedding ring.

I had known Wendy's plans for a while but hadn't foreseen how her actual leaving was going to set me adrift. My parents and siblings were packing for a trip abroad. I'd gone with them to Europe before, upon my graduation from high school, but now I was too old for a family vacation. What was I going to do with my summer then? Where could I go? My father had a suggestion: I could go to Venezuela, where someone owed him a favor.

That my father was a very important dentist had always been made clear to me, and I looked up to him. A pioneer in the field of dental implants, he'd gone all over the globe lecturing, and he was especially popular in Caracas. There he had many ties to dentists, and that is where, as it happened, the international dental convention was to be held in the fall, an event for which there was much to do to prepare. I had taken two years of college Spanish, and so my father arranged for me to be hired by the International Dental Association to go down to Caracas for the summer to translate important dental documents.

On my way, I stopped over one night in Curaçao, at a pink stucco hotel with a trembling fountain in its courtyard and palm trees rushing overhead. As soon as I registered, I scanned the lobby. At that moment, my primary goal was to get laid, as quickly as possible. After months of doing everything just short of copulation with Wendy, I was ready to go.

At this point, I had only consummated the love act twice in my life. The second time was when some of my fraternity brothers rented a prostitute, and we went into a room with her one after the other. I cringe when I think about this now, how overtaxed the poor whore must have been, and also how gross it was for me to occupy the same vagina my fraternity brothers had just been enjoying. At the time, however, I had been too drunk to think.

"Are you a virgin, too?" the whore had asked me when it was my turn, but actually, my deflowering had occurred two summers before, on that family vacation to Europe, one day in Paris. After touring the city all day, our guide had brought us to the Place Pigalle, and there my father started winking at me furiously. At first I didn't know what he was trying to tell me, but he soon made it clear with a few lewd gestures while my mother gazed at the Basilica du Sacré Coeur. So that evening I told my mother I was going to hear some jazz in a cellar on the Left Bank where people applauded by snapping their fingers, but instead I made my way back to the Place Pigalle, to a strip club I had noticed when my father had winked earlier that day.

The striptease had been going on for hours, and there was still a lot to come off when I lost patience and went for the door. The proprietor rushed up to me and asked me why I was leaving, but I couldn't explain it to him in my high school French. I didn't know how to tell him that I felt teased. Wrenching myself from his grasp, I made my way to the street.

Across the way was what looked to be a small hotel with a sea of men gathered in front. Every so often, a woman came out and stood

The Brothel

in the doorway, causing tremendous excitement in the crowd. "How much do they charge here?" I asked a man standing next to me in my high school French. By saying *ici* I was implying that I knew how much a whore charged *là*, in New York. This, of course, was not true. The man did not seem to understand what I was saying. But it didn't matter. Whatever the price was, I was going to pay it. If I didn't, I wouldn't be able to look my father in the eye when I returned to the hotel.

A short, stocky woman with a pretty face like a kitten came and stood in the doorway just then, and I crossed the street to her, causing a great ripple to go through the crowd. After we had done our negotiation and she had taken a towel from an older woman, she led me up a steep staircase to a spare small room. I was terrified, but I tried not to let on. "I am Marie," she told me, taking off her pleated skirt and squatting on the bidet. Then she took a washcloth and gently washed my genitals until I was aroused. When I took off my shirt, she said, "Ah! *Sportif*!" flattering me that I looked like an athlete.

She left her blouse and stockings on, but she was tender with me, knowing it was my first time. I didn't exactly know what to do or how to proceed, but she took matters into her own hands, and so very soon I had passed through my own personal Arc de Triomphe and found myself navigating my engorged Bateau Mouche down the river opening up inside of her. It surprised me how at home I felt there, as if I had been able to climb back inside my mother, whom Marie resembled slightly with her dazzling smile. Alternately, I felt myself reuniting with my other half, the missing puzzle piece I knew I had been searching for my whole life. Now that I had arrived, I wished to remain here in perpetuity, but a force larger than I was took over, and I expended myself. *Et voilà.*

Marie very kindly allowed me to stay with her for a few moments afterward, and she let me talk to her, although I don't know if she could understand what I was saying. I was trying to tell her how grateful I was to her, how complete I felt inside of her, how she smelled like a jewel box, with undertones of the aquarium in my

Johns, Marks, Tricks, and Chickenhawks

room at home, overdue to be cleaned, but I didn't have the words for any of this.

Now here in Curaçao, after putting my things in my hotel room, I went back down to the lobby and out the door to look for a cab. When the driver asked me where I wanted to go, I harumphed for a few minutes, and then, in my best Spanish, I told him that I wanted a woman, *una mujer.*

"No problema," he said, and he drove me to what looked like a set of institutional bungalows behind barbed wire, El Campamento. It was an encampment of whores. The government regulated prostitution, and perhaps consequently, El Campamento had all the glamour of crumbling government buildings. The cab driver explained to me that I would need to bargain once I was inside. He cautioned me to be tough.

In a large room full of women, I chose a tall, willowy *mulata* who reminded me of a girl I had been in love with at Penn before I met Wendy. Randi had not been interested in me. She only liked mean, older guys. She had fixed me up with Wendy. I started bargaining with the *mulata* Randi over her price. How cavalier I sounded to myself, how mean, how crass, and I immediately saw what a turnoff this was to the *mulata.*

I was sorry; I thought this was how it was done, but it was too late. In the sterile institutional cell with its gray walls and metal furniture where she took me after we had completed this transaction, she went about her duties in what seemed to me a rather unfriendly manner, looking away when I attempted to kiss her.

This time I knew the drill, however, or my penis did, probing its way into her furry purse without any assistance from either of us. One again, I was amazed to find myself propelled headlong down the silky river I had so briefly enjoyed with Marie. It was flowing on, independent of the chagrin I felt over my shameful treatment of this woman, whose name I hadn't even caught. I closed my eyes, and for a few moments the prostitute and the cell we occupied together in our dank entangled suits of skin ceased to exist, but

319

before I knew it, the wave I had been riding rose up abruptly several stories and crashed.

The next morning, still filled with shame for the way I had bargained with the prostitute, I was on the plane to Caracas when a man I had been idly observing across the aisle moved next to me and started rubbing his leg against mine. I tried to tell myself it was an accident, but when he started putting his hands on me, it became clear what was happening. I pushed him away. "What are you doing?" I asked.

"You don't want me to?" he asked.

"What gave you that idea?" I said.

"You gave me the look!" he said, indignant.

Yes, I had looked at him, but I looked at everyone. I didn't mean anything by it. I had to spend the whole rest of the flight trying to fight the man off.

Roberto, the dentist who was to be my host, was there at the airport with his wife and young son to greet me. As I got into their yellow Mercedes, I noticed it was riddled with bullet holes. Caracas was a beautiful modern city full of elegant new high-rise apartments where all the cars were riddled with bullet holes. Though Venezuela with its oil was one of the richest countries in South America, most of the people were living in abject poverty, in cardboard boxes called *ranchos* that covered the mountainsides surrounding the city, and earning their livings by violent crime.

The dentists, however, were among the richest people in Caracas. They lived in palatial houses, and they all had second houses in the mountains, where they went on alternate weekends, and third houses at the beach, where they went on the other alternate weekends. There was no middle class to speak of in Venezuela, but out of the four or five people who occupied this stratum, my host Roberto's brother, Alberto, and their old mother, Consuela, could be counted as two. Now Roberto was rapidly driving me to the middle-class apartment where his mother and brother lived. This was where I was to be housed all summer while I worked at the convention center translating important dental documents.

Johns, Marks, Tricks, and Chickenhawks

I was not a dental student, however; I was not even pre-dental, and I had not done particularly well in my college Spanish courses, so it was very soon clear that I was completely hopeless as a translator of the important dental documents that needed to be prepared for the upcoming International Dental Convention. My supervisor, Ernesto, a pleasant homosexual who, to my relief, did not come on to me, very soon stopped giving me important dental documents to translate and simply allowed me to come to the office every morning to do nothing, and then, at the end of the day, to go home, because my father was a revered dentist, the president of the International Implant Association.

Various important dentists who were friends of my father, like Julius La Rosa-Werner, would take me along with their families in their Mercedes riddled with bullet holes on alternate weekends to their houses in the mountains or their houses at the beach. During the week, of course, I slept in one of the bedrooms of the two-bedroom apartment of Alberto and Consuela, who slept in the other.

Their flat was on the fourth floor, high above the street. Nonetheless, there were bars on the windows. One night I was lying on my bed reading a letter penned on pale blue airmail stationary, the kind that is its own envelope. It was from Wendy. She was having just a terrific time in Israel. She'd met an American guy who'd gone there to live, and he was showing her all around the country. His name was Marvin. I looked up and noticed there was a man outside, clinging to the bars on the window. The bars are keeping him out, I told myself. There is nothing to worry about.

The next day I was sitting at my desk in my office in the cavernous Caracas Convention Center when a big important dentist named Maurice walked in and invited me to go with him to the military ball. He was a man of about 40 who had a wife and family, but his wife was in the mountains, so there was space at his table.

The night of the ball, he came for me at Alberto and Consuela's. On the way to the ball, he took me for a few drinks. The men in the bar, and there were only men in the bar, came up to me and smirked.

"Oh, Maurice, you have such a handsome date!" they said, pinching me on the cheek, and that was when I realized this was a homosexual bar, and I was Maurice's date for the military ball. Maurice had brought me to this bar to show me off.

So by the time we arrived at the ball, I was thoroughly pissed. The ball was being held in a fantastically ornate, mirrored and gold-leafed palace. Maurice and I were seated at a table full of glamorous people. Next to me was the editor of the Venezuelan *Life* magazine, a blond and bejeweled carcass my grandmother's age in a low-cut gold lamé gown, who in short order took me out on the dance floor and started squeezing my behind. A married woman with grown children and three houses, she had come to the ball with a young escort who chatted with Maurice as she moved me around to the music. Having imbibed several glasses of liquor, I was apparently willing to go along with this.

All during the ball, Maurice kept seeing that my glass was refilled, and when the ball was over, he took me back to the homosexual bar for a few more drinks, and the men there leered at me and pinched me again. By this time, I was so drunk I could barely stand up. "I just have to make a stop back at my house before I bring you home," Maurice told me.

"Good," I said. "I really have to pee."

Maurice's house was luxurious and richly decorated, like all the grand residences of the Venezuelan dentists. Upstairs, children and a maid were sleeping, or so he told me. I went into the bathroom, took out my dick, and began to relieve myself. Then, through the loud sound of the urine tumbling into the bowl, I heard another sound and turned my head. Maurice was in the bathroom. His face was in my face, his tongue was in my mouth, and his hand was on my cock.

I pushed his hand away in disgust, but to my shock, humiliation, and outrage, I now had a hard-on. This was when I realized that everyone has every kind of sexual impulse. "I'm not a homosexual! Why did you think I was a homosexual?" I protested to Maurice.

"I'm sorry," Maurice said. "It was the way you looked at me when I first walked into the office. It was the sign."

"No, it wasn't!" I said. "I just like to look at people!"

"You are a people watcher?" he asked.

"But now I'm really horny!" I exclaimed. "Now you have to get me a woman! Bring me your maid!"

"I can't really do that!" Maurice said. "She's 70 years old. Just calm down; tomorrow I'll take you to a prostitute."

The next day Maurice introduced me to a whore he himself had frequented who lived in a nice apartment with shuttered windows not far from Alberto and Consuela's. Her name was Inez, she was very cheerful, and in her arms I at last felt the fulfillment of all the desire I had repressed as I labored over Wendy's tight unblemished body.

Inez had dark eyes and an open mouth. When I was making love to her, I felt that my penis was enormous, that I had impaled her on the end of a long sword. Other times I found myself swimming inside her, exploring the vast interior of an underground grotto.

I patronized Inez regularly for the rest of the summer, arranging to see her by calling her from the *mercado* beneath Alberto and Consuela's. Alberto and Consuela had no phone. The proprietors of the *mercado* clearly knew what I was transacting, but if they sat in judgment of me, I didn't know by what standards.

It seemed to me that there was no reason I should have to feel guilty when I was in Inez's bed, and that accounted for a great deal of the happiness of being with her. Inez was extremely nice to me, and we would have long talks after the performance of the act. Eventually, I told her about Wendy, how I couldn't go all the way with her because nice single girls in New York had to preserve their hymens for their wedding nights.

"Are you going to marry her then?" Inez asked, and for a moment I wondered if that was where all the frustration I had been suffering with Wendy had been leading.

Then Inez told me about her own life. She had one great love, an officer in the army. Sometimes they would go to stay at a charming hotel by the sea where they would make love twelve times a night. When he made love to her she experienced the exact happiness that is promised in birthday candles. Other times during the love act she would feel that she was sitting on a yellow cushion in the window of a modern house, and that there were trees outside, and that the late afternoon sun slanting through the trees and in through the window was warming her, and that there was a book in her hands, but she was not reading because there was no need to do anything.

I went to see Inez so often that I began to run out of money, and I felt very bad that I was not going to have enough to buy gifts for my hosts before I left. Then one night toward the end of the summer, I realized I was sick. I lay in my bed at Alberto and Consuela's, shaking. I knew I had a fever, and a high one, and in the middle of the night I began to worry that I was going to die. I needed Alberto to call me a doctor, so I stumbled into the room where he lay sleeping in a twin bed across from his old mother, but when I started to ask him for help, he leapt up and started punching me as hard as he could until I collapsed on the floor.

At this point, he put on his glasses and saw what he had done. It was me, his guest, not a burglar, as he had supposed. I whimpered from the rug, begging him to send for a doctor.

Alberto put on his clothes and went out, but in a little while he returned.

"Is the doctor coming?" I asked.

"No, he is not," Alberto said.

"Then you have to take me to the hospital!" I begged. "I'm burning up!"

So Alberto took me to the emergency room of the hospital. There they knew immediately what it was that was the matter with me. An insect in the jungle had bitten me, they explained, taking out a very long needle. Didn't I go into the jungle every weekend either on my way to some rich dentist's house in the mountains or some other rich dentist's house at the seashore? Now I was going to have to pay.

But I did not have jungle fever, and so the injection didn't help me,

324

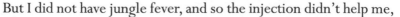

Johns, Marks, Tricks, and Chickenhawks

and I became even sicker than I had been before. What I had was one of the first cases of poisoning from a contaminated batch of bottled water. One had to be careful not to drink the tap water in Venezuela.

I remained too sick to go downstairs to the *mercado* to call Inez until the day of my departure, so she never knew about my illness, and, in the end, I never said goodbye to her, but because ours was a business arrangement and not a real relationship, as I understood it, no civilities were expected of me nor any concern from her. I lay delirious and feverish at Alberto and Consuela's until Roberto came to drive me to the airport to catch my plane home. He entered my room just as I was struggling to get out of bed to dress for the trip, came over to me, and began to unbutton my pajama top. I thought he was going to help me to get dressed, that he could see that the fever was making me weak and felt sympathy for me. But Roberto was not helping me to get dressed; Roberto was taping pieces of gold to my chest.

"When you get to New York, call my brother who lives in Queens at this number that I will give you," Roberto instructed me. "He will come and get the gold."

I flew back to New York on the verge of vomiting for the entire flight, the gold taped to my chest hairs adding to my discomfort, and I continued to feel ill for the next six months, waking up drenched in sweat several times every night.

Yet I did not call Roberto's brother who lived in Queens to tell him to come and get the gold. I was angry at the way I had been treated. But very soon Roberto's brother who lived in Queens came and found me, and so I gave him all the gold, which I had been keeping at the bottom of my underwear drawer. Wendy had returned before me, and for a few days I felt awkward around her, but then we started up our relationship right where we left off, making out and petting heavily, but still preserving her hymen for her wedding night.

She would never go all the way with me unless I married her, and my parents were all for it. It was not lost on them that Wendy came from a very wealthy family. Wendy's father owned a chain of

325

department stores in the Midwest. "It doesn't hurt," my father said, and, one more time, he winked at me salaciously.

SHERRIL JAFFE was born in Walla Walla, Washington, in 1945. Her dad was a publisher, her mom a bookkeeper; she has lived mainly in San Francisco, but also L.A., Beverly Hills, Berkeley, Sebastopol, New York City, Monroe, New York, and Jerusalem. She is the author of ten works of fiction, including *The Unexamined Wife*, *Expiration Date*, and *You Are Not Alone and Other Stories*, winner of the 2011 Spokane Award for the short story. She received the Josephine Miles Award for Literary Excellence, a PEN award in 2000, and a MacDowell Fellowship in 2010. She has an MFA from Bennington and works as a professor of creative writing at Sonoma State University. "El Campamento" is based upon incidents recounted to her by her late husband, Alan Lew. She lives in San Francisco and walks in Golden Gate Park every day.

ONCE A CLIENT

Jane Whatshername

I met Barry during the time I was working at 333, which was both the name and street number of a typical suburban brothel in Adelaide, Australia. Four bedrooms, one bathroom, client waiting room, girls' (staff) room, receptionist, and us sex workers. It was clean, safe, sparse, and far from high class. I was a 25-year-old single mother and university student with average looks and average attitude, dressed in a wig, a hooker dress, and trashy stay-up stockings. I was halfway through a fourteen-hour shift one Sunday evening when Barry rung the brothel doorbell. Brushing our hair and applying another layer of lipstick, us three workers on shift clip-clopped in our high heels one at a time into the waiting room where Barry sat. We introduced ourselves, smiled, sussed him out, did our best to impress, and then clip-clopped back to the staff room. It is impossible to predict which worker a client will choose, so I always got a bit of a thrill when the receptionist called my name, especially when it was a slow night.

Barry booked me for an hour and I provided my service in one of the dimly lit, no-frills brothel rooms. An hour can be a long time to spend shut away with a stranger within four small walls, especially if you don't get along. Fitted out with nothing but a double ensemble bed, a bedside table, a clock radio, and a wooden chair, time could drag on and those rooms could end up feeling claustrophobic. But Barry and I clicked and the hour passed quickly. The sex was over early in session and we spent the rest of the hour lying around naked

327

telling silly stories. Just before the hour was up, Barry got aroused again and he happily offered to extend the booking. During the second hour I got to hear Barry's story: He worked out at the mines in central Australia and had a fly-in/fly-out contract, working solidly for two and a half weeks and then having ten days off. He came to Adelaide during his downtime and spent all his money on five-star accommodations and partying.

Still in the tiny room, the second hour went by quickly and easily. We were having fun and Barry didn't want to say goodbye, so with only three more hours left until I finished work he decided to pay the fee to book me out for the rest of my shift. We spent the whole night in that room fucking, laughing, and talking. I can't deny I was attracted to Barry's obvious disposable income, and I was flattered that he was willing to spend so much of it on time with me. I also enjoyed his company and his sense of humor, so at the end of the five hours I agreed to meet him after work and hang out in the bar of his hotel—for free.

Mixing business with pleasure is widely warned against in many businesses, and the sex industry is no different. In the circles I mixed and worked in, it was considered a big no-no. My friends would have called me crazy and my boss would have sacked me, so I kept it to myself. I was crossing a lot of lines. I might have spent hours alone naked in a room with this guy, but he didn't know my real name and he hadn't seen the real me or even my real hair! I surprised myself when without too much thought I agreed to meet him in the lobby of his hotel. Nothing but the time and place had been confirmed or negotiated, and I felt vulnerable but excited.

After spending five hours with me, Barry left the brothel and went back to his hotel while I packed up my work gear, collected my pay, and headed home. Once home, I had about half an hour to pretty myself up before calling a taxi into town. I noted in my head that the taxi was going to be at my expense, and I felt a bit annoyed with myself for not only agreeing to give away my time for free but also spending my own money in order to do it. Then I consoled myself with the knowledge that I had made good money on this night, largely because of Barry.

I let the butterflies take over. What will I wear? He only knows me as the hooker in a trashy short dress and too much cleavage. What I chose to wear would represent the real me, and what about my hair! He only knew me with the sexy sleek stylish wig hairdo, but my real hair underneath was more like punk rock chick. I was all nervous and excited. I showered, put on my expensive perfume and my matching girly undies and bra, the ones I kept only for my personal life. Then I put on my jeans, sneakers, and hoodie. I looked in the mirror and tried to see myself through his eyes. I looked like a more wholesome version of the person he met in the brothel hours before, more like the girl next door than a sultry sex kitten. With just a brush of mascara and lip gloss, my crazy hair looking cute and my clothes comfortable, I still felt sexy with my favorite underwear and scent on my skin.

I hoped Barry appreciated that he was getting the real me, in my real clothes. I hoped he knew that he was lucky. I wanted him to understand the significance. But when I met up with him he didn't seem concerned with my changed appearance one way or the other.

That night was fun. We partied with his money until it was time for me to return to my child and real life. We made plans to catch up the next time he was in town, and then the time after that. This hotel room romance continued for only a few weeks before Barry made me an offer. He wanted commitment, he wanted me to stop working, and he was prepared to put his money where his mouth was. I didn't want to give up sex work, but if he was prepared to financially support me, I would consider it. Who wouldn't be tempted by not having to go to work, right? He told me he was sick of hotel rooms and after working hard all month he wanted to come back to a home. He offered to rent a nice house for me and my son so that he could stay there during his downtime. It sounded perfect to me—ten days of fun while he was in party mode followed by twenty days of the house to myself while he went back to work four hundred kilometers away. I jumped at the offer.

329

For the first time our fling shifted from hotel rooms and bars into the public and domestic domain. We looked at houses together and visited friends. He spent time with my son and he met my mum. Everything went well, and our new home was gorgeous. He was happily paying all the rent because it was still cheaper than the expensive hotels he used to pay for, and I got to live somewhere beautiful rent-free. We spent his first visit home playing house; I cooked, he bought me flowers, we cuddled on the sofa and watched movies. It was fun. His second time home was less enchanting. He was less appreciative and I was less excited by cooking. We bickered for the first time, but when we kissed each other goodbye, I had hope that the next time would be better.

While he was gone, things were good. We talked on the phone and sent e-mails; he paid my bills and we missed each other. But when he returned it didn't seem so much fun anymore. Real life got in the way of the sex, romance, and indulgence that had bought us together. We did dishes instead of ordering room service. We sat on the couch and read the paper instead of rolling around on the crisp white sheets of hotel beds. We talked about bills and shopping lists instead of fantasies and fears. Once domesticity set in, our true colors began to shine. I had thought that all those hours spent alone together surrounded by four walls would have given us an opportunity to really get to know each other. I thought all that talking and laughing and exploring and confessing would have meant I understood what I was getting myself into. But it was the outside world, the real life pressures and the daily distractions, that really tested our compatibility, or lack of.

We continued our relationship together for about six months, but it felt like six years. By the end of it, I was bored and he was demanding. I was broke and he was sick of paying for my expensive phone bills. We still had fun, but the shine had worn off and there were lots of times when we would argue or just ignore each other.

Instead of missing him, I was happy when it was time for him to go, but we both pretended to be sad. We had settled into the house;

my son and I were happy in our new home and there was no way I could afford the rent by myself. I had a part-time job, but Barry had made me give up sex work so my income was small. I wanted to go back. I missed the money, the independence of making my own money, the other workers, the attention from clients, and the excuse to wear trashy dresses and high heels. I wanted out of this deal with Barry, and sex work was going to be my way out. I fantasized about returning to work for a few weeks, but I didn't take it any further initially because I wasn't sure if it was a good idea and I didn't want to hurt Barry. During his next visit home I tried to reconnect with him, but he seemed distant. Then he bluntly told me he wanted me to "make my hair normal," and I knew for sure that we were not suited for each other. I liked my cute pink hair, and if there is one thing being a hooker has taught me, it's that everyone is someone's type. I didn't want to stick around with Barry if I wasn't his type. And then when I thought about it, I realized he wasn't really my type either—he had a temper and he was often quite chauvinistic. We spent the rest of his stay going through the motions until he left early. He always left at 4 PM after making a big song and dance about how much he was going to miss me, and he always wanted sex before he left because it was a while in between. But this time he left at 2 PM with barely a kiss goodbye, saying that he was tired and wanted to get back in time for an early night.

Now, it was obvious to me that leaving early wasn't about him needing sleep. He was always tired when he headed back to work, but that had never stopped him from dragging the process out as long as possible. I didn't know why he was leaving early this time. I just presumed he had come to the same conclusions about our relationship as I had, but I didn't dwell on it. I didn't really care what his reasons were. I was just relieved to get my house back two hours earlier than expected so I could plot my escape.

I had made my mind up. It was over. I still didn't know how I was going to tell Barry, but first things first. I needed to make some money. I was going to go back to sex work and pay my own rent, and

331

then I would call Barry and tell him my decision. Sometime before his next visit.

When Barry had been reading the paper earlier that day, I had noticed the sex industry ad pages in the classifieds section. As soon as he walked out the door, I poured myself a glass of wine, grabbed the paper, and sat down ready to find myself a job in a brothel. I flicked through looking for the "adult relaxation" section. I knew there would be plenty of "looking for staff" ads among the columns and columns of names, numbers, and promises of a good time. I looked through the paper three times, but I couldn't find the page with the ads. They had been there before; I had seen them. I found the section and page number listed in the contents table—page 16. I turned the pages, but page 16 was not there. On further inspection, I realized that page 16 had been removed. Presumably by Barry. Barry, who had left my house two hours earlier than necessary, without hassling me for sex, with a list of local hookers and their phone numbers.

The penny dropped, but I wasn't mad. Instead, I saw my out. The irony of catching my boyfriend sneaking around with hookers only because I was trying to sneak around and be a hooker myself was not lost on me. I was just annoyed with myself for crossing the line with a client in the first place. I should have known better. I am paid to be the professional. My clients should be able to fall in love all they want, safe in the knowledge that their sex worker will not let them take it any further. But I let us both down. If I had maintained my professional boundaries, Barry could still be paying me by the hour instead of sneaking around paying someone else by the hour—and we would all be happy.

JANE WHATSERNAME is a sex worker in her 30s, born, raised, and currently sex-working in South Australia. She's the only child of a single mum, who was and is a nurse and artist. She's lived most of her life in and around Adelaide, South Australia, but she has traveled a lot around Australia. Her first job was at 12 years old selling lollies door to door, and then later a checkout

Johns, Marks, Tricks, and Chickenhawks

chick at Woolworths. She's done sex work on and off and in the background since she was 19, but she has also worked in aged care, community health, and social welfare sectors in various roles from support worker to project manager. Currently, sex work is her only source of income. Jane is neither her real name or her working name, but a name she uses to tell her story through her blog. Jane hides her identity to protect herself and her family from discrimination, harassment, and the law. A real person with a real family, Jane volunteers at her kids' school canteen one day a fortnight and sells sex on the other days. She writes about her job, her life, her thoughts, the stuff that goes on around her, and the meanings she makes of it all. Sex work is illegal in South Australia, and Jane has been through many raids, so she is forced to remain anonymous but not silent. She has a lot to say and she wants you to listen. She's always been passionate about social justice and has always been active in campaigns that promote that. In her downtime she enjoys a red wine and her laptop. She also loves good food, great views, and sunshine. And she loves hanging out with other hookers.

The Brothel

I LOVE MY WIFE
AND I LOVE FUCKING TAMMY

Anonymous

Tammy is posing in front of the mirror in her black stiletto heels that look like wolves. She's five-foot-eight but in the heels she's almost six feet tall. She has the most perfect 22-year-old tits I've ever seen in my life. I hate to be one of those guys who say that kind of thing, but it's true. It takes my breath away just to look at them. And her ass is so tight. Everything is all shaved and oiled, and toned, like she just stepped out of some magazine. She's looking at me in the mirror. Posing. She's got thick red lipstick on. And her hair is done perfect. She smells good. If you look close you can see she shaved her pussy recently. It looks fascinating. You can really see everything. Which I like. And I like picturing her shaving. Knowing that I would be looking. I've known her since she was 19. I've seen her driver's license. She weighs 119 pounds. She told me that earlier. She likes to tell me how much she weighs. Her mom is a vain pain in the ass, but Tammy loves her. Bitches and moans about her constantly. But she loves her. Her mom's from the old country. So is her dad. He's a very successful lunatic. Her sister's a drug addict. Either in or out of recovery depending on what day it is. She does fellatio better than anyone I've ever known. She has incredibly powerful muscles all over her body. But especially in her pussy. I just gave her $250. Well, actually, I put it on the table. Then she picked it up and put it into her little bag. Then she got undressed. Then she started posing. I have no idea why, but a picture of my wife flashes in my mind.

We were skinny-dipping up in the mountains. She got out of the water. And the sun was shining on her. And I realize again how much Tammy looks like my wife when she was that age. I mean it's ridiculous. It's so psychologically fucked up. Of course I know it is. But that doesn't stop the fact that Tammy, right now, just looking at her, takes my breath away and gets my dick hard in a way that my wife can't possibly do now.

I love my wife. She's my best friend. We've been together since we were kids, really. It was the smartest thing I ever did. She's so much better than me. Seriously. She's better-looking. She's smarter. She's nicer. She takes their care of things better. She has better hair. I could go on. But I won't. She's the mother of my children, for God's sake. We have three kids. They're teenagers. They're great kids. Not because of me. Believe me. Because of her. Don't get me wrong, I work my ass off. But she's the one. She made sure they grew up right. Please and thank you, all that stuff. But also, just knowing the difference between right and wrong. Knowing that when you promise to do something you should actually do it. That you're not supposed to lie and cheat and steal. But I am a liar and a cheater and a stealer. Because I've been paying the incredibly talented and enthusiastic prostitute Tammy to give me ridiculous amounts of pleasure. My wife's body, it's just all old and saggy-droopy now. She's not really interested in working out. The kids are always around. Or need to be picked up. Or need to be dropped off. It's exhausting. We're always tired. And she doesn't have nearly the skills that Tammy does. I still have sex with my wife. Don't get me wrong. And I like it. I love it. I love my wife. This is not the same. Not that it's worse or better. In many ways it is better than having sex with Tammy. Because I feel totally connected to my wife. I love looking at her while making her cum. Seriously, it's something I really love doing. I want to add more. Our lives are just so ridiculously busy.

I don't feel guilty. I thought about this a lot. Like, what if she came to me and she said, my wife this is, that she'd been paying some stupidly handsome gigolo $250 to have sex with her for three years.

What would I do? In one way, I would think, *Good for you!* I hope, honestly, that would be what I'd say. Because, let's face it, I'm no spring chicken. I'm definitely not the man she married. My hair is basically extinct. But of course it's pouring out of my ears and nose at an alarming rate. I don't shower enough. Looking at my doughboy gut, you'd never guess I once had a six-pack. But of course on the other hand if she told me that she'd been banging some young stud and paying for it, I'd be horrified. I'm not a violent person. But if I was, there's a chance I might get violent. This does bother me. That I think somehow it's okay for me, but it's not okay for her. If it's okay for me, it should be okay for her too. But is it okay for me? I keep trying to figure out if I'm doing something wrong. If I'm sinning. Who am I hurting? I make sure I'm always condomed up. I keep it completely separate from my life. I feel no great need to confess. In fact, I don't feel any need at all to confess. It's just like getting a foot massage. Or going to a chiropractor. Or getting a haircut. I really don't think I'm doing anything wrong here. So long as she doesn't find out. And there's no way she's gonna find out. I'm a very careful person. That's part of how I make my living. Believe me, if I wasn't careful in my line of work, I'd be a dead man. Because to me, the only sin is doing something that hurts somebody. If I was hurting her in some way, I wouldn't do it. I feel this tremendous desire to make her life good. Because she's made my life so good. That is my wife of course.

Tammy is crawling up the bed now. On all fours. With a funny kitty cat smile on her face. She is so fucking beautiful it makes me feel incredibly lucky to be alive in a world where I get to fuck Tammy. She's about to work me over, ring my bell and rock my world like the well-trained, incredibly skillful, beautifully souled professional she is. And after I'm done, I'll go home and have dinner with my wife and my family. We're trying to figure out where to go on vacation this year. Bermuda or Paris. I'm gonna tell her we can go wherever she wants to go.

JOHNS AND JILLS WENT UP MY HILLS

Dr. Annie Sprinkle as told to David Sterry

What I did for love . . . For twenty years, from 1973 until 1993, I had many different gigs in the sex industry. I made porn movies, did live sex shows, burlesque, pin-up modeling, phone sex recordings . . . But throughout those years I always relied on prostitution. In the '70s and '80s, making porn wasn't the full-time job and moneymaker like it is today. Porn was more of a hobby and political activist statement. We had to supplement our porn star income with another steady job, so I chose prostitution. Or prostitution chose me. Eventually I became the first porn star to bridge into the art world, and to get a PhD. This year marks my fortieth year doing sex-related work. I'm so proud of the prostitution work I did. However, the sessions I did were invisible; there isn't the documentation. Just as home making, housekeeping, motherhood, and care giving are not appreciated or well documented in our society . . . Same with prostitution. It's like "women's work."

About my johns . . . Mostly I worked in Manhattan massage parlors. I loved my johns and they loved me. I always preferred the men that touched my heart in some way. I wasn't into the young, studly, hunky guys but was more into the differently abled, blind, scarred, ampu-tees, messed-up vets, widowers, and the socially handicapped, the awkward, the shy . . . I had all kinds of johns: rich, middle class, poor, fat, skinny, funny, sad, Hassidic, Saudis, vets, virgins, Mafiosos, police,

337

The Brothel

accountants, artists . . . I met and pleasured all kinds. On some rare occasions, women came along with their men. We called them "jills." They were "swingers" and pretty cool women.

In a more compassionate sex-positive society, prostitutes and johns would be government-subsidized. It would be a social welfare health and wellness thing. In Holland, I heard that the government used to pay for prostitutes to service some of the lonely, home-bound people on welfare, which I thought was so compassionate and valued touch and sex. With the budget cuts, and all the talk about "trafficking," I doubt they do it anymore. But at least these days there is Internet porn at least. Porn stars have likely replaced the real live girls.

My favorite john? I didn't call them "johns" but clients. So I had this client I'll call Samuel. Not his real name. I saw him steadily for twenty years, usually twice a month. Over twenty years you really get to know someone. When I met him originally, he had three little kids, then they started growing up, getting married, then they'd have their drugs and alcohol problems, then they got divorced . . . When-ever we would get together I'd ask him, "How are things? How are the kids?" He was someone that I wouldn't have been having sex with had he not been paying me. But I cared about him deeply and genu-inely wanted to know about how his life was going. When his business took a turn for the worse, I lowered my price for him. Looking back I'd have to say it was definitely a type of long-term relationship. The only reason it ended was because I moved out of New York. He was a great guy. He owned camera stores. I met him when I was 18. We split up when I was 38. He saw me grow up too. He was a client, and also a friend. Such things are more common than people might think. This arrangement was not so different than many American relation-ships. That's why the laws against prostitution have got to go. They are totally unfair and mean.

Clients and orgasms. Sure, I had orgasms with clients, even though it was kind of a taboo at that time to admit it. Women weren't sup-posed to enjoy sex that much! Today, whores are much more open about enjoying the sex. I usually kissed my clients if they wanted to kiss. I thought it was just way too weird to say "no kissing allowed," That to me was uncomfortable. Blow jobs are okay, but kissing clients is still a taboo.

Respect. A lot of women I worked with really didn't respect their clients. I respected my clients, as I tend to see the intrinsic, unique worth of every person. I was raised Unitarian by humanist parents. I think the whore-client relationship is very influenced by our childhoods, our parents, what we bring to the table as it were. I had many clients who didn't respect me, probably because of how *they* were raised. We're all the walking wounded. But still, magically, somehow you made it all work. It was still a win-win situation even when it was all screwy and convoluted. We are all complex creatures.

My reactions to my clients sometimes surprised me. One guy was quite disrespectful. He was from a country that is known to be very misogynist—which will remain unnamed. He kept trying to have anal sex with me, even though I told him "NO!" I didn't want to have anal sex with him. He kept trying to provoke me, make me angry. He was being manipulative and mean and grabby. Still I felt inclined to be nice to him. I felt like, *Ugh, this guy needs to learn how to love. Gee, I'll model love for him,* I thought. *I'll kill him with kindness.* I don't know if my strategy had any effect or not. Perhaps it was simply my way of coping with a challenging situation, and I needed to pay my bills. Other women might have kicked him in the balls and thrown him out. But then whores have the ability to put up with behaviors other women would never manage to put up with. That's why we deserve to be generously compensated. Some men can be very rude. On the other hand, some clients are absolute angels.

A whore and a client can have a complicated relationship. One john always brought me a gift every time he came to see me. He brought me a pearl necklace, a ring, a bra, or something. But eventually, as much as I really loved all the gifts, he fell in love with me, and he tried to weasel his way into my life. It was too much, and I sort of had to "break up with him." Yes, whores do sometimes break up with their johns. He was pretty devastated. He was in love and that was not okay. That was uncomfortable for me. I'm sure he soon found another whore to buy gifts for.

There have been times where I have definitely felt like I was a john. As a pin-up photographer for ten years, when I was photographing men and women, to be honest, sometimes I felt like I was a john, especially when I was shooting guys because they—you know—they had to have big erections in the photos. So they would jerk off for me for hours sometimes, and then I'd pay them. I sometimes felt like a "dirty old man" and a "voyeur." Because they were younger than I was, and I'd pay them, and they were working it. But that was okay. I didn't mind being a john!

I heard about a recent study where some researcher did a survey and discovered that people who have been prostitutes are ten times more willing to be johns than the average person. So, if you've been paid for sex you understand the value of that experience on some level.

As a prostitute, you can also be getting a sort of sexual thrill, by the sheer kinkiness and humanity of it all. Lots of clients want to eat a whore's pussy. It's part of the job. In those instances, perhaps the whore becomes the john. There is a momentary role reversal. The whore is using the john for her pleasure. He's paying her, but perhaps she is subsidizing his purchase. She's paying the john by surrendering her bodily pleasure, which makes him the whore, working to please her. Its all so deliciously twisted.

My johns adored and worshipped me, therefore they empowered me. When I was 18, 19, and 20, I had a poor self-image and needed attention. It's hard for people who haven't been prostitutes to imagine, but I think it's often true. There can be a very symbiotic relationship happening.

Being a whore was great preparation for being an artist. Beth Stephens, my partner and collaborator, and I just did a live art piece in a Brooklyn gallery—Grace Exhibition Space. Our work is exploring the earth as lover, instead of earth as mother. So we built a bed frame and poured fifty-five big bags of fresh dirt into it. We took off our clothes and got into the bed of dirt. Then we invited our audience to take off their clothes and join us. On one hand, it's very different than being a prostitute. But then again it's not. We were paid to get in bed with total strangers, naked. In a sense we are turning art patrons into johns and jills. It's fun to play in these realms. I think that in some ways, we are all whores, johns and jills.

It's a pity that there's such a negative connotation about paying for sex. There are very few out johns in the world. I really respect those few. Fred Cherry, who passed away, Hugh Loebner, and Charlie Sheen are the only out johns I can think of, after all these years. They are very brave. No one wants to admit they pay for sex. Yet millions of people do, one way or another. Being a john is actually far more stigmatized than being a sex worker.

The laws against prostitution are beyond screwy. I absolutely think more women paying for sex is in the future. It's part of women's empowerment. It's part of having some of that privilege men have enjoyed for centuries.

I'm interested in this idea of expanding the idea of what a john is, or a jill. I also did a masturbation ritual, which was called "The Legend of the Ancient Secret Prostitute," in a theater piece called *Post Porn Modernist*. I was just fresh out of prostitution, so it was just an extension of that. Now that work is studied in many universities. In my theater pieces, I would do "Tits on the Head"—Polaroid photos for $10 on the stage. There would be a line of folks paying me $10 for their turn. It was public prostitution. I turned my whole audience into johns. But because it was in a theater context, an art context, it was socially acceptable.

I've become a pimp for the earth. I sell erotic experiences with nature. My partner Beth Stephens and I have been doing "Ecosex Walking Tours." People pay us to show them how to have an erotic and sensual experience with nature. If people loved the earth more, and took more pleasure in nature, they might take better care of our resources and stop polluting so much. Our work is at sexecology.org

A happy ending . . . Once when I was touring a show on the road, the houseboat where I lived accidentally burnt down. I lost most of what I owned, my cats died, and it sent me reeling. Although I didn't ask anyone for help, people started sending me money to help me get back on my feet. Which I did very quickly. Old clients and porn fans heard about it and sent money anonymously. It was so touching. So if anyone tells you that old whores always have tragic endings, and that johns are cruel, horrible people, they are wrong.

ANNIE M. SPRINKLE was born in Philadelphia in 1954. She was raised in L.A., was a psychedelic teen in Panama City, Panama, spent her "wonder years"—from the ages of 18 to 40—in Manhattan, then returned to California where she has been based for the past twelve years. Her mother was one of the top ESL (English as a second language) teachers in Southern California. Her father was a playwright and social worker. He was with the U.S. Embassy's aid program in Panama for four years, where she went to high school. Then he became a PhD and university professor specializing in gerontology. He wrote and produced numerous plays and text books. Both parents were feminists, antiwar protestors, civil rights activists, and politically engaged. Sprinkle earned a BA at School of Visual Arts then became the first porn star to earn a PhD (IASHS). She has been an activist in sex worker rights for forty years, founded Occupy Bernal, and is currently a passionate environmental activist pioneering the ecosex movement. A former prostitute and "porn legend," she has proudly had sex with over 3,500 people. She has also written and done photography for most every '80s to '90s sex magazine as well as many non-sex publications like *Newsweek* and *The New York Times,* and has published five books with Tarcher/Penguin, Continuum, and Cleis Press. Annie has appeared on many TV shows, including HBO's *Real Sex* four times. She has toured five theater pieces about her life and work in sex. Her work as a performance artist and "radical sex educator" is studied in many universities. Her private pleasures are cuddling her black lab, Bob, swimming, walking in nature, hot tubbing, getting as many massages as possible, and spending time with her elderly

342

mother and blood family. Her guiltiest pleasure is reading the National Enquirer every week. For the past ten years she has collaborated with her life partner, artist Elizabeth Stephens. Visit Anniesprinkle.org, loveartlab.org, and her new site, sexecology.org.

PAYING FOR IT

David Henry Sterry interviews Chester Brown

David Henry Sterry: I'm talking to Chester Brown. So you wrote the book *Paying for It*, which was about paying for It. "It" being sex, of course. So, I was curious about something. I've been trying to get men to talk about paying for sex and it seems like at this time in history, it's much easier for people to admit that they sell sex then that they buy sex. I wondered if you had any thoughts about why you think that is.

Chester Brown: Obviously there's a stigma against both. I would think it would be about equal. But I suppose it's obvious why there are guys who don't want to come forward.

D: Why do you think that is?

C: Maybe it's the idea of what you're supposed to be like as a man, and, of course, most people who pay for sex are men. Although there are some women who do, but, yeah, it's this idea that men are supposed to be able to get sex if they want without paying for it. You're supposed to be able to seduce women or be appealing in some way and, if you're not able to do those things, if you're not able to get sex without paying for it, you're not the sort of man our culture thinks you should be. I've certainly heard guys say, "I don't have to pay for it," as if that's some kind of significant thing.

D: Yeah, I've heard the exact same thing from so many men that I've asked. They puff up their chests and say, "Hey dude, I never had to pay for it!"

C: Also, it occurs to me that there's been a relatively recent tendency in the media to see prostitutes as victims and johns as exploiters. I don't think most prostitutes see themselves as victims or see their clients as exploiters, but that way of seeing prostitutes and johns is pretty common now outside of sex-work circles, and it's more shameful to be the exploiter than the exploited.

D: So what was your first experience, buying sex?

C: I think it was late '99. No, no, no . . . early '99. I'd gone without sex for a couple of years. My girlfriend, my last girlfriend, had broken up with me, and a few years passed, and finally I was so sexually frustrated that I decided to go ahead and pay for it. It was at a brothel here in Toronto. It turned out to be a really positive experience with a very nice woman who was very attractive. It was such a positive experience that I was sold on the lifestyle or whatever you want to call it. There was no turning back. I don't know what would have happened if that first time hadn't been as positive as it was.

D: And what was this woman like?

C: Like a lot of prostitutes, she was very good socially. She had good conversational skills, and she was chatty, but not too chatty. She could initiate a conversation if there wasn't one going on, or, you know, she just knew how to talk and make me feel comfortable, and a lot of that isn't in the book because I didn't feel . . . Actually, a lot of what she told me was stuff about her family and, uh, you know, personal stuff. It got personal really quickly, which surprised me. I thought these women would be more guarded, but she told me a lot about herself that I couldn't put in the book. Her willingness to be open put me at ease.

345

D: Yeah, I've noticed that the best sex workers that I've purchased sex from have a way of just making you feel at ease and comfortable.

C: Yeah-yeah.

D: I guess that's true in almost all sorts of service industries you know, like from a psychiatrist to a nurse to a bartender. The best in their field, they just make you feel like you can let your guard down 'cause they let their guard down a little bit. It's kind of a fascinating dynamic.

C: Yeah.

D: So did you see that woman again? Or was this just a one-time thing?

C: I saw her three times. And unfortunately there was a little bit of an uncomfortable situation the third time. I guess I was just going on a bit too long sexually, and she didn't like it. There was a bit of poor communication. I didn't quite get what was going on. So, unfortunately, things ended on kind of a strange note between us, and I didn't see her again. I didn't want to go back because it had been a bit uncomfortable and strange. You know, I see one woman regularly now.

D: Right.

C: And if something like that happened with her—I call her Denise in the book so I'll call her that for this interview too—if something like that happened with Denise, we would probably be able to deal with it because our relationship has been going on longer. Plus, I was new to paying for sex, and probably, if I was seeing someone for the first time now, I'd know how to handle an awkward situation like that better.

D: I also think that's one of the, I hesitate to say "pleasures," but advantages to having a relationship with a professional like that is that you get to walk away with honor. There's no expectation. Because you paid for it.

Whereas with civilians, you're invested in this relationship, there's a social contract that says you can't just walk away after most civilian sex.

C: Yeah, that's true, although [chuckle] as I said, I'm paying only Denise for sex now and it's been years. I couldn't just walk away now.

D: Really?

C: If I did want to end the relationship with Denise, for whatever reason, we would have to have a conversation about it. Not that I'm thinking of ending it, I'm very happy in it, but it's not a casual relationship anymore. It's not casual the way a prostitute-john relationship would be if you saw each other once or a few times.

D: Yeah, absolutely. Have you ever had any experiences with a prostitute that . . . um . . . that were bad . . . that didn't go well?

C: Not really bad, certainly not where anger was expressed. Probably with that first prostitute, the third time I saw her was as bad as it got. Well, she did get angry, but she got over it and apologized pretty quickly. It didn't escalate into any kind of argument. But there was no situation where it seemed like there was really lingering anger . . . certainly not on my part. It didn't seem like on their part. Oh, okay, now something is coming to mind. There was a situation where a woman used her hair to hide her face while we were having sex. That wasn't a situation where either of us was angry, but it was clear that she was ashamed. She didn't want me to see her face and that certainly made me feel badly. I felt bad for her. So, probably that was the worst situation. No one ever stole my money. Although [chuckle] now that I say that, I'm remembering another situation where there was a prostitute who I gave money to, and then it turned out she didn't have condoms, and we couldn't have sex, and she didn't give me my money back. But I didn't ask for it back; I basically let her get away with taking my money without giving me anything.

D: Yes, in my experience it's very hard to get money back from a prostitute once you've given it to her.

C: Yep. And getting back to anger, now that I think about it, there have been several times that Denise has been upset with me. We do argue from time to time. But it never gets really serious, and we make up easily and quickly. Our arguments never get intense like the arguments I would have had with girlfriends or like the hellish fights you see married couples having.

D: So do you find a different quality in civilian sex than in professional sex?

C: Huh. Well, the best unpaid sex—where you and the woman are really into each other, and there's a lot of really intense passion, and things are really hot between you—yeah, I've never had that kind of sex when I was paying for it. The best unpaid sex is going to be, I think, more passionate and more hot than the best unpaid sex . . . er, sorry, the best paid sex. The best paid sex can still be really great and really intense, but, you know, without the emotional passion there, it's not going to be quite at the same level as the best unpaid sex.

D: Yeah, I agree with that. But sometimes sex workers have the most amazing skills. I enjoy that.

C: That's true. The best blow-jobs I've had have been from prostitutes.

D: Yes, I'd say that's true, and I have a large data pool to pull from. Has there been any fallout from you coming out about being a john, about paying for it, from friends, family, or people online?

C: Not that I can tell. No real negative fallout. I mean, certainly not all my friends or family think what I'm doing is good, they might have a somewhat negative take on prostitution, but it seems like they're all still willing to hang out with me. No one has shunned me or shut me out of their lives. The relatives that I thought might have the most negative take on it still seem to love me.

D: Ha-ha, that's great! I know when I wrote my book about selling sex, my family did shun me. They said it was because my parents are characters, minor characters, in the book but I said such nice things about them!

C: Okay.

D: When you were writing the book, was it an easy process? Was it difficult to write about this stuff?

C: It was pretty easy. It was no more difficult than writing and drawing any other book. In a lot of ways it was a lot of fun; I'm passionate about the subject of advocating for the rights of prostitutes and johns. It's fun creating a book you really care about.

D: And how many sex workers do you think that you've been with in the course of say, the decade or so?

C: Huh. I *paid* twenty-three women for sex, but there was the one who then didn't have sex with me, so, if we're talking about some sort of sexual contact, it would be twenty-two prostitutes. Actually, that's the lifetime total. If we're talking about just the last decade, I've only been with . . . how many? Maybe five prostitutes. Eight years ago was when I began seeing Denise exclusively.

D: So for the last eight years you've only paid one woman for sex.

C: That's right. The first time Denise and I had sex would've been back in 2003, and in early 2004 I started seeing her exclusively. Although, at that point, back in 2004, I had no idea I'd still be having sex with her eight years later. She's managed to keep me fascinated all this time. I'm

349

never tempted to call anyone else or search for anyone else. And she's basically left the profession. She stopped seeing other clients several years ago. And she doesn't have a boyfriend; she's monogamous with me. But I do still pay her for sex.

D: And do you ever have to explain this to like civilians that you are dating or anything?

C: To civilians that I'm dating?

D: Yeah.

C: No. I don't date civilians. I don't even try. I'm, like, totally out of the game of dating, or trying to get a girlfriend, or anything like that. I'm very happy with the situation I'm in with Denise. I'm not looking to get married or anything like that. I'm just a john now. I'm gonna be paying for sex for the rest of my life.

D: That's very interesting. It's definitely outside the norm. As a society, we're programmed so that at a certain age, you have to have a girlfriend, you have to have a wife, you have to have a kid, you have to have a house. These things, they seem so arbitrary to me, but it's like our culture wants us desperately to fall into this mold of conventional relationships.

C: Well, after my last girlfriend broke up with me, I looked at how our relationship had gone and how my previous relationships had gone and, even though those girlfriends had all been very nice women, I realized that I did not like being a boyfriend. I didn't like that role, so I thought I had to figure out some other way to, you know, have sex. And I much prefer paying for sex than being a boyfriend.

350

D: And what didn't you like about being a boyfriend?

C: A lot of things. When you're in a relationship, the dynamic seems to change over time. I only had two long-term girlfriends, but with both of them, as time went on, the sex tapered off in terms of frequency. We had sex less and less often. And talking with friends or whatever, hearing other people's stories, that seems to be the case with a lot of romantic relationships. You know, if a relationship has gone on for five or six years, that couple is not having as much sex as they were at the beginning of the relationship. In a lot of marriages, the sex stops altogether. So that's a very common thing, you know, even if they still like each other. And I just didn't feel free. I felt like I was reporting to someone else all the time, accountable to them. Like, if I wanted to buy something expensive, I had to get permission from her. Another thing was, I felt like, when I was in a romantic relationship, I was responsible for the other person's happiness, and maybe that's my own peculiarity, but I didn't like that feeling. You can't be everything for another person.

D: I find myself overwhelmed by that from time to time. There are many cultures, contemporary and historically, where the social norm is for a married person to have a spouse and then to have a lover who tends to be more the sexual partner than the spouse. But that doesn't seem to be the case for us North Americans.

C: Yeah, well, that's one way other cultures have handled it, but there's also polygamy.

D: Yes.

C: There are a lot of cultures where it was normal for a guy to have multiple wives.

D: Yes.

C: I don't think our system, where we have one romantic partner, where we get married and we're only supposed to have sex with one person—that doesn't make a lot of sense. Not that polygamy makes any more sense. I've found a system that seems to work for me, and it doesn't require monogamous commitment from anyone. I think the big problem is what I call possessive monogamy. I think we should have a lot more freedom in our sexual lives. We should stop making monogamous commitments. Trying to get your sexual partner to make a monogamous commitment to you is not a loving thing to do; it's selfish. And having said that, though, I have been monogamous for the last eight years with Denise, and it's working for me. But one of the reasons it works is because there isn't any heavy pressure on the relationship.

D: Well I think the word you used, "possessive," is a very telling one. And it doesn't sound like that is present in this relationship that you have.

C: No, not at all. We haven't made vows to each other to be monogamous; monogamy just happened. But if she wanted to start having sex with some other guy—if she thought that would make her happier—that would be fine by me. I want her to be happy. Not that she's *not* happy now. Anyway, if she did have sex with someone else, I doubt I'd be jealous; I wasn't jealous before when she was having sex with other guys, clients, and boyfriends.

D: Well, thank you so much for speaking with me, I appreciate it.

C: You too, David!

D: By the way I LOVED your book, *Paying for It: A Comic-Strip Memoir About Being a John*. I want to play you in the movie.

CHESTER BROWN was born in 1960 in Montreal and grew up nearby, in Chateauguay. His dad was an electrical engineer. His mom was a housewife. Before he was born, she was a schoolteacher for a short while. The art school he went to in his late teens is not worth naming because it was a waste of his time. In 1979, he moved to Toronto because he never learned to speak French, despite growing up with so many Francophones around him. He readily admits to being embarrassed that he never learned to speak French. He's lived in Toronto since then, except for a two-year period in the '90s when he lived in Vancouver. He worked in a photo lab for seven years before becoming a cartoonist. For a year he worked one night a week putting comic books into boxes and shipping them out to comic shops. He began self-publishing his work in 1983. In 1986, he became a professional cartoonist and has had six graphic novels published since then, including *Louis Riel* and *Paying for It*. He's won some awards, but won't pretend that they'd be meaningful to anyone outside the comic-book industry. He doesn't really have a hobby, unless it's reading. Most of his time is spent working, and he loves his work. Cartooning is fun for him. For many years, while he worked at the photo lab, his hobby was drawing comics; he managed to turn his hobby into a job.

The Brothel

Johns, Marks, Tricks and Chickenhawks

The Brothel

Tricks, Johns, Marks, and Chickenhawks

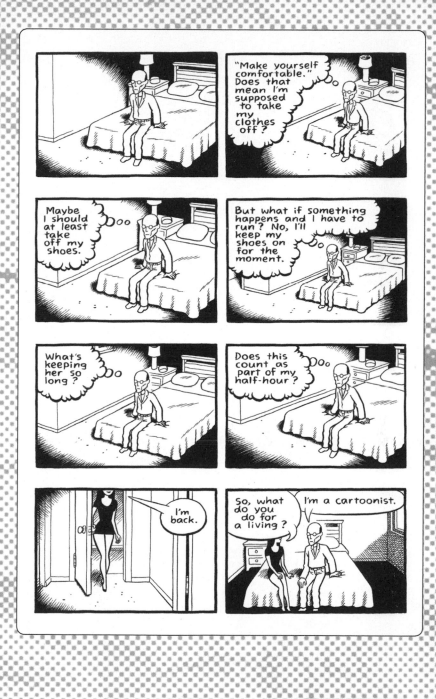

357

The Brothel

Tricks, Johns, Marks, and Chickenhawks

359

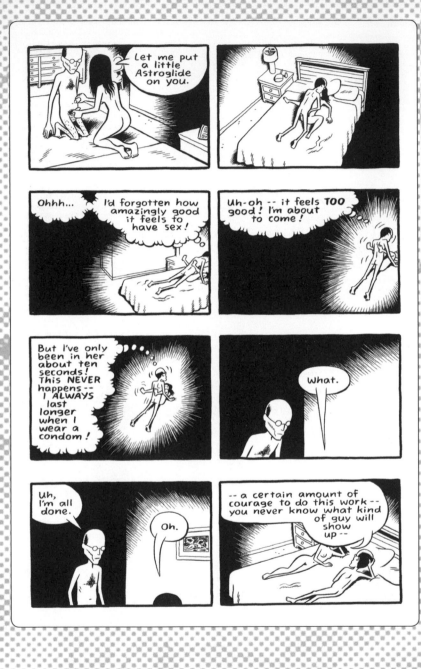

Tricks, Johns, Marks, and Chickenhawks

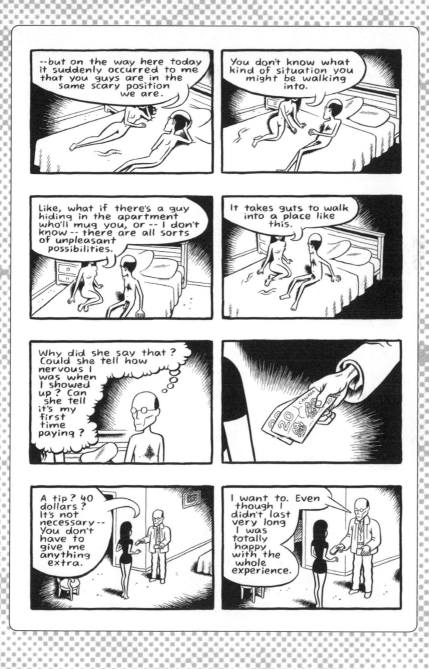

The Brothel

Tricks, Johns, Marks, and Chickenhawks

THE BURDEN HAS NEVER RETURNED.

The Brothel

THE NIRVANA OF SEX WORKERS

Hugh Loebner

Prostitution has made my life so much happier. Mainly because it has meant having so much more sex. Sex isn't that important to me. Unless I'm not getting any. I'm not a sugar daddy. I'm more like a NutraSweet daddy. A sugar daddy will buy a woman a horse and stables; I'd buy her riding lessons. A sugar daddy would buy a woman a car. I'll give her taxi fare. However, I'm very conscientious about being fair with the women I pay to have sex with me. I suppose that's why I've had so many good experiences with sex workers. In the end, it wasn't just about all the sex I had, which was great, don't get me wrong; it was also about making friends with lots of really amazing people. I remember Emily: She was a dancer from Baltimore. She was slender, very cute, quiet, alluring. I really had the hots for her. She was dancing for me, I bought her some drinks, and eventually we went back to my place. She was incredibly generous with her time. Again, we had some great sex together, but I also really enjoyed having dinner with her, shooting pool. She was just a great person to have in my life. A few years later I was on vacation and she called me. Her truck broke down and she needed some money to fix it. She had been so generous to me I thought, *Why not?* I sent her money to fix her truck.

I guess one of the big advantages to having sex with a prostitute is that you don't have to worry about being charming, which actually makes me much more charming. I don't want to be "on" all the time.

I can just be relaxed and be myself. How much is that worth? How much would you pay for that?

Sometimes while watching nude dancing I get into this very re-laxed state, it's kind of like Nirvana; it's blissful, like I'm in the presence of the most beautiful *objet d'art*.

HUGH LOEBNER has been a college professor, director of computing (academic and administrative) and consultant, and vice president and president of Crown Industries. His father started Crown Industries, Inc. He was as sleazy a character as Hugh is. Prior to starting Crown Industries, he started Crown Party Service, a party rental agency. Hugh's lived in New York City; the Catskills; Miami, and Miami Beach, Florida; Baltimore; and Norfolk, Virginia. He is notable as the sponsor of the Loebner Prize, an embodiment of the Turing test. He is an American inventor, holding six United States patents. He is also an outspoken social activist for the decriminalization of prostitution. For fun, he invent things and spends too much time on the Internet reading liberal blogs.

6

Peep Shows,
Strip Clubs, and
Adult Theaters

IMPROBABLE GOD: A TRUE STORY FROM THE LUSTY LADY, CA. 1990

Carol Queen

At the Lusty Lady Theater there were two work stations: the stage, where half a dozen women strolled languidly around, barely clothed (there was a management rule that you could wear a garment that covered your breasts OR your puss, but never both at once), surrounded by windowed booths where the men peered in to look; and the Private Pleasures booth, where you got to have the as-advertised one-on-one "Talk to a Real Live Nude Girl" experience—the window between the booth and the hallway could be closed with a curtain once a customer had been lured inside, and the window and intercom between the customer and the live nude, etc. left nothing to the imagination except the sense of touch. And of course, we provided that ourselves: The entire place was a temple to masturbation, except that the girls on the main stage couldn't as easily devote themselves to this practice as we could in Private Pleasures; onstage we were encouraged to stay on the move and finger ourselves only desultorily, and even that was a problem until I began to encourage the use of baby wipes between bouts, otherwise we would also leave our own pussy flora on the handlebars between the windows and give each other yeast infections.

I liked the stage, where I was surrounded by wild-child women of every stripe—shaved-headed dykes wearing femmie wigs; rocker chick girlfriends who almost all, as stereotype predicted,

369

were helping to fund their no-good boyfriends' bands; punk zine-makers; women's studies majors taking postmodern feminist theory to the streets, or rather to the bank; exactly one moonlighting downtown San Francisco executive secretary, who—bonus!—was still nursing her four-year-old, so she lactated; a pack of aspiring performance artists; and me, a grad student in sexology. Well, it was like a lab! Plus, as a bi-dyke who had recently reintegrated the mysterious male of the species into her repertoire, I got to study up on penis variety, right- and left-handed male masturbation techniques, and other interesting details I'd forgotten since high school or never knew.

Onstage, and backstage, the women had an easy camaraderie that eluded most all-women's spaces I'd ever been part of. Our lockers back there were piled high with wigs and drag, and we shared makeup tips, stories, and sometimes intimate time after work, though most of the women who liked women had outside girlfriends already—it was just beginning to be a big status symbol for S.F. dykes to be able to date a stripper. Some of my best friends, twenty years later, are women I met on that stage; my very first day I met my dear friend Wasabi, lately emigrated from Santa Cruz, who surprised me by pointing out another dancer, Zizi, and informing a customer who was watching her hungrily that Zizi had been "raised by wolves!" Wasabi—hotter than anything—was also so named because she wore one of those stretchy sleeveless dresses you could buy in 1989, the whole thing the perfect celadon green color of a dab of wasabi. She strolled across the stage in it, her splendid ass rolling it up her thighs and over her cheeks as she went. I never did figure out how she was able to do it, but it was a stunning crowd-pleaser of a move; on one side of the stage she'd be clothed, and by the time she got across she'd be half-naked.

I liked the stage all right. But I liked the Private Pleasures booth even better. Onstage we couldn't easily talk to the customers—the rock music we "danced," or rather, writhed, to was way too loud, and you couldn't tell someone your name without shouting—and as it turned out, I liked talking to the customers almost as much as masturbating for a living. I was incredulous when a few of the less sexually identified girls said they faked orgasms when they did this—good God, it was bad enough to do it with your lousy lay of a rocker boyfriend (you were only reinforcing bad behavior), but faking it on yourself? That was just incomprehensible to me. In my view, that and the women made this the best job I'd ever had, and the only real downside was having to punch a time clock, which I considered—there and at the pizza place where I'd worked years ago—fundamentally insulting.

The booth worked like this: Picture a small five-by-five square room covered, floor to ceiling, with red shag carpeting. I entered by a door in the back that attached to a tiny dressing room. In front of me, a large window allowed me to see my customer, sitting on a bench in a small, plain booth of his own, its only other furnishings a box of tissues and a trash can. To my right, another window let onto the hallway, where I could survey the scene when I didn't have a customer in with me. When I did, red curtains obscured the view. Between me and my visitor there was a contraption where he could put money and I could hit a switch that turned on the lights and intercom, the better to see and hear each other with, my dear. When alone, I had another intercom I could use to broadcast my availability down the hallway and into the lobby: "Hey gents, it's Minx in the talk booth, and I am *sooo* lonely in here! Come brighten up my night and tell me a story!" (Strictly speaking, it was not always night; the Lusty Lady opened at 7 AM, supporting hordes of downtown worker bees with that necessary wank to calm them down before the big meeting, and lunchtime was busier than most of the evening hours. Customers were not always white collar, though those who were had all developed the knack—did they advise each other to do this, I wonder, or each develop the idea by himself?—of tossing their ties over their shoulders the way men do when they're in a restaurant eating soup.)

My stage name was Minx Manx. Stage names were not optional,

but required, and I wanted a cat name, but all the feline ones were taken. There was a Kitten, a Tigress, a Kitty, and a Cat. Manx wasn't spoken for, though, and while not sexy enough for a first name, it worked fine paired with Minx, the moniker I'd grown fond of when reading the tragically brilliant *A Confederacy of Dunces*. There were also many women named after exotic spices—Wasabi was one of this group—and a surprising number whose names referenced the great rivers of the world.

One night I *was* lonely in the booth; it had been slow, and time ticked past much faster while engaged in talking, masturbating, or both, so I hoped to lure in a customer with my trusty intercom. There were few guys in the place, and one, who kept looking at me around the corner of the hallway, would vanish behind a pillar whenever he saw me looking at him, hiding out. But then he'd pop out again. He was a furtive, ratty little man of indeterminate middle age, the kind of fellow whose suit coat elbow patches covered actual holes, not a professorial look he'd affected on purpose. I realized at last, as I tried to sweet-talk him in—"C'mon, baby, I see you! Why are you so shy? Come in and talk to me, I can just tell you have something special you want to talk to me about"—that he was trying not to be observed by any of the other men in the place as he made his way down the hallway towards me. At last he covered the last few feet of open ground and scurried into the booth, locking its door.

He seemed just as nervous in private; he stammered and hemmed as I welcomed him in. "Um, um, um, is it—is it true that I can, can m-m-m-masturbate in here?"

"Why, yes, baby! Of course! Please make yourself comfortable, unzip, and let's start feeling good together. Do you have anything special you want us to talk about tonight?"

Did he ever.

"I, I, I was hoping I could ask you to say something for me while I, I, m-m-masturbated—can I ask you just to say it and repeat it until I'm,

I'm, I'm all done?" This was very common in Private Pleasures—
most men had some sort of fantasy they liked to experience through
narration while they jerked off, or a particular kind of language they
wanted to hear as an aural accompaniment to the feelings they could
generate with their hand. Since they were essentially paying to do
what they could do at home for free, the visuals and the auditory part
of the experience became supremely important, the real reason they
were there.

"Of course, baby! I'll say pretty much anything you like. What
would you like me to say?"

"Plea-plea-please just repeat this until I'm done," he said again,
"the words, 'I do not believe in the improbable God of the Eighth
Commandment.'"

"Pardon me?"

But I'd heard him right the first time: "I do not believe in the improbable God of the Eighth Commandment."

"Um, okay, baby! Let's get to it!" I pulled my panties off and stood up
so I could sway my hips and bring my pussy over near his eye level—actually, since he was such a small man, I towered a little. And as I wiggled
my ass and began to stroke my mound, and he pulled his furtive little
dick through his zipper and began going to town, I purred, "I do not
believe . . . in the improbable God . . . of the Eighth Commandment."

Backwards, for the ass view, and then bent over, so I could see
him between my spread thighs: like almost all of them, he stared
fixedly at whatever pink bit I showed him, and again, sing-songily,
I repeated: "I do not believe . . . in the improbable God . . . of the
Eighth Commandment."

All the while I was scrolling through distant memories like they
were microfiche: Eighth Commandment! Eighth Commandment!
What the fuck is the Eighth Commandment?

Now, I'm not a big Bible-reader. I do have one, though, and I
have studied up a little. I've not broken all of the commandments, although I believe I do not have a perfect record, either,

commandment-wise. As my ass swayed, mentally I picked up my dad's old 1926 Bible from the shelf where I kept it and turned to the commandments—what the fuck chapter were they in, anyway?—and tried to visualize the page. This seemed deeply important to me, because as I told you, I was a sexology student, and I wanted to know *how on earth* such a phrase came to be eroticized. I pictured my visitor as a tiny little boy, before the elbow patches and the furtive mien. A little boy under a pew, maybe, diddling himself while the preacher thundered? Could that experience capture a phrase as in erotic amber, always and ever-after a trigger for sexual arousal? I tried to remember my Havelock Ellis; this theory *did* sound a lot like early sexology. Eighth Commandment: Was that the one about lying? "Thou shalt not bear false witness"? Maybe the child had been caught up in a lie and punished. Maybe he played with his little penis to feel better. Maybe . . .

I was masturbating along with him by now, fingers flashing between my labia in front of his eyes. "I do not believe . . . in the improbable God . . . of the Eighth Commandment . . ." It came out a little breathier now.

But by God, this was weird! Kittenish as my voice was, I really found myself wishing I had that Bible with me in the booth; I wanted to pound my fist on it! I wanted to preach!: *"I do NOT BELIEVE! in the IMPROBABLE GOD! of the EIGHTH! COMMANDMENT!"*

Jeez!

My mental culmination seemed to cause his literal one. He spurted into his hand, gave a small sound, and then hastened, as they so often do, to grab a tissue and wipe up and get the hell out of there. He thanked me before leaving, though; some, jizz expelled, lose their social skills altogether.

I kept my curtains, and the booth, closed for a while longer, going over this encounter. I didn't want to mutually masturbate with any kind of normal person right then; I was too occupied with the mystery of Improbable God, as I began calling him in my head right away.

Eighth Commandment! Eighth Commandment! What the fuck is the Eighth Commandment? How the fuck did he come to be a furtive little man in San Francisco who masturbated to this phrase? (I saw him once again and this time he also wanted me to dangle my shoe off my foot so he could see lots of toe cleavage, so maybe my under-the-pew theory was correct after all.)

There is a postscript to my story. I have been telling this tale for over twenty years now, performing it in front of audiences, leavening my book readings with spoken word between the essays. And one year, in Eugene, two little dykes approached me after my reading. One was dragging the other, who seemed more reserved, but the one young woman was intent: "That guy! That guy! The one in the peep show!"

Immediately I thought, as I always do, *Oh shit—that wasn't her dad, I hope!* I realize I am bringing the most intimate stories out of the confessional of the peep show booth and sharing them with everyone, stories the people who shared them with me never imagined I would take onstage or onto the page—I try to stay as mindful as I can about privacy.

"That guy! Her ex-girlfriend came from that exact same cult!"
Cult?
"Yeah, every time she did anything that she got punished for, she had to say, 'I believe in the improbable God of . . . ' Well, whatever she did."

Is that so? Mystery, perhaps, partly revealed.

I think of Improbable God to this day: He is like an avatar to me, not a newfangled online self, but the old-school kind—"an incarnate divine teacher." Whatever had happened to him, punished for lying or whatever he did—this puzzle remains inscrutable because someone tells me different editions of the Bible move the commandments around so they're not always in the same order, so for all I know he was coveting his neighbor's wife—whatever profound moment seared this line into his psyche, he does NOT *believe* in the

Improbable God. He's saying *no!* to him, and he's doing it through the medium of his cock, linking the pleasure he can get from it to his ability to speak up, speak for himself, say the forbidden. A helpless little kid, punished, maybe abused, grabbed his cock to feel better, and has never let it go. Thinking of him gives me strength, affirms how powerfully the erotic impulse insinuates into our experience, and reminds me that, if we look at it from enough different angles, all of sexuality is really just as inscrutable as his own strange and fantastic example.

CAROL QUEEN, PhD is a writer and cultural sexologist and is the founder, with her partner, Dr. Robert Lawrence, of the Center for Sex & Culture (www.sexandculture.org). Her father was an elementary school teacher. Her mother was a bookkeeper. She has worked as a waitress, Gay People's Alliance director (University of Oregon), restaurant manager, graduate teaching fellow (sociology), catering penguin, education director of a small AIDS organization, Lusty Lady peep show performer, San Francisco Sex Information training coordinator, and sexologist. And writer. And call girl, but she reckons that's not a job, it's an adventure. Plus, she does public performance and speaking all over the place. Her erotic novel *The Leather Daddy and the Femme* (1998) won a Firecracker Alternative Book Award; a "director's cut" edition came out in 2003. Her first book, *Exhibitionism for the Shy* (1995, 2009), explores issues of erotic self-esteem and enhancement, and she also authored an essay collection entitled *Real Live Nude Girl: Chronicles of Sex-Positive Culture* (1997, 2002). She's also edited several volumes of erotica and essays and has appeared in explicit educational videos, notably *Bend Over Boyfriend*. She has addressed scholarly conferences, including the International Conference on Prostitution and the International Conference on Pornography. In 2009, she debated the question of promiscuity ("Virtue or vice?") for the Oxford Union at Oxford University, England. Perhaps most closely affiliated with the bisexual and sex work communities, Carol has been speaking publicly about non-mainstream sexualities, from lesbian to leather, for thirty-five years. She's an Oregon-raised, twenty-five-year San Francisco transplant. She makes collages, usually involving the Virgin Mary and vulvas. She loves to travel, especially by train. She and her partner, Robert, haunt estate sales, where they keep an eye out for materials for the CSC archive—like your great-grandfather's mimeographed WWII porn stories. She got to San Francisco by heeding a long-ago storyteller's advice: "Follow what fascinates you!" When not doing sex-positive stuff, she loves to travel and go junking.

HOW TO DATE
A STRIPPER IN FIVE EASY STEPS

Essence Revealed

If rule number one for sex workers is get the money first, then rule
number two is don't date the customers. Most people assume that
strippers must have men clamoring to date them. Not true. The job
makes it truly difficult to have a long-term relationship. "Stripper" is
such a stigmatized term. The media has done a great job at portraying
us as damaged, valueless goods. Most men won't admit it, but they
cannot handle that their girlfriend is the "S" word—a stripper.

I never break rule number one, but I have broken rule number
two. It leads to predictable and disappointing results. Meet a guy
at club, thus ensuring he knows what you do out of the gate. Go on
date. Start dating exclusively. Get asked to quit dancing. Cue in issues
all stemming from partner not being able to handle dating a stripper.
Relationship ends, sometimes with no warning or arguments whatsoever. And repeat.

Yet, every night at strip clubs, guys kill themselves trying to get
a stripper's number. I can count on one hand with fingers left over
how many guys I've given my number to at work. Many ladies have
a separate work phone that they use to give regulars. I never got a
work phone.

One night at work I sit with Brian and his boss. Brian and I end
up going into the V.I.P. room. We spend our time back there mostly
talking and flirting between me dancing for him.

RULE NUMBER 1: Respect My Time at Work

We stayed back there for three hours. If I meet someone who I may truly be interested in at work, it sucks. I'm at work, so I cannot stop working to hang out with someone I am crushing on. I won't just give someone my number or bother to take theirs if I have barely had time to talk to them and feel them out. Brian gets this without being told and respectfully pays for the time that we spend talking. We can chat and get to know each other without me feeling obligated to leave him to get back to hustling.

RULE NUMBER 2: Don't Try to Get Me to Break Club Rules Because You Sense That You Are Different Than the Other Customers.

There are huge sparks flying in the V.I.P. room, but I do not break club rules. No touching and definitely no kissing! The only contact we make is through the chemistry that is shooting back and forth between us. After three hours we wrap up our time. Because of us having such a long conversation, I am clear that he is not an axe murderer. I take his number. For some reason when I give people my number they do not call me. I don't want to risk not being able to connect with him outside of work. I'm sure that he does not think I am going to call. I do.

RULE NUMBER 3: If You Do Not Try Anything on the First Date, I'm Going to Want to Jump on You More from the Sexual Tension Created

On our first date, we go to dinner. He is the perfect open-car door, pull-chair-out-for-me-first-to-sit-down gentleman. The sparks are growing to an all-time high. If they could be touched, they would singe the fingertips. He does not try so much as to hold my hand. Oh.

My. God. I want him to hold my hand. I would let him. I want him to touch my arm. That would be respectful enough. Good gracious, I want to jump all over him with my hands, lips, hips. We only hug goodbye.

RULE NUMBER 4: Treat Me With Genuine Human Respect and Dignity

He doesn't act like he is ashamed for me to be around. I've experienced being a "secret" that never gets told to family or friends. Magically, I never meet anyone in his circle save maybe one best friend (one must brag to *someone* about getting a stripper, right?). I meet his brother right away. I actually drag the two of them to see *What the Bleep Do We Know?!* Before we ever have our first kiss, he makes sure that I am clear about the fact that he is interested in me for more than just the physical attraction. "I'm sure guys come at you sexually all the time," he says. It had been weeks since we first met. Finally we share our first kiss. It is slow, sweet, and lingering. He later admits to being nervous about touching me for fear of scaring me away. He wants to do everything right.

RULE NUMBER 5: Don't Ask Me to Quit (Especially If We Met AT the Club) and Let Your Insecurities Get in the Way of Our Relationship

We have a great time every time we are together. We speak on the phone every day. We live about an hour's drive away from each other. Therefore, we take turns driving to see each other. Never once does he treat me as if I am less than a person. Never once is "stripper" hurled like an insult meant to cut. Never once does he ask me to quit. Never once does he seem ashamed by me. A year later, we still can talk for hours about everything and nothing. We always laugh in each other's presence.

I will never forget this particular night. We are at his place. He is in the kitchen cooking me dinner. I am in the living room putting together a new shelving unit. We share a moment laughing at the irony. After dinner, before we go to sleep, we are sitting on the bed. "I have to tell you something," he says. The look on his face makes me start to wonder what I did wrong. I don't think I did anything wrong. Did he do something wrong? Is this the part where out of nowhere he tells me he can't see me anymore? Is this the "I can't see myself dating a stripper long term but I'll never admit it so I'll break up with you for no reason" talk? I brace myself.

"I got a promotion at work," he says. Relief, that's great news. He has a pretty high-up position now and works really hard so he deserves it. "Congrats," I say as I move to hug him, happy for both of us. "It means I'm moving to Detroit," he says. Without any delay or reaction time, tears burst from my eyes. My heart shatters into millions of pieces and fall, piercing my stomach from the inside. Finally, finally I meet someone secure enough to get that stripping is just a job. I finally meet someone who doesn't keep me isolated from the rest of his world like a dirty little secret. This is someone who doesn't hinge my human value onto a stigmatized label, and he's leaving me. This is not how I want the story to end. I want to tell you that we lived happily ever after. However, we never even got the chance to see if we could last that long. Tears still well up and overflow from my eyes when I recount the night. The media and limited views of morality have done such a good job of dehumanizing strippers that no one can see our humanity. No one cares that I am someone's first-born girl child, a sister, a really good best friend, a favorite aunty, a nerdy student, etc. Very few people truly want to honestly know how to date a stripper. Brian is the first person that I met who did. For this I will love him forever.

I am not able to attract and have a healthy long-term relationship until after I quit being a stripper full time. Everyone wants the trophy of being successful at getting the stripper's number. They may even want to parade you on their arm. They definitely want to have sex with you. But no one that I met besides Brian truly wants to know how to date a stripper in any amount of steps.

ESSENCE REVEALED is first-generation West Indian born and raised in Boston. She Got her BFA at NYU's Tisch School of the Arts and MA at NYU's Steinhardt School of Education. Her writing has appeared places such as $pread, Corset, BurlesqueBible.com, and 21st Century Burlesque. After about a decade in upscale gentlemen's clubs, she hung up the stilettos and picked up sparkly gloves and feathery boas. For the past three years she has performed nationally and internationally both solo and as a member of Brown Girls Burlesque. Her favorite thing to do besides reading is to lie on the beach in Barbados to rest up for a night of calypso dancing.

Johns, Marks, Tricks, and Chickenhawks

RULES OF ENGAGEMENT—
SPECIAL REQUESTS

Berta Avila

A virgin at heart, your flesh seared in sin.
Pain, tears & sorrow—burrowed within.
Rage & defiance—your shield and your sword,
To yield unto those who call you a whore.

I was showing them all that I didn't need one fucking thing from them, sticking my tongue out at society, my mother, all men, and God. I was "woman, hear me roar." Never mind how I felt the morning after. I'd feel better after my first glass of sangria—wasn't that made with fruit? Well then, that was my breakfast of champions.

This was just another day for a 17-year-old single mom trying to survive. I pressed the gas pedal on my rundown blue Chevy Malibu. Old girl was hanging in there by a thread, new girl, me, was hanging by a thread too. I couldn't wait to get to work so I could down my first double scotch and soda. It had been a hard day: My toddler had a butt rash, my rent was due, and the babysitter was late. Coming up to my exit I could see the big neon sign flashing in bright fuchsia letters, The Doll House. Yeah, that was my place of employment. I liked the fact that I was working at The Doll House. It made me feel like I was . . . well, a doll. I felt like a woman, all self-dependent, supporting my kid, my sister, and myself. I liked that I could slip out of my black tasseled bra with ease, after my second double scotch, that is. I liked the wolf calls, the whistles, and the admiration in the men's eyes as I flaunted my stuff onstage. I liked the fact that I was now, officially, a topless dancer.

I grabbed my purse and walked as fast as my stilettos would allow. With the wind in my hair, and my slinky red dress clinging tightly around my body, I had the whole world in my hands. I walked into the club and slipped into my lioness stride. Smooth, sexy, young, and mean. Suddenly, my joy of anticipation dropped like a cement brick down to the dirty carpeted hallway that led to the dressing rooms. My "red carpet" turned into a grubby, grimy, booze-stained brown rug. There was Mike standing at the end of the bar with a big grin on his face. He reminded me of the big bad wolf waiting for Little Red Riding Hood. I swear I saw him lick his lips. I shuddered inside; the thought of him feasting on me was repulsive.

"There's my girl, the belle of the ball," he hollered out from across the end of the bar.

I remember thinking, *What the fuck is he doing here? Oh yeah, he owns the damn place.* He was holding the "you owe me" card over my head every chance he got. After all, not just anybody would hire a 17-year-old to dance topless. I better not forget his benevolence, and I knew exactly what the price was. I just didn't know if there was enough scotch in the world to load up on before screwing him.

I downed my drink while reaching down behind myself with one hand to make sure my thong was neatly tucked in my butt crack. I walked up to the stage in all my glory. It was a long, narrow stage about the size of two banquet tables, but to me, it was *Showtime at the Apollo*. It was lined with mirrors, and a shiny carousel-type pole sat in the middle. I stepped out onto the stage to the tune of "R-E-S-P-E-C-T, find out what it means to me," Aretha Franklin's soulful voice—"Respect," how ironic, how moronic too. It was a busy night, and tips were good. These dumb G.I.'s didn't know if they were putting twenties or ones in my thong as they slobbered at the edge of the stage with glassy eyes. They were way too fucked up to care. I was way too fucked up to care, either. But not too fucked up to not cringe every time Mike breathed his hot, boozy smelling whispers in my ear between sets.

"You're looking good, honey; have you given some thought to our little business deal?" he said as he leaned over me from behind and grabbed two handfuls of tit.

He had been talking to me about these so called "friends" he had who ran an escort service. They were supposedly a "legit respectable wife and husband team" who ran a good ole ma and pa business. Like they were selling fucking teddy bears or something like that. Mike ran it down for me like a pro; you sit around looking pretty until someone calls for an escort, then you just show up and escort them anywhere they want to go. Never mind the only place they wanted to go was three feet ahead to the hotel bed. No, these gentlemen didn't really want to go—they wanted to come! So, before we went anywhere, I would need to collect for either half an hour or a whole hour of my company—this was the agency's cut. Anything else besides my lovely company was considered a tip and that was mine to keep. The arrangement would then be strictly between the client and me. Then I would have the "choice" of where, how, and how much it would cost him. Oh, and by the way, I must always remember it's business before pleasure, money first.

"Yeah, I thought about it, but I'm having problems with my baby-sitter," I said as nonchalantly as I could muster.

"Come on, baby, you're a gold mine. You can make $300 to $500 per client," he added.

I don't know what behooved me to say, "Fine, I'll give it a try, but if it doesn't really pay, I ain't doing it."

Mike's face lit up like the neon sign outside. He had this slimy, sly smile on his face like I'd imagine a starved man would have when presented with a T-bone steak. *Ugh . . . what the fuck am I doing?* I thought to myself. At that moment I wanted to run, to spit in his face and run as fast and far as I could. But my feet were like cement blocks, my butt glued to the barstool. This tiny glimmer of sanity in the back of my head kept saying, *Don't, don't do it!* I downed my nth scotch. The voice faded away.

"Alright then, that's my girl. I'll take you down tomorrow before

385

you start your shift and I'll introduce you to them," Mike said. "But you do know what that means, don't you?"

"What," I said, dreading what was about to pour out of his filthy mouth.

"Well, that means you gotta be initiated," he added.

"Oh yeah?" I asked in a feigned "I don't give a shit" attitude.

"Well honey, tonight I'm gonna take you for a ride and show you the ropes," he said.

Scotch don't fail me now! I thought as I shrugged my shoulders and ordered another drink. The bar started to close down. A good thing cause I was far too wasted to dance again. In a haze I got dressed, thought for a second I could slip by Mike and make it out of there unscathed. Too late, Mike was standing right in my path, keys in hand, salivating. We drove around for a while and he kept talking a mile a minute in his usual coked-up speed, schooling me about the game, what to do, what not to do. I was so loaded I couldn't have made sense of it even if I had wanted to. I peered out the car's window as we pulled into this rundown motel. I remember thinking *You cheap SOB, you brought me all the way to J Town to get a cheap room?* J Town, as we locals called it, was short for Cuidad Juarez—as in Mexico where nobody gave a shit about a 40-year-old coked-up man and a drunk minor, not to mention everything was cheap. Rooms, booze, sex, all were cheap in J Town. Mike went and paid for the room, came back and opened my door as if he were a fancy doorman at the Ritz. I felt cheap.

"Now slide that pretty ass of yours in here," he said while opening the creaky door to the cheap rat hole.

The stench was unbearable, like rotting meat left in the fridge too long. In my drunken stupor I tried to hold my breath; impossible, it penetrated my nostrils and punctured my brain. Mike closed the door behind him and double locked it. For a split second I panicked. *I'm dead,* I thought to myself tripping over my own heels. I fell flat on my face unto the bed. Mike tore into me like a famished hyena. At the speed of lightning he pulled down the zipper on my jeans and peeled them off, heels and all. He then yanked my sweater over my head and ripped my bra off. Before I could catch my breath, he was on top of me, squeezing my breasts hard while trying to pry my legs open with his knees. I wanted to say, "Stop you asshole," but the words wouldn't come out. He kissed me, his tongue long, cold, wet, like a dead sardine. I tried pushing him off again but he grabbed my wrists and held me down tightly.

"Don't fight me, honey, that's not part of the deal," he said while breathing his rancid breath on my face.

Suddenly, he sunk his teeth into the fleshiness of my breast like a lion tearing into a gazelle. It hurt deeply, worse than when Mother would bite my fingers when I couldn't memorize my multiplication tables.

"Stop it, you're fucking hurting me, and don't kiss me on my lips!" I screeched and screamed out in pain. Where I found my courage, I'll never know.

"Good girl, that's rule number two: no kissing on the lips," he said.

With that he stopped abruptly and got up off me. I was both shocked and relieved. Maybe it was over; maybe he would take me back to my Chevy. Oh God, no, maybe now he's gonna strangle me and leave me here in this shithole where the rats can feed off me. I lay there quietly, playing dead. It worked with Mother's ass-kickings, maybe it would work now. I heard Mike's pants buckle and fly being undone. He walked into the bathroom, peed, and flushed.

"Come here, honey, I got a special request for you," he called out from the bathroom.

Shit, what now? I thought as I realized, to my dismay, I was sobering up. I walked naked and barefooted into the dingy bathroom. The walls were a pukey green; the once-white toilet was a dingy gray with crusty, rusty crud all in and around it. The tile floor was cold and grimy. I wondered how many different people had pissed and done other things on it. I stood at the entrance; I stared, amazed and nauseated—too much reality. There was Mike, butt-naked inside the claw footed, ancient-looking tub. He was crouched down like a frog, balls and penis swinging below him. Living through the songs in my head all I could think of was "goodness, gracious, great balls of fire" as I looked at him with all the wide-eyed wonder of a 17-year-old.

Puzzled, I asked him, "You want me to take a bath with you?"

"No, honey, just get in here. Don't you gotta pee?" he asked as if asking a toddler who was being potty-trained.

"I guess," I said, stumbling toward the dirty toilet.

"No, no, get in here. I want a golden shower," he said with a tone of impatience in his voice.

I crawled into the tub and sat down on the cold enamel. I pulled up my knees and hugged them against my chest. Mike pried them open with one hand while jerking off at the same time.

"Now, when I say go, you go. I want you to pee on me," he said with heavy breathing, "You got it?"

I nodded and waited for his command. I could remember reading some kind of crap regarding peeing and sex in one of the *Playboy* magazines my daughter's father had, so I had an idea about it. I sure as hell never thought I'd be peeing on someone. He just kept jerking off and mumbling obscenities under his breath.

"Now—go—now!" he said forcefully.

For a quick second I panicked. *What if I can't pee?* I thought to myself, but just as the thought came so did my pee. Mike leaned over me, balancing himself with his arm outstretched behind me grabbing the tub's edge. He kept jerking off while holding his penis directly under the stream of my pee. He started groaning and moaning as he ejaculated over me. I sat there in a puddle of cum and pee, marinating in sinful sludge. He stood up slowly and hopped out of the tub as he grabbed one of the towels.

"Why don't you clean up, honey, and come have a smoke with me," he said.

I was shivering and, what's worse, stone sober. I quickly turned on the water and splashed it over my lower body as best I could. I wrapped another one of the grimy towels around myself and I stepped out into the room. Dressing as fast as I could, from the side

I watched Mike reach into his back pocket and pull out some money from his wallet. He folded the bills, walked over to me, and stuck them in my bra.

"That, my dear, was a special request, and you always charge extra for special requests," he said as he buttoned up his shirt, cigar hanging out the corner of his mouth.

I kept my eyes lowered, afraid to look him in the eye, afraid that he might see my disgust. The ride back to The Doll House was silent except for the sound of the radio. I tuned into "I can see her laying there in her satin dress in a room where you do what you don't confess, sundown . . ." Gordon Lightfoot singing my song. I closed my eyes; sadness pierced through my heart.

"That was great, sugar; we'll have to do it again soon. I'll see you tomorrow," Mike said when we arrived back at the club's parking lot.

I couldn't get out of Mike's Caddy fast enough. "Sure, anytime, see you then," I said as I slammed the car door and ran to my blue Chevy.

I must have driven home in a daze. I quietly opened the door and took off my heels. I tiptoed in the dark, peeked in on my daughter and Pamela, the babysitter. They were both fast asleep. Usually, I would lean over my baby and kiss her on the forehead, but tonight I felt so dirty. Somehow, it was as if I was undeserving of kissing her, of tainting her with spiritual sewage. I was afraid I'd contaminate her with whore's spores. I went into the bathroom, locked the door, and undressed. My breast was hurting, so I turned on the light and took my bra off. I saw myself in the mirror.

"Mirror, mirror on the wall, who's the smuttiest of them all," I said to myself.

I touched my breast with my fingertips ran them over the soreness while I cupped it in my other hand. I sure had forgotten—Mike had sunk his teeth into my tit. I could see his teeth marks. He broke my skin and there was some dry, caked-on blood on the tiny incisions. It was red and swollen, tender to the touch.

I went down to my knees and started crying, *Fucking slimy bastard, he bit me.*

As I sat there holding my tit and crying I noticed some bills next to my bra. I reached out to grab them as I wiped tears and snot off my face with my forearm. I looked at the three bills, did a double-take. They were three crisp hundred-dollar bills. My eyes got big, my tears dried off. All of a sudden, my breast didn't hurt quite as much. I showered and scrubbed long and hard, and I budgeted in my head my newfound money. I lay down on my couch while visions of sugar-plums danced in my head.

I never did go back to The Doll House. I never went back to see Mike, although he must have called at least fifteen times in the following days. Every time the phone rang, my stomach would tighten up. I couldn't go back to dance anytime soon either, what with a bruised tit and all. Who wants to see that? Later I'd reminisce over that thought—oh yes, there were other freaks who would find that "erotic." Eventually, I made my way to the Pussycat Lounge, and yes, eventually I did make my way into the escort service scene.

My opening line on all my outcalls: "Listen up: four rules: 1) business before pleasure, money first; 2) no kissing on the lips; 3) no biting; and 4) No! I won't pee on you or let you pee on me!

I never forgot the rules.

BERTA AVILA is a Chicana who grew up in an impoverished West Texas barrio speaking Caló, the Spanish gypsy language of her mother. Berta is a gypsy rose with a spark of Jewish heritage from her absent father, who was born in 1899. The son of exiled Jews from Spain, Berta's father was a runner for the mob in the '40s in Chicago, then a shoemaker who eventually opened his own shop, where Berta got her first pair of stilettos. The very essence of her unique persona instigated endless torture long before bullying became a "topic of interest." Her rage morphed her into an independent, undaunted woman who learned to use tongue and pen as her shield and sword. In youth, her nomadic nature impelled her on cross-country, hitchhiking travels, tugging along her four-year-old. She holds a master's in urban survival and a minor in sarcasm, which is most useful in the art of single motherhood. She has lived in El Paso and Fort Bliss, Texas; Fort

Johns, Marks, Tricks, and Chickenhawks

Benning and Columbus, Georgia; Dunkirk and Rochester, New York; Fort Carson, Colorado; Albuquerque, New Mexico; Hercules, El Cerrito, Oakland, San Leandro, and Los Angeles, California. Her work is featured in *This Bridge We Call Home*; *Hos, Hookers, Call Girls, and Rent Boys* (Soft Skull, 2009); and on Scribd. She presently lives in the Bay Area, where she works as a linguist. Her writings are forever fueled by her ex-professions as an exotic dancer, escort service worker, "harlot by the side of the road" worker, brothel worker, and all-around vamp. She has also worked as a masseuse, waitress, medical legal assistant, medical transcriber, bilingual teaching assistant, interpreter, and translator. She is a spiritual warrior who finds respite in her passion for writing and her love for her daughters. She likes reading, writing, belly dancing, yoga, silk embroidery, and beading.

END OF A STRIPPER

Alvin Orloff

All good things come to an end, not least careers in the sex industry—
but I didn't want to think about that. Stripping at the Campus Theater,
a gay smut palace in San Francisco's trashy Tenderloin, was easy, fun,
lucrative, and strangely therapeutic. Here's how it went: I'd come out
on stage dressed in a skimpy outfit and dance around for five minutes
while flinging off my clothes. Once down to shoes and socks, I'd love
myself up a bit, then hop down into the auditorium to work the audience for tips. The men would ogle my nether regions (it was against
the law to touch) while running their hands over my firm young body
and stuffing cold hard cash into my socks. I had twenty minutes to do
this before it was time to get back on stage and climax (or pretend
to), bow, and exit.

For me, extracting money from the audience became a game of
skill with dollars for points. I had to figure out which dance moves
showed me to my best advantage, guess which audience members
were big spenders, and judge how long to stay with each fellow. The
money was not only an abstract score; it also paid my rent, freeing me
from the nightmare of a "real" job and providing welcome assurance
I wasn't quite as hideous as I'd always previously feared. We Campus
strippers weren't the tanned, handsome, beefcake Adonises who strip
for ladies, but we were all at least doable. Having been chubby and
392   homely enough while growing up to make it through high school
without a single date, the validation was important to me.

I'd been at the Campus for eight contented years when a downward trend in my tips became noticeable. It wasn't hard to figure out why: Stripping is a young man's game, and by that point I was one of the oldest guys working there. Now, sure, some genetically gifted fellows stay buff and sexy into middle age, but I clearly wasn't going to be one of them. At 35 I was already manifesting the decrepitude typical of elderly Eastern European Jews: The corners of my mouth turned down, giving me a permanently disappointed look; my body began storing fat for long, brutal Russian winters; dark bags of woe appeared under my eyes; and my shoulders slumped as if weighted down by centuries of anti-Semitism. I was starting to look less *ooh, la, la* than *oy, oy, oy*. I'd have to quit soon, or face the humiliation of getting fired.

The thought of reverting to the state of un-sexiness was depressing, but the thought of getting a "real" job induced panic. I couldn't type or drive a car, held no trade license or advanced degree, spoke no foreign languages, played no musical instruments, and was terrible at math. I had trouble waking before noon, mixed up times and dates, didn't know a thing about computers, and couldn't cook. True, I'd graduated Phi Beta Kappa from a good university, but I'd never once used the words "heuristic" or "ontological" in a sentence. One look at my résumé (nightclub DJ, telemarketer, exotic dancer) and anyone could see I was as a frivolous wastrel. Stripping, once a source of pride and pleasure, began making me feel anxious and doomed. It probably didn't help that Campus's matte-black, décor-free interior made it look like a theatrical set for *No Exit* or some other bleak, existentialist drama.

Considering my dilemma invariably rendered me so overwhelmed and exhausted that I had to lie down. Why did that feel so nice? Oh, right, *aging*. Oldsters are always getting tired. My fatigue would get worse and worse until finally I'd be sitting in a chair at some home gazing vacantly out a window wondering if Joe and Morty would be up for pinochle later. Actually, retirement sounded quite appealing—until I looked around. Even in my little circle of friends, freaky queens and anarcho-punks all, there were conspicuous signs of not just career activity, but success. People owned *cars* and even *houses*. People bought insurance and went on international vacations. They put money in IRAs (not, I was surprised to discover, the Irish Republican Army, but some sort of tax-free savings account) and 401(k) plans (I'm still not sure what those are). Far from retiring, my peers were entering their prime. I didn't know how, but I badly wanted to join them.

Or rather, I felt I *should* want to join them. In reality, my few scrapes with legitimate employment had been wretched. Restaurant work felt like a cross between the treadmill at the gym and one of those Japanese game shows where contestants get abused and humiliated in front of a sadistic audience. Office work was even worse, reminding me of a B-movie I'd seen as a child in which some hapless soul (bound and gagged, but eyes wide with a hysterical terror) was slowly, brick by brick, walled up in a dungeon. A single morning under the glaring fluorescent lights of a typical office left me feeling as if I, too, was being interred alive—albeit in a warren of gray cubicles rather than the basement of a castle.

Sometimes, while fondling my flesh, guys at the Campus would make improper suggestions. "I'm from Iowa, and we don't have places like this one here, no siree. I always drop by when I'm in town on business. Wanna come back with me to my hotel?" No, I never did. First, management forbade leaving with customers because they didn't want the place to look like a takeout brothel. Second, I usually had some very important nightlife event to rush off to after my show. Third, I didn't like thinking about such men. They were an alien and mysterious species to me, and one I strongly suspected of being dull and depressing.

Just once, though, a pair of guys got me tempted. They were younger than the usual customers, not much over 20, and wore the schleppy discount clothes of guys who aren't caught up in trying to look hip or sexy. They were quite chatty while pawing me, which I found super-cute because of their thick New Yawk accents. "We tink

Johns, Marks, Tricks, and Chickenhawks

you're real sexy!" one said. "Dats a great dance you do up dere!" said the other. The first was chunky, the second a string bean, and in my mind I nicknamed them Ralph and Ed after the Jackie Gleason and Art Carney characters from *The Honeymooners*. After I'd finished my show and was in the corridor leading to the lobby, I saw Ralph shoving Ed in my direction. The two of them were whispering to each other.

"Ask him, ask him!"

"No, you ask him."

"Nuh-uh, *you* do it."

"No way, *you*!"

It felt weird realizing that to them I was an intimidating, worldly whore. Couldn't they see I was just a shy kid like them underneath my brash exterior? Finally, Ralph screwed up enough courage to query (with blushing cheeks, no less), "Wouldja wanna do a private show for us?" Now, the Campus had a room in the basement where enterprising dancers were allowed— encouraged even—to take customers for . . . well, pretty much *whatever*. Don't ask. Don't tell. Normally I had no use for the space. I had no moral objection to prostitution, but since the dawn of the AIDS crisis, I'd become so sexually squeamish I wasn't willing to do with strangers most of the things guys wanted to do in that room. Ralph and Ed, however, were kind of utterly adorable, so I decided to make an exception.

"Okay," I said. "Follow me." I led the boys down the steep steps to the basement past the pool table, past the darkened maze for sex cruising, and through the door to the private room. To call the space skuzzy doesn't do it justice. This was a Stygian, crypt-like den of Dickensian squalor. The furniture-free space was tiny, perhaps six by nine feet, and illuminated by a single, weak, uncovered light bulb. The dank walls were hewn from solid rock while the floor was bare cement. The air smelled ancient and earthy, like the fetid exhalation of some subterranean beast, and one could hear the intermittent whoosh of wastewater from the rusty old pipes crisscrossing the ceiling. If not for the fakey-fake moans and hyper-repetitive disco

395

soundtracks from the movies being screened upstairs, I could've easily believed myself in hell's foyer.

The boys, unfazed by the ghastly surroundings, handed over some cash (I forget how much, but not much), and we began to mess around. Ralph took one side of me, Ed the other, and they shared the middle. Somehow, this all felt less like a couple of dudes getting it on with a stripper than what might happen at a Boy Scout sleepover, innocent and playful. I felt flattered that two guys a decade my junior were hot for me and was starting to think maybe I wasn't too old for my job after all when Ralph and Ed began whispering to each other again.

"You got the money?"

"Sure, sure."

"Ask him!"

"No, *you* ask him!"

Finally Ralph popped the question. "Wanna go back with us to our hotel?"

I did, actually. Before I could say "sure," though, something stopped me. My heart was breaking. I could see that Ralph and Ed loved each other with the unspoken, everlasting affection of best buddies. They were a dynamic duo of swashbuckling schlubs, forever embroiled in crazy shenanigans and madcap misadventures. The world might see them as low-status losers, but they could never really lose so long as they had each other. I'd had a friend like that once, a kooky co-conspirator and soul mate. We'd been inseparable for sixteen years, but a few months previously he'd died of AIDS. Since losing him I'd become prone to bouts of severe melancholy, and seeing the boys together was bringing one on. I worried Ralph and Ed would spot my mood, stop seeing me as a sex object, and start seeing a sad, lonely guy. If there's one thing a vain, narcissistic stripper doesn't want, it's being seen as a sad, lonely guy. I regretfully declined their kind offer and went home alone.

After that night, stripping was never the same for me. Seeing the Ralph and Ed as human accidentally demolished the emotional wall

Johns, Marks, Tricks, and Chickenhawks

I'd erected between my audience and myself. It had been easy to ignore the humanity of customers when they'd always been older and unattractive to me, but I could no longer take that dynamic for granted. Gazing out from the stage, I saw faces belonging to real men with real sexual needs and tragically limited prospects of getting those needs met. Sure, a few were probably content to ogle and paw attractive strangers, but how many were secretly yearning for something *more*, a sex object they could also talk to or someone to find *them* sexy? And how long would it be before I found myself in their shoes? I'd had plenty of boyfriends since shedding my childhood pudge, but would anyone want to touch me once it came back? In ten or twenty years, might I be sitting in some darkened theater hoping to bribe a stranger for a caress? Along with making me anxious, stripping also began making me sad. It may be unrealistic to hope for a world where sex always walks hand in hand with love, but does sex really belong in bed with commerce? Capitalism doesn't dehumanize sex more than it does other human interactions, but isn't that bad enough? Figuring old age would end my career soon anyway, I took the step I'd dreaded for oh so long and quit.

ALVIN ONLOFF spent his childhood in New Jersey, his teen years in Berkeley, and his entire adulthood in San Francisco—with one year off (for bad behavior) in Manhattan. His father was a newspaper editor; his mother was a potter (ceramicist, if you prefer). Before his latest gig as a bookstore manager, he worked as an exotic dancer, bicycle messenger, forklift driver, babysitter, and telephone interviewer. He began writing in 1977 as a teenage lyricist for the Blowdryers, perhaps the campiest of all the early San Francisco punk bands. His writing can be found in numerous zines and anthologies, including *Beyond Definition* (Manic D Press, 1994), *Tricks and Treats* (Harrington Park Press, 2000), and *Pills, Chills, Thrills, and Heartache* (Alyson Press, 2004). Alvin is also the co-author of a transsexual showbiz memoir, *The Unsinkable Bambi Lake* (Manic D Press, 1996). His novels include *I Married an Earthling* (Manic D Press, 2000), a sci-fi send-up; *Gutter Boys* (Manic D Press, 2004), a twisted tale of debauchery and unrequited

397

love set in early '80s new wave Manhattan; and *Why Aren't You Smiling?*, from which "The End of a Stripper" is excerpted. Alvin lives in San Francisco's über-trendy Mission District, works at a used bookstore, and is up for just about anything. His hobbies include strolling, napping, and snacking. His only passion is the reading and writing of fine literature.

Johns, Marks, Tricks, and Chickenhawks

THE GERMAPHOBE'S GUIDE TO SEX WORK

Aimee DeLong

People tell me that I have a fat ass like it's a compliment. In shows with other girls, they all say the same thing. First, the dude drops his pants. Then the other girl shows her tits, usually with spacious nipples, cuz most of them have popped a kid by now, and I turn around, bend over, and shake that ass.

"Oh yeah, baby. She's got a fat ass," is what the other girl always generally says. "You like that? Yeah, baby. Look at that fat ass." The dude's mouth usually drops a little more as he starts looking like he just came from the dentist. That slack-jawed, post-Novocain mouth as he pumps his dick a little harder.

So, this black dude comes into the peep show. And Betty (a lot of the girls pick old-lady names), a delicious-looking, supple-skinned Filipino chick with a navel ring and a back tattoo, turns to me and says, "You better watch out, Violet. He likes the chocolate. And he only likes white girls with fat asses."

Chocolate? I think, *What in the hell does that mean? I'm not shitting for anybody.* I cringe.

"Girl, you gotta do it. It's just chocolate, and he pays extra."

I'm confused, but I attempt to at least seem mentally present as the black man that likes the chocolate and the fat, white asses approaches me.

"You know me? You know who I am?" he asks.

"Uh, yeah," I answer.

399

"You know what I like?" he whispers.

"Sure," I say casually.

"Can you do that?" his voice vanishes into a hush.

"You mean the chocolate?"

"Yeah," he confirms.

I'm thoroughly confused now. In this line of work it's always best to play it cool, but I can't agree to do a brown in front of this guy if I'm not going to do it, which I am not. But another general rule in this line of work is that if you can't play cool, the next best thing is playing dumb.

I look at him, twirling my hair around my finger. "Do you mean actual chocolate, like candy?"

He takes a step back, almost insulted. "Of course, what did you think I meant?"

I laugh it off. "Oh, I just wanted to make sure we were on the same page."

"Okay. Well I just need to grab some cash and I'll be right back," he tells me.

I nod, as if I'm prepared for the mission, me and my fat ass.

While he's off at the cash machine, I have a few minutes to try to prepare for this experience. But he's a fast motherfucker, because by the time I can even situate my bottle of hand sanitizer so that I can directly douse it onto my skin after he hands me cash that has been in his hands after his hands have probably touched his cock at some point over the last hour, he's already on his way back up the stairs, walking toward me.

I'm semi-strung-out-exhausted from a late night at a goth club where I only fit in cuz all my clothes are black, and then there's my gnawing, relentless dissatisfaction with life and most things around me. To remedy my hangover, I drink a double espresso which has a tendency to make me more jittery than awake. So, when fat-ass-dude hands me a Mounds bar that is already open with only one remaining Mound, I don't have a lot of mental clarity to process the mystery of the missing half. *What the fuck? I guess he ate it.* The other one appears to be completely pure and untouched, so I take it. If I were more alert, I would straight up tell him that he needs to hand me an unopened candy bar. And also not to mention the disturbing fact that he actually brought me chocolate in solid candy form. I mean, what does he exactly—EXACTLY—expect me to do with it? Wouldn't chocolate sauce be more efficient, not to mention logical? I couldn't say after all, because I've never really done this before. I have also never really asked anyone else to do it before either. I take the Mound and go into my side of the fantasy booth, sitting the candy bar down and rubbing my hands with sanitizer.

He whispers through the money slot, "What's your name?"

"Violet."

"Just put it between your cheeks, and let it melt. Then tell me when you're done so I know when to put the money in."

I eyeball my container of baby wipes, thankful that I just bought a new pack this week, and then go for it. I stick the Mounds bar between my fat ass cheeks and just stand there for a couple minutes, not saying anything to the man on the other side, although I can hear him breathing. I wonder what he's thinking. I wonder what I'm thinking. It all feels blank.

"Alright, I'm done," I announce as I pull the smeary candy bar out from the grip of my ass cheeks.

"Yeah, why don't you take a bite of that nasty candy bar, Violet?"

I flip him off behind the covered window and shake my head viscerally like this dude is one gross, kinky bastard.

"Okay," I tell him as I throw the candy bar on the floor in disgust.

"You took a bite, Violet?"

"Yes," I lie, "why don't you put the money in, and then maybe we can talk some more." I'm losing patience a lot less quickly than I should be.

He slides me some cash as I grab it between my left pinky and ring finger from the backside of my hand, place it on the intercom box, then slather on more sanitizer. I hear him insert his money. The curtain rises slowly.

"Take your clothes and shoes off, Violet, and turn around."

I comply. I'm tired, and the more he directs me the less I have to think.

"Now bend over and spread your legs, and arch your back."

I follow his instructions.

"Yeah, like that. Um-hum . . . very nice. Now take your hands, and spread those cheeks as far as you can. I wanna stare right into that tight little anus of yours."

I complete his directions.

"Oh, yeah. Just stay like that."

I hear him jerking off.

"Violet, how old are you?"

"Twenty-two." I concoct an age that sounds young enough to be shocking but old enough to be realistic.

"Oh yeah, look at that nice, round ass. Do you care if I call you a slut?"

"No, not at all," I tell him. I could fucking care less. I'm so tired that I'm about to fall over. My leg muscles start to shake in this physical position that has the sustainability of a plastic-bag factory. I balance the crown of my head against the wall in front of me.

"Pull those elbows back, fucking slut," he commands in a soft, low porno voice, slow and easy. Dirty.

I start shaking my ass from side to side more out of discomfort than arousal, but he can't tell the difference.

"Oh yeah, Violet. Do you mind if I call you stupid?"

"Go right ahead," I say, wondering if the show is almost over. And then I hear the curtain start to descend in its rickety, mechanical glory.

"Don't move!" he tells me, "I'm going to put more money in."

"You have to give me more money up front too," I tell him.

"Alright, just hang on a second," he says in a panic as if his valuable jerk-off time is being horribly disturbed. He hands me the cash. I frantically rub not only a dime-size amount of sanitizer on this time, but a fucking Canadian-dollar-size, hurrying so I can get back into

position before he puts the money in the machine. Right as the curtain starts to scroll back up, my head re-roots itself against the wall.

"Oh yeah, Violet. There's that round, fat, white ass. I just wanna lick that chocolate all up for you. Would you like that, you stupid slut?"

"Uh-huh," I dramatize a moan.

"Do you like it up the ass, Violet?"

"Oh yeah," I tell him, "I like big black dicks up there, but I don't let anyone fuck me in the ass even though I want it *sooo* bad."

"Why is that, you fucking dumb whore?"

"I wanna keep it tight. You know what I'm saying, baby?"

"Oh yeah . . . you're just a dumb, white tease with a hot ass."

"That's right." I feel my muscles giving way and my hyper-erotic-posture collapsing the tiniest bit, but it's not imperceptible to him.

"Pull those elbows back up, Violet, and keep spreading those chocolaty cheeks. I wanna clean that all up for you. You look like you need a little help wiping, baby."

This is getting old fast. Even though it's all a fantasy, it's not my fantasy and I just wanna say, *No, douche bag. I don't want your help, and if you weren't such a freak I wouldn't have a Mounds chocolate bar all over my ass, smelling like coconut and looking like a very un-hot, hot mess. It's probably going to take half a pack of baby wipes to get this junk off. Fuck you and your fat-white-ass fetish!*

But I guess some of my fantasy is actually being fulfilled *too*. I'm being paid money for my sexuality, which is taken from me in small bits all the time for free anyway, on the subway, walking down the street, in the bodegas, at clubs, as men say crass things to me, or touch me inappropriately before I even have a chance to see it coming.

"I sure do need some help," I tell him as I wiggle my ass back and forth.

"Oh yeah, Violet. That's it, you dumb, white bitch . . . Oh . . . damn, damn, Oh . . . UGH!" The curtain goes down right as he comes.

I straighten up in one rapid motion to relieve my muscles. He talks to me through the money slot.

"Goddamn, Violet," he says. "Have you done this type of thing before?"

I'm not sure if he's referring to the Mounds bar specifically, or if he's just wondering if I bend over, completely naked, for strange men all the time.

"Why don't we discuss it during another show on another day," I answer.

I spend the next ten minutes cleaning my ass with baby wipes. I have to laugh to myself about the absurdity of it all. But honestly I think I'm too tired to know if I think it's funny in theory, or reality, or at all. The memory of the opened Mounds bar floats through my brain as I sit on the train, making my way home. I think about the twenties that he slid to me after I knew for sure he was touching his cock. I think about that pile of money that is now quarantined safely into the special pocket of my purse that I keep for tainted cash. I attempt to reassure myself by mentally running through all the times I used the hand sanitizer.

Why in the fuck did I agree to accept an unsealed candy bar? I feel like a germaphobic failure, on Whore-O-Ween. But, like any employee, a sex worker gets tired on the job too, and can't always catch every little detail. People think, *Wow, you get paid to masturbate?! That's easy, I could do that!* They never stop to consider just how *oh-so-easy* it would be to do it fifteen times in six-hour shifts, several days a week. They don't think about how you constantly have to keep up a level of attractiveness that surpasses how you feel on fat days, or rag days, or days when you don't feel sexy because your boyfriend is too tired to fuck you. They don't think about all the times you have to say no to eating pizza because you have to work the next day, and you don't want to be all swollen and bloated from the grease, and the cheese, and that goddamn golden New York–style crust. And they don't think about how your ass is more likely to eat a Mounds bar than your face is.

The bugs in my nerves start to crawl as I try to run through all the possible plagues and diseases that could have been settled into the creaminess of that soft dark chocolate. I try to convince myself that I'm being ridiculous. I know I'm being ridiculous. And, I create a new mantra for the day to make the bugs go away. I relax my fidgeting ankles, take a deep breath, sigh, and silently say to myself, *Violet, it's important to remember that you can't get herpes from a candy bar.*

AIMEE DELONG is a writer of fiction, living in San Francisco. Her work has appeared in such places as *3:AM Magazine, Brown Bunny Magazine, and Everyday Genius.*

HAIRY ANNIVERSARY

Chris Moore

Walter, the squirrelly cashier, spanks a grown man in a dress. This is not the legend of Saturday night. This is Tuesday morning. 11:40 AM. I find myself thinking about the theme song from *Different Strokes,* and I visualize every letter of every word while some inner voice sings along as if it's karaoke.

Katrina snaps her fingers and takes back her whip. She looks over me and thrusts its handle in my direction.

"HIT HIM!" she says.

I try not to laugh in her face and offer up no excuse. "No thanks. I've got to go to lunch in a few minutes."

She looks at her slave on his hands and knees on the carpeted floor of the Mitchell Brothers lobby and lashes him across the back and ass as if to make a point, then she stares at Walter and me like we're next.

"WELL!" she says. "GO AHEAD, LAUGH!"

Then she lashes him again, HARD! The slave whimpers a little this time.

"GO AHEAD, LAUGH!" she repeats. "LAUGH AT HIM, HE LIKES IT WHEN YOU LAUGH!" The words fall from her cruel mouth. It's hard not to think of her as an insane person when she's like this.

We stand with stone faces like the statues on Easter Island. I notice a damp area where the slave's sweat has made his dress an even darker shade of purple. Then I wonder how much money he's paying her for this shit anyway. Essentially, if we laugh, we would be participating

406

in this guy's humiliation fantasy. And this is something I'm just not willing to do . . .

FOR FREE.

Ten dollars an hour isn't enough to make me want to get involved in this kind of debauchery. If the guy threw in a hundred bucks, well, I'd laugh all he wanted. This idea made me feel a little dirty. Luckily it didn't last very long.

As if it were some divine intervention, the business telephone rang. Walter and I both went for it with great enthusiasm, as if answering the phone would transport us out of this terrible situation for just a second. Even if it was a wrong number, or a telemarketer, we could put some kind of distance between our world and theirs. Sometimes a two-foot Formica counter just isn't enough. Ask any bartender.

As for my own personal boundaries, if I can stay at least ten feet away from a person spurting and ejaculating bodily fluids, that's enough for me. Walter beat me to answering the phone. I just stood there awkwardly trying to ignore the heightened level of weirdo-ism.

Luckily, by this point Katrina had grown bored with us. She was yanking the choke collar, leading her slave on his hands and knees, marching over the semen-encrusted jungle green carpet. Soon off in the darkness, we could hear her spanking the slave way down that hallway. The crack of the whip, the whimper of the man in red lipstick and high heels.

Finally, it felt okay to laugh. But not at the slave.

"You idiot," I said. "Do your mommy and daddy know what you do for a living?"

Walter looked like he just found out his girlfriend was actually a man. "Aaaaaaggghhh, CHRIST!" he groaned.

"Do you feel dirty?" I asked.

He was silent.

"Well, you ought to. You just helped that poor, rich, miserable fool get off . . . FOR FREE!"

"I feel kinda sick," he whispered.

"Walter, you are sick! Is this how you thought your life would turn out? Spanking tricks in the lobby of a goddamn whorehouse in San Francisco? FOR FREE!?"

He was slumping in his chair. Any aura of machismo he'd once held had long since left him. "I wish I'd thought about it before I did it," he whispered. Then he was silent.

He was a decent worker and all of that, but he was very young and full of the idealism that ten-plus years of this business has robbed from me. He was just doing what I always did, doing things just to do them. Living, experiencing things for good or ill. However, in this case, it was the ill. Hopefully he had learned something of value at not too great a personal or mental price.

"Ah hell, Walter," I said, "don't feel too bad." I lied to make him feel a little better, "We've all spanked that guy."

He could see I was just trying to make him cheer up. I could see it wasn't working.

"Fuck it," I said, "it's almost noon. Wanna get some Chinese for lunch?"

He didn't respond. He seemed lost in his own little world of self-doubt and pity.

I decided to go it alone for my break. I got my coat and went for the front doors and the world that lay just beyond the lobby.

"The Tenderloin," I giggled and spoke to no one, "there's nothing tender about it."

It was the twenty-first day of September. My anniversary of working at the theater. All I could think about was that I had spent another 365 days in the whorehouse. I had the general's chicken and some fried rice while I watched news of the war in Iraq on a giant television and pondered the day-to-day life of the enlisted professional soldier.

This made the horror show of my work somehow less terrifying.

CHRIS MOORE was born in Eastern Tennessee and raised by a television and drug-abusing wolves called parents, who were legally blind vendors in government buildings—they ran snack bars and such. He's lived in

Johns, Marks, Tricks, and Chickenhawks

Chattanooga, Gatlingburg, and Nashville, Tennessee; Atlanta; Portland, Oregon; New Orleans; Seattle; San Francisco; and Barcelona, Spain. With no formal education and a healthy dose of wanderlust, he packed up his skateboard and headed for the West Coast, where he has studied extensively in bars, strip clubs, drunk tanks, tattoo parlors, libraries, and the gutters of the notorious Tenderloin. He's worked as a caterer, dishwasher, production assistant, director of live sex shows, carnival barker, hustler, valet, men's room attendant, pizza guy, doorman in nightclubs and bars, bartender, jack of all trades and master of none. His passions are being with his dog Roo, art in all its forms, learning new languages, travel, skateboarding, friends, bartenders, tattoo artists, and strange women. His work has appeared in tiny, crude, obscure zines and on bathroom stalls. These days, he can be found in San Francisco.

WHORENECOPIA

Xavio Octavier

As the '80s wore on, the prayers of the poor heterosexually oriented
males of San Francisco had wafted up to heaven and we were granted
a place called the Lusty Lady Theater. This place was the apotheosis
of the 25-cent woman show. The center ring of this attraction was
and is an oblong room with a series of window booths on three sides.
Unlike the earlier 25-cent woman shows in the Tenderloin, there
would be several ladies in the room at once. For the slightly more af-
fluent or those who "fell in love" with particular entertainers, down
the hall was and is a "private show" room where a patron can sit "one
on one" with a Lusty Lady behind the glass. Across from the lavato-
ries, for the shy are a few dirty movie or video booths as well. The
bathrooms are male and female, and couples and women are always
welcome in the show booths.

Another difference from the earlier 25-cent woman shows is that
the ladies are positioned slightly above the viewer in the booth and
lit from below as well as above. There are a few poles for the more
athletic girls and the walls are lined with mirrors.

In those days before the union was formed, 25 cents brought down
the screen and one could gaze at the loveliness for a minute or less
until the screen went back up. The machine accepts ones, fives, tens,
and twenties today as it did then, but I think they phased out the 25-
cent action. For a few dollars, you could have beautiful girls show
you their tits, spread their asses, dance, jump on and off the pole,

come over and look down into the booth to see your dick if you were jerking off, and put their pussy up to the glass for a closer look. In other words: paradise.

Of course, you had to arrive at the right time of day or night. That would be after and not before the swabbers went through mopping up the floors of the booths of the spilled semen. Ideally, you would get a nice clean freshly swabbed booth where your shoes did not stick to the floor and your nose was filled with the pleasant smell of fresh disinfectant instead of the stale stench of man essence. If one of the Lusty Ladies' ugly hairy dyke girlfriends appeared when the screen went down, you could switch booths or let the time run out, and if a goddess appeared you could slip in a five or a ten and hope she wasn't about to go on break. Timing was essential because the goddesses were always behind the screens in the booths with the most come on the floor. So you had to be the first to find them after the swabbing. There was only one swabber at a time. The swabs were a lazy, indifferent bunch of punks with tattoos and pins through various parts of their faces, and often giant rings in their earlobes as is the modern custom of many young people today.

It was here I first learned to recognize a woman only by looking at her ass regardless of what color wig she might be wearing. It was here also that I learned that if a woman has a beautiful face she also has a beautiful pussy, and vice versa.

God doles out beauty from top to bottom as it were. Or vice versa. I also learned for the first time in my life that it was possible to get an erection and or have an orgasm without the aid of alcohol or drugs. That was the most amazing thing of all.

Since the ad agency was a few blocks away, I began going to the Lusty Lady during lunch and going up to Broadway to buy porn mags at the cigar store, which is now gone. Tuesdays and Thursdays were the days the new mags arrived except for the super-deluxe Chinese girlie mags printed in Hong Kong on super-high-gloss high-quality paper with high-definition printing. These mags ceased publication when the British turned Hong Kong over to the communist mainland.

411

San Francisco's Broadway stretches the length of the city, from the Embarcadero to the Presidio, but it is mostly residential except for a three- or four-block stretch in the North Beach district, where the strip clubs and music clubs are located along with restaurants and Chinese dollar stores. There are other strip club areas in the Tenderloin, with a few isolated "gentlemen's clubs" with valet parking and a dinner menu and strippers sprinkled about, but I am not talking about strip clubs. I am talking about whores, which brings me to the point of my story.

Walking through this area regularly at lunch or after work or at night puts one under the surveillance of the panhandlers, the denizens of the local residence hotels, the barkers in front of the strip clubs, the local pimps and prostitutes, and any other sharks cruising for suckers. I soon found myself being stalked by a young whore who seemed to be a recent high school graduate. By this time I had won an Acura Integra at work, which I occasionally drove up Broadway on my way home. This did nothing to improve my disposable income, as maintenance was expensive, but for the first time I knew why men loved their cars. The little whore and her pimp could not help practicing their arithmetic skills on me as I went to the Lusty Lady several times a week, albeit often only spending a dollar or two, and as I walked down Broadway Tuesdays and Thursdays with a plain brown wrapper of fresh porn, although I often stuck it under my armpit beneath my sweater if I was going back to work. So as I walked down Broadway at lunchtime or after work or in the evening, I found myself continually confronting my perseverant stalker. If she had put as much energy into wage slavery as she did into prostitution she might have had a decent job, but that is another issue. She was not the most beautiful woman in the world, but she was cute, with freckles and blue-grey eyes. She had a large mouth with brown hair pulled tightly and what looked like painfully into an attempt at some kind of cornrow-type ornamentation. Medium-size breasts and a pudgy but cuddly looking body. Always in jeans.

Over the course of the next several years, she made it one of her hobbies to try and get me to, what shall I say . . . hire her? Commission her? You get the picture. Every time I went to Broadway she would suddenly be walking beside me or walk out in front of me and get sociable. She rarely said, "Ya wanna date?" Maybe whores didn't do that anymore, but she would talk to me and ask me for money and so forth. Eventually she asked me to buy her a drink at a bar on the corner of Broadway and Kearney. She showed me her ID to prove she was 21 and that her name was really what she said it was. "Jennifer," I think, but I don't remember exactly. Over drinks she told me she was studying to be a dental assistant and that her mother was abusive to her. After a while I said, "Let's go," and she said, "Where are we going?" I said, "I don't know where you are going, but I'm going home." She *tsk*ed, and I said, "G'night."

Many moons passed, and one night I loaded up my wallet and headed over to Broadway for some fun. I was hoping it would be goddess night at the Lusty Lady, and I was prepared to spend some time there if it was. Then I was going to have some drinks at Specs' Twelve Adler Museum and Cafe down the street and then maybe buy some porn at the cigar store or maybe a three-for-the-price-of-two pack at the adult bookstore. I found a parking place right on Broadway at Kearny. You could park on Broadway at night in those days, which is not permitted today. I had no sooner stepped up onto the sidewalk than my stalker appeared and grabbed my arm and said, "Let's go watch a movie," meaning a porn film in a booth at the adult bookstore. In a moment of weakness I hesitated, and finally after years of relentless harassment I said, "Okay, how much?"

She told me it would be $60 and she took me into the adult store. She told me to buy a rubber and give the guy behind the counter $20. We went into the movie booth and closed the door. She unbuttoned my trousers and pulled down my shorts. She opened the package and put the rubber on my erect penis. Then she opened the door and left. I don't know where she went, but as I have pointed out earlier,

413

whores have a remarkable ability to appear out of nowhere or completely vanish in less than a split second.

I was not surprised but I kind of kicked myself for letting her work me when I certainly knew better than to give a prostitute money on the pretense of receiving some kind of sex experience. I had spent all my money and couldn't afford the Lusty Lady or the drinks or the mags, so I pulled up my pants and went home. After that, she still kept bugging me every time I saw her, but I think she had forgotten she had already reminded me of what was behind that particular scam called "prostitution." Maybe she thought I would be tempted to spend more to get more. I don't know. My friend Darryl Victor Dubin told me he used to get blowjobs from transsexual hookers in doorways for $35, but then that is a different thing. Transgenders may step over the line, but they are still too close to their previous gender for my taste and it is the unattainable "attractive woman" that one craves anyway, so I don't see the point. I once saw her with her pimp. He was a young black kid in his early twenties.

One night I was driving up Broadway on my way home when I saw her standing on that same corner in a pouring rainstorm looking like a drowned mouse. I was stuck in traffic at a red light so I honked my horn and motioned her over. I gave her an extra umbrella I had in the car so she didn't have to stand there in the rain. Sometime later I saw her standing out in the rain again without an umbrella. Several years later I was walking down Van Ness Avenue on my way home to an apartment I was staying at when I came upon a whore standing in a doorway wearing nothing but a flimsy bra and panties. It was a cold San Francisco night in the forties or low fifties and I was wearing an undershirt, a flannel shirt, at least one sweatshirt, maybe two, a black Levi's jacket, and a hat. I was also warmed from having walked from Specs' through the Broadway tunnel and down Van Ness, but I wasn't sweating. I said something about it being a bad night to be out dressed like that, and she smiled as she stood there shivering.

After these experiences I came to realize that pimps are not only masters of female psychology (not feminist fantasies and myths about women but actual women's real psychology), but they are also masters of male psychology. What man can resist that poor girl standing in the rain or freezing in a doorway nearly naked? I almost gave her my shirt, but I realized her pimp would strip it off her and send her back out. Men who would never approach a prostitute will certainly be moved by their instinct to protect and defend a "lady in distress." As it is in the animal kingdom where the male pig spits in the female pig's face, which is her cue to spread her legs for mounting, so it is in the human world, where the male is irresistibly moved to protect and defend the female. These pimps know their stuff. They are also masters of invisibility.

The last time I saw the persistent prostitute was three or four years ago. She had aged perceptibly and was much thinner. I've seen whores on Broadway over the years decay into drug-rotted remnants of their former selves. She seemed to be going in that direction, which worried and saddened me. If she remembered me, it was only as a john and not as the person with whom she had had interactions over the years. In my life she loomed large as one of the only if not the only woman who repeatedly pursued me sexually, even if it was only to get my money for her pimp. To her I must have blended into the thousands of men she worked on over the years. I asked her how she was, and she made some reference to how "good" she was in a sexual sense. I said I meant how her health was, because I hadn't seen her for some years since I left San Francisco and she looked like she was doing meth or had AIDS or something. She stopped. Shocked. "You think I look like I have AIDS?" she said. She burst into tears and went running away up the street. I haven't seen her since. I certainly have a "way" with women. Most women sense that and avoid me. I should have tried to develop a different "way," but we are what we are. What can I say? On the outside, I'm a nice guy. On the inside, I'm a cruel monster. Or maybe it is the other way around.

My final encounter with a prostitute occurred as we entered the twenty-first century. I was sitting at the bar in the aforementioned Specs' Adler Museum and Cafe when a young, beautiful black girl entered. She was goddess-beautiful and very light-skinned. Not that looking African or European is particularly a trait of beauty in itself, but she just happened to be light-complected. So in walked this beautiful, sexy young lady and sat down beside me as I was drinking my curds and whey.

"I wish somebody would eat my pussy and lick my ass," she said rhetorically. I turned to her and I said, "Well, I'd love to eat your pussy, but I don't know about the ass-licking." I had been thinking of licking a girl's ass and still do from time to time, even in my old age, and I know that it is another technique of pimps to inspire dedication from their whores since most men balk at a rim job. But then or now I would have to approach that kind of thing cautiously, since an actual ass, no matter how beautiful, might not be so appetizing as a picture of one in a porn mag or a fine Lusty Lady's ass on the other side of the window.

I asked the beauty if she was a prostitute, because I didn't have any money and the whole thing would end right there. I actually had $40 in my wallet but I considered that the same as nothing to a prostitute. This was now the twenty-first century after all.

"No, I'm not a prostitute," she replied.

"Are you a stripper or, I mean, a dancer?"

"Do you like dancers?"

It appeared that this was like winning $100 million in a lottery I hadn't even bought a ticket for. Suddenly from heaven had come a beautiful woman who didn't want anything from me I didn't have! All she wanted was cunnilingus! And maybe to have her ass licked. Incredible! Unbelievable! A once-in-a-lifetime miracle! Social status, money, muscles, handsomeness, a large penis, a cruel and brutal personality. I needed none of the usual requirements for a man to get some poontang!

All I needed was the will to eat some pussy. And maybe lick a girl's ass. And I had that. "That's one thing that I got plenty of, baby!" as the song goes.

Off we went. "Let's take my car," she said. Who am I to argue with an angel?

416

She drove three blocks and parked in front of the Old Spaghetti Factory, which by then was some restaurant but had been famous among comics and improv people as the Old Spaghetti Factory for decades. It seemed a little odd to only drive three blocks from Specs' and then park in such a conspicuous place, but she suggested we get in the back seat, so I did. She pulled down her jeans and I began the sacred task. There was a little bit of ass smell there that made me think I might not have been the first person to take her up on this offer that night.

It was very late and I was very drunk and very tired. I was no longer working at this time and I was only in my forties, so I had been staying up late every night jerking off four or five times till dawn. After a while that catches up with you. I couldn't pass up this miracle, though, and so I kept up my end of the business while she pushed my head down into her pussy, making moans and groans of pleasure. We had both pulled our pants down but not off, and I began to feel a cool breeze on my buttocks that puzzled me because the window had been rolled up when we got in the back, though the front windows were half open. She continued pulling my head down and moaning and complimented me as we finished. I told her I'd like to do it again sometime. She said, "Sure," and drove me back to Specs', which was emptying out at closing time. Before I could get any contact info she peeled out through the intersection with a squeal of burning rubber. When I got home, my wallet was empty. The $40 was gone!

My only explanation is this: She actually was a prostitute although she denied it, probably thinking I might be a cop. Although San Francisco cops and prostitutes are like cake and icing, or windows and curtains, or—well, you get the idea. She had driven me to where her pimp was waiting, possibly saving the parking place. As she kept my head down and my ass in the air, he reached in through the front window, deftly lowered the back window, reached into my pants pocket with the skill of a master pickpocket, and, while the whore distracted me, removed my wallet and took out the cash, and then so I wouldn't suspect anything, returned the wallet to my pocket and signaled the whore to finish. She offered to do me something, but I was too drunk and tired for my own arousal and, anyway, it's pleasuring a beautiful woman that is the impossible dream. A man's orgasm is an easy thing to give himself. Getting a gorgeous woman to let you turn her on is like winning the lottery. Especially without the money, muscles, social status, etc.—the things that will impress her girlfriends when she tells them about you. And though it was certainly worth the $40, I probably wouldn't have done it at all if I had known it would cost me that much.

Now my only problem is trying to figure out if this picking of my pocket counts as "sex" when I try to remember if it has been twenty-six, twenty-seven, or twenty-eight years since I've had sex. I mean sex with another person there at the same time. Or should I say I've had sex once in the last twenty-odd years? Dear Playboy Advisor, can you help?

Since I left San Francisco and moved to Pennsylvania, the only whores I am in contact with are on the Internet. They pester me constantly, but I figure they are not real whores, just robot pro-grams designed to get into my computer to plant spyware and malware and steal my personal information. I pity the crook who steals my personal info. It'll ruin his credit completely. I suppose if I responded, I'd be switched over to a real whore who would come over to case my house and steal any cash or jewelry or credit cards I might have laying around. Since I don't have much cash left, no jewelry, and no credit cards, I figure I'll save them the trouble. If all men were like me, women would have given up prostitution in 7000 BC.

Oh, I almost forgot. Once in the '80s, my roommate told me that he and his drug dealer friend brought a couple of hookers over to my flat and fucked them in the living room while I was sleeping in the back bedroom. So there may be such a thing as sex for money outside of Nevada and Amsterdam. Either that or he was a lying sack of shit with Kool-Aid drippin' out his mouth.

Johns, Marks, Tricks, and Chickenhawks

XAVIO OCTAVIER was born and raised in a small town in the Northeast. He has a bachelor of arts degree in philosophy from the local college. He lived for most of his adult life in San Francisco, where his greatest accomplishment was staying out of the small town where he was born for over twenty years. He has performed comedy in San Francisco for many years and enjoys playing music. He was a co-writer of the poster that says, "All I need to know about life I learned from *Star Trek*."

PORTRAIT OF THE PORNOGRAPHER
AS A YOUNG MAN

Sam Benjamin

At the age of twenty-four, I was an aspiring pornographer, new to Los Angeles, loaded down with a bloated rucksack of idiot dreams. My goal was to shoot and direct ethical, intelligent sex films, ones so skillfully rendered they couldn't help but satisfy a whole kind of person. Horrendously broke, I nonetheless refused to get any sort of real job. If it wasn't porno, I didn't want to hear about it.

But a guy can't just breeze into Hollywood and immediately start shifting paradigms. First he must observe. I spent a month pounding the unforgiving sex industry pavement, finally landing a one-day job shooting behind the scenes on a soft-core feature bound for German cable. The day's work netted me $35 cash, a sleazy sum even by porno standards. Sure, my camera work was top-notch, and I waited for the job to evolve into a regular thing. It never happened.

Undaunted, I convinced a webmaster from San Jose to let me produce a pair of short videos for his website, the focus of which turned out to be ejaculate, unrealistically enormous amounts thereof. From ten feet off-camera, a plastic Petco syringe, slightly smaller than a turkey-baster, sprayed swinish glop on the contestant of the day. The effect was dramatic, but what I'd mixed up in my kitchen laboratory proved too runny—more sauce than stew. In the end, it fooled no one.

Dollars dribbled to dimes. A well-intentioned friend took me on a drive out to the beach. Hungry, he stopped off at a restaurant and got some chili, served in a bread bowl. I didn't have any money, so when he was done he let me eat the goddamn soggy bowl. It was humiliating.

The game was on. I was losing. Was it *possible* that I was bad at sex work? The bar seemed set so absurdly low. And yet, here I was, limboing dangerously close.

I would have to start at the bottom, I realized. The very entry level of the sex industry. There were a few gay bars in West Hollywood that hired go-go dancers. Seized by an odd recklessness, I bulled my way into Micky's and asked to try out for the team. The manager sized me up for a moment and then agreed to a trial session. I danced for an hour in front of a tiny, bored crowd, wearing boxer shorts and a Metallica T-shirt with three-quarter-length sleeves. Seven dollar bills in the black, thighs quivering, I dismounted, feeling like a total idiot.

"So, what do you think?" the manager asked. "Ready to make this a regular thing?"

"Not yet," I choked, running past him. "I need to practice my footwork."

I slunk home and curled up in a soft ball. Depression runneth over my cup. My failure to even *compete* in the sex industry, much less change it for the better, hit me like a humiliating slap to the face.

But the next day, my luck turned. I received a call from a buddy who did box-cover design. There was an opening at one of the companies he worked for.

"It's a videographer position. Steam Productions. I could probably get you an interview, if you're interested."

"Terrific," I said. "But who's Steam? I never heard of them."

"Gay company, one of the biggest. Probably pay pretty well. What do you think?"

Shooting gay gave me some pause. My idea of groundbreaking sex-positive entertainment generally also included perky tits. But I was trapped into a corner here. It seemed unwise to be overly picky.

"See what you can do."

He got me a meeting, in North Hollywood. I was mildly surprised. I'd assumed the top gay companies would all be located in glitzy West Hollywood; North Hollywood had a deadened, drunk-at-ten-o'clock-in-the-morning feel to it. I chugged out there, feeling sleepy. I pushed open a heavy, unmarked door, and was greeted almost instantly by a bright-eyed female receptionist.

"Hi!" she beamed. "Are you *Sam?*"

"That's me," I mumbled.

"Lawrence is *busy* right now. He told me to tell you to hang on and he'll be *right* with you." She motioned to a row of leather-covered chairs. "Please make yourself at home."

I settled into one of the chairs, assessing my surroundings. The place had a definite porno feel to it, as if the air had been sprayed thick with synthetic dishwater desire. And yet, the place was clean. The paint job was new. The air conditioning worked. But for the many glossy placards of half-naked, muscular young men with nipple rings staring down upon me from the walls, it looked quite a bit like a dentist's waiting room.

"Hi. Are you Sam?" A hefty, pink-faced man, about 50 years old, stood over me, grimacing. He had the white, wig-like hair of a young Phil Donahue.

"Lawrence?"

"Come on in," he said grimly. We walked into his office, where he slipped behind an expensive-looking desk and settled into his chair, motioning for me to do likewise.

"Sorry about the wait. I was on the phone with my lawyer. Some really unfortunate stuff happened this weekend. I'm in some hot water." He looked at me for a moment, as if deciding whether or not to trust me.

I stared at him, kind of curious, against my will.

"Driving under the influence," he confessed, finally. "Second time in six months. They take away your license for that, you know."

"That's too bad," I said, sympathetically.

"Just bad decision-making, Sam." He exhaled a mighty breath, and then spread his hands out on the desk with finality, as if to clear the topic from his mind. "Did you bring me a sample of your work?"

"Nope," I said. "I hadn't thought about it."

"Mind if I ask you what's your sexual orientation?"

"I'm basically straight," I said.

"*Basically* straight?" he said. "What's that supposed to mean?"

"I guess it means . . . I want to fuck women?"

Lawrence appeared to weigh the statement.

"Well, let me ask you this, Sam: Would you have a problem shooting men having sex? You know, butt-fucking." He seemed to savor the word, and paused for a moment, as if allowing it room to glow.

"No, I don't have a problem with that. I can shoot anything."

"I just wonder if someone who's not gay can really understand what we're trying to do here. Technically, you might be able to shoot all day, and make it look great. But if you can't understand what's going to turn my viewer on, then you're not going to be much good to me."

I nodded. He had a bit of a point there.

Lawrence stared at me baldly. "How old are you?"

"I'm 24."

"You look about 16."

I laughed. "What are you talking about?"

"Listen, in this business, that's a *good* thing."

"Except when I'm trying to get someone to take me seriously. Anyway, I don't look 16."

"Listen, Sam," Lawrence said, in a no-bullshit kind of tone. "I've interviewed about fifty people for this position. I had some guys in my office last week. Two brothers. They brought me a goddamn film. It was in Sundance. It was amazing."

I had never had a film in Sundance, I realized. Nor in any kind of festival. I slunk a bit lower in my seat, feeling mildly ashamed.

"And yet, I see something in you."

"Really?" I said, hopefully.

"Oh, absolutely," Lawrence said. "Now, this might sound strange, but have you ever done any modeling?"

"Oh, a little, I suppose." The Petco syringe tapes. That counted.

"Really." He settled back in his chair and gave me an appraising look. "Well, that's very interesting. Let me ask you something, Sam. Would you be interested in doing a video for *us*?"

"No, I don't think so," I said. "I'm kind of a behind-the-camera kind of guy."

"Why don't you let me see your body a little?" said Lawrence, casually.

"Nah," I said. "I don't really feel comfortable."

"Sam, you're *here*. You're gotten yourself a meeting with the president of one of the biggest companies in Los *Angeles*. This is what's known as a golden opportunity. Are you going to turn me down without even exploring it?"

He had a point there. And how different was this from go-go dancing, after all?

"Well, okay," I relented. I stood up. There, in an air-conditioned North Hollywood porno office, at ten thirty in the morning, I took off my shirt.

"Well, don't just stop *there*," he said exasperatedly. "They're not paying to see your *chest*, you know!"

"Oh," I said. "You want me to take off the pants, huh?"

"Yes . . ." he said, as if I were retarded.

I did. Lawrence craned his neck, staring down at my penis seriously.

"How big is it erect?" he said, looking closely at my cock, then back up at my face.

"I think about six inches," I said.

"It looks like it'd be bigger than that," he said seriously. "I should know; I've been in this business for a long time."

"Yeah?" I said, my pants still down.

"Twenty years." He smiled at me, crossing his arms. As if to say, *How do you like that?*

I put my pants back on and sat back down, amused. I sort of liked the guy now. Maybe it was because he hadn't extended any sleazy I-must-fuck-you-now tendrils when he'd examined my naked body. I felt rather *appreciated*, actually. Clearly—just like me—the guy was a professional.

"We'd have to get you to shave that goatee, that's for sure," he said, meditatively. "You have a problem doing that?"

"No."

"Let me ask you this: Did you play any sports in high school?"

"I played soccer."

"Great. We haven't done soccer yet . . ."

"In what?"

"In the *College Studs* line. Right. Here's the deal: You and another guy play soccer. Then maybe you go to the pool to cool off. Then, you start doing your thing." He pantomimed a wrist-wriggling motion, his fingers cupping inwards, toward his palm.

"We don't do it to each other, do we?" I said, mildly concerned.

"No, no. You look over at each other every once in a while. That's all. How does that sound to you?"

It sounded all right. "How much does it pay?" I asked, suspiciously.

"It'd pay a thousand dollars."

I was slightly taken aback. "Sign me up," I said. No, I *sung* that phrase, in a greed-inspired half-jive: *Sign me up* . . .

The thought of money trumped my feelings of embarrassment. At present, my leaky refrigerator bore a fistful of wet brussel sprouts and basically nothing else. I was ready to move into normality.

Lawrence noticed. "You know, we should shoot this video. But I could probably make you a lot more money than that."

"Huh?"

"See, I have these clients. They're friends of mine. They would probably pay five hundred bucks for a guy like you. A guy with your look. A few might even pay a *thousand*."

"For what?"

"Massage. Sensual massages. You go to their house, give them a good rubdown, the last two minutes, you reach around and jack 'em off. It's easy."

"Oh . . ." I said.

"You could get flown out to St. Louis. Stay in a hotel for a weekend, spend one night with the guy, and come back with a thousand bucks in your pocket. Or just stay around here. You could make an extra grand a week doing it."

"Huh," I said. "Sounds . . . weird."

"Oh, come on! Now listen, if you're interested, what you've got to do is come out to my house. You can practice on me."

"I can *practice* on you?"

"Yeah! You have to know what you're doing! What if sent you to some huge Hollywood star's house, and you freaked out? He'd never speak to me again. No, I train all my models. I teach you what to do."

"So, let me get this straight," I said. "I . . . *massage* you. For free."

"Yes, for free! And then I get you work!"

"And then you get me work." I laughed. I thought for a second. "Okay."

"You want to come out to my house?"

"Yeah, okay."

"Well, the best time is tonight. That's probably the best time."

So he drew me a map. "Come at eight."

"Okay," I said. I looked at the map. Simple. "Okay." Granted, I hadn't expected things to work out this way. But now I saw the light: The gods of porn, apparently, worked in mysterious ways.

This is it, I said to myself as I drove home. *The opportunity you've been waiting for. You'll earn the money for your own porno films by whoring it. You'll go to some lawyer's house, jack his old-man peter, and he'll give you five hundred bucks. Then you hire San Fernando's next rising star to come over and take a tantric bubble bath with you—and you give her the five hundred bucks. You don't even have to put the money in the bank. My God, this has a certain poetic, mathematical, karmic beauty to it, doesn't it?*

A weird kind of symmetry seemed to be in effect here. As an aspiring director, should I not first endeavor to become the object of the gaze? Doling out a few hand jobs here and there would get me in the door.

Think of it like therapy, I reasoned. *You've got this guy on a table, he's all bent out of shape from a long, hellish day in his personal rat race. His spine is twisted up in crunchy knots. His neck meets his upper back in a toxic bunch. His lower belly is a flab-twisted sac of poison.*

But you, I told myself, *you slip into the room in a cool white robe and greet him solemnly, like a resourceful Japanese geisha. Then you turn on the soothing jazz sounds of Louis Armstrong on your portable black jam box and begin to massage his body deftly, sending out rich, healing energy until all of his worries and pent-up grief dissipates like steam into the netherworld.*

And then you give him a reach-around.

That evening I drove out to the deep Valley. Lawrence greeted me with cautious approval. "I wasn't sure if you'd turn up."

I shrugged. "Here I am."

"Well, good. Come on in."

His house was highly leathered and gross. The Valley killed me. Semi-rich people of all ethnic varieties paired schmaltz-heavy design with a boneheaded belief in exterior stucco. Porn homes, in particular, surged with hauntingly bad taste. All those carpeted toilet seats. All that asbestos.

I took a seat on Lawrence's black leather couch. He sunk into a fat white leather chair next to me. He didn't offer me anything to drink. We were about to begin our negotiation when he got a call from Hawaii. "Excuse me. I have to take this." He spoke for some minutes as I fidgeted, then ended the conversation.

"I'm sorry," Lawrence apologized. "I had some pressing business matters to attend to. A friend of mine just found this new kid with a ten-inch dick. You understand."

"I do." I did.

"So," said Lawrence. "I'm sure you have things to do tonight. We may as well get started."

"That sounds good," I said. "Listen, I wonder if I could ask you for some food?"

Lawrence sighed, but he dutifully trudged to the kitchen, where he rustled up a tub of cheese and a box of crackers. I started spreading cheese on wheat, steadily demolishing Lawrence's limited cracker supply.

"You been doing this for a long time?" I said, my mouth full. I motioned with my hand. "Making movies?"

"I told you, I've been around the business long enough to know it backwards and forwards. How about yourself?"

"I'm just getting started," I told him. "But I want to direct."

Lawrence laughed. "You know, you might think this is funny. But before I got started in porn, I was a basketball coach."

"What?"

"Assistant head coach. University of Dayton."

I stared at him. "You're kidding me," I said, laughing.

He stared right back, serious as death. Something was shining in his eyes, and I recognized it as pride. "Ten years."

We shared a small, meditative silence, both of us undoubtedly envisioning various locker room scenarios. Pieces were beginning to fit together. The *College Studs* line. Of course.

"So." He was ready to get down to business. "You have any questions?"

I shook my head, still eating. *Best to act like it's all second nature*, I thought, *like I was born doing it*.

"Let's go upstairs."

I followed him up the ugly, spiraling staircase, and at the top of the landing we turned right on the soft shag carpet and headed straight for Lawrence's bedroom.

There was no massage table. No Louis Armstrong. No dignified sensual therapist's robe for me. Lawrence had a big bed in the center of the room, and there was a shabby green comforter draped on top of it. Immediately, he began taking off his clothes.

"Go ahead and strip, Sam," he called back over his shoulder.

Lawrence, naked, was pear-shaped, full of blubber. He flopped down onto his bed forcefully.

"Straddle me."

428

Now also nude, I did. My tan body contrasted starkly with the enormous pink tortoise below me. I rocked from side to side, uneasily, staking my balance.

"Now, what you'll do when you go to a client's house," said Lawrence, "you'll start rubbing their shoulders. Go ahead, rub my shoulders. That's it."

Lawrence was so fat, I could hardly feel the muscles underneath the pink blubber. I searched in the flesh for something living, something I could tenderize and bring back to life.

"If you get stimulated, don't be embarrassed," said Lawrence. "It's a perfectly natural thing."

Underneath me, he began to slowly hump the bed.

"You know," I said, my voice rising nervously, "I think I could give you a better massage if I stood up for a while. I could get more leverage."

"No," said Lawrence, his voice muffled by the pillow his face was buried in. "They want to feel your thighs on their back."

"*They* do?" I mumbled. The tortoise rolled back and forth. Up and down. I kept kneading, desperately trying to pierce the hard blubber coating that congealed around his musculature.

"Now," Lawrence announced, "what you'll do next is reach back and start playing with their balls."

"What?" I said. My hands stopped their kneading. "I thought that comes at the end of the massage."

"No. It's all the way through. So, you reach back and get the balls, just gently . . ."

"Hold on, hold on," I said. I dismounted the massive porn producer's body and knelt next to him on the bed. My knees sunk into the mattress. "You *said* it was just the last two minutes of the massage."

"Well, of course I didn't say that. Here, give me your hand . . ."

"No, hold on, just *tell* me what you want me to do . . ."

Lawrence propped himself up on his elbows and craned his head back so he could see me. "Sam, you're being stupid. *Give me your hand.*"

He reached across the divide and took my hand. I bristled.

"Hold up, man," I said, my jaw tightening angrily, my fists balling. Things were spiraling out of control. "Just hold the fuck up."

"*You* calm down," said Lawrence, still gripping my arm tightly. With his free hand, he pointed at me, and I saw him for the assistant head coach that he was. "Just *calm down*. Now, can I just show you, Sam, what the heck I'm talking about? Can I just *do* that?"

"Yeah." I said. For some reason I was near tears. "Go. Do it."

He looked at me, disappointed.

"You just *take* their dick . . ."

"So how the fuck am I supposed to know? You know?"

"And stroke it like this . . . just like this . . . You just stroke it. That's all." He released my hand and I took it back from the imaginary penis that he had transformed it into.

I nodded. My lips pursed tightly, my arms folded protectively over my bare chest. There was a weird lump in my throat.

"Sam, why the heck do you think you're getting paid $500?" said Lawrence, tiredly.

I shrugged. There was nothing to say. I felt like a goddamn fool.

"What you've got to understand," said Lawrence, leaning back against the headboard, exhausted, his hand folded over his potbelly, "is that this is not about sex. It's about *money*."

"I get it. Money."

"Exactly. You go in there, you get it done quickly, and then you leave, Sam." He frowned, thoughtfully. "Now, I don't want you feeling like something *bad* happened here. I never close doors, and this one's always open to you."

"Uh, thanks, I think," I said. "Good luck."

That evening, safe at home, I took stock of my situation, feeling surprised to find myself vaguely cheered. I was just as broke as before, but I understood my mission a bit more clearly. If I was truly going to make sex films that subverted any of the stupid nonsense around me, I'd have to find a few people who actually kind of liked what they were doing. If not, then I'd just repeat the mistakes of our elders.

430

Johns, Marks, Tricks, and Chickenhawks

"You'll do it, too," I promised myself. "Porn *visionary*. Doctor of the bone."

It was also a great relief to understand that I was not cut out for all acts of sex-work duty. Nobody wants a half-hearted, poorly administered hand job. They are, quite possibly, the worst things in the world.

SAM BENJAMIN attended Brown University from 1995 to 1999, where he spent his time deciphering postmodern theory, drawing comic books, and making self-indulgent videos. Post-school life led Sam to Santa Cruz, California, where he discovered an impressive network of marijuana farmers but not much in the way of a contemporary arts scene. Yet it was in this town that he first hatched his pornographic destiny. A stoned midnight revelation led him to believe he would produce "feel-good" erotic films and sell them on eBay, garnering a modest fame for his efforts, revolutionizing a dying genre, and making a small killing in the process. Sam is a graduate of the Cal Arts MFA writing program and the author of the memoir *American Gangbang: A Love Story* (Gallery Books, 2011).

PORNOGRAPHER, LAP DANCER, AND SEX-POSITIVE FEMINIST

Nina Hartley

Even though I don't currently have direct sexual contact with paying customers as many sex workers do, as a pornographer I have a measure of intimacy with the end users of my product. Before porn, I was a nursing student who moonlighted as a stripper/lap dancer at San Francisco's O'Farrell Theater. Besides the good tippers, my favorite fans there were the ones who came wearing sweat pants with no underwear, as it made my job much more fun and enjoyable. I knew I was cut out for this line of work when I discovered through conversation with the women in the club that I was the only dancer there who didn't think those guys weren't disgusting, pathetic losers. As a lap dancer, I just found that sweat pants were a much more comfy ride for me than zippered denim and belt buckles. As a sex-positive feminist, I was happy to help men get off safely with an enthusiastic partner, and as a kinky person I got off on not knowing who they were. I stopped lap dancing in 1985, when I graduated from nursing school.

I started in porn in 1984, and as a performer/star I've been meeting my fans in person since 1985, at conventions, public appearances, on the street, and at feature dancing gigs at strip clubs. I'm as sexual with them at these venues as the law allows (being nude or topless, hugging them, letting them grab my butt, taking Polaroid pictures), and they're very open with me about their lives and sexual

432

experiences. It helps that they know I'm a nurse, and they're surprisingly honest about themselves.

My erotic services provider friends tell me that most of their labor is emotional rather than directly sexual, and I'd say the same holds true for what I do. I offer authentic, if temporary, emotional connection to my fans. I really do wish I could fuck each one once, as I know how life-changing it could be. It's heartbreaking at times to contemplate the level and depth of isolation and loneliness that most people live with day to day, and I do my best to alleviate it in my own way. I really wish sex work were decriminalized, as it would make my life much easier.

I have met, in person, about three-quarters of a million people over the course of my career. They fall into many categories or types, and I have my favorites and most-disliked, as would anybody in my line of work.

Besides the obvious, such as finding drunken fans completely obnoxious and annoying, my least-liked fans are the racists, who hate that I do hardcore scenes with black men. I've lost many a fan that fell in love/lust with my big blue eyes, blonde hair, golden tan (in my younger days—I'm pale now), and Germanic features and made me the star of their erotic Aryan daydreams. Imagine their shock and dismay when they find a scene of me enthusiastically engaging in raunchy sex with a black man. It's very disconcerting to them, like the day they discovered that there is no Santa Claus. I don't lose sleep over losing money from these jerks.

My favorite fan, without a doubt, is Carl Sumner, from Maine. I met Carl and his wife, Mary, when they came to see me at Alex's Supper Club in Stoughton, Massachusetts, a little south of Boston. It was the late '90s. The club is so small that everyone who enters is visible to the whole room. Into a space filled with men in their twenties to forties and pretty, young dancers steps a retired couple with gray hair and sparkling smiles. Fans asked me if they were my grandparents, as they looked like they were in their seventies.

433

They may have looked like Sunday school teachers but they were just longtime married grandparents who had always enjoyed a robust sex life. They would drive down from Maine, making a weekend getaway out of it by spending the nights away in bed-and-breakfast places.

Carl was a dedicated nudist and would often call me when he and Mary were getting ready for a romp. He'd say, "I'm naked and we have on one of your movies. Mother's got on her red baby-doll nightie and her highs!"—her high heels. Even though they couldn't fuck anymore, they always had fun with movies, masturbation, and oral sex.

After over fifty years of marriage, Carl was widowed, and he and I developed a phone sex relationship. He was always so chipper and happy, naked and masturbating in his recliner and watching one of my tapes. He especially liked the orgy and swinging movies. I would send him naked Polaroids of my adventures on the road with my playmates, and it always made me feel good to be able to help a fellow out that way. His fondest wish was to find a way to get to Dark Odyssey sex camp so he could cavort naked with hundreds of people, but we could never figure out what to tell his son about where he was going.

One cold and snowy February, I was in New Hampshire for a conference and Carl drove down from Maine to spend the night with me. He was 90 at the time and drove himself. I had the best time with him, playing naked all evening and late into the night. He was so happy, clear, present, and appreciative that he made the perfect fan. People laugh and snigger when I say I had sex with a 90-year-old guy, but I tell them Carl is a great example of how sex can be fun for a person's entire life. As of this writing Carl is 93, still hale, hearty, and horny. I do wonder what his kids will think, though, when they find his considerable porn stash when he's gone. A lot of it is inscribed from me to him. I hope they think it's great, not gross. I also hope they understand that their mother, and for some of them grandmother, was fully onboard for their adventures.

So, the worst fans are really awful: drunk, ignorant jerks who really do look at me like I'm a thing. The best fans are warm, wonderful, loving men and women who know that I have their best interests at heart. As I tell them all: I'd be there in person but I can't be, so I send the movies.

NINA HARTLEY is a pornographic actress, pornographic film director, sex educator, feminist, and author. Her mother was a statistician for the California State Department of Public Health. She took a double major at UC Davis in chemistry and statistics. Her father was a writer and, until his blacklisting in 1957 (one of the last to be caught in the Red Scare), a popular radio personality—"Jim Grady"—in San Francisco. He hosted the show *This Is San Francisco* and a radio version of *You Were There.* After he lost that job, he never had a steady one again, becoming a househusband twenty-five years before it was fashionable. In 1969, Nina's parents discovered Zen Buddhism and haven't stopped sitting meditation yet. Their teacher was the amazing Suzuki Roshi *(Zen Mind, Beginner's Mind).* Her parents were ordained as Zen priests in 1977, and her mother went on to become the first woman abbess of an American Zen temple. Her father died in 2011, at the age of 95. Her mother still lives in the Zen Center in San Francisco. Hartley has three older siblings, eight nieces and nephews, seven great-nieces and great-nephews, with one more on the way. She's done food service and sex work. She trained as a nurse and got her degree and license, but has never earned a paycheck in that profession, though she uses her education in her line of work all the time. She's been a sex worker since 1982 and an adult movie performer since 1984. She still works in porn today. She also teaches and writes. She likes to cook, read (mainly nonfiction, science, and history), watch movies, have sex with her husband and any of their playmates, listen to jazz, and dance.

THE END OF MY FAIRYTALE

Madison Young

Not all fairy tales are pretty. In fact, some are downright gruesome.
I was no stranger to the exchange of intense energetic sensation that most mortal human beings classify as pain. In fact, I got off on it. I was a slut for the rush of endorphins, the pushing and pulling of pointed and thick thuds of energy that swirled and swooshed through my small curvy frame. My back arched while cuffed to a Saint Andrew's cross, my ass open, and my body and mind in a space of complete surrender awaiting my Daddy's hands, his whip, his cane, his touch. This was how I lived my life, dedicated to service and facilitating and documenting human affection, relationships, and intimate connections. I'm a sex expert. I'll step in front of the camera with lights blaring hot onto my naked skin and reveal my most vulnerable and honest sexual self. Over the years, I've found great joy in facilitating that same safe environment for other women, men, and persons of variant gender identities to explore their deepest fantasies while I capture those moments on video to share with the world, to share that magic, like catching lightning bugs on a summer evening and crossing your fingers that their light shines just as bright in that glass jam jar as it did flying in the dark night sky. They never look as magical in that jam jar, but there is a glimmer of light and magic, enough to make us believe in something.

I can never quite capture the absolute intimacy, power, and thick, sweaty, animal energy that builds as you are leaning over a person who is staring into their partner's eyes and coming with complete vulnerability and trust in the moment. Those soft words of "I love you, slut" as a woman's fist exits her male partners' asshole covered in ass juices and lube remnants on her black latex glove. I can shoot these moments, I can be a part of that magic as a performer, but it loses just a little bit of its magic by the time it gets to the consumer. I get to live the fairytale; the viewer or porn consumer only gets to read the fairytale from their bed with a warm glass of milk. I make fantasies a reality.

I've been performing in the adult industry for over a decade now and directing since 2005, producing over twenty-six films and guiding millions of viewers to moments of orgasmic glory. There are some folks that watch my films from home and they need more. They believe so deeply in the fantasy that I've created for them that they want to step into that fantasy. They want the fantasy to come knocking on their door. Many girls are happy to be that fantasy.

There are women in the adult film industry that also work as professional dominatrices or escorts, providing the personal fantasies for these men and women that they desire and on their own terms. Personally, I have always found immense gratification in the very clear-cut negotiated boundaries that exist within porn. A very safe space has been created for one or more persons to open themselves up and connect in an erotic way with the other performers and the camera, or in a solo masturbation scene just with the camera. The performers realize that you are not going to go out on a date with them afterward, this is not a relationship, and there is no confusion of personal and business.

We are here to communicate about our desires, connect and divulge our most intimate selves to one another and to the camera and then go home to our families, our partners, etc. It's a well-communicated agreement with clear boundaries. But within personalized sex work, those lines get blurry.

Before my foray into the world of pornography, I dabbled in everything from cake sitting and golden showers to nude house cleaning and peep show performance. I was a sexual adventurer and doing an anthropological study of my own fetishes and other peoples. These experiences dwindled away as my life became consumed with making pornographic films and creating a more global discussion and impact in the realm of sexuality. I was fascinated with documenting my journey, and porn was the simplest way to capture my rapidly changing life on film for the world to watch.

One day I got an e-mail from a gentleman who was a fan of my kinky adult films. He was a client of a friend of mine who worked as a dominatrix. His proposal was simple. He wanted to fly me to Cleveland where he worked as a big shot lawyer. He would introduce me to his mistress and if we seemed comfortable with one another, his mistress and I would engage in a BDSM scene, while he watched. He just wanted to watch.

I was skeptical of flying anywhere to meet anyone that wasn't a reputable producer, so I told him that I needed to talk with my friend Linny, whom he had worked with before.

I called Linny up on the phone. "He's safe. He's annoying as hell and I have to keep him in line, but he's safe. He has a huge ego but you have a greater tolerance for ego than I do. He can be rude but he pays incredibly well, and if you are able to put up with his bullshit he could be a steady stream of extra income for you. I suggest asking for more than you would on any film. He's a handful."

It was not exactly a stellar recommendation, but I was accustomed to inflated egos from my plentiful work in Los Angeles, where egos rivaled the size of some of the girls' breast implants. If he was in need of a compliant submissive with good communication skills, I was his gal.

Two thousand dollars was the agreed-upon number. It would take a day to get there, a day of submission, and a day to get back. My average rate for performing in a film was $1,000, so doubling that for an in-person experience seemed more than reasonable.

With that my flight was booked. First-class with champagne in real glass stemware. I boarded in the early morning along with business men and women off to work on the cross-country flight. I stuck out like a sore thumb making my way down the jetway with my stuffed L.L. Bean backpack full of vibrators, dildos, toiletries, fetish heels, stockings, garter belts, and a black silky evening gown that I had rolled up into a tootsie roll formation. I only bought clothes that didn't require an iron. I sat back in my big leather first-class seat sipping champagne and awaiting my rendezvous with Jackson and his mistress.

When I arrived, there was a car waiting for me. The driver stood next to the luggage carousel holding a sign that read my legal name, Tina Butcher. The name seemed foreign, old, and unused. No one left in my life called me by that name, and I always found it a little jarring whenever it arose in conversation or legal documents, like an old childhood nickname that no longer fit the person that you had grown into.

The driver was dressed in black slacks, a black suit jacket, button-up white shirt, and cap.

"Hello, miss. Are you Ms. Butcher?"

"Yes, I am, but you can call me Maddie."

"Okay, Maddie. Can I help you with your bag?"

George, the driver, assisted me with my bag and led us to the awaiting black Lincoln Town Car with caramel-colored leather seats.

It was a short drive to the hotel. I was staying at a Westin. My grandmother used to work at a Westin. She cleaned dishes in the kitchen for fifteen years. She was a hard-working woman that would do anything for her five children. She worked odd jobs and was in and out of relationships. She was a fiery woman who had three different husbands throughout her life, including Ed. Ed was her last husband. A good man. Ed was African-American and Grandma Virginia had two children with Ed. It was the '60s in Southern Ohio, and mixed-race families were more than frowned upon. It was outright dangerous. My grandmother was a spitfire—there was no dictating rules

439

or proper social protocol to her. Love saw no colors, and my grand-mother wasn't shy about her perspectives. She was a vocal woman. She passed away twelve years ago. I missed her and I thought of her as the driver pulled up to the hotel and opened the car door for me, handing me my bulky, awkward backpack.

I walked up to the check-in counter. It was late, and I was tired from the long flight. I showed the woman my ID and received my key before heading up to my room. The woman at the counter told me that my room and all amenities had been taken care of. Any room service that I might want, just call down and sign it to the room. I thanked her and headed up to the suite. It was a large, comfortable suite with a Jacuzzi, living area, bedroom, bathroom, and a bottle of expensive champagne sitting chilled on the table, with a note. "Looking forward to meeting you. Love, Jackson."

I undressed and slipped into a comfortable terry cloth robe and slippers that the hotel had provided, and threw my clothes on the floor. I retreated to the bathroom and ran hot water into the tub. I need a nice long soak.

Who is Jackson? What makes him tick?

Jackson called me at 9 AM the next morning. He was on his way to pick me up and would arrive in ten minutes and would like me to be standing in the parking garage awaiting his arrival. I didn't know what he looked like, but he knew what I looked like. He has reached into his pants many times while gazing at dirty films of my darkest desires being played out on his computer. For him this was simply a continuation of our sexual relationship. The one that started the moment that he clicked the play button on his torrent download, the one where I was revealed as Daddy's little slut puppy who wants a big fat cock deep inside my ass. Yes, that torrent download.

I finished my makeup, adding deep red lipstick to pursed lips. I eased my thigh-high stockings on my curvy legs and slipped into my black patent leather high heels before grabbing the same navy blue backpack that made me look like I was headed off to high school. Ironically, the bag was sent to me by my mother and bore an anagram of my initials from my birth name. TMB. They might as well have been archaic primitive markings with lost meanings.

Jackson pulled up outside the hotel in his silver Lexus. Jackson was in his early fifties and had silver hair. He was tanned, coifed, well manicured, and well dressed, and had an air of success and arrogance that reeked worse than his Armani cologne. His mistress was blond, blue-eyed, and in her forties. She appeared to be dressed like an advertising executive in a suit dress with heels and pearl earrings and necklace. She was classy and sophisticated, and I was curious to discover their story and how I would fit into it.

What did Jackson like? Jackson wanted to feel adored. He was a switch. He wanted to feel like he wasn't the only one in the world that liked to be beaten severely. He wanted someone to tell him that he is not alone.

Jackson wanted to feed me. Make me soup. Amy's vegetable soup and oven-warm pita bread and hummus. He would take phone calls from his law office while we were in session, screaming at the peons that work for him while his mistress flogged me in the background. He refused to buy a smart phone. He used a small flip phone that was at least ten years old. Jackson would drink more champagne than he should, pouring glass after glass into his champagne flute. Eventually he would fall asleep from food and drink, and his mistress would discontinue fucking me in the ass with her strap-on cock so that we could provide a pillow and blanket to cover Jackson. Jackson would have AndroGel for my nipples and his, to make them sensitive. An arousal gel that makes you really turned on, or so Jackson claimed. It was what worked for Jackson. He would touch his nipples and so would his mistress, and if I was feeling so inclined I would touch them as well.

Jackson had always been kinky. He told me of traveling through Europe as a teenager and meeting an older woman who seduced him and turned him on to the pleasure of pain. He stayed in Europe for a summer enraptured in her wiles, beaten daily, serving her every need. Now as a father of three and a well-known attorney taking on prominent cases with major media attention, he found it impossible

441

to be out among any kind of BDSM community. So he erred on the side of professionalism. Professional dominatrices, mistresses with a kinky side, and submissives. The submissives are always the hardest to find. A strong yet empowered submissive, bright yet tolerant of his ego and arrogance. Often he met with dommes on his own. His was a bossy bottom, a masochist that would order his pain like he ordered his drink at Starbucks. He was particular.

Jackson was a dedicated and loving father. He talked often of his children, one of whom had opened a business. He was seven years old. It was a lemonade stand. The young boy mixed the lemonade and then put his younger five-year-old brother to work serving the lemonade and taking orders while the seven-year-old took all the profits. Jackson laughed at his child's entrepreneurial efforts, proud and amused. His wife knew about his affinity for kinky sex, and their marriage was not one based on sexual chemistry and passion but one of mutual respect, appearances, and parenting of their three adopted children.

His laugh was comical and loud, throaty, and nasal, like that of a Jim Henson creation. He scrunched his lips and made funny faces fixing his hair. He was an amusing character, a caricature of himself. He was tender-hearted and yet he was a vessel for sadistic desire that could only surface in a commercial arena of his life, compartmentalized and put away in the closet after monies have been exchanged and doors to his secret kinky condo had been locked. It wasn't that secret. He is known about town. Cleveland was a small city with small-town heroes with recognizable faces, like his.

Jackson wanted to see blood. He wanted to watch as skin was broken and canes split in two over bruised blue hard flesh. Green, pink, blue-like pastel sorbet about to sour and melt into one big mess. Jackson wanted vibrated orgasms until my vulva was big and pink and swollen to the size of a grapefruit. He wanted to watch as his mistress pounded her large black strap-on cock deep inside my asshole and she pounded her fists down onto my bruised and bloody ass. He wanted drama and he wanted to dictate our desires from behind the curtain. Jackson would watch from the sidelines barking orders: "Fuck her in her ass. Madison really wants you to fill her ass up. Really deep. Now spank her. Madison wants a severe spanking. Make it severe."

I smiled and breathed as the domme and I put on a good show for Jackson at our own pacing and communicated about our next act in S&M theater while he took a boisterous phone call from work again.

After five years of working with one another, I think we can say that there is an established relationship. I took a brief pause in meeting with Jackson during my pregnancy with my daughter. I resurfaced in his life about nine months after the birth of my daughter, and he was eager to see me. I had lost the sixty pounds that I had put on during the pregnancy, but a few stretch marks still remained, along with loose belly skin, reminding me that I had changed. I was no longer the kinky girl next door but the MILF who called her own shots and knew what she wanted.

When we arrived at Jackson's condo, I met his new mistress. She was young and her name was April. She lived in New York and had started her own latex design company. She had been working as a pro-domme and fetish performer for about four years. She was 24. I had a bad feeling about the session but proceeded. I shouldn't have. I felt old. With over a decade of work in the BDSM community and sex industry, this young woman had never heard of me. She also wasn't familiar with any BDSM educators, instructors, writers, or elders. She was young and inexperienced, and I was insulted to have her there to "dominate" me.

I lay belly down on the bed, cuffed and chained to the bedposts by my wrists. My ass was filled with a large silicone butt plug that I had brought from home. After cleaning my ass with a thorough enema, I filled it with lubricant, using my fingers and then fist to warm up my anus for a welcoming insertion of the butt plug. My ass sucked in the plug. The young girl, Mistress April, wore a short latex dress and heels. I was not in a submissive headspace. I didn't like this girl, I didn't trust her, and I just wanted to be home with my Daddy and my daughter. My breasts started leaking milk when I thought about

443

my little girl, and my eyes started to water a little. I buried my face into my pillow, breathing in and telling myself that it was just one afternoon, that I could get through this.

Jackson sat perched on his throne-like chair that sat beside the bed. "I want you to cane Madison severely. She wants to be severely beaten. Madison, I want you to count the strokes. April, Madison gets one thousand strokes."

Slowly, I gritted my teeth and breathed in and out, with each cane stroke, counting upward to one thousand. My eyes began to water and all I could think about was how much I despised this girl that was giving me this negative energy. I didn't want the energy that she was giving me, and I didn't have the power to convert all of what she was giving me into some juicy love from those in the world that I give a damn about. I just couldn't do it. So with every strike I struggled. I felt the jaggedness and inaccuracy of a wounded child playing dress-up and beating down on me. My mind ran to comforting thoughts. Thoughts of rocking back and forth holding my child, nursing my little girl to sleep. I missed her. My mind ran to pain and anger toward my partner, my Daddy, who had been cheating on me during the pregnancy with his coworker, Sheryl. I pictured Sheryl beating down on me with the cane. I felt deep, deep pain. Pain that needed to get out. I needed a deep emotional cleaning and right now I was being led down this dark and scary alleyway not by a trusted spiritual guide or an elder in the BDSM community but by a novice with a stick and some cheap latex. I had been down the road of cathartic BDSM experiences many times before in positive, well-supported environments, but this was not one of them. The strokes quickly followed one after another, and I counted to the beat of the sharp sting upon my hardened ass. I could tell that I was badly bruised. I could feel the cane beating down on the tenderized flesh and something liquid and wet forming puddles on my abused bottom that the cane seemed to come splashing down into. I glanced up from the pillow toward the wall above the headboard and noticed that the wall was covered in splashes of blood. The cane had broken my skin, and blood would splash toward the wall with every new stroke. I started to cry hard, sobbing tears, just wanting to stop, just wanting to endure.

"997, 998, 999, 1,000." I collapsed upon the bed, my breast covered in milk that I had leaked during the scene, my entire bottom half covered in blood and bruises, my face covered in smeared lipstick, smeared mascara, and tears.

"I want out," I declared, still sobbing and a little surprised by my own hoarse voice.

"What? You want out? I think, just for that, you deserve another five hundred strokes, Madison." Jackson stood up and grabbed my hair, looking into my eyes.

"Jackson. Get these cuffs off of me right now. Game over." I was serious. The session was over. I had given all I could and needed to decompress back in the hotel. I needed a delicate warm shower and to curl up watching pay-per-view movies and eating room service.

April looked at Jackson and undid my cuffs. I quickly showered, got dressed, and waited for April and Jackson to clean up the condo before he drove me back to the hotel.

"I'm sorry, Jackson. I don't think I'm willing to go there any more with you. My life is just too complicated right now. The fairytale of Madison, the young princess who secretly desires to be kidnapped and tortured—she doesn't exist. I'm sorry." It felt like I was breaking up with a lover of many years and at the same time like I was telling a little boy that there is no Santa Claus. The truth is sometimes, I am that princess that wants to be kidnapped, but only on my terms, and my terms have changed. Maybe it's because I'm a mother. Maybe I've just reached a level of maturity in my thirties where I'm appreciating smaller circles of deeper intimacy. But regardless of reason, I'm shelving my fairytales for another reading that involves me and Daddy.

MADISON YOUNG is a sex-positive Tasmanian devil. This sexpert grew up in the suburban landscape of Southern Ohio before moving to San Francisco in 2000. Since then, this Midwestern gal has dedicated her days to facilitating safe space to dialogue on the topic of fringe identities and cultures as well as documenting healthy expression of sexuality. Madison's breadth of work in the realm of sexuality spans from documenting our sexual culture in her feminist erotic films to serving as the artistic director of the forward-thinking nonprofit arts organization Femina Potens Art Gallery. Madison values sexual education in her work and has taught workshops and lectures, and has acted as a panelist on the topics of sexuality, feminism and pornography, and kink around the world, including at Yale University, Hampshire College, the University of Minnesota, and UC Berkeley. Her writings have been published in books such as *The Ultimate Guide to Kinky Sex*; *Baby Remember My Name*; *Rope*; *Bondage, and Power*; and *In/Soumises*.

Johns, Marks, Tricks, and Chickenhawks

SEEKING

Dylan Ryan

I wasn't sure that I wanted him to touch me. No, that's wishy-washy. I was pretty sure I didn't want him to touch me, but it was really just about too late for that kind of uncertainty.

Hanging above the headboard and each matching side table were photographs in matching black lacquer frames, each one featuring a different girl in some state of repose; naked, eyes aimed anywhere but at the camera. Back to him, I examined each photo, looking for similarities and typifying factors. I, sitting, bottom resting on my heels, haunches nestled, hands cradling each other in the warm crevice between my thighs, compared them. To one another. To me.

Thing is, he wasn't a bad man. He wasn't the kind of guy that co-erced the desperate youth of America to get naked for his camera. I had met that guy and this one bore no resemblance. This one was a neuropsychologist, the head of said program at the most prestigious university in the province. He was married but she knew all about his escapades, and had regular ones of her own. He was smart, unhurried, and deliberate in most instances I had witnessed, both big and inconsequential. I had to imagine, therefore, that all that suppleness had presented itself rather willingly to him, much the way I was now. For the right price. And then there, I had it, our shared characteristic. None of those glass enshrined girls looked like me. But we were all the same.

This was our fifth "date." It was at another exceptionally fancy restaurant of his choosing where I had thoroughly enjoyed my five-course meal. He spoke in calm, metered tones about his work, while I interjected with overlapping experiences from my social work career. He asked me about graduate school, I found instances to show off my wine knowledge. Well past the, "Why are you doing this, how much, how often" portion of our program, I had begun to find his company genuinely enjoyable, and was discovering the subtle pleasure in the parry and thrust of talking with a person who was smarter than me in many esoteric areas. By then I had come to know what kind of clothing he appreciated, and took pains to present myself in a pleasing way: legs, manicured fingers, hair off my face, a dress that revealed itself out from under several layers of necessary Toronto winter accessories. I could say it was good. I will say it was good. And with goodness came the time to make good on our arrangement.

It's called Seeking Arrangements, a very apropos name. That's exactly what I was seeking each and every time. A form of relationship mutually beneficial for all involved. They have money, I need money; they need what I have, I have it to give. It's called an arrangement but you can call it whatever you want. And don't say you never will because you would. I wouldn't but I did. And I did again.

And here I was, uncertain and supple and un-coerced. He moved up behind me and gently pulled a blindfold over my eyes and I stretched out long across the soft grey sheets. It was all soft domination and the quiet click of the camera shutter and the room was warm and clean and I didn't mind him touching me at all. His touch felt smart like his words had and as I listened to his breathing quicken, I focused on the black and white images of those girls burned into the backs of my eyes and wondered if any of them had slept with his wife, too.

Some girls say they disconnect, but I never left the warmth of that room, the "Yes Sir" and "Thank You Sir," coming with ease, just like the rest of our arrangement. After my blindfold was lifted, I pulled the same warm gray sheets over me and drifted off to sleep. He had made it clear that the bed was for me, and he left to head home to his real life arrangement.

Johns, Marks, Tricks, and Chickenhawks

The next afternoon, deep in a class about ethics in social work practice I opened my email to find one from him. In an attachment were four photos from the night before. All in black and white; three of me blindfolded in full stretch on the bed the last with the blindfold off. Looking right into the camera. Smiling.

The message in the email: "I'm saddened to tell you that I'm going to have to end our arrangement. You are simply not submissive enough for me."

And I thought of the girls.

Maybe I was different after all.

DYLAN RYAN is a porn star, writer, performance artist, social worker, body working yoga teacher, and bacon lover. Born and raised in the wilds of suburban Southern California, Dylan has wander-lusted as far as Europe and Canada, and ultimately settled in the only city that ever truly held her heart, San Francisco. A big believer in doing way too many things at once, Dylan has made a career teaching people about sex, writing for a variety of print publishers and online media such *Bitch* magazine, *Huffington Post,* and CNN, and assisting the sex work community through harm reduction-focused organizations, all whilst dipping her toes in and out of academia and graduate school. Dylan's fondest wish is that people will feel their feelings about what she does.